ISO 14001

CASE STUDIES AND PRACTICAL EXPERIENCES

Edited by Ruth Hillary

ISO 14001

CASE STUDIES AND PRACTICAL EXPERIENCES

EDITED BY RUTH HILLARY

Greenleaf
PUBLISHING
2 0 0 0

To the lovely children: Max, Zak and Jessica

Published by Greenleaf Publishing Limited
Aizlewood's Mill
Nursery Street
Sheffield S3 8GG
UK

Typeset by Greenleaf Publishing.
Printed and bound, using acid-free paper from managed forests, by
The Cromwell Press, Trowbridge, Wiltshire, UK

British Library Cataloguing in Publication Data:
    ISO 14001 : case studies and practical experiences
        1. ISO 14000 Series Standards   2. Environmental protection -
        Standards   3. Industrial management - Environmental aspects
        I. Hillary, Ruth
        658.4'08'0218

    ISBN 1874719276

CONTENTS

FOREWORD

Oswald A. Dodds, MBE

Chairman, ISO TC 207/SC 1:
Environmental Management Systems (EMS)

As we enter the 21st century, few doubt the need to conserve the Earth, although a number challenge the proposed remedies! When ISO, the International Organization for Standardization, set about developing standards to assist (mainly) business in managing their environmental affairs, few of those who became involved realised what would result. ISO TC 207—the parent committee for the ISO 14000 series of standards—came into being in 1993 and its members each have their own agendas, expertise and backgrounds. The fact that consensus is reached on anything is remarkable, as is the fact that a number of ISO 14000 standards have been published. It is also the case that our critics point out some weaknesses in the standards. They may even be correct, but the fact is that we have several agreed standards—where none previously existed—which are being used. They are also to be reviewed, using an established process that should help improve them and keep them relevant.

We also have evidence of acceptance and use in diverse situations and activities: for example, exponential growth in certification/registration to ISO 14001 as well as evidence of other widespread uses not involving third-party certification (second- and first-party declarations of conformity are both recognised by the standard). This is very heartening and should encourage those not yet involved, as well as providing feedback opportunities to the standard-writers.

The examples of different uses of ISO 14001, collected together in this book by Dr Ruth Hillary, demonstrate that the standard-writers have designed an environmental management system (EMS) that is applicable in all situations. The book will help non-users, particularly small and medium-sized enterprises (SMEs), many of which struggle to find the time, resources or expertise to implement such a system, however worthwhile the effort may be. Best of all, the examples show what can be achieved by the thoughtful use of ISO 14001 to improve individual users' environmental performance—a worthwhile outcome in itself.

Dr Hillary and all of the contributors and implementing organisations are to be congratulated for their efforts to inform and advise us all. I wish their endeavours every success.

Oswald Dodds, October 2000

INTRODUCTION

Ruth Hillary

Network for Environmental
Management and Auditing (NEMA), UK;
UK expert to ISO TC207/SC1 Working Group 2

ISO 14001 is the star standard among the International Organization for Standardization's ISO 14000 series of environmental management standards. It has seen spectacular growth since its launch in September 1996. Worldwide registrations are set to pass the 20,000 mark in 2000 with 20 times that number reportedly waiting in the wings. It's the gold medal winner among environmental management systems (EMSs): liked by the market, internationally available and recognised, not too difficult to achieve (especially if you're a big company) and it satisfies the users. Other arguably better approaches—because they are more transparent and more accountable to stakeholders—are falling, not at the first hurdle but at the last, outstripped by the sheer weight of numbers and popularity of ISO 14001. Its de facto status as *the* EMS to have is silencing some critics. Claims that it is élitist, that it is an Anglo-Saxon approach, that it is designed to exclude trade from developing countries, that it is not relevant to smaller firms, that it is a club for the 'good' boys, that it is a whitewash for stakeholders have all been subdued as its success across the globe has grown.

When I first thought about putting together a book on ISO 14001 case studies, I had in mind the standard's phenomenal growth, its undoubted success in some quarters and the gradual quietening of its critics. I wanted to find out what was really happening to ISO 14001 in the organisations that were so readily adopting it. I had read enough implementation guides; I was now looking for those juicy cases where the real experiences of organisations would unravel the standard. I wanted more than just stories about the step-by-step approach taken to implement it; I wanted to hear about the issues tackled, the problems faced and overcome, and the directions taken. Were organisations adapting and shaping the standard? Were they driving a path beyond the ISO 14001 straitjacket? And who was doing all this and in what type of organisation?

I was not to be disappointed. In the call for papers for this book I had an overwhelming response from around the world—cases set in diverse geographical, political, economic and social situations. This book represents the best of these. They were chosen because of their ability to demonstrate novel and unique approaches to ISO 14001, because they tackled new techniques and overcame thorny issues, because they engaged and explained and challenged the view of what made ISO 14001 tick, and because they had visions of where they wanted to take ISO 14001. The readers are treated to the wisdom of those that have taken what is a jargon-riddled standard, deconstructed it and then built workable systems applicable to their requirements. These ISO 14001 implementation 'experts' expose their successes and failures. We learn from both. They are not uncritical of the standard. Many found it cumbersome and time-consuming but all applied it to meet their needs. *ISO 14001: Case Studies and Practical Experiences* seeks to unravel the truth behind what can and cannot be achieved by ISO 14001 and aims to provide readers with enough knowledge to make choices about its relevance and importance, not only to their worlds but also to society.

To understand the diversity of ISO 14001 implementation practice the reader is first introduced to four EMS cases in Part 1, 'Implementation, Maintenance and Integration'. Here, practitioners present the techniques employed to make ISO 14001 operational, maintainable and beneficial. Scott Houthuysen introduces Lucent Technologies Micro-electronics Group's **business-wide ISO 14001**; built on a single EMS platform and integrated into business cycles, the system reaps commonly cited benefits. In the next chapter, consideration is given to how to maintain the enthusiasm for and momentum of EMSs once the euphoria of the first wave of benefits has died down and the certifiers have left (Pedersen and Nielsen). The authors highlight the flexibility in second- and **third-generation** EMS. This contrasts sharply with Bruce Cockrean's discussion of the restrictions placed on EMS development in New Zealand local authorities where the central paradigm is **legislation**. In the final chapter of the section, Anne Randmer points to the absence of years of enforced legislation in Estonia to show how the application of environmental programmes including technology and EMS can be effective tools to improve poor **environmental performance** where legislation is failing.

Diverse environmental and management objectives are satisfied in the case studies in Part 1; however, certification is often, although not always, an objective of organisations implementing ISO 14001. Part 2, 'Certification and Registration Experiences', takes a deeper look at the subject with stories from three different players in the certification arena: small enterprises, a multinational corporation and assessors. Jonas Ammenberg and colleagues present a novel case study of a joint EMS and **group certification** of 30 small and medium-sized enterprises (SMEs) in Sweden. By networking and utilising a group implementation model, the smaller firms established a workable and cost-effective method to achieve ISO 14001 and, importantly, obtain certification at reduced cost. This simple model may provide a means to successfully engage more SMEs in EMS implemen-tation. At the other end of the size spectrum, Furrer and Hugenschmidt discuss the **global certification** of UBS's banking business, highlighting ISO 14001 as a useful tool when integrating diverse cultural and country perspectives into its EMS. Every company seeking ISO 14001 certification wants to know what the certifier is looking for. Robinson and Gould address this, describing the **assessor view** and the certification process, the key requirements of the standard and the common failures in registration to ISO 14001.

Equipped with information on ISO 14001 implementation and certification, the reader moves onto Part 3 in which five case studies show the use of tools and technology to either streamline the ISO 14001 process or to beef up its environmental performance credentials. **Information technology** (IT) use in EMS implementation is currently limited but potentially powerful. The Waterford Crystal and ALSTOM Power cases (Harwood *et al.*) demonstrate the potential of IT to automate the integration of many management systems—including quality, environment, health and safety, and occupational health and safety. While IT is not readily applied in smaller firms' EMSs, another potential route to engage smaller firms in EMSs is shown by the application of the **environmental performance evaluation** (EPE) guidelines in ISO 14031 (Løkkegaard). Adoption of EPE guidelines by smaller enterprises shows they can develop better indicators for environmental performance and simpler EMSs. In the subsequent chapter, Cagno and Trucco are concerned with why poor environmental performance objectives in EMS arise and present a rigorous **review methodology**, which they claim produces a quality of information that results in strategic objectives that fit well into other company objectives. The last two chapters in the section are concerned with the lack of performance standards stipulated in ISO 14001. Johannes Fresner cites three Austrian companies that have based their EMS on **cleaner production** techniques. He asserts that this approach leads to a **'living EMS'** directed at significant emission reductions as well as cost reduction and increased profits. Nonita Yap takes up the theme that ISO 14001 is about conformance not performance in her cases from Taiwan, which also utilise cleaner production techniques to integrate measurable environmental performance targets. Yap argues that this is not only desirable but also technically feasible.

A feature of ISO 14001 in comparison with standards in the ISO 9000 series is its high demand for training and communication. Part 4 concentrates on this aspect of the standard from differing cultural and organisational settings. It starts with an account of the Czysty Biznes project in Poland (Serafin *et al.*). The project aims to enhance the environmental performance of SMEs. In Poland, pressure for the standard is rare, as is pressure to comply with legislation, therefore raising **employee awareness** to environmental issues is crucial in bringing about environmental programmes and nurturing local accountability and responsibility. **Training and communication** is key to maintaining the stability and progress of EMSs in the Spanish hotels, as discussed by Anguera and colleagues, because seasonality and fluctuations in both employee and customer numbers disrupt implementation. In the final chapter of the section, Pam Evers examines the influence of **cultural and social factors** in the EMS implementation in an American Indian reservation. Here the tribal government, cultural ties with the natural environment and a complex web of federal, state and tribal regulations result in the development of a unique environmental policy.

Part 5 takes the reader into the topic of stakeholders and their role and engagement in ISO 14001. It begins with Michael Toffel's case study of one Southeast Asian packaging company's journey to ISO 14001 registration. The company anticipates **customer demands**, and the growing trend of multinational companies certifying to ISO 14001, in order to plan ahead and become ISO 14001-registered. In doing so it engenders greater staff participation in environmental initiatives and a shift in focus to preventative actions.

Next, Adrian Carter details the integration of management systems at an offshore service contractor, Amec Process & Energy. The interaction with clients' management systems and the high level of influence exerted by the company over **subcontractors** influenced implementation and shaped the EMS. Jean-Pierre Tack discusses the role of formalised EMSs as efficient tools to improve environmental performance and better communicate with stakeholders in the following case of the electricity-generating company Electrabel. He notes that the company considered the EU's Eco-management and Audit Scheme (**EMAS**) as more stringent than ISO 14001 and a better mechanism for communicating with the public: a key consideration for Electrabel's nuclear site where the scheme was piloted. Utilising EMS in a novel and imaginative way is the remit of the next case. Quentin Farmar-Bowers explores the potential to facilitate co-operation and co-ordination between the differing **stakeholders** as they impact on the biodiversity of Australian road reserves. Maintaining what is a disappearing biodiversity from verges is complex and fraught with problems as the variety of vested interests interact. The EMS appears to have the potential to draw together these unco-operative stakeholders to provide a partial solution to better manage biodiversity.

With ISO 14001's origins in the manufacturing sector and process, the three chapters in Part 6 investigate how products, design and technology can be successfully accommodated into the EMS model. The first case, by Matthew Mehalik, is of a uniquely ambitious partnership between a design and textile firm, DesignTex, and a small mill, Rohner Textil, to create an environmentally sustainable fabric. To do this, a collection of tools and techniques was employed: **life-cycle assessment**, EMSs, life-cycle cost accounting, etc. A fabric was produced that was suitable for disposal by composting, aesthetically appealing, met industry standards and was price-competitive. Reconciling environmental and economic concerns in this case paid dividends. Next, Krut and Strycharz present details of ISO 14001 implementation in the Capital Program Management department of the New York City Transit Authority. By necessity, this required the focus of the EMS to look upstream to design and downstream to suppliers and contractors. Implementation highlighted a critical issue: how to customise the EMS to incorporate **design for the environment** (DfE) and contractor management. In the final case study of Part 6, Western Australian companies certified to ISO 14001 are revealed to be more innovative and open to the adoption of **environmental technologies** than other non-registered companies (Marinova and Altham). This receptiveness to new technologies can be seen as a positive outcome from ISO 14001 implementation.

Environmental and economic benefits are the subject of Part 7 of this book. Switzer *et al.* begin the section with evidence from US firms that **environmental goals** are not necessarily more stringent in ISO 14001-registered firms but that their commitment to attain them and to use more measurable targets was enhanced, as was their desire to set goals beyond compliance standards. The following study, also located in the United States, seeks to reveal whether implementation of formal EMSs improves environmental performance—a preoccupation of US regulators (Bridgen and Helm). Some state regulators are exploring **non-regulatory approaches** to improve environmental performance. The ability of ISO 14001 to increase top management commitment to integrating environmental activities into companies' day-to-day operations may play a role in future non-regulatory schemes. The final two chapters look at the cost savings and marketing advantages often cited as benefits of ISO 14001 implementation. Andy Hughes and Vicky Kemp investigate whether ISO 14001 can impact on **economic value added**. They conclude that it can, but with a lot of preconditions. In Brazil, where environmental awareness is still limited, the uptake of ISO 14001 by eight companies (Maimon) reflects the **globalisation** of multinational companies' environmental policies and the efforts of export companies to obtain a competitive advantage.

The final part of this book considers sustainability and how organisations use ISO 14001 to meet the broader needs of **sustainable development.** Bekkering and McCallum start the section by discussing how ISO 14001 can be used as a tool to achieve **Agenda 21** goals in local government in Canada. Here, political considerations can overtake management ones, but the standard provides a means of making operational the municipality's sustainability vision. The next case addresses SMEs' engagement in sustainable development. Proyecto Guadalajara is a project to promote sustainable development through the adoption of ISO 14001 by smaller firms in Mexico (Wells and Galbraith). The case reveals many failings of the **network approach** used, but it does demonstrate the potential to capture firms currently out of the environmental action loop, allowing them to contribute to sustainability. Another way of incorporating enterprises in sustainable development is through the **supply chain**. The Nike Inc. case (Valero *et al.*) shows how a large company can mobilise its suppliers in effective management and move them closer to sustainable values. The incentive for both customers and suppliers is a mutual dependency they have in their drive toward becoming sustainable companies. ISO 14001 devotes little attention to sustainability, so in the final chapter of this book Susan Burns describes a framework—**The Natural Step**—which provides an overarching vision and guide for EMSs, steering these towards sustainability.

All the contributors to this book present lessons about ISO 14001 born out of real-life practical experience. They show the diversity of applications for ISO 14001, not just to different organisational types but also to different geographical locations and political and economic settings. What these cases tell us is that ISO 14001 is adaptable, popular and workable. It can be stretched and pulled to meet the needs of many different users. We learn that it can be applied at both the global and local level of organisations; that it works for large and small organisations, for private and public entities, for communities and industrial groups, up and down the supply chain, and for contractors. We learn that its process-oriented stance can be modified to integrate product and design issues and that technology adoption is promoted by it. We are exposed to its limitations and lack of environmental performance specificity and shown that the use of other tools such as cleaner production, environmental performance evaluation and life-cycle assessment can strengthen the standard. We are buoyed up by the raft of benefits, both economic and environmental, that are described in the cases and downhearted by its lack of vision on sustainable development.

ISO 14001 is not a thoroughbred. It is a workhorse of a standard, designed to get you started and going down the right path. What is apparent from the thoughtful and explicit contributions to this book is that it motivates and allows those implementing it to do with it what they want. This is ISO 14001's greatest strength—and weakness. Implementers can set ambitious objectives, define clear visions of where they want their organisations to go or they can sit on the fence and be content with compliance with legislation and improving systems. Its critics have valid points: it can be used to exclude; it is not always appropriate to all firms, especially not to SMEs; it is ambiguous on how environmental performance improvements are achieved; and it is weak on stakeholder involvement and sustainable development. However, ISO 14001 is currently the most acceptable badge of achievement on environmental management.

I believe there are two issues of paramount importance to the development of ISO 14001 if it is to contribute to the wider societal demand for sustainable development. The first is: how will the greater involvement of stakeholders and the wider societal demands for the provision of environmental information be incorporated into EMSs? The second issue is the broadening of EMSs to incorporate and capture social and sustainability issues. For, while it is clear that the international forum of ISO is restricting the current revision of ISO 14001, the case studies in this book show that the key factors for the development of EMSs are: stakeholders' involvement and the more imaginative provision of environmental information; tangible and measurable environmental performance improvements; and, above all, the broadening of EMSs to include social, ethical and sustainability goals. In the end, ISO 14001 is about people and what they want. This book shows they want more from the standard and, as a result, the evolution of the EMS into a more sustainability-focused tool—an SMS (sustainability management system)—is already on the horizon.

Part 1
IMPLEMENTATION, MAINTENANCE AND INTEGRATION

DEPLOYMENT AND OPERATION OF A BUSINESS-WIDE EMS

Scott D. Houthuysen
Lucent Technologies Microelectronics Group, USA

This chapter discusses one company's approach to deploying and operating a business-wide, third-party-registered ISO 14001 environmental management system (EMS). The term 'business-wide' as used here means implementation of a common global approach to environmental management which is specified under a *single* EMS platform.

Lucent Technologies Microelectronics Group (Microelectronics) is a business unit of Lucent Technologies, with over 12,000 employees worldwide. It grew out of Western Electric's semiconductor components business, which was the first in the world to manufacture transistors. Microelectronics is a market leader in the design and manufacture of optoelectronic and integrated circuit products. These products provide our customers with clear-cut, innovative application solutions for worldwide data, voice and video communications. They include:

☐ Digital signal processors for modems, wired, cordless and cellular phones

☐ Standard-cell application-specific integrated circuits for disk drives and other applications

☐ Field-programmable gate arrays for telecommunications networks

☐ Components and subsystems such as photodetectors, laser modules, receivers, and transmitters for fibre-optic telecommunications networks

◢ Why implement a business-wide EMS?

Since 1991, Microelectronics has had a formal team called EnAcT (*En*vironmental *Act*ion Team) to address environmental issues that affect the business. The EnAcT consists of environmental management representatives from all Microelectronics manufacturing locations worldwide. While the international community was debating the final details of ISO 14001 during 1995, Microelectronics—working through the EnAcT—determined that environmental management needed a more formalised definition and structure if further improvements in Microelectronics' global environmental management and performance were to be realised.

Environmental performance included complying with all legal and other environmental requirements (e.g. governmental voluntary programme agreements, customer specifications, etc.), establishing and meeting environmental objectives and targets that go well beyond legal compliance, and formally including community environmental concerns and issues in decision-making on environmental improvement projects. It was also determined that implementation of a Microelectronics-defined business-wide, global EMS, meeting the ISO 14001 standard elements, was key to improving environmental management and performance. ISO 14001 was also viewed as the quality tool needed to implement Microelectronics' environment, health and safety (EHS) vision:

> To fully integrate environmental, health and safety considerations into the business decision-making process, thus making these endeavours a value-added proposition to the customer, company and community.

Business benefits

In 1995, Lucent Technologies established a goal that required its operating units to implement an EMS based on recognised standards by the end of 1999. In addition to allowing Microelectronics to be the first Lucent unit to meet this goal, implementation of a business-wide, ISO 14001-certified EMS also provided a number of benefits to the business.

Market research indicated that a number of Microelectronics' customers (e.g. Siemens, Ericsson) were interested in using ISO 14001 as a tool to improve the environmental performance of their suppliers. As many companies work to present themselves as environmentally responsible organisations, they also want to ensure that their suppliers are too. Microelectronics receives many supply chain questionnaires asking if it has implemented ISO 14001 or other EMS standards.

One Microelectronics

Establishment of a business-wide EMS has allowed Microelectronics to fully enhance its 'One Microelectronics' approach to environmental management. This enables environmental issues affecting more than one location/product to be elevated to group level and addressed in a cost-effective manner for implementation at all applicable locations. Aspect action teams address such environmental issues. These teams consist of employees who are closest to the environmental issue and are most likely to succeed in making the change.

A 'One Microelectronics' business approach allowed us to integrate into the existing ISO 9000 quality management system infrastructure and capitalise on lessons learned

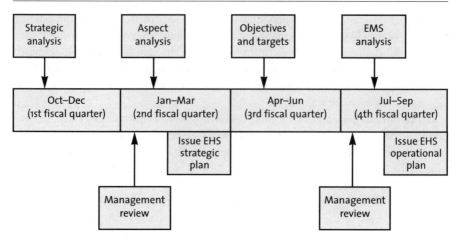

Figure 1.1 **Microelectronics EMS planning calendar**

associated with gaining ISO 9000 certification. For example, proven ISO 9000 processes for documentation control, auditing and corrective/preventative action programmes were readily adapted for ISO 14001 implementation, thus lowering implementation costs.

The Microelectronics EMS was designed to allow more formal involvement with the local community, including local and state regulators, in the company's EMS and environmental decision-making through its local environmental advisory groups (LEAGs). LEAGs are further discussed under the *Communication with community and customers* section.

In the past, cross-organisational roles and responsibilities were loosely defined, which led to some confusion and wasted resources from duplication of effort. Documentation of environmental management roles and responsibilities across the business and locations led to clearly defined expectations and improved human resource utilisation. As part of this effort, Microelectronics specified the services required of Lucent Technologies Global EHS Centre[1] in a contractual agreement.

The Microelectronics EMS was designed so that it coincides and integrates environmental decision-making into the annual business planning cycle. As shown in Figure 1.1, technological advancements and new legal or other environmental requirements are reviewed to formulate a draft EHS strategy during the first fiscal quarter. This strategic input, taken with significant environmental aspect analyses, is then discussed among EnAcT members during the second fiscal quarter to determine group and location objectives and targets. These are formulated, along with project plans, and then reviewed by management for funding and approval. Additionally, the Microelectronics EMS is reviewed by EnAcT members and management during the last fiscal quarter. Finally, project plans to accomplish objectives and targets are documented in an annual EHS

---

1   The Centre provides services such as developing global summaries of legal environmental requirements, training programmes, company-wide environment, health and safety standards, and performing audits.

operational plan, issued during the last fiscal quarter. Further discussion on implementation of relevant ISO 14001 planning elements can be found later in this chapter.

A business case, covering implementation and operation of a third-party-certified ISO 14001-based EMS, was prepared and approved by the Microelectronics executive committee. The committee consisted of the Microelectronics group president, the vice-presidents and directors of key business operational functions. Following business case approval, a Microelectronics ISO 14001 implementation team was formed. This ISO 14001 team was tasked to formalise and document the Microelectronics EMS platform requirements and processes needed to gain business-wide ISO 14001 certification. There were two factors that motivated the team:

☐ Top management support and endorsement for Microelectronics to be an environmental leader (e.g. the president participated in Microelectronics' ISO 14001 awareness video)

☐ Desire to meet Lucent Technologies EHS goals for 2000, and set an example as the first operating unit in Lucent Technologies to gain ISO 14001 certification

During initial development of Microelectronics EMS processes, the ISO team worked with the US Environmental Protection Agency (EPA) as part of Project XL[2] to address their EMS concerns. Project XL is an EPA voluntary programme designed to reinvent US 'command-and-control' environmental regulation with innovative solutions to improve company environmental performance.

The entire process from ISO 14001 business case development to receipt of ISO 14001 certification took 18 months (see Fig. 1.2).

On 2 April 1997, Microelectronics obtained one of the world's first known 'business-wide' ISO 14001 certifications. The certification covers Microelectronics' EMS which ties all Microelectronics locations together with corporate support organisations under one ISO 14001 certificate. This type of EMS was established so that common environmental improvement opportunities could be identified and solved in one go for all locations through deployment of the aspect action teams. To obtain this business-wide ISO 14001 certification, Microelectronics headquarters and its ten global manufacturing/design locations in six countries, with five US locations in four different states, received ISO 14001 audits by Lloyds Register Quality Assurance. In addition, the Lucent Technologies Global EHS Centre was reviewed since it had documented responsibilities as a supplier to support the Microelectronics EMS.

◢ Design of the business-wide EMS

The Microelectronics EMS is based on ISO 14001 principles and comprises five major components:

---

2   Meaning eXcellence in Leadership.

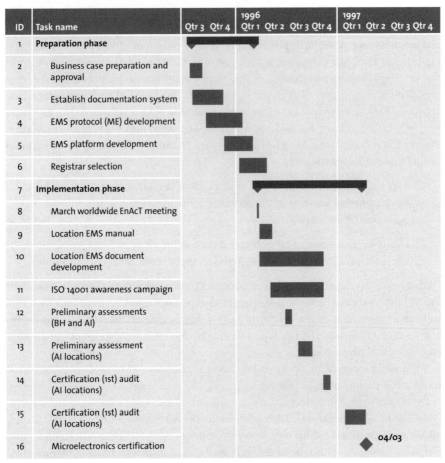

ID	Task name	Qtr 3	Qtr 4	1996 Qtr 1	Qtr 2	Qtr 3	Qtr 4	1997 Qtr 1	Qtr 2	Qtr 3	Qtr 4
1	**Preparation phase**										
2	Business case preparation and approval										
3	Establish documentation system										
4	EMS protocol (ME) development										
5	EMS platform development										
6	Registrar selection										
7	**Implementation phase**										
8	March worldwide EnAcT meeting										
9	Location EMS manual										
10	Location EMS document development										
11	ISO 14001 awareness campaign										
12	Preliminary assessments (BH and AI)										
13	Preliminary assessment (AI locations)										
14	Certification (1st) audit (AI locations)										
15	Certification (1st) audit (AI locations)										
16	Microelectronics certification								04/03			

ME = Microelectronics; BH = Berkeley Heights; AI = Allentown locations

Figure 1.2 **Microelectronics ISO 14001 certification time-line**

- ☐ Environmental policy
- ☐ Planning
- ☐ Implementation and operation
- ☐ Checking and corrective action
- ☐ Management review

As previously discussed, the Microelectronics EMS planning and management review elements (e.g. significant environmental aspects determination, objectives and targets identification, EMS reviews) are tied to the annual business cycle, thus ensuring that environmental management is continually improved.

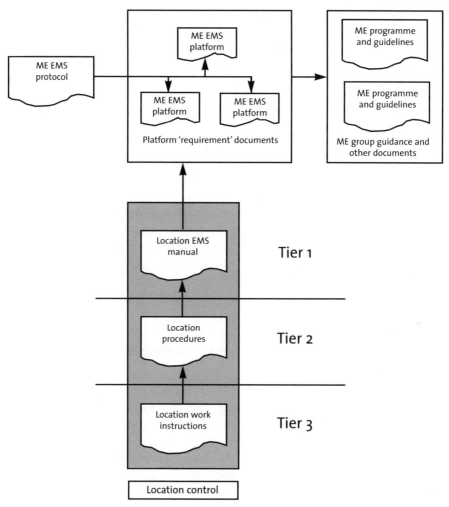

Figure 1.3 **EMS documentation structure**

As with all EMSs, the Microelectronics EMS is defined by an environmental policy which is signed by the group president. This policy applies to all employees worldwide. The Microelectronics group environmental policy was later changed to an EHS policy.[3]

The specific requirements of the Microelectronics EMS are defined in a Microelectronics EMS protocol document that links to a series of Microelectronics EMS platform documents (see Fig. 1.3). To ensure real-time availability of the documents by employees, the documents are controlled and made accessible via the company's intranet. These platform documents address each ISO 14001 element and specify Microelectronics' EMS requirements and processes of the 'One Microelectronics' approach to environmental

3   See www.lucent.com/micro/environ.html

management. Companion documents known as Microelectronics programme and guideline documents provide guidance on implementation of specific environmental programmes and are also made available on the intranet. All locations were required to prepare an EMS manual which ties the Microelectronics EMS platform document requirements to location EMS procedures.

In developing the Microelectronics EMS, many existing processes such as environmental training and awareness, and emergency preparedness and response were documented. New Microelectronics EMS processes were also documented and implemented, such as defining environmental aspects and conducting EMS audits) The key to building a business-wide EMS was to define a strong, common approach to the planning elements of ISO 14001. In doing so, significant environmental aspects are similarly defined and thus managed through the Microelectronics EMS worldwide. This framework allows locations a degree of flexibility in implementation such as how best to define operational controls and training programmes to ensure adequate environmental management. Allowing flexibility for implementation recognises the fact that cultural variations exist across the business and that many current location-specific environmental management programmes can continue working as long as the EMS recognises them.

◢ Microelectronics EMS planning elements

Environmental aspects

The Microelectronics EMS prescribes a common methodology for determining environmental aspects and minimum criteria that must be applied to define significant environmental aspects.

Environmental aspects are identified by the location based on the aspect classes shown in Figure 1.4. The classes are defined to encompass all actual and potential location interactions with the environment. These include consumption of resources such as energy, water and materials, releases to air and water, wastes, and local environmental interactions such as those affecting the land or surrounding community. The classes are defined such that they group similar types of aspects and are convenient given typical location organisation, record-keeping routines, etc.

Environmental aspects are further characterised by the location in terms of quantitative and qualitative factors such as amount of materials consumed or emitted, applicable regulations, etc. Based on defined qualitative and quantitative factors, the aspects are evaluated by the location to determine which aspects are significant. Significance is ned on an absolute rather than relative basis, i.e. regardless of how an aspect to any other aspects, including those at other locations. Given the chemically ture of the Microelectronics business operations, significance criteria focused management activities. The Microelectronics EMS specifies an aspect as ulfils specific minimum conditions such as:

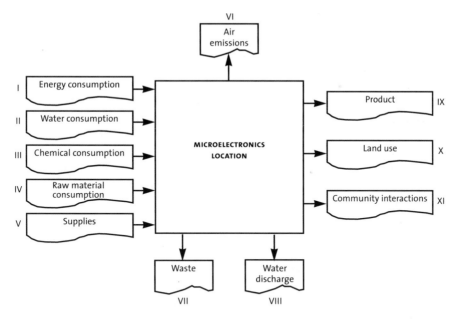

Figure 1.4 **Environmental aspect classes**

☐ The aspect is subject to Lucent goals or Microelectronics environmental objectives.

☐ The aspect is subject to environmental laws or regulations.

☐ The aspect is subject to requirements of the Lucent Technologies worldwide EHS standards (global standards for all Lucent locations) or other environmental requirements to which the Microelectronics group or location explicitly subscribes.

☐ The aspect involves a material that poses significant risk due to toxicity or other hazardous characteristics. 'Significant risk' is defined as a hazard level equivalent to a rating of three or higher in any of the National Fire Protection Association Hazardous Material Identification System, or other similar programme categories for health, flammability and reactivity.

☐ The aspect was identified by the LEAG.

Once significant environmental aspects have been identified, they are reviewed. Using the synergistic effect of EnAcT members, significant environmental aspects are identified which will serve as input to determine group-level objectives and targets. The Microelectronics EMS requires that significant environmental aspects be managed by either improvement objectives and targets or maintained under existing documented environmental management programmes (discussed below).

Legal and other requirements

Microelectronics Group utilises the Lucent Technologies Group EHS Centre to identify and communicate environmental legal requirement information that may be applicable to the Microelectronics products and location activities. The Centre also identifies and communicates 'company environmental requirement' information to Microelectronics in the form of Lucent Technologies environmental policies, goals, standards and other company adopted environmental programmes (e.g. voluntary governmental environmental programmes). This information is reviewed by the Microelectronics Environment, Health and Safety Assurance Organisation and by location subject matter personnel for relevance to the group and its locations. The Assurance Organisation, working through the EnAcT, identifies and communicates those requirements which can be addressed by a Microelectronics group level programme.

Objectives and targets

Every significant environmental aspect must be managed in accordance with Microelectronics' EMS requirements, including the setting of objectives and targets. At both group and location levels, each significant aspect is assessed to determine if the aspect must be improved or maintained based on current environmental performance and adequacy of existing management programmes. This assessment is made through a sequential series of questions. Formalised EMS procedures, to identify and document environmental objectives and targets for significant environmental aspects which are based on a specific tiered prioritisation process, drive a 'One Microelectronics' approach to environmental performance. A sample of the questions is given below:

☐ Are operations associated with significant aspects in compliance with all applicable requirements of the Lucent Technologies worldwide EHS standards and environmental laws and regulations for the last two years?

☐ Are associated risks and potential liabilities being managed successfully?

☐ Are relevant environmental objectives (e.g. Lucent corporate goals), associated documented concerns of the LEAG, and other environmental requirements, to which the Microelectronics group or location subscribes, being addressed satisfactorily by existing programmes with specific objectives and targets?

☐ Are important environmental factors identified during or subsequent to the environmental aspect analysis process and other relevant environmental information (e.g. pending legislation, proximity of operating conditions to permit limits, level of environmental impact, opportunities for pollution prevention or enhanced legal compliance, customer requirements) being satisfactorily addressed?

As part of the objectives- and targets-setting process, information to be considered when answering the questions for each significant aspect includes the following:

☐ Quantitative/qualitative information and environmental risks associated with significant environmental aspects

☐ The Microelectronics group EHS policy

☐ Requirements of the ISO 14001 standard and the Microelectronics EMS

☐ Legal and other requirements, such as relevant Lucent Technologies EHS standards

☐ Interested-party views obtained using the LEAG process

☐ Audit results

☐ Technological options

☐ Financial requirements, operational data and business case analyses

If the answer to any question is 'yes', an improvement objective and target may have to be established for the significant environmental aspect. If the answer to all questions is 'no', it means that the significant environmental aspect has adequate environmental management programme(s) already in place and the objective is to maintain existing programmes and performance. Final improvement objectives and targets are selected for implementation during the current planning cycle, based pending management review at the location and group levels.

Environmental management programmes

The Microelectronics EMS requires that environmental management programmes for achieving objectives and targets be established and documented in group and location EHS plans. The purpose of the EHS plan is to provide a compilation of the environmental projects and ongoing management programmes that will drive environmental performance during the current fiscal planning cycle. In general, the details regarding responsibilities, schedules and the tasks that must be undertaken to achieve 'improvement' objectives and targets are described in the EHS plan. Management programmes designed to maintain performance take the form of other documents (e.g. operational controls contained in Tier 3 EMS work instructions or procedures). Where an objective and target is to maintain existing management practices or performance, the EHS plan may simply identify the objective and target and then refer to the specific existing documents that contain the necessary details regarding responsibility, schedules and tasks. The EHS plan is implemented, monitored and reviewed with top management during the fiscal year.

Communication with community and customers

ISO 14001 specifies that 'organisations establish and maintain procedures for receiving, documenting and responding to relevant communication from external interested parties.' One very unique element of the Microelectronics EMS is the establishment of

LEAGs to ensure that local community environmental issues and concerns are included into the decision-making process.

LEAGs were established to allow external interested parties to provide input to the Microelectronics location regarding its significant environmental aspects and the setting of its objectives and targets. The LEAG process is also used to increase community understanding of location operations and communicate planned changes such as facility expansions. LEAG members typically include people who live and/or work in the area around the Microelectronics location, as well as local government representatives. Microelectronics locations host periodic LEAG meetings in which location personnel solicit LEAG input after discussing their significant environmental aspects and objectives and targets. Discussion of significant environmental aspects and objectives/targets has led to interesting LEAG input and discussions. For example, Microelectronics Allentown location discussed with their LEAG the Microelectronics group-wide objective to implement water conservation projects that will reduce the need for one billion gallons of water per year by the end of 2001. For that Microelectronics location, it translated to an absolute reduction of its water use by about 40%, representing about 3%–4% of the total city water production. Overall, the LEAG agreed and applauded the effort but one member who worked for the local water utility expressed concern at its impact on the utility's revenue. The following year, a severe drought occurred and water restrictions were imposed on the local community. Due to Microelectronics' water conservation efforts, the local water utility did not impose water restrictions that could have impaired business operations.

With the implementation of Microelectronics' EMS, the company is better able to certify business-wide responses to environment-related questionnaires from customers. Suppliers' questionnaires typically address one or more of the following issues: EMS standard registration, actual environmental performance, product composition such as use of banned or restricted substances, chemical use in manufacturing activities, and legal environmental compliance certifications.

◢ Environmental performance

As a result of implementation of the Microelectronics EMS, business efficiencies (e.g. integration of environmental planning into the business cycle), internal communications between company locations and functions, as well as external communications with customers and the local community through the LEAGs, have improved. Many location- and group-level environmental objectives and targets were set and realised under this newly documented Microelectronics EMS (e.g. waste and energy reduction projects, water conservation projects, etc.).

Through the ISO 14001-based EMS, Microelectronics continues to demonstrate its commitment to the group-wide EHS policy, set group and location objectives and targets, and establish programmes to drive environmental performance throughout the business. Microelectronics efforts to integrate environmental decision-making into the business planning cycle have resulted in a number of accomplishments, thus demonstrating what this high performance business-wide EMS model can achieve.

Through a 1996 EnAcT meeting, water conservation was identified as an area for improvement across Microelectronics. As a result, a cross-location water team was formed composed of representatives from locations consuming more than 200 million gallons a year. An objective was established to implement water conservation projects that will reduce the company's need for one billion gallons of water per year by the end of 2001 (about 50% of 1996 usage). Microelectronics anticipates meeting this objective. During 1997–1999, Microelectronics implemented water conservation/recycling projects that resulted in total annual savings of 750 million gallons and over US$2 million annually.

Similarly, group energy efficiency was identified as an area requiring improvement to meet a Lucent Technologies objective. A cross-location Microelectronics energy team was established which set an objective to improve the energy efficiency of Microelectronics' operations by what would otherwise be the emission of at least 50,000 tons of greenhouse gas emissions (CO_2) by the end of 1999. This objective has been achieved with implementation of over 160 energy reduction projects that also resulted in annual savings of US$4.8 million.

Recognising that perfluorocompounds (PFCs) used in semiconductor manufacturing are long-lived greenhouse gases that contribute to global warming, Microelectronics signed a Memorandum of Understanding with the US EPA in an endeavour to reduce the emission of certain PFCs on a voluntary basis. A PFC team was initiated to look at ways of reducing PFC emissions in a manner that is both technologically feasible and cost-effective. Microelectronics has also agreed to co-operate and share technological information related to PFC emissions reductions with other semiconductor manufacturers and is a participant in a global effort to reduce PFC emissions with the World Semiconductor Council. This effort by the Council was recently acknowledged by the US EPA with the award of a 1998 Climate Protection Award. Microelectronics has started to convert its downstream etch operations from CF_4 to NF_3.[4] Although both chemicals are PFCs, NF_3 is almost completely destroyed in the process and CF_4 is barely consumed, hence an appreciable reduction in PFC emissions can be realised. By mid-2000, all planned conversions have been completed and Microelectronics has reduced its PFC emissions by about 15%. In conjunction with semiconductor tool manufacturers, Microelectronics is exploring other technological options to further reduce PFC emissions.

As a result of gaining ISO 14001 certification, the third-party ISO 14001 certifier identified a weakness in the Microelectronics EMS relating to the identification and communication of EHS requirements to a special class of suppliers—contract manufacturers. As a result, Microelectronics put together a team consisting of members from the relevant departments (such as purchasing and EHS) to address the issue. A formalised management programme in the form of a Microelectronics EMS platform document was subsequently developed. This document contains definitions, procedures and tools necessary for process implementation that started during 1998. The supplier evaluation process requires an assessment of these suppliers in four key areas:

---

4   CF_4 = carbon tetrafluoride; NF_3 = nitrogen trifluoride.

☐ Environmental management systems

☐ Environmental performance

☐ Environmental restricted substances

☐ EHS compliance with legal requirements.

Once the assessment is complete, requirements are prepared based on the supplier's response and incorporated into the supplier contract by Lucent's purchasing organisation.

In response to customer requests, during 1998 Microelectronics set an objective to develop a product composition guide (PCG) for integrated circuits with the intention of providing a reference for determining the chemical composition of our products. The guide provides quantitative estimates of significant materials contained in Microelectronics integrated circuits. The PCG also identifies specific chemicals that are intentionally not contained in our products, their distribution packaging, or their manufacture. Through the PCG, Microelectronics hopes to provide data to customers who request this information so that they can evaluate the potential environmental impacts of their products. The information can also be used for end-of-life assessments. A similar PCG for optoelectronic devices was also recently developed and released.[5]

◢ Conclusion

The Microelectronics EMS framework has been successful in reducing the environmental impact of Microelectronics's activities and products. In line with its long-term vision, Microelectronics continues to drive environmental decision-making into its product realisation process. By integrating environmental considerations in the concept stage of the product realisation process, Microelectronics can prevent pollution more effectively and design out potential problems before they occur. Microelectronics believes that the discipline of the EMS will help it accomplish this task.

5   See www.lucent.com/micro/iccomp and www.lucent.com/micro/optocomp.

MAINTAINING THE MOMENTUM
EMS after the certifier has left

Charlotte Pedersen
Deloitte & Touche, Denmark

Birgitte B. Nielsen
Valør & Tinge A/S, Denmark

A Danish survey shows that companies achieve various different advantages through their environmental management systems (EMSs). Some of the main advantages are that:

☐ Their clients find them more reliable.

☐ Their environmental impacts are reduced considerably, and some even removed through implementation of cleaner production.

☐ Investments are paid back in the short term, and often faster than expected.

These companies are scotching the myth about environmental management being nothing but paperwork.

The following chapter illustrates how 18 Danish companies have gained added value through implementing and maintaining their EMSs. The chapter also describes the problems they had to overcome.

◢ Maintaining the momentum

EMS certification/verification is a climax: a milestone where there is a chance to celebrate and where the certificate itself is the reward. After this, the EMS changes from being a special project to becoming integrated into the daily routine. Following certification, the main task is to keep the momentum going by continuing to focus on environmental issues in order to create new opportunities and values.

A key task is to update and maintain the system so that it continues to be an active tool, resulting in environmental improvements and supporting the company's general development.

In the autumn of 1998, 18 Danish companies that had been verified to the EU Eco-management and Audit Scheme (EMAS) or certified to ISO 14001 were invited to take part in a survey carried out by Deloitte & Touche Environmental Services and Valør & Tinge A/S with the purpose of sharing experiences on how they continue to maintain enthusiasm for environmental improvements and environmental management following initial certification.

The experiences of the companies were shared at two one-day seminars and, afterwards, their views and experiences were included in a booklet to which each of the companies also dedicated a short case history (Nielsen and Pedersen 1999).

The main survey themes and topics of discussions among the companies were:

☐ What are the most significant issues and elements in the EMS after certification?

☐ What are the new challenges?

☐ Which tasks of an EMS change and which don't?

☐ What results can be achieved?

☐ What are the pitfalls?

◢ Environmental management for continuous improvement

The main experience at Danish companies is that the first environmental improvements can be achieved simply by good housekeeping and common sense. The improvements can be extensive and yet also financially advantageous. But there is a limit on how far the companies can get with good housekeeping alone.

A number of the companies in the survey have reached that limit. Of course, this does not mean the end of environmental improvement opportunities. It does, nevertheless, mean larger projects, more extensive investigations of available opportunities, possibly investment in new technology and pilot plants, changes in production flow and product design, etc. All these matters demand management commitment and assertive decision-making.

Several of the companies in the survey have already introduced, or are about to introduce, cleaner production; for example:

☐ Saloprint, a printing firm, recycled water in its film-processing machine, which resulted in a reduction in water use by 90%. Likewise, it has also replaced about 90% of the mineral printing ink with a non-toxic vegetable-based ink.

☐ R98, a waste collector, has established a new cleaning unit for washing sanitation trucks that has resulted in the use of less water and soap.

☐ Paper manufacturer Stora Dalum has replaced many large pumps with smaller ones and changed its frequency regulators. It has also reduced the amount of time that the paper mass is stirred (pulped) by half, resulting in a 50% energy saving.

❑ Glasuld, an insulation materials manufacturer, has replaced one of its product's raw materials (sodium nitrite) with another (manganese dioxide), which has resulted in a 70% reduction in nitrous oxide emissions.

Implementing new, innovative and cleaner production technologies does not exclude a company from still valuing good housekeeping among employees. Good housekeeping is a way of educating employees on their environmental responsibilities. Some employees prefer smaller projects concerning good housekeeping, while others find it easier to grasp projects with a longer development time. These differences are part of the challenge in environmental work.

Generally, leading Danish companies and the companies in the survey tend to expand the scope of the environmental work from the site to the entire product cycle, embracing raw material usage, production, distribution, consumption and disposal. Some stakeholders, in particular consumers, are more interested in the product's environmental impact while it is being used than in the production conditions. Environmental impacts related to the company's products during use, product development, transport, distribution and services, are now drawn into the EMS. Because of this, the product's environmental impacts and product development play a more dominant role in the management system than first intended.

◢ Market-oriented environmental management

Many companies had expected to attract more customers due to their adoption of EMSs. Primarily, there are two reasons why this expectation has not been fulfilled. First, the market in Denmark for 'environmentally sound' solutions is still quite small. Although public- and private-sector organisations are increasingly adopting 'green' policies, these are often not properly implemented.

The other reason is that the certified companies have focused on getting their own house in order, and have simply expected the market to develop more or less by itself. Today, companies in the survey admit that it takes a serious and targeted contribution to convert a high environmental profile into market advantage (Møller-Jørgensen *et al.* 1999). Due to this, they have expanded their EMS to include co-operation between environmental managers and sales and marketing employees, so that the salespeople improve their ability to communicate the company's environmental initiatives to customers and, conversely, the customer's environmental requirements to the environment manager.

The first EMAS-registered companies had many requests for their environmental statements. Initially, such requests came primarily from students and consultants, but subsequently many companies have increasingly received requests from stock market analysts and financiers.

In the view of the participating companies, it is not sufficient for them just to work with environmental issues within the company's own boundaries. Co-operation with suppliers is increasingly important, but obtaining information on suppliers' environmental performance can be very resource-intensive, for both parties. Regardless of how the company chooses to deal with supply chain management, dialogue is recommended and the use of different tools to communicate performance is crucial.

Both nationally and internationally, there is a general tendency for customers and suppliers to work together over several years; over time their co-operation becomes closer and closer, enabling the development of joint solutions to common problems. The co-operation develops from issues relating to money and products, to include service, information, knowledge development and favours. In order to work even more closely together, both parties need to be observant and nurture teamwork. This trend also applies to the environmental area, in part because many environmentally friendly solutions can only be developed along the production chain.

Detergent manufacturer Henkel-Ecolab, for example, works with some of its biggest customers to develop solutions that reduce the collective environmental strain. Such an approach is beneficial because the parties can take advantage of each other's skills, while environmental improvements arise out of the whole process. One of Henkel-Ecolab's objectives is partly to improve communication with interested parties and also to establish co-operative relationships with its suppliers and customers. During these collaborations, joint goals are defined and action plans prepared.

Such initiatives rely on long-term planning, which is why co-operation agreements are often up to seven years long. Henkel-Ecolab assesses that this type of agreement opens up greater possibilities for environmental improvements than do shorter-term arrangements.

As noted earlier, the management of suppliers and the collection of information on their environmental performance can be a very resource-intensive task—both for the company and the supplier; but co-operation can work in many ways and the company can provide suppliers with more guidance and help. For example:

- An audit can be carried out at the supplier's premises, with the company and the supplier working together and exchanging experiences.

- Training courses can be held with the supplier on subjects of relevance to both the supplier and the customer.

- Questionnaires can be sent out, and suppliers ranked according to their environmental performance.

◢ Motivation, training and organisation

Many of the companies in the survey experienced difficulties in maintaining momentum, year after year. This is due, among other things, to the fact that the number of obvious environmental improvements that employees take part in decreases—and immediate results are, therefore, not always noticeable.

Usually, it is visible targets, actions and results that provide effective motivation, and it is a big challenge to keep having something on the agenda that will do this. Environmental work needs to be real and visible for the individual—as shown in the examples below.

Training and education is still important, but after EMS certification several companies changed from classroom to on-the-job training or to monthly or quarterly meetings with discussions and presentations, where it is possible to involve employees and discuss their suggestions. Information concerning environmental activities is vital for employees' understanding and participation.

Unimerco, a custom tools manufacturer, does a lot to improve the environmental consciousness of its employees, with a view to encouraging them to think, 'What does my work mean for the environment?' At Unimerco, all employees are given a better understanding of which environmental impacts they can help to reduce. Among other things, Unimerco asks all staff to make an environmental mass balance of their own workplaces. Indeed, the establishment of an environmental mass balance is a part of new employees' induction procedures.

Several of the participating companies have had positive experiences in deriving inspiration from external bodies or initiatives—in the shape of visiting speakers or from fact-finding visits to other firms. Other companies have found that their environmental audits are the best form of employee training.

◢ The system in operation

As companies gradually get more confident with ISO 14001, EMAS, EMSs and their own company's capacity, the system adapts more and more to the company—and companies learn how to use the standard more flexibly.

At the beginning of ISO 14001 and/or EMAS implementation, companies in the survey were very conscientious, especially with regard to completing paperwork. With time, however, the environment manager and other employees became more familiar with the requirements and with their own capabilities, which means they were better at reasoning and explaining their choices and priorities to the external auditors.

For the majority, it has been a positive experience to see how the system's second and third generations become increasingly flexible and less bureaucratic. In many cases, the second and third draft of the EMS manual has resulted in its decreasing in length by a half, and the long descriptions and detailed explanations have been removed. In the early stages, there was a clear tendency to write too much. Some companies have chosen to display the instructions on the wall instead of having them in the manual. Finally, some have chosen to minimise the amount of enclosures and instead produce outlines, flow diagrams, etc. of the procedures to reduce documents to one page, thus shortening the manual.

Just as the system becomes more flexible with time, the environmental auditing method also changes. Where, in the beginning, most companies undertook compliance audits to evaluate whether the system and activities were in agreement with the standard specifications, compliance moves away from being the primary purpose of the audits. Now the main purpose is to investigate whether the system and the activities that have been put in place fulfil the company's requirements.

All 18 companies in the survey pointed out that the challenge is in getting the environmental auditing away from being a control function. They have found that it is much more beneficial to use the audit to find out where the system is not working properly and to identify how the specific tasks can be undertaken more flexibly and efficiently. Therefore, an audit must always ask employees for their suggestions to improve the EMS. The best input for improvement often turns up in this way and it is easier to keep environmental auditors if they undertake this type of approach because their role is perceived as more constructive.

Environmental auditing is carried out in a variety of ways. Some companies audit using an individual procedure/instruction as a base; some audit using a flow throughout the production; while others do one department at a time. Insulation manufacturers, Glasuld, use a method known as 'grab a tail and follow it', where the audit is carried out in all directions of the system. The way the audit is carried out depends, among other things, on the auditors' preferences and on how they achieve the best results.

Several of the companies in the survey choose to let the management and/or the people responsible for the system be audited by external auditors in order to acquire input from outside the company. How often environmental audits are carried out depends on the company's culture. Some undertake small audits constantly while others assess the entire company in a month, after which there are no audits until the following year. In several companies, the employees prefer internal audits just before the arrival of the external auditors, so that they feel more at ease when the external auditors arrive. Others have removed this nervousness of external auditors by carrying out several smaller internal audits, so that the employees get used to being audited.

Finally, while only a few of the companies in the survey have done this, many are showing a lot of interest in creating an electronic version of the environmental manual. There are many advantages to this, in particular the ease of updating the manual and making it available to all employees.

◢ Results and pitfalls

All 18 companies in the survey have achieved usable results from their EMSs. The results have been achieved at different levels—some are strictly environmental, some financial, others organisational.

The following selection of statements, which the companies made during the study, reflects some of the main outcomes:

> The increased responsibility we have achieved due to the environmental management system has come off internally and caused a generally greater obligation—in other areas as well.

The fact that a third party checks the systems has meant increased credibility towards customers.

Environmental impacts have been remarkably reduced—some even removed.

All environmental investments have short payback periods—from months to a maximum of 3.8 years—and this is quicker than expected.

We do not drown in paperwork—this is a myth!

The environmental manual needs to be revised after the certification—and it becomes smaller.

We get new orders due to our environmental efforts.

We have created a better working environment—the inclusion of health and safety aspects in the environmental management system motivates employees to actively contribute to the . . . system.

The integration of systems is a good idea for us—it saves resources and optimises routines.

There are no cost savings from the reduction of noise, dust and odour.

It is nice to document that we are doing something.

Our inspection frequency from the regulators has been halved after we became EMAS-registered.

We have started co-operating with the authorities.

Our environmental work has become part of the everyday routine.

Through maintaining the EMS and keeping up the motivation, the companies in the survey discovered several pitfalls that others should be aware of:

Environmental improvements

- ☐ It is easy enough to find cost-neutral environmental improvements in the beginning, but it gets more and more difficult as time goes by.

- ☐ Too many designated major environmental impacts increase the risk of not paying enough attention to individual impacts.

- ☐ It is difficult to specify the expected results—and even harder to put them into financial terms.

The market

- ☐ It takes an applied effort to turn the company's impressive environmental profile into market advantages.

- ☐ Lack of external demands from customers, officials, etc. reduces the company's commitment.

- ☐ Suppliers can be difficult to influence if the company is not a large customer.

Motivation

☐ Most often, visible goals, actions and results give motivation, but it is difficult to continuously have something on the 'agenda'.

☐ Correct attitude is one thing—but do we necessarily abide by it?

☐ It is hard to engage new employees because they have not experienced the enthusiasm of certification.

System appendices

☐ The manual often becomes too big, with lots of graphs and flow charts.

☐ Internal auditors have found that they and their work are not respected, which has caused some to drop out of the audit team.

☐ Some procedures are so complicated that they are almost guaranteed to result in a deviation at the next audit.

◢ Beyond environmental management

The next step is working towards sustainable development and that goal is a huge challenge for all parties. Sustainability is defined as the principle that our actions today should not limit the economic, environmental and social possibilities for future generations. In the future, all participants in society can expect that they will be confronted with attitudes towards sustainable development from many of their partners, and that they will be measured in relation to economic abilities, environmental performance and social responsibility (i.e. welfare and social equity). In the long run, the strongest companies will be those that are now going on the offensive and taking responsibility for the development of the sustainable society.

The three elements of the sustainability concept—environmental, economic and social—have always existed for companies. However, their meaning for each company differs, depending on the political, social, environmental, etc. development of society. Economic conditions and demands will, as a consequence of our capitalistic global economy, always create the boundaries for companies. However, in the long run, a company's commercial survival can be greatly dependent on the social and environmental aspects of its reputation.

SUCCESS AND FAILURES
National guidance on ISO 14001 for New Zealand local authorities

Bruce Cockrean
Global to Local Ltd, Tisbury, UK

In 1997, following consultation with local authorities and Local Government New Zealand, the New Zealand Ministry for the Environment provided Sustainable Management Fund[1] support for the development of a guide to environmental management systems (EMSs) and ISO 14001 for local government.

The two-and-a-half-year project comprised the following elements:

☐ Publication of a report on international best practice in production of national guidance on EMS for local authorities

☐ Case study ISO 14001 training programme

☐ Development of EMS by case study local authorities

☐ Production of guidance document based on case study experiences

☐ National training and dissemination programme

The development of the EMSs and the resulting guidance had to reflect the impact of the Resource Management Act 1991 (RMA) on local government's approach to environmental management and its ability to move beyond legislative compliance towards continual improvement in the management of wider environmental impacts.

1   The Fund provides financial support for practical initiatives that help to achieve the sustainable management of New Zealand's resources. The Fund normally provides between 40% and 70% support for projects, with the remainder being provided by project participants and beneficiaries. To receive funding, the projects need to be practical, of national benefit and include extensive consultation with stakeholders. A summary of funded projects is available from the Ministry for the Environment, Wellington, New Zealand.

This chapter describes:

☐ The relationship between local government, the RMA and ISO 14001

☐ The drivers for ISO 14001 by the case study local authorities

☐ The EMS development process by the case studies

☐ The development of the national guidance document

☐ An assessment of the failures and successes in case study development of ISO 14001

☐ Conclusions

◢ The RMA and local government: a legislative approach to sustainable management

The RMA was established as the principal legislation for the management of New Zealand's natural resources, through rationalising and integrating previous environmental management legislation and reforming the role of local government in the process of environmental management.

The purpose of the Act is 'to promote the sustainable management of natural and physical resources'. At the heart of the RMA approach to sustainable management is the focus on controlling the effects of activities rather than the activities themselves, through the issue of 'resource consents'. The need for any person to obtain a resource consent is set out in the Act under the headings of land, coastal marine area, river and lake beds, water and discharges. Activity related to these areas needs a resource consent unless expressly identified as a permitted activity in the appropriate regional or district plan.

The RMA recognises the Treaty of Waitangi and the partnership that exists between the Crown and the Maori. In 1840 the Maori ceded 'kawanatanga' (governance) in exchange for 'rangatiritanga' (absolute guardianship of resources) (Freider 1997).

The development of the RMA went hand in hand with a major reform of local government. The Local Government Act Amendments of 1989 brought in a series of amalgamations that rationalised over 800 local authorities, elected boroughs, regional bodies and special boards to just 86 authorities. The 86 authorities comprise 12 regional councils (based on water catchment areas) and 74 local councils, including cities, districts and unitary authorities.

The RMA establishes the hierarchy of roles and responsibilities for resource management as follows:

☐ **Central government**: setting policy on matters of national significance; 'calling-in' proposals of national significance and monitoring implementation of the RMA

- ☐ **Regional government**: establishing regional plans; managing water, soil and geothermal resources; controlling land use as it effects natural resources; monitoring plan effectiveness; consent compliance; the state of the environment and the outcome of transfers of power

- ☐ **Territorial local authorities**: developing district plans consistent with relevant regional and national plans

New Zealand local and regional authorities are also responsible for a range of other services in addition to resource management. These include: waste management, utilities management, parks and reserves, pest management, libraries, road maintenance and asset management.

There is no requirement in the RMA to have an EMS in place, although the implementation of an EMS is consistent with the philosophy and purpose of the RMA and an 'EMS-type method' is also provided for in a number of sections of the RMA. (Cockrean 1999). In general terms, however, the relationship between EMSs and the RMA is as follows:

- ☐ The output of a council's EMS provides other regulators with evidence of environmental performance.

- ☐ An EMS demonstrates legislative compliance as a baseline for environmental performance. Councils can therefore use an EMS as a framework for a self-regulatory approach to legislation. Regional councils are increasingly favouring such self-regulatory approaches.

- ☐ An EMS leads to a greater understanding of environmental risk factors associated with the operations carried out by local authorities, thereby providing the potential for reducing the risk of pollution, contamination and environmental accidents as a result of council activities.

- ☐ Operational control and emergency preparedness and response procedures form part of an EMS. As such, an EMS may provide for a defence of due diligence in the case of an incident under sections 341(2)(b)(I)&(ii) of the RMA.

- ☐ An EMS demonstrates corporate consistency in all areas of operation with the objectives and policies in district and regional plans.

◢ The development of EMS by case study local authorities

The eight case studies shown in Table 3.1 were chosen to represent the range of regional, unitary, rural and urban local authorities and the range of local authority activities.

Case study local authority	Case study activity
Hamilton City Council	Hamilton Zoo
Manukau City Council	Waste management
Marlborough City Council	Environmental Policy and Monitoring Unit
Matamata-Piako District Council	Utility assets
New Plymouth District Council	Planning division
Palmerston North City Council	Water supply
Wellington Regional Council	Soil conservation
Western Bay of Plenty District Council	Parks and property management

Table 3.1 **Case study local authorities**

Drivers

The main reasons the case studies gave for wanting to develop an EMS were:

- ☐ To provide evidence of due diligence
- ☐ To help identify cost savings in resource use and waste management
- ☐ To improve resource consent management processes
- ☐ To act as an example to local businesses and resource consent applicants
- ☐ To assist with legislative compliance

The drivers identified are, in many ways, similar to those that might apply to business. In the UK, by comparison, while local authorities can be expected to want to use EMSs to identify resource savings and help with due diligence, there are a range of other drivers that were not identified explicitly in New Zealand. These include:

- ☐ As an implementation method for corporate environmental policies (HMSO 1993)
- ☐ As an element in the response to the Local Agenda 21 (LA 21) process
- ☐ Following assistance from local government organisations
- ☐ To help deliver best value[2]

At the beginning of the New Zealand local government project, many of the case study participants were looking to develop ISO 14001 to identify resource savings and to assist with legislative compliance rather then to help improve the overall environmental performance of service delivery. This may at first appear to be a rather restricted approach, but such an initial attitude is understandable in the context of the evolution of sustainable management debate and practice in New Zealand local government.

---

2   *Integrating Sustainable Development into Best Value: Preliminary Guidance* (1998) LGA/LGMB.

First, local authorities' strategic and policy responses to sustainable resource management are governed by their roles and responsibilities identified in the RMA and, at the same time, the environmental impacts of many of their operational activities are also controlled by the requirements of resource consents under the RMA. Many local authorities have therefore assumed that executing their roles and responsibilities under the RMA and applying for resource consents at the operational level means they are managing their organisation in a sustainable way. This has meant that many authorities have not looked at the wider environmental aspects of their activities, such as purchasing, contract management, transport, waste minimisation and energy use.

Second, local authorities have received very little guidance and direction to date on issues such as LA 21, EMS and the many other issues associated with developing 'greener' local government organisations. In 1994, the Ministry for the Environment and the New Zealand Local Government Association produced an Agenda 21 guide for local government (New Zealand Ministry for the Environment 1994). This provided a number of case studies on LA 21 implementation and explained the background and New Zealand context. Many local authorities have incorporated the concept of LA 21 into their strategic planning documents and have undertaken community consultation exercises inherent in the LA 21 process. A couple have implemented sustainable city programmes—the 'eco-city' approach of Waitakere City Council is, perhaps, the most successful example to date. There has, however, been little other clear guidance and information provided by national government agencies or non-governmental organisations on LA 21 and how it relates to other initiatives such as EMS for local government. This poor level of support is not surprising given the small size of the local government sector as a whole and the fact that the limited resources available have been focused on getting to grips with the requirements of the RMA.

The level of guidance and direction provided to New Zealand local authorities to date on issues such as LA 21 and EMS contrasts with approaches taken in other countries. For example, the Australian Local Government Association has produced guidance (ALGA 1996) and training for local authorities on how to develop EMS, and there is a co-ordinated approach to LA 21. In the UK, the Improvement and Development Agency's Sustainable Development Unit, together with many other agencies, has provided extensive guidance, training and direction for local government on the EU Eco-management and Audit Scheme (EMAS) and LA 21[3] and this effort is supported by commitment to the principles of LA 21 by national government.

The drivers for EMS in New Zealand local authorities will evolve with time. Local government should become increasingly confident in looking at sustainable management beyond the implementation of the RMA and should receive clearer direction at the national level rather then merely responding to market forces. An increasingly concerned and environmentally conscious population would also provide drivers for local government to adopt EMS for their own organisations.

---

3   See The Improvement and Development Agency's Sustainable Development Unit publication list.

◢ The case study implementation process

Comments on the key stages of EMS development by the eight case studies are shown below.

Policies

Only one case study had an existing corporate environmental policy 'signed off 'by the chief executive, while another had pulled together a range of environmental policies from the strategic plan. Two others had long standing 'draft' corporate environmental policies which had not passed through the committee phase, had not been signed off by senior management nor implemented. The four remaining case studies did not have corporate environmental policies in place, but had tended to develop single-page policies that identified the uniqueness and values of the individual councils while intending to ensure that the requirements for ISO 14001 were met.

Environmental aspects

Many authorities found it hard to identify indirect effects. Direct effects were identified as part of the resource consent process and were being managed through that process. As a result, it was initially difficult for the case studies to see how EMS was adding value to sustainable management.

The only other direct effects that were readily identified related to health and safety issues. Direct effects such as transport use, energy use, material use and disposal were not generally identified, perhaps because their management is not controlled by the RMA. Indirect effects, when identified, were not seen as significant at first, again perhaps because their management is not controlled by the RMA.

Possible indirect effects could include purchasing policy, contractor and supplier management, contract management and specification, environmental education, economic redevelopment and business planning, community partnerships, consultation processes, etc. However, the training, consultation and drafting processes required by the project led to a greater appreciation of the significance of many of these indirect environmental effects and the potential influence that local authorities have in controlling them.

Objectives and targets

Given the influence of the RMA on local government environmental management, it was important to see if the case studies would set objectives and targets that took them beyond legislative compliance. In the first instance, many of the objectives and targets set related to the undertaking of monitoring conditions attached to resource consents. But the case studies did seek to set targets above and beyond legislative compliance in the following two key areas:

☐ Seeking ways of requiring contractors or consultants to identify the environmental impacts of their operations and to have mechanisms in place to minimise potential impacts

☐ Developing procedures for identifying and reporting on the environmental impacts of reports and policy proposals not governed by the RMA procedures

Management systems

Wherever possible, existing management systems were used to reduce the EMS development time and to help with an integrated management approach. Two of the operational case study units already had ISO 9001 in place which they used as the basis of the implementation and monitoring elements of the EMS. All the case studies operated within an annual planning and reporting structure which could incorporate environmental programme setting and performance monitoring. They all also had to establish auditing and management review procedures from scratch. The success of such approaches will need to be assessed over time.

◢ The guidance document

The guidance document was designed as a hands-on 'how to' guide for local authorities to be able to develop their own ISO 14001 EMS. The introduction provided the context for New Zealand local government and identified the relationship between the RMA and EMS development. The second part laid out the steps local authorities should take to getting started, with a special focus on ensuring commitment and developing staff awareness. The third part presented a step-by-step guide on how to develop, with case study examples and system development worksheets and templates.

A national training programme was initiated to introduce all local authorities to the guide and to an environmental performance management tool for use above and beyond the implementation of the RMA. The guide (Cockrean 1999) is now available to all New Zealand local authorities for use as the basis for EMS development.

◢ Failures and successes

There were a number of failures and successes in the ISO 14001 development process by the case studies. These are examined below.

Failures

Eight local authorities started the process of developing an ISO 14001 EMS at the start of the project. By the end of the case study development phase only five had developed or partially developed a complete EMS or had plans to do so. The reasons given by the three local authorities for dropping out of the study are listed below.

☐ **Insufficient resource availability**. Having committed to the project and undertaken training, some of the authorities felt that they could not find the amount of time necessary to see the process through to completion. This was especially true for the authorities that did not have corporate environmental policies in place, had not identified and quantified their environmental aspects and did not already have formalised operational control and reporting systems.

☐ **Lack of priority**. EMS development was not a priority for those case studies that dropped out. New priorities always came first and the work never got off the ground. The lack of priority was due in part to lack of recognised drivers and lack of senior management support and commitment.

☐ **Lack of perceived benefits**. Staff in several of the failed case studies did not appreciate the wider environmental impacts of their activities and therefore could not see beyond the control of direct environmental aspects through the consent management process. As discussed earlier, this focus on the direct environmental aspects may be due to a perception that meeting the requirements of the RMA will result in all significant environmental aspects being adequately controlled. By not appreciating the wider impact of their organisation's operations (such as supply chain management, contract management, education, awareness-raising, etc.) they could not appreciate the value added by an EMS. A greater focus in training on the importance of managing these indirect environmental impacts may have resulted in fewer failed case studies.

These reasons are by no means unique to New Zealand local authorities, but they highlight the importance of making sure that senior management is fully involved in the process and can provide all the strategic support and leadership necessary to make sure individual units can make ISO 14001 a priority.

For those case studies that were still developing their EMS there were also a number of 'technical' stumbling blocks which slowed up the EMS development process. The main ones are described below.

☐ **Focus on direct operational environmental aspects**. Implementation of the RMA has focused local authorities' attention on the management of direct operational impacts on the environment, with little consideration given to wider environmental aspects. This lack of a wider perspective and knowledge of indirect environmental aspects caused particular problems when developing environmental policies that were 'appropriate to the nature, scale and environmental impacts of its activities, products or services'[4] and when identifying the environmental aspects of its activities 'which it can be expected to influence'.[5]

---

4   'Requirements for an environmental policy', ISO 14001, section 4.2a (ISO 1996d).
5   'Identification of environmental aspects', ISO 14001, section 4.3.1. (ISO 1996d).

☐ **Lack of quantification of environmental aspects.** While the successful case studies were able to identify many of their environmental aspects, there was often no monitoring of whether the impacts were increasing year on year. This was particularly true of environmental aspects related to transport use, energy use, office waste management and herbicide and pesticide use. This was due in part to the relative newness of some of the roles and responsibilities of local government with regard to monitoring of environmental impacts, and the fact that the wider environmental impacts of their operations had not been recognised and were, therefore, neither monitored nor managed.

☐ **Identification of significance.** The initial approach taken to identifying significance by many of the case studies was based on whether the aspect was controlled by a resource consent. Such a focus on significance based on legislation is not surprising given the importance of the RMA and the lack of documented monitoring of indirect aspects. As a result of the project, some of the case studies were developing a risk-based approach to significance testing which incorporated an assessment of the amount of influence they could be expected to have on the environmental aspect. Such an approach should be of particular value when assessing indirect effects and the management of contractors and suppliers.

Successes

To date, none of the case study local authorities have chosen to certify their EMS and it is still too early to be able to identify resource savings and reduced environmental impacts, especially as many of the case studies had not been monitoring these areas previous to the EMS development. No clear indication was sought during the course of the project as to whether the case studies were intending to seek certification at the end of the project. There may be a number of reasons why none of the case studies has chosen to certify its EMS as yet:

☐ They were never intending to seek certification but wanted to develop a system that would help identify resource savings and help with resource consent management.

☐ They are waiting to fully embed the EMS into the organisation before seeking certification at a later date.

☐ They perceive no benefit in gaining certification because they feel no pressure to do so from regulators, community, pressure groups, central government or other stakeholders.

There are, however, a number of areas where the development of ISO 14001 can be seen as beneficial for the case study organisations.

☐ **A broader appreciation of environmental impacts.** One of the major reasons why Local Government New Zealand supported the project was because it was felt that the development of EMSs would help local authorities appreciate the full breadth of their organisations' environmental impacts other than those controlled by the RMA. The systems developed by the case studies have shown this to be true, although a greater level of senior management support would be needed to turn the broader appreciation of organisational impacts into real improvements in performance.

☐ **The integration of environmental performance management into existing management structures**. The case studies identified the potential of integrating EMS programme setting and performance management into the annual plan development and monitoring process, and the operational control procedures into existing quality control systems. Such approaches at integration with existing management structures should help with the organisational change necessary if an EMS is to help deliver continual improvement in performance in the long term.

◢ Conclusions

The approach to environmental management within New Zealand local government is presently focused on the implementation of, and compliance with, the RMA which requires an effects-based assessment of environmental impacts. There has not been a focus on identifying and managing wider (indirect) environmental impacts. Very few local authorities have stand-alone corporate environmental polices, LA 21 initiatives or EMSs.

As local authorities start to appreciate their influence in improving environmental performance in such areas as supply chain management, contract management, budget management, and environmental education and awareness-raising, their approach to environmental management will evolve beyond resource savings and legislative compliance. This may enable them to become increasingly confident in looking at sustainable management beyond the implementation of the RMA

Many of the case studies involved in developing the guidance struggled with identifying and managing indirect environmental aspects and setting improvement targets beyond compliance with the RMA. Significantly, they also suffered from a lack of senior management commitment to the EMS development process. As a consequence, the effectiveness of ISO 14001 for New Zealand local government to create environmental performance improvements beyond legislative compliance is, presently, limited.

The effectiveness of ISO 14001 as a tool for managing the process of continual improvement in environmental performance can be realised only with senior management commitment and leadership along with an appreciation of the organisational change that needs to occur to deal with the wider environmental issues of importance to local government. In the absence of wider organisational change and commitment, the development of ISO 14001 alone will not achieve long-term improvements in the management of the wider environmental effects of local government.

Nevertheless, ISO 14001 is an appropriate tool for helping local authorities meet their present perceived environmental management needs of legislative compliance and resource savings. It is hoped that local authorities' appreciation of their role in influencing the environmental performance of organisational processes such as supply chain management, contract management and facilities management will grow over time. If it does, the relevance of ISO 14001 for New Zealand local government will also be recognised.

ENVIRONMENTAL INITIATIVES TO IMPROVE THE QUALITY OF THE LOCAL ENVIRONMENT
Kunda Nordic Cement AS, Estonia

Anne Randmer
Centre for Development Programmes, Estonia

This chapter discusses some of the implementation experiences of environmental management programmes at an old cement plant—Kunda Nordic Cement Ltd in Estonia. The overview of the implementation process is given and some immediate outcomes analysed.

◢ Background

Kunda Nordic Cement is located in Kunda, north-east Estonia, on the south coast of the Gulf of Finland. The company is more than a hundred years old. It underwent major reconstruction and modernisation in the 1970s, and was privatised in 1992. The company is a large-scale industry in Estonian terms, with annual sales of around US$27 million in 1998 (around 660,000 tonnes of clinker produced out of which around 320,000 tonnes of cement is manufactured). The value of sales in 1999 was around US$24 million, with the fall mainly due to changes in world markets, particularly the strength of US dollar, although 590,000 tonnes of clinker and 360,000 tonnes of cement were produced; 75% of the clinker and cement is exported to both Western and Eastern markets.

The town of Kunda is heavily dependent on the company, both economically and environmentally. The company is the largest employer in town, providing around 360 jobs. Like most industries in Central and Eastern European countries, Kunda Nordic Cement was owned by the state, which planned all investments centrally according to 'command economy rules'; environmental investments were given no priority during the Soviet era.

Emissions released by Kunda Nordic Cement make up the major part of the pollution in the town and neighbourhood. Local residents, the town's government and regional environmental officials made continuous and serious complaints about environmental pollution from the plant. The air pollution from the plant has also caused international problems as the major winds spread the dust to Finland.

Due to severe air pollution—dust emissions were as high as 80,000 tonnes (146 kg per tonne of production; see also Fig. 4.1)—consideration was given to shutting the company down. However, taking into account social considerations, the municipal and environmental authorities gave Kunda Nordic Cement permission to continue production but only on the condition that it established an efficient environmental programme to reduce environmental pollution and implement it according to an agreed schedule.

Although in a very weak economic and environmental shape, the company was privatised by international financial intermediaries: the International Finance Corporation (IFC), the European Investment Bank (EIB), the Nordic Environment Finance Corporation (NEFCO) and some multinational corporations.

◢ Implementing the environmental programme at Kunda Nordic Cement

The first environmental investment programme of about US$7 million was carried out between 1993 and 1997. The programme mainly consisted of 'end-of-pipe' solutions to reduce air pollution, i.e. installing electric and sack filters and renovating a kiln, financed by the new shareholders of the company (EIB, IFC, NEFCO). After implementation of this 'first-aid' environmental programme, dust emissions from the plant's stacks were

Figure 4.1 **Dynamics of dust emissions realised by Kunda Cement Plant (kg per tonne of production)**

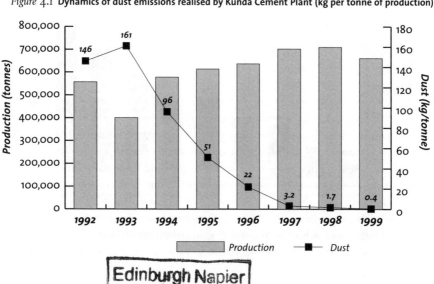

drastically reduced. In 1993, more than 70,000 tonnes of dust was emitted by Kunda Nordic Cement (161 kg per tonne of production), while in 1997 the total dust emission was only 2,250 tonnes (3.2 kg per tonne of production).

When developing the next environmental investment programme, an environmental audit was carried out in 1997 by Estonian auditors under the guidance of consultants of the internationally recognised firm, Det Norske Veritas. The audit findings indicated that environmental problems at the company remained severe, and large investments were required to solve them (see Fig. 4.2). Management of the company recognised that a special study needed to be carried out to optimise investments.

Based on recommendations made in the audit report, the company accepted the proposal of the Estonian Ministry of Environment to join the Estonian–Finnish bilateral co-operation programme as a pilot company to implement an environmental management system (EMS) that fulfils the requirements of the international standard ISO 14001. The aim of the co-operation programme was to build local capacity to assist Estonian industries in implementing EMSs based on either ISO 14001 or the EU Eco-management and Audit Scheme (EMAS).

Local consultants were selected to carry out the EMS implementation at the pilot company under the supervision of a Finnish consultant. The total cost of the pilot project was US$75,000 which was shared between the Ministry of Environment of Finland (80% of costs) and Kunda Nordic Cement (20%). The project was implemented during 1998–99.

The main goal of the pilot project at Kunda Nordic Cement was to train all key personnel (top management, line managers, environmental and quality managers, and laboratory staff) to prepare a company-specific EMS that fits as much as possible with the routine management system of the company and not to create any additional bureau-

Figure 4.2 **Dynamics of resource fees and pollution charges at Kunda Nordic Cement, 1993–2001**

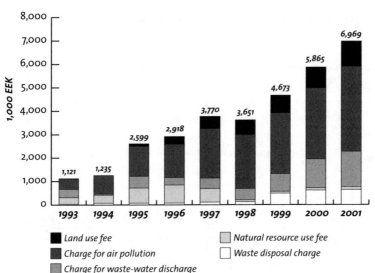

cracy. Also, a special training and practice programme for all employees of the company was tailored to ensure that the company was ready for the certification audit and that it would be able to maintain the system after the consultants left.

The implementation scheme

For practical reasons, the project was divided into several modules based on the structure and elements of the ISO 14001 standard itself. The modules were:

- ☐ Design an environmental policy

- ☐ Develop appropriate methodology to identify environmental issues and environmental aspects

- ☐ Develop company-specific criteria to assess environmental aspects and impacts in order to select significant aspects

- ☐ Elaborate an environmental programme and action plan

- ☐ Establish a documentation and records system

- ☐ Design a communication (both external and internal) system and carry out in-service training

- ☐ Establish a self-monitoring and internal auditing system

- ☐ Provide special training for internal auditors

- ☐ Carry out an internal audit (conducted by internal auditors)

- ☐ Conduct a management review

As the main aim of the project was to give the company team hands-on skills to implement the EMS, it not only required strong commitment from top management, but also from every employee who were required to dedicate themselves to the project and, importantly, to maintain and develop the EMS after the project was closed. We would point out how important it is not to allow the environmental manager alone to implement the EMS because its operation depends on the involvement and dedication of *all* employees. We have witnessed many cases where the elaboration and maintenance of an EMS was the environmental manager's personal responsibility. As a result, after a while the EMS ceased to operate, and the money spent on certification was wasted.

Based on their previous experience, the consultants planned the practical work of EMS implementation in Kunda Nordic Cement through a series of two-day workshops, conducted every six weeks. Twenty-five key personnel were selected by the consultants and nominated by top management to participate in the design and implementation of the EMS. The group was headed by the management representative, the administration director and involved all line managers, quality and environment managers, heads of maintenance divisions, the financial manager, the head of laboratory and the captain of the harbour (the harbour belongs to the company).

The workshops gave the key personnel a very good opportunity to discuss openly all environmental matters on a regular basis. Also, they allowed the essence of the standard to be interpreted and understood in a common-sense way; especially the practical identification procedure and analysis of environmental aspects. This was positively highlighted as a useful exercise to evaluate the potential impacts on the environment of an individual's activities.

In the workshops the consultants 'interpreted' the ISO 14001 definitions and elements into language that was easy to understand taking into account the context of the company. After explaining the elements of the standard in the plenary session, participants were divided into smaller groups, each facilitated by a consultant. In these groups participants were given the opportunity to practise relevant issues, such as defining environmental policy for Kunda Nordic Cement, identifying environmental aspects, elaborating criteria to prioritise the aspects, designing appropriate external and internal communication, reviewing monitoring and defining the measurement system for the company. The small group work proved very useful as the consultants could easily see if something remained misunderstood and had a good chance to make the necessary amendments to the training programme.

A very important component of the whole project was the training of the company's internal auditors. Fifteen employees, including line managers, the captain of harbour, the environmental manager and the head of the laboratory, were nominated as internal auditors. Having more than two or three internal auditors in the company gives it the potential to plan internal audits on a regular basis, covering all operations and relevant documentation at least once a year. The work is divided so that the auditing of a particular part of the process and reporting of the findings does not take more than a day.

Looking back at the work done already, we would point out some of the critical moments in the implementation of Kunda Nordic Cement's EMS:

☐ **Identification of environmental aspects and defining their impacts**. It is essential to divide the production process into small parts (activities) and let company staff analyse for themselves the existing or potential environmental issues that are arising or could arise from these activities. Acting in this way, more than 300 environmental aspects, of which 25 were considered as significant, were identified in two days. We believe this would not have been the case if external consultants worked without the input of company personnel who knew, in detail, the processes and products of the company. The close involvement of key personnel also made it easy to integrate the environmental programme (projects to approach goals and targets) into the company's investment plan.

☐ **Setting realistic goals and targets**. The group work method is a very efficient way of identifying, negotiating and getting a consensus, as these goals and targets are never reached without committed employees. It is also very useful to have financial managers in the team.

☐ **Elaboration of easily understood training programmes for all employees**. Employee training should not be delivered as boring lectures but should include practical work to identify how each employee can influence the environment. It is better to conduct the training in small groups (15–20 persons) based on their similar production activities. Although it might seem too time-consuming, we felt it was very useful to give a short introduction to the key elements of the EMS and then let the employees discuss in smaller groups of four to five the potential environmental impacts of the operations they run every day. It was also quite surprising for top management that more than a hundred project proposals to improve the environment, most of them at no cost or low cost, were made by employees. As a result, the company got many new 'champions' in addition to the staff who were supposed to be leaders because of their job description.

☐ **Realistic time-frame and proper evaluation of possible risks.** Implementing an EMS from scratch, i.e. organisations that have not implemented a quality management system before, usually takes more time than expected. The top management of the company and the consultants were pretty confident that Kunda Nordic Cement would be ready for an external audit by the summer of 1999. The company will be ready for certification some time in 2000.

◢ Conclusions

To conclude, we would like to report some cost figures. The direct expenses for implementation of the EMS based on ISO 14001 were around US$75,000 which were the consultants' fees. In addition, the company allocated more than 500 person-days to the work performed by key personnel/team members. It is very difficult, if not impossible, to estimate the work done by every employee.

So far, the environmental policy has been defined and the main environmental goals set up. More than 300 environmental aspects were identified and recorded, of which 25 were ranked as significant. The environmental programme is being elaborated to reduce the plant's adverse environmental impacts. The tentative programme for the year 2000 includes environmental investments of more than US$2.7 million, mainly to solve the solid waste problems.

Implemented environmental projects from 1999 include: 63 tonnes of clinker dust were recycled as a valuable mineral fertiliser; and the boilerhouse was reconstructed to use natural gas instead of the oil shale that resulted in reduced air pollution and solid waste generation.

As a result of this intensive EMS implementation exercise it is expected that Kunda Nordic Cement will be certified to ISO 14001 in 2000 and will be able to maintain and continuously improve the system in the future.

As a follow-up to the established EMS, and to demonstrate the continuous improvement approach, the company has started to prepare its integrated pollution prevention and control system based on best available techniques.

Finally, the approach worked out within this pilot project will be applied to the implementation of an ISO 14001-based EMS in the furniture industry in Estonia in 2001–2002.

Part 2
CERTIFICATION AND
REGISTRATION EXPERIENCES

5

JOINT EMS AND GROUP CERTIFICATION
A cost-effective route for SMEs to achieve ISO 14001*

Jonas Ammenberg
Linköping University, Sweden

Berit Börjesson
Altea AB, Sweden

Olof Hjelm
Linköping University, Sweden

At Hackefors Industrial District in Sweden, 30 small and medium-sized enterprises (SMEs) are co-operating on environmental issues. Uniquely, this group has formed a network and established a joint EMS in accordance with ISO 14001. In this chapter, the EMS model used at Hackefors is presented and the cost savings that have resulted are analysed. Environmental improvements are also briefly discussed.

It can be concluded that, by networking and implementing a joint EMS, the SMEs (mostly small and 'micro' enterprises[1]) at Hackefors have established a rational and cost-effective solution that has facilitated both the implementation and maintenance of EMSs. Although the EMSs were only recently certified, many environmental and commercial improvements have already been observed. Many of the companies have received positive responses from their customers and believe that the EMS improves their ability to obtain contracts for the sale of products and/or services. Furthermore, the companies at Hackefors believe that having an EMS based on ISO 14001 results in commercial and environmental benefits.

---

* This study was financed by NUTEK, Swedish National Board for Industrial and Technical Development.
1   Micro enterprises are defined as those with fewer than ten employees.

◢ Introduction

Worldwide, companies are developing EMSs according to the requirements of ISO 14001 and/or the EU Eco-management and Audit Scheme (EMAS). The number of certified companies is increasing rapidly. By August 1999, nearly 11,000 companies were certified to ISO 14001 (Peglau 1999) and, by September 1999, roughly 2,500 were registered to EMAS (European Commission 1999). Both ISO 14001 and EMAS require environmental procedures and requirements to be communicated to suppliers and contractors, including requirements for EMSs. SMEs often supply large organisations.

SMEs are defined by the European Commission as independent companies employing fewer than 250 employees, with a turnover of less than €40 million or an annual balance sheet total not exceeding €27 million (CEC 1996). Independent enterprises are those not owned as to 25% or more of the capital or the voting rights by other enterprises. Small enterprises are further defined as independent companies with fewer than 50 employees and a turnover smaller than €7 million or an annual balance sheet total not exceeding €5 million. There are no official Swedish statistics on the definition of SMEs, which is why it has not been possible to ascertain the exact number of SMEs or their turnover in accordance with the EC definition. Official statistics from Statistic Sweden show that 99.5% of Swedish companies have fewer than 250 employees and a turnover of no more than €40 million. It seems reasonable to assume that many of these companies are SMEs. Together they have a combined annual sales figure that represents 42% of total annual sales of Swedish companies. Even if it is not proved that there is, in general, a connection between a company's turnover and its environmental impact, the fact that SMEs represent a considerable part of the total annual sales suggests that they are important economically and likely to have an associated importance from an environmental point of view. It should also be observed that SMEs in Sweden, and probably elsewhere, are not subject to environmental regulation to the same extent as are larger companies (see e.g. SFS 1998: 899) and, therefore, their environmental impacts may be poorly controlled.

Implementation of EMSs requires substantial resources, both financially and in terms of staff, and many SMEs are hesitant of implementing EMSs. In a study of SMEs in the UK, all of the companies studied found the initial stages, such as the environmental review, register of significant environmental aspects and policy requirements, difficult (Hillary 1996). It is essential to find a cost-effective solution that facilitates the implementation and maintenance of EMSs in SMEs. It is also important that such a solution is not regarded as a 'light version' of ISO 14001 or EMAS, but involves a complete EMS.

By working together, 30 SMEs at the Hackefors Industrial District in Sweden have overcome many of the difficulties mentioned above and were certified according to ISO 14001 at the beginning of 1999. This chapter discusses how the joint EMS has affected commercial and business-related matters. Based on the experiences gained from this network, the possibilities for SMEs to use group certification to gain ISO 14001 are analysed. It has been asked whether or not implementation of EMSs leads to environmental improvements or if it is just a new method for 'greenwashing' companies. Therefore, the effect the joint EMS has had on environmental performance is briefly discussed.

◢ Formation of the network

Hackefors Industrial District in Linköping, Sweden, consists of about 90 SMEs with 1,500 employees. Of these, 50% have fewer than eight employees while the largest has 70. They represent a wide range of businesses, including manufacturing, waste recycling, transportation, construction and graphic industries.

A common trend in Sweden in the late 1980s was to form business associations, and this is what happened at Hackefors. The objectives of these associations varied considerably. The main objective at Hackefors was to stop the closure of the local post office. Over the following years the business association worked on various issues, such as an information post and, later, environmental matters.

The starting point for the environmental work was in 1996 when an inventory of waste generated at all 90 companies was carried out. The following year a central unit for collection, separation and utilisation of waste was created. This work raised awareness of environmental issues in many of the companies and some of them decided to go one step further. They wanted to establish an environmental profile for the district and find a means of publicising their environmental achievements and credentials. During discussions with environmental organisations, the possibilities of EMSs and ISO 14001 were considered. Over 30 companies formed the Hackefors Environmental Group (HEG) and started to develop a joint EMS according to ISO 14001. Of these enterprises, 17 have five or fewer employees, four have between six and 10 employees, two have between 11 and 20 employees, five between 21 and 30 employees and four have more than 30 employees. This means that a majority of the enterprises are 'micro'.

An additional group at Hackefors consisting of 20 companies is following the HEG example. At present, several industrial districts in the Linköping region, as well as other parts of Sweden, have started to implement joint EMSs.

◢ The joint EMS

The EMS model used at Hackefors Industrial District is called the Hackefors model. Each enterprise within the HEG has an EMS of its own that fulfils the requirements of ISO 14001 and thus holds its own certificate. In this way, the Hackefors model does not differ from other EMSs. There are, however, many unique factors that are of interest for further study, such as the small size of the enterprises, the way the EMS has been implemented, the system administration and group certification. The overall organisation, interpretation of requirements, documentation, training and internal auditing will be presented in more detail.

Organisation

The joint EMS is organised in a way that is very similar to the organisation of systems for larger industrial concerns (see Fig. 5.1). All companies have an environmental co-ordina-

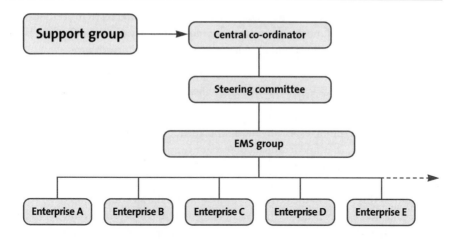

Figure 5.1 **Organisation of the Hackefors Environmental Group in accordance with the Hackefors model**

tor and these together form the EMS group. From this group a steering committee is chosen, consisting of seven of the environmental co-ordinators, which in turn selects a central co-ordinator. A few individuals (i.e. the support group) support the central co-ordinator and the steering committee and assist the co-ordinators with their duties. Decisions are prepared in the steering committee and taken by the EMS group. The steering committee, together with the central co-ordinator and the support group, can be compared to a core environmental department in an industrial concern.

The central co-ordinator can be selected from the companies in the network or from outside. At Hackefors, the co-ordinator is employed by a consulting firm which is a member of the HEG. Personnel from this firm have supported the central co-ordinator and the steering committee, and assisted the environmental co-ordinators regarding the accomplishment of environmental reviews, documentation, training, etc. The central co-ordinator has many important functions, such as preparing documents, identifying and communicating common legal requirements, raising interest and commitment, calling meetings, handling minutes and dispatches, and planning environmental training.

The steering committee is led by the central co-ordinator. Important functions for the committee are to develop the EMS and to plan environmental auditing. It also inspects and discusses new or revised documents, especially the central document—the EMS manual—which is identical for all the enterprises. The steering committee examines training needs, what the training should include, etc. During the implementation process, the committee met twice a month. After the certification it has meetings when necessary, but at least once every three months.

The environmental co-ordinators are responsible for their enterprise's environmental matters. Together they meet on a regular basis within the EMS group. The purpose of these meetings is to make decisions, train and educate the co-ordinators, and provide information about and discuss new or revised procedures or documents. During the implementation phase the EMS group met once a month, but after receiving certification they meet every second month. In order to promote efficiency, a maximum time is set on the length of the meetings, and agendas are distributed well in advance.

Interpretation of requirements and documentation

It is our experience that many environmental managers find it difficult to interpret the requirements of ISO 14001, especially those who are not accustomed to reading standard or legal documents. They find it difficult to prepare, control and update all the documents needed to fulfil the requirements of ISO 14001. Smaller enterprises often lack competence and resources, both financial and human.

To address this problem the central co-ordinator and the steering committee prepare many of the documents needed. The EMS documentation consists of two main binders, one of which is identical for all the enterprises—the EMS manual. The other main binder contains documents that are specific for each enterprise. For a majority of these specific documents, the central co-ordinator and the steering committee prepare documentary templates, which simplify document completion. Centralised handling and steering of many of the EMS documents saves the SMEs much of the administrative work. This, however, requires good communication, so that each enterprise understands the function of the documents and why they are needed. In addition to the two main binders, there are binders for each enterprise's records.

Environmental review and assessment of environmental aspects

The central co-ordinator and the steering committee prepare guidelines for environmental reviews that facilitate the identification of environmental aspects. An important, and often difficult, part of the review is the assessment of environmental aspects. A joint assessment method is used by the enterprises at HEG. Each company carries out its own assessment according to this method, but the co-ordinator and the support group assist and supervise in this process.

One of ISO 14001's main requirements is compliance to legal requirements (see e.g. Rosenbaum 1997; Wilson and Thomas 1998). The companies together subscribe to the latest issue of environmental legislation on CD-ROM and every company has a register of environmentally relevant legal paragraphs that affect its activities. The central co-ordinator is responsible for the identification of legal requirements that are generally applicable (to many of the companies within HEG), while the environmental co-ordinators are responsible for individually applicable legal and other requirements.

Environmental targets

Each enterprise has individual objectives and targets. There are also collective environmental objectives for the HEG, which are not quantified. It is not mandatory for the individual companies to have objectives or targets that support the collective objectives. Rather, these objectives are to be seen as guidelines.

Training

Environmental training is considered to be vital. Knowledge of environmental matters and EMSs is necessary to motivate the staff and to make them understand how to cope with environmentally related tasks. Therefore, the Hackefors model puts great emphasis and substantial resources on environmental training. Each employee receives at least 30 hours' training. This large amount of training was partially made possible by government subsidies. The training included basic environmental information, education on EMSs and ISO 14001, waste management, environmental impact of industries in general and legal and other requirements.

Internal auditing

All the environmental co-ordinators were offered training in internal auditing, which the auditing authority arranged. Fifteen participated, and ten completed the training and were approved (certified as internal auditors). These internal auditors conduct all internal audits within HEG at a set price per hour (€58), which they decide together. At small or micro enterprises it might be difficult to use the personnel as internal auditors since the auditors should be independent and objective. At Hackefors the auditors do not audit their own companies, so this solution circumvents the problem of ensuring independence.

Certification and external audits

As noted previously, each enterprise has an individual certificate. The term 'group certification' refers to the fact that all of the companies were certified at the same time and much of the work was co-ordinated within the group. Each enterprise was audited at the time of certification. This will not be the case for the follow-up audits, however. Since the documentation and procedures conform for enterprises within the same line of business, the external auditing authority has agreed to audit only one enterprise within each line of business at a time. Each company, however, must have been externally audited within a period of three years.

The fact that enterprises within the HEG have many identical documents and procedures ought to result in similar judgements by the auditors. However, the external auditing procedure at HEG proved that auditors interpret the requirements of ISO 14001 differently, and so make different demands. During the certification audit, several identical or very similar documents/procedures were judged differently. This indicates a serious problem—inconsistent interpretation of the standard's requirements by assessors. Inconsistency may result in loss of confidence in certification to an EMS standard in general. The auditors at Hackefors represent the same firm. It is probable that the way requirements are interpreted varies even more between different auditing authorities. The external audit procedure at Hackefors also showed that some auditors lack experience and competence regarding auditing of EMSs.

Costs

Since the Hackefors joint EMS is a pilot project, some of the costs for the implementation are not known (or are, for various reasons, not allowed to be made public). The consulting firm, where the central co-ordinator and the support group are employed, runs similar projects with joint EMSs at other industrial districts. The costs connected with these projects are more representative and hence more interesting. Therefore, where known, the amounts presented below are from the Hackefors joint EMS, while others relate to similar and probably more valid projects.

For the implementation of the EMS, the participating enterprises pay a stipulated amount per employee to finance the work of the central co-ordinator and the support group. This amount does not include training, certification or internal audits. At Hackefors, this amount was roughly €195. Regarding the later projects, the figure was set at €345 per employee for enterprises with no more than 50 employees and considerably lower (somewhere between €25 and €155) for larger enterprises. Of HEG's costs for training, 50% was covered by governmental subsidies. The remaining cost was €58 per employee.

In Sweden, there is another project without any kind of subsidies where the Hackefors model is used. For that project the number of hours for training has roughly been halved (16 hours). This shows that the model works without subsidies, with the caveat that the amount of training has to be reduced or the budget for training increased.

Concerning the maintenance of the EMSs, together the companies finance the central administration, i.e. the work done by the central co-ordinator and the support group. As for the implementation side, the costs for each enterprise depend on the number of employees. The co-ordinators in the steering committee get no payment from the other companies.

◢ Cost savings and commercial effects

The Hackefors model has certainly led to significant cost savings compared to individual certification. For many reasons, however, it is difficult to estimate how much money the joint EMS has saved at Hackefors. Comparisons have indicated that the price for this group certification is at least 50% lower than for individual certification. Many of the cost savings are because a majority of the expenses have been shared between 30 enterprises. Furthermore, HEG was at an advantage when negotiating the choice of an external auditing authority because of the large number of involved enterprises and the fact that the joint EMS was such a novel approach. The use of internal auditors was also cost-effective compared to having one internal auditor at every company or using external consultants. The co-ordinated training was advantageous from a financial point of view, and the government subsidies played an important role. Since follow-up audits are carried out less frequently than for individual certification, auditing costs are lower for some enterprises within HEG. Effective and rational administration has led to further savings.

In a recent study, 12 of the environmental co-ordinators were interviewed to see if the co-operation and joint EMS have lead to any changes regarding environmental performance or commercial and business-related matters (Ammenberg and Hjelm 1999). This study indicates that an absolute majority of the environmental co-ordinators believe that the EMS has made it easier to win contracts for products and services, and that ISO 14001-based EMSs lead to commercial and environmental improvements in general.

◢ Environmental effects

The Ammenberg and Hjelm study (1999) revealed that the joint EMS at Hackefors has already led to many environmental improvements. The main improvements were identified within the area of waste management, on which the companies had co-operated before the EMSs were implemented. Therefore, these improvements must be seen as a consequence of networking, rather than of the EMS per se (this finding is supported by the co-ordinators). Previously, there were in general only two waste categories, one for incineration and one for non-combustible waste (and, in some cases, one for special waste). Today, there are about 20 waste categories separated at the central unit, some of which are re-used by other companies. Before, the fraction for incineration included waste that should not be incinerated, such as electronics, etc.

Other areas where improvements have been found, or environmental targets promise positive effects, are emissions, energy, goods and transportation. Examples of improvements are: reduced emissions of solvents; reduced emissions to air and water; more effective use of energy; substitution for more environmentally sound goods; and co-ordinated transportation. Many of these improvements are, according to the co-ordinators, a direct consequence of the EMS implementation.

◢ Other benefits

In addition to the mentioned environmental improvements, many other benefits have occurred as a consequence of the network, with the companies co-operating in many areas. Electricity is bought jointly and the companies have managed to get district heating to Hackefors. There is a common pool of workers, collective caretakers and security guards, while some office equipment (photocopiers, etc.) is also shared.

The environmental training has brought about an increased interest in education. Today 144 employees are studying computers and 60 take English lessons. A few are also studying German, French, chemistry and natural sciences.

◢ Conclusions

It can be concluded that networking and group certification have led to a rational and cost-effective solution for the SMEs (mostly small or micro enterprises) at Hackefors. The Hackefors model has facilitated both implementation and maintenance of EMSs according to ISO 14001. Several industrial districts in the Linköping region as well as other parts of Sweden have started to work according to the Hackefors model. It remains to be seen if the outcome of these joint efforts will be successful, but the prospects are promising. This indicates, at least on a national level and for small enterprises, that many obstacles for SMEs might be overcome through the use of the Hackefors model or similar approaches.

The role of the central co-ordinator is of great importance. The presence of a dedicated person was crucial for the successful outcome of the Hackefors project, especially since this was a pilot project with no equivalent experiences to learn from. This could be considered the model's weak point, with so much depending on one person. The central co-ordinator must be a good communicator who is able to convince the leaders of the SMEs that environmental issues are important, both from an environmental and commercial point of view. Experiences from Hackefors also show that this person must have a good understanding of the entire district.

Although a relatively short period of time (six months) has passed since group certification, the EMSs have resulted in many positive environmental changes. The main environmental improvements seem to have occurred in the area of waste management, where the companies within HEG had already co-operated for a few years prior to the implementation of the EMSs. There are also environmental improvements that are direct consequences of the EMSs, notably in relation to emissions, energy, goods and transportation.

Many of the companies have received positive responses from their customers and believe the EMS has improved their ability to win contracts for the sale of products and/or services. A clear majority of the environmental co-ordinators at HEG are of the opinion that EMSs based on ISO 14001 lead to positive commercial *and* environmental effects.

It is reasonable to assume that, by virtue of their numbers, SMEs are an important group from an environmental point of view. It is clear that these firms, in Sweden at least, are not subject to the same extent of regulatory control as larger companies. Hence, group certifications and joint EMSs similar to the Hackefors model could provide an important means for reducing environmental damage caused by the activities of SMEs.

FINANCIAL SERVICES AND ISO 14001
The challenge of determining indirect environmental aspects in a global certification*

Bettina Furrer and Heinrich Hugenschmidt

UBS AG, Switzerland

In 1998, after the merger (see Box 6.1), UBS's environmental management system (EMS) was completed in accordance with the international ISO 14001 standard for environmental management systems. In May 1999, UBS AG received certification according to the ISO 14001 environmental standard. This makes UBS the first bank in the world to have its environmental management system in banking operations certified according to ISO 14001 on a worldwide basis. The bank's in-house operations in Switzerland were also recognised as being in accordance with ISO 14001. Certification was carried out by SGS International Certification Services AG.

UBS AG (see Box 6.1) is a globally active financial institution and, as such, subject to continual change. It is therefore crucial for the EMS to be established along banking processes and not to form an independent management system. However, this also means that the EMS is dependent on the design of internal banking procedures. In a merger situation, this can be both an advantage and a disadvantage. On one hand, when banking processes are redesigned it is possible to systematically integrate environmental aspects. On the other hand, the constant reorganisation can also destroy past efforts made to implement environmental operational procedures. However, the bank's organisational changes have influenced the development of the EMS, and the work on it is continuous as banking procedures are constantly subject to change. Furthermore, the bank's reorganisation may also influence the implementation schedule of environmental measures in both a positive and a negative sense.

---

* Opinions expressed in this chapter are the authors' and do not necessarily reflect the opinions of UBS.

UBS IS ONE OF THE WORLD'S LEADING FINANCIAL SERVICES GROUPS. UBS WAS formed in 1998 through the merger of Union Bank of Switzerland and Swiss Bank Corporation. Today, UBS is represented in over 50 countries. UBS Group consists of three divisions: UBS Switzerland, UBS Asset Management and UBS Warburg.

☐ UBS Switzerland covers the Private Banking and the Private and Corporate Clients businesses. The former provides Swiss-based banking for high-net-worth international individuals, while the latter offers standardised banking products for both private customers and small and medium-sized enterprises.

☐ UBS Asset Management specialises in asset management, including institutional investors and mutual funds. It is a major global investment management player in a number of segments, with a particularly strong market position in the USA, the UK, Japan and Switzerland.

☐ UBS Warburg consists of three businesses: Corporate and Institutional Clients, Private Equity, and International Investment Services, including e-services. UBS Warburg offers a comprehensive spectrum of investment banking services on a global basis. Corporate clients of UBS Warburg have access to various services: funding and advice for mergers and acquisitions; for equity and bond issues; for foreign currency transactions; for financial risk management; and for fixed-income and treasury products. Private clients have access to international onshore private banking and e-services.

Box 6.1 **UBS's global business activities**

UBS experienced the integration of environmental issues in banking processes as being much easier than a geographical approach that focuses on single locations. The reason for this is that banking processes are often managed from one organisational unit and the regional sub-units report directly to this central unit. It is therefore easier and more efficient to focus on these key interfaces. However, as soon as it is a matter of evaluation of legal compliance, a more geographic approach is necessary. In Switzerland, for example, environmental regulations can vary from region to region.

In a multinational company, the perception of environmental challenges contrast from business area to business area and from country to country. The different divisions have distinct perceptions of risks and business opportunities. Time-frames are set in either the short or long term, depending on the products and services. Likewise, clients may have divergent expectations as to how far environmental commitment should go. Furthermore, in different regions of the world, the political and regulatory systems vary and the infrastructure is more or less developed. Evidently, this also affects the integration of environmental issues into our activities.

Within a multinational company it is imperative that the responsibility for environmental matters lies with every single employee. UBS therefore integrates environmental aspects into training in accordance with its environmental policy. The aim is to create awareness, motivation and competence with regard to environmentally friendly conduct. This requires awareness of environmental issues affecting the function concerned. Environmental modules are therefore incorporated systematically into all three levels of UBS training—junior trainees, training for established staff and management training.

Our environmental training focuses on environmental issues in Swiss commercial banking and in international investment banking, environmental aspects of asset management (e.g. the 'investment game') as well as 'banking and ecology as management responsibilities'. In 1997 and 1998, approximately 1,200 UBS employees attended environmental course modules. Roughly half were trainees, while the other half were established staff. Executive training courses were attended by 142 staff in 1997 and 33 in 1998.

The new UBS AG environmental policy was passed by the Group Executive Board in July 1998 (UBS AG 1998a). Our environmental policy concentrates on the fields of banking, in-house ecology and environmental management. In banking, we aim to take advantage of environmental opportunities and duly take environmental risks into account in our risk management. With regard to in-house ecology, we focus on the reduction of greenhouse gas emissions. We strive to ensure the efficient implementation of our measures by a lean and effective environmental management system (see Fig. 6.1). In all our efforts, we seek open and active dialogue with all stakeholders concerned (e.g. clients, shareholders, employees, authorities, environmental partners, organisations and experts).

Based on this environmental policy, the Private and Corporate Clients and Warburg Dillon Read (WDR) divisions have each formulated additional policies as the basis for

Figure 6.1 **UBS's environmental management system**

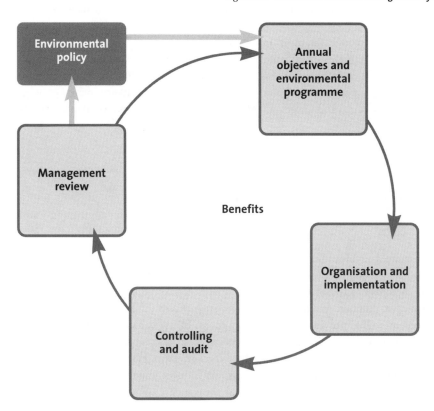

their annual planning procedures. In the divisions, annual targets and environmental programmes and measures are developed. These are being drawn up by means of intensive discussions between the specialist environmental units and the line units. Final decisions are taken by the responsible corporate units.

Our planning procedure is based on the annual analysis of the environmental impact of bank products, the environmental performance evaluation of in-house operations (i.e. analysis of the most important energy and material flows), and also the monitoring of compliance with legal and other requirements.

Ultimate responsibility for all environmental issues rests with the group chief executive officer. Within the framework of their functions, all executives and employees are responsible for the implementation of the environmental policy; the environmental functional units support the work of the line units. For example, ecological aspects affecting credit rating are, wherever appropriate, integrated into the general credit rating system. Where necessary, credit specialists are supported by the unit for environmental credit risks.

The annual and extensive internal environmental audits relating to the full spectrum of banking activities and in-house operations are of special significance. Their results provide an important basis for the evaluation of the environmental management system and planning for future programmes. In 1998, about 100 environmental audits of banking activities in the divisions Private and Corporate Clients, WDR, Private Banking and UBS Brinson took place, in addition to approximately 35 audits on energy management and in-house ecology.

The Group Executive Board is informed on an annual basis of the degree of implementation of the environmental policy and decides, based on the internal audit results, on general environmental objectives. Individual heads of divisions decide their environmental programmes and objectives on the basis of their environmental policies, the results of the audits and the general environmental objectives as passed by corporate management.

◢ Banking and the environment: indirect environmental impacts

For any service provider, the most pertinent environmental impacts can be indirect; such impacts may be influenced, but are hard to control. For many of our clients, environmental considerations not only represent financial risks—they can also mean new business opportunities. As a bank, we can give such clients the advice and information they need, as well as providing support in the form of our bank products and services. We therefore integrate environmental aspects into our various banking activities (commercial banking, asset management and investment banking) (see Fig. 6.2).

Furthermore, UBS, like any other business, has a direct impact on the environment through its own in-house operations. By far the greatest environmental pollution is

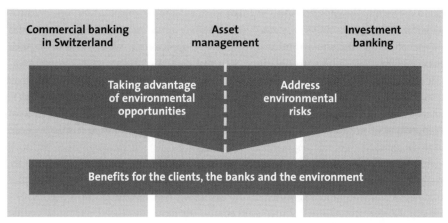

Figure 6.2 **Bank and environment**

caused by energy consumption, especially in the form of power generation. For UBS, sustainable development is, therefore, a significant component of sound management.

UBS' environmental management system has consequently been designed to predominantly focus on its core businesses, financial products and services, while still including direct environmental impacts resulting from its in-house operations.

◢ Evaluation of environmental aspects

A detailed process to identify the environmental aspects of UBS's activities, products and services has been established. The environmental impact for each banking activity has been evaluated and rated 'high', 'medium' or 'low', using the following criteria:

- ❑ Business risk

- ❑ Liability risk

- ❑ Reputation risk

- ❑ Potential for business opportunities

- ❑ Impact on the environment

The sub-ratings for each of these criteria are aggregated to an overall significance rating by using the highest ranking for each aspect considered. The aspects with overall significance 'high' are estimated to be relevant. This procedure is re-conducted annually for new or modified activities, products or services that may affect the environment.

The environmental aspects in investment banking can be outlined as follows. Environmental problems can become financial risks for the bank. The viability of our clients' businesses may be affected by poor environmental performance. Moreover, the necessity to comply with new environmental regulations, or the obligation to clean up contaminated sites, may result in high costs and may diminish future cash flows. Regarding initial public offerings and equity underwriting, where appropriate, we endeavour to take environmental risks into consideration when pricing and placing with potential investors. The bank may also have to take into consideration investors' requirements, such as compliance with World Bank standards. Finally, environmentally controversial transactions are increasingly being targeted by pressure groups. We are sensitive to public opinion and we are aware of the efforts being made by pressure groups to raise the profile of these issues.

As far as commercial banking is concerned, environmentally oriented businesses can profit from new commercial opportunities and reduced costs. On the other hand, the environmental risks to which our credit clients are exposed can also have consequences for UBS. Contaminated and polluted sites change the basis on which UBS grants credits. The often high costs of site decontamination or of disposing of hazardous waste reduce the value of collateral. The need to conduct investigations and the resulting delay in the project may also lead to disruptions to our clients' income stream. If the bank becomes the owner of a contaminated site, it may be held liable for the subsequent clean-up costs. In contrast, companies with systematic environmental management and innovative, environmentally sound products enjoy new market opportunities and competitive advantages. For UBS, this helps to improve a credit rating of a client.

◢ Monitoring continuous improvement with environmental performance indicators

The evaluation of environmental aspects gives a clear indication of our working priorities and leads to the establishment of our environmental objectives and programmes. However, the efficiency of our environmental management system and the status of the implementation of our environmental policy needs to be assessed by other means such as internal audits and informal reviews and environmental performance indicators (EPIs).

Internal audits

Internal audits aim to determine whether the EMS conforms to defined procedures and whether it has been properly implemented. They give a picture as to what extent the EMS is implemented at a particular moment. Within UBS, the annually internal environmental audits are performed on the full spectrum of bank activities and in-house operations, and are realised worldwide in key locations. To ensure a valid result, the sample of the audit partners should be representative and a relevant number of interviews should be conducted. The selection of the audit partners is therefore a crucial step in the EMS cycle. Furthermore, the audits need to be carried out in a standardised way; this can be achieved by using a checklist. Internal audits are a very useful tool in order to determine the overall status of the implementation of the EMS. However, they are not able to outline company-wide environmental performance.

Besides internal audits, informal reviews and regular exchange of know-how with relevant people throughout the bank can be useful in evaluating the overall status of the EMS.

Environmental performance indicators (EPIs)

Quantified EPIs are the most important management tool for planning, monitoring and controlling environmental procedures within the bank, as they perpetually map our environmental performance. Additionally, they effectively demonstrate the continuous improvement of an EMS, as required by ISO 14001, to both the management and the certifying company.

The starting point for the development of EPIs is the draft international standard ISO 14031 which distinguishes between management performance indicators (MPIs) and operational performance indicators (OPIs) (ISO 1998b).[1]

- ☐ MPIs measure the efficiency of the EMS in the field of product ecology. Such indicators can also map the organisation (e.g. headcount for environmental management), training (e.g. time spent in functional training per employee) or control (e.g. number of internal audits conducted).

- ☐ OPIs measure the environmental performance of products and environmental procedures, and their relevance in comparison with traditional banking products (e.g. the performance of procedures for the systematic analysis of environmental aspects in credit assessment or 'green assets' under management).

The environmental control of our activities is at different stages of development within the different divisions, the level reached being largely dependent on how long and how intensively environmental issues have been integrated into daily routines. Thus, control of the Swiss credit rating and in-house energy management are well advanced. In other areas, systematic environmental control is still in its early stages.

Eco-controlling of in-house operations

As far as the bank's in-house operations are concerned, EPIs have been used for many years. From an environmental point of view, absolute performance indicators are crucial as they indicate the total consumption of resources and emissions caused by the bank. For internal control and external benchmarking, these figures should be related to other relevant process parameters. These relative performance indicators express the environmental effort of a company independent of its size or production output. Both the development of absolute and relative performance indicators is important.

UBS's energy management functional unit annually drafts energy reports, which contain internal energy and water consumption figures for all 700-plus UBS locations in

---

1 Full standard published on 15 November 1999.

Switzerland. The progress of energy consumption over the previous five years is shown for each separate building. The majority of records for these reports have been kept continuously since 1980. Between 1990 and 1997, the volume of electricity consumed by UBS in Switzerland shrank by 18%. Over the same period, staff numbers fell slightly (by 3.5%). In absolute terms, heating energy consumption rose by 15%, compared with a 28% increase in the energy-relevant office space.

On the basis of energy and material flows, the in-house ecology functional unit produces the in-house environmental performance evaluation (EPE)—a comprehensive survey of all environment impacts. Future measures are planned on the basis of the results of this in-house EPE. According to the EPE, the greatest impact on the environment resulting from our in-house operations comes from electricity consumption and also from running our heating systems. We view ongoing energy management, the use of energy-saving appliances and eco-efficient building design as providing opportunities to optimise our energy consumption.

Measuring the environmental performance of banking activities

For UBS, one of the most important current objectives is to further develop the EPIs in banking. The work has been started, but systematic environmental control is still in its early stages. To further broaden our knowledge in the field of environmental performance measurements, UBS is actively engaged in the eco-efficiency metrics working group of the World Business Council for Sustainable Development (WBCSD). Furthermore, we are currently developing EPIs in an international working group jointly lead by Credit Suisse, Swiss Re and UBS.

EPIs should consider two aspects. First, the indicator should testify whether or not, or to what extent, the environmental procedure is executed. Second, the quality of the assessment of environmental issues should be measured.

◢ **Example: commercial banking**

In 1994, UBS developed and implemented a three-stage procedure for the systematic analysis of environmental aspects in credit assessment. During consultations with the client, we discuss potential environmental opportunities and risks. To this end, our customer advisers are provided with checklists and other tools. If environmental risks are identified, our client adviser discusses these with the internal credit officer and assesses their impact on the loan's viability. This may then be followed by an in-depth assessment of environmental risks, with UBS supported by an external specialist organisation.

Furthermore, financially relevant environmental aspects have a well-established role in UBS credit rating procedures, along with traditional rating factors such as financial performance indicators, sector allocation or management quality. When determining the value of the loan collateral put forward, potential clean-up costs and loss of value caused by soil contamination are also taken into account. The results of the environmental analysis may also affect the financial conditions attached to the loan.

In co-operation with Ecofact AG, the outsourced domestic environmental credit risk functional unit, EPIs for commercial banking are now being developed. Based on pilot-testing, these EPIs will be implemented within the next two years. Indicators to monitor the execution of the procedure could be:

- ☐ Percentage of loans that have been assessed according to the UBS environmental risk assessment directive (UBS AG 1998b)

- ☐ Number of requests addressed to Ecofact AG

- ☐ Volume of environmental loans

- ☐ Volume of prevented credit loss due to environmental credit assessment

- ☐ Distribution of environmental rating in the loan portfolio

To monitor the quality of the processes, the data should be set in comparison with information gained from 'traditional' credit process control; for example:

- ☐ Total loans or loans per sector

- ☐ Sector risk distribution in the loan portfolio

- ☐ Distribution of ratings in the loan portfolio

- ☐ Volume of recovery

and external environmental data in a region or country, such as:

- ☐ Number of contaminated sites

- ☐ Number of estimated remediations according to legal requirements

- ☐ Number of high-environmental-risk companies

- ☐ Number of environmental accidents per sector

At the moment, we are investigating the possibility of an IT-based evaluation of EPI in commercial banking. There are different challenges to be met at this stage. First, the necessary environmental and credit-related information needs to be collected and included in the risk measurement system. Furthermore, some IT tools need to be redesigned in order to map environmental procedures. Last, but not least, internal political issues relating to which data are integrated in risk measurement tools have also to be addressed.

◢ Conclusion

UBS regards ISO 14001 as a very useful tool to implement its environmental policy. As a large, multinational company, UBS found the design of the EMS in the structured way of ISO 14001 useful in implementing environmental objectives and operational procedures throughout different business units and cultures. Furthermore, during the dynamic situation resulting from a merger, the ISO guidance and framework aided the successful implementation of an efficient EMS.

Quantified EPIs are the most important management tool for planning, monitoring and controlling environmental procedures within the bank. However, the measurement of environmental performance of banking processes is still at its early stages.

For any service provider, the most pertinent environmental impacts can be indirect, and although they may be influenced they are also hard to control. Consequently, UBS's EMS has been designed to predominantly focus on its core businesses, financial products and services. It was found that ISO 14001, which was originally used in industry, can easily be adapted for use in the service sector.

◢ Future challenges

As described, UBS's EMS is generally well developed and broadly implemented along internal banking processes. Quantified EPIs are the most important management tool for planning, monitoring and controlling environmental procedures within the bank. However, the measurement of environmental performance of banking processes— compared to EPIs in industry—is still in its early stages. To further increase its efficiency,

Box 6.2 **Sustainable financial innovation**

SUSTAINABLE PRIVATE EQUITY

On the one hand, banks, investors, politics and science show growing interest in private equity and venture capital. On the other hand, sustainable development plays a considerable part in management practices. We think that sustainable private equity has a considerable business potential because companies that develop and market environmental business opportunities can experience substantial growth. In order to benefit from those opportunities, they need strong investment partners—sustainable private equity investors.

THE KYOTO PROTOCOL AND FINANCIAL SERVICES

The basis for an emerging global market was created in late 1997 when more than 150 governments adopted the market-based mechanisms of the Kyoto Protocol. As the Kyoto Protocol is an agreement between countries and nations, the question might be raised how companies will be affected. Governments will most likely pass on their commitments to greenhouse gas-emitting companies. From the perspective of a private-sector company, greenhouse gas emissions will affect the cash flow negatively while emission reductions might create extra income. In other words: there will be a strong incentive to reduce net greenhouse gas emissions. Companies can respond to these requirements not only by directly reducing their emissions but also by taking advantage of the so-called Kyoto Mechanisms. Banks that are able to provide sound services to these companies may gain from a new, emerging market for financial services in the context of the Kyoto Protocol.

the EMS should be even better integrated in management processes such as budgeting, accounting or 'management by objectives'.

As indicated earlier, an EMS is very helpful in the implementation of existing policies. However, we found that innovation (see examples in Box 6.2) is not really covered by the ISO framework.

This is especially the case with innovations that are not based on continuous improvement (e.g. increased energy efficiency of the heating system), but on external changes in the environment. Examples are the new Kyoto framework or the growing importance of non-credit finance techniques. In general, we think that strategic product/ market innovations cannot be directly facilitated by ISO 14001, as the standard is more focused on translating policies into operational procedures. This strategic gap might be considered as the main drawback of ISO 14001.

7

REGISTRATION TO ISO 14001
The view of assessors

David Robinson
British Standards Institution, UK

Richard Gould
Environment Agency, UK

Since the launch of ISO 14001, several thousand organisations have registered to the standard through external assessment (ISO 1996a). Furthermore, for every company registered, there are many more seeking registration. While there have been several publications providing guidance on implementing environmental management systems (EMSs) (Sheldon and Yoxon 1999; Jackson 1997; Gilbert and Gould 1998), there is little guidance on the certification process itself.

This means that many organisations misunderstand the requirements of the EMS standard and assessors. Furthermore, research at BSI has shown that there are common trends in the causes of unsuccessful registration to ISO 14001 (see Appendix). This chapter describes the certification process, the key requirements of the standard, and what assessors expect to see.

◢ Key documents

There are several registration (or certification) bodies in the UK that undertake ISO 14001 assessments. All assessments follow a consistent theme because each registration body follows the same rules. The key standard for assessment bodies is ISO Guide 62 (ISO 1998a), which specifies two things. First, the registration body must have its own management system to serve as a robust framework of controlled procedures for assessing other organisations. Second, the guide specifies, in generic terms, the evidence required to recommend registration to a standard.

So who assesses the registration bodies? In the UK, this role is undertaken by the United Kingdom Accreditation Service (UKAS), which determines whether the registration body meets the requirements of ISO Guide 62. Worldwide, accreditation bodies such as UKAS have agreed international frameworks for accrediting registration bodies, as well as writing more specific guidance on assessing to particular standards. Thus in Europe, a forum of accreditation bodies such as UKAS, known as the European Co-operation for Accreditation (EA), has published several important guidance notes, and the key document of these for ISO 14001 assessments is known as EA 7-02 (EA 1998).

◢ The assessment process

EA 7-02 describes how an assessment body must structure the audit. These are minimum requirements, so the assessors have a degree of freedom to apply their own methods and styles, but there will always be a foundation of similarity between different assessment bodies. UKAS audits all the assessment bodies using ISO Guide 62 and EA 7-02 as audit criteria.

The EMS initial assessment must include at least two site visits and, therefore, most assessment bodies divide the audits into two stages (see Fig. 7.1). The first of these is typically an **audit of intent**, where the assessors see if the organisation's management system is appropriate for managing the environmental performance of its operations, and also addresses all the clauses of ISO 14001. The second stage of the audit is typically an audit of **implementation and effectiveness**; having established that the EMS is appropriate and meets all the requirements of ISO 14001, the assessors now determine if the system has been implemented and is effective at managing environmental performance. Hence, the stage 1 audits use ISO 14001 and EA 7-02 as audit criteria, while the assessors will refer to the organisation's EMS procedures and work instructions during stage 2.

Stage 1 will typically involve a detailed site tour so that the assessors can see the organisation's environmental aspects and impacts. In real terms, this means use of

Figure 7.1 **The two stages of the assessment process**

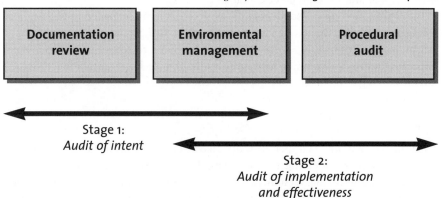

resources, supply chain impacts and, most importantly, releases to air, land and water. Then the assessors will examine the documented system to see how it matches the needs of environmental performance management.

The first stage will also typically examine the organisation's internal audits as well as a detailed look at the aspects and impacts. As both of these are very important, the next three sections discuss them in more detail.

Effective management of environmental risk

The most important element of successful ISO 14001 registration is the identification of environmental aspects and impacts. If this exercise is incomplete, then the EMS will have insecure foundations. ISO 14001 requires the organisation to have a procedure that allows it to identify the significant aspects and impacts that it can either control or influence.

Therefore, the first thing the assessors need to see is a documented procedure that identifies all the environmental aspects and impacts. This procedure must include a robust means of determining significance; there is not a prescribed method for this, and the methods used are diverse in their complexity. However, research at Lancaster University, UK (Crowther 1999), examined a spectrum of methods and found that all produced similar results.

According to EA 7-02, 'a significant impact is one which must be managed'. Therefore, the converse is also true: if an impact has to be managed, then it must be significant. Hence, any licensed or regulated processes, such as air emissions, waste management and effluent discharges, are significant by default.

Many assessments have shown that the simpler the methodology, the more robust it is. Complex risk-based analyses may have a role where there are a lot of significant impacts and the organisation needs to prioritise dealing with them, but this exercise also requires substantial skills and experience in environmental science and risk analysis, otherwise the results can be nonsensical. For example, a small producer of offshore chemicals used a series of equations and probability factors to determine significance, and ranked a domestic central heating boiler as having a higher environmental risk than a storage area containing several tonnes of hydrocarbons, with no secondary containment and a drainage system that led straight to the sea.

The organisation must also identify the aspects that it can influence, as well as those it can control. Supply chains often fit into this category. Contract conditions, for example, can be used to strongly influence or control a supplier to reduce its environmental impacts. However, it is common for many organisations seeking registration to overlook this area.

Containment, control and compliance

When many environmental specialists are asked in a few words to summarise the key things they need to see during an assessment, then the three most common words are **containment**, **control** and **compliance**. Many assessors expect the organisation to have identified all the significant releases to air, land and water. One assessor, for example, draws a large input–process–output diagram of each company he audits, and divides the area outside the process into a containment zone and an impact zone (Fig. 7.2). The auditees must know and understand how any releases from the containment zone affect the impact zone, and, if the impacts are significant, then the organisation must take proactive steps to prevent or reduce those impacts.

Similarly, the assessors will take a close look at regulated processes. An auditee must have licences for all these processes and be able to produce verifiable evidence to demonstrate compliance with all the licence conditions. The same applies to cascaded legislation; for example, if the organisation uses licensed waste carriers to transport waste to transfer stations and disposal sites, then the auditee must be able to produce evidence showing that the waste service providers not only have the correct licences, but can demonstrate that they have met their co-operative requirements under the Environmental Protection (Duty of Care) Regulations 1991. In simple terms, unless the auditees can demonstrate compliance by the second stage of the assessment, then the assessors cannot recommend registration. There is only one mitigating circumstance here and that is if the regulatory authorities have agreed to a programme to remedy any non-compliance. However, the auditees must be able to prove this.

The importance of internal auditing

Effective internal audits can both demonstrate the effectiveness of the EMS and improve environmental management. During the first stage of the initial assessment, the assessors of the registration body determine, by detailed analysis, the reliability of the internal audit. So the organisation's records of the internal audits should be sufficiently comprehensive to provide evidence that the registration body can validate to confirm the effectiveness of the audit process.

Figure 7.2 **Containment and impact zones**

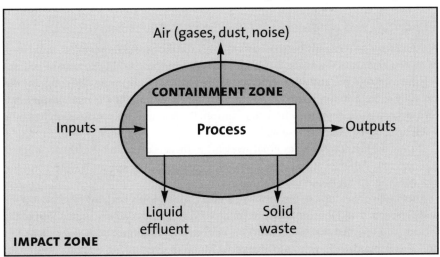

More specifically, the external assessors will look for objective evidence of the competence, experience, training and independence of assessors. They will also evaluate the organisation's auditing procedure and methodology, such as the extent of the audit, references to relevant standards such as ISO 14011 (ISO 1996b), the resources available for the audit, the checks performed, findings and follow-up.

◢ Case studies

The following case studies describe some experiences of EMS assessors, illustrating typical pitfalls that prevent registration, and an example of good practice.

Use of untrained EMS auditors

External assessors expect an organisation to have competent and trained internal auditors. This was not the case in an organisation in the building and construction industry which used a quality systems auditor to undertake an integrated quality, environment and safety audit before the full certification assessment. During this audit, instead of defining a scope that covered all the clauses of the standard, the auditor's plan only looked at areas that were common to both ISO 14001 and the quality standard ISO 9001 (ISO 1994), such as document control.

However, the audit failed to address site issues such as leaking diesel barrels lying next to a canal and a clearly visible oil spill on the ground because the organisation had not identified the significance of the issue during its own internal audits. The lack of control and containment was still evident during the external assessment; furthermore, the company did not respond appropriately. Hence the EMS was clearly not effective in terms of audit competency, audit methodology and corrective and preventative actions.

Abnormal and emergency situations: a product-line focus

A manufacturing company had based its EMS around the production process. Evaluation of aspects and impacts was also based around the production facility, instead of examining the complete site and all its environmental aspects. Furthermore, the company did not fully address abnormal and emergency situations. As a result, the main factory yard area lacked appropriate environmental controls. For example, the organisation had little knowledge of the drainage system.

During the first stage of an external assessment, there was a power cut. The factory was plunged into darkness and alarms sounded. People were unclear on how to react and evacuation from the building was slow.

After finding the cause of the problem and allowing people back into the factory, the audit continued and the assessment team decided to do a second site tour. A visit to the factory yard revealed that the production machines had dumped plastic raw materials and these found their way into drains which were overflowing with the materials.

Evidence suggested that the drains must be the surface drains, meaning that the raw materials could leave the site via the surface drainage system. The company agreed with this finding and the audit continued.

About two hours later, however, the company had not started to clear the materials from the drains, demonstrating the inadequacy of the emergency response. This meant that there were major non-conformities during the first stage of the external assessment and the registration body stated that the company would have to completely rectify these by the second stage of the assessment.

The company then did a comprehensive site drains inspection and produced a drainage plan detailing the surface and foul drains. The company also evaluated the environmental risks outside the factory under normal, abnormal and emergency conditions, and implemented the appropriate controls to deal with these risks.

Ineffective spill response and the time-bomb

A ball-bearing manufacturer used several tonnes of lubricating oils every year, which a supplier delivered in 205-litre drums. The full drums were stored in a bunded enclosure with an isolated drainage system leading to a sump, while the empty drums were stored next to the enclosure, in the open yard. The nearest drain led to an oil interceptor, which in turn led to a local river.

During the last stage of an initial assessment, the team of assessors saw that many of the empty drums were stored upside down. Furthermore, several trails of dark and clear liquids were seeping from the base of some of the drums, into the drains. However, the company representatives were not concerned because they were convinced that the oil interceptor would prevent the leaking liquids—which were water soluble cutting fluids—from reaching the river.

The drums continued leaking into the drains for an hour. When the assessor asked about the solubility of the leaking substances, the company realised that the oil interceptors would be ineffective.

Their response to dealing with the leaks was also ineffective, however, because of a lack of actual practice using spill kits. Further investigations showed that the drums were stored upside down because of gaps in the training.

Belts-and-braces for the worst-case scenario

During the first stage of an initial assessment at a metal components factory, two auditees explained to the assessor how spent cutting oil was pumped to underground storage tanks within submerged, metal bunds. The tanks served as reservoirs and one of the company guides then explained that this pumping system was automatic, and would cut off the supply to one tank, and fill an emptier one. Meanwhile, another automatic pumping system would take spent cutting fluid to a recycling system.

When the assessor asked about all the things that could go wrong, the auditees explained in great detail how there were several fail-safe mechanisms. Then the assessor pointed out a potential weakness in the system, and asked what would happen if the fail-safe systems all failed. The auditees replied that the underground bund could overflow and pollute the river.

At the closing meeting, the auditees and assessor discussed this, and the managing director made an instant decision to build an extra bund above ground, as it would cost very little—certainly substantially less than a pollution incident.

Six months later, when the assessor returned for the second stage of the assessment, there was a catastrophic breakdown of the fail-safe mechanism and the pump did not stop sending cutting fluid to a full tank. As a result, the underground bund overflowed, releasing over two tonnes of waste oil.

However, the new bund contained the overflow. Furthermore, the factory staff responded rapidly and effectively. The assessor observed the response to this incident for two hours. After the incident, the auditees asked whether it was worth continuing the assessment. The assessor replied that it was, because the company had demonstrated a proactive approach, effective training, and an excellent responsiveness to emergencies. The company was soon registered to ISO 14001.

◢ Appendix: examples of pitfalls in ISO 14001

See following tables.

CLAUSE IN ISO 14001	EVIDENCE EXPECTED	EXAMPLES
4.2	Documented policy addressing all of the requirements listed in 4.2 (a)–(f). The policy should briefly describe the activities of the organisation.	▶ Often a reluctance to reference pollution in the policy dependent on industry sector ▶ Significant environmental aspects often overlooked when documenting the policy ▶ Items in policy do not have associated objectives and targets or are not addressed anywhere in the EMS. ▶ Misunderstanding the term 'available to the public'—often referred to as being publicly available ▶ Often the only form of communication to the employees is via a notice board with no explanation as to what the organisation is trying to achieve ▶ Not many organisations reference the commitment to comply with 'other requirements' to which they subscribe.
4.3.1	Procedures defining responsibility for identifying environmental aspects that it can control or influence and for keeping the information up to date. Procedures should provide a methodology for assigning significance to identified environmental impacts.	▶ Often a misunderstanding of what are environmental aspects and impacts ▶ Not all activities addressed (offices often overlooked—disposal of IT equipment, disposal of cleaning effluent from floor scrubbers, etc.) ▶ Failure to recognise indirect aspects (suppliers, on-site tenants, canteens, customers, disposal of product, etc.) ▶ Failure to recognise services or activities that are not completely within the scope of the EMS (e.g. common site effluent treatment plants) ▶ Failure to address products within the evaluation ▶ Often a focus on the manufacturing process itself (following the QMS) and ignoring external factory/site issues ▶ Site-wide issues often overlooked as methodologies only address specific activities ▶ Methodology described in procedures not followed or no evidence to demonstrate that the evaluation was actually carried out ▶ Abnormal and emergency situations overlooked in high-risk activities
4.3.2	Procedure for the identification of, and access to, legal and other requirements The organisation should be able to demonstrate that it is aware of the legislation that is applicable to its activities, products and services.	▶ Auditee believes that subscribing to an environmental publication and having it on the shelf is evidence of identifying the legal requirements. ▶ Long lists of legislation that are not relevant ▶ 'Other requirements' often get overlooked. ▶ The register is a 'one-off' and does not get reviewed. ▶ A belief that it is up to the certification body to tell the auditee what is relevant or to prove that auditee is not aware of legislation ▶ Legislation has been identified for the organisation but they have little understanding of the content or have not had access to the legislation to evaluate applicability.
4.3.3	Documented objectives and targets	▶ Legal and other requirements overlooked ▶ Objectives and targets bear no resemblance to the identified significant aspects. ▶ Policy items not addressed by objectives and targets or within the EMS ▶ Objectives and targets are not clear—e.g. reduce waste by 5% (5% of what and by when?) ▶ Objectives and targets are 'soft' and have very long lead times.

(continued over)

CLAUSE IN ISO 14001	EVIDENCE EXPECTED	EXAMPLES
4.3.4	Programmes to demonstrate progress towards or achievement of the objectives and targets	▶ Often no evidence to support that the objectives and targets have been taken on board ▶ New developments and new or modified activities, products or services are often overlooked.
4.4.1	Structure and responsibility defined within the EMS either in the manual, procedures, work instructions, job descriptions, etc.	▶ Usually addressed adequately but often employees have not been told of their responsibilities.
4.4.2	Identification of training needs and a procedure(s) to support ongoing identification of training requirements and raising of awareness	▶ Employees are often not aware of the significant environmental impact(s) that relates to their work activities and potential departure from specified operating procedures. ▶ Not aware of the emergency response requirements ▶ Unaware of policy requirements and how it relates to them
4.4.3	Procedure(s) for internal and external communications Recorded decision on the processes for external communication on the organisation's significant environmental aspects.	▶ Procedures only capture the negative—e.g. complaints ▶ Communications with regulators not recorded ▶ This decision is often omitted from the EMS and usually organisations do not know how to interpret this part of the standard.
4.4.4	An overview document describing the EMS and giving direction to related documents	▶ The manual often does not give direction to related documentation. ▶ It is believed by small organisations that the certification body must see a manual and procedures together with work instructions, and so the EMS becomes a paper chase: complex and difficult to manage.
4.4.5	Procedure(s) to provide control of documentation so that all of the requirements within the clause are met	▶ Procedures often do not allow for periodic review. ▶ Procedures often not available at essential locations. ▶ Amended documents are left in someone's in-tray and obsolete documents not removed from the working manual.
4.4.6	Procedures relating to the identified significant environmental aspects and in line with the policy, objectives and targets Communication of relevant procedures to suppliers and contractors for those goods and services with significant environmental aspects	▶ Procedures do not give guidance for when things go wrong ▶ Responsibilities not clear ▶ Misunderstanding that all suppliers must be sent environmental questionnaires ▶ When questionnaires are sent, nothing is done with the information. ▶ No procedures/guidance to control key activities such as safe storage: for example, of hazardous materials/oils ▶ Procedures documented but not communicated
4.4.7	Procedures to identify potential for and respond to accidents and emergency situations Periodic testing where practicable	▶ Procedures very lengthy and difficult to follow in an emergency situation ▶ Procedures not available where required ▶ No spill response equipment nearby ▶ Spill procedures do not give important contact numbers or define responsibilities. ▶ This is often not addressed within the EMS.

(from previous page; continued opposite)

CLAUSE IN ISO 14001	EVIDENCE EXPECTED	EXAMPLES
4.5.1	Procedures to monitor and measure key characteristics of the operations and activities that can have a significant impact on the environment	▶ Monitoring procedures do not specify frequency or responsibilities. ▶ Key parameters often overlooked: e.g. no presence of oils in effluent discharge, daily volume limits of effluent, and noise levels in planning consents
	Evidence of monitoring/ measurement results identifying where parameters have been breached	▶ Results out of specified limits not identified, therefore action not taken by company ▶ Samples taken but results recorded in units different to those specified in consent limits
	Calibration records	▶ Monitoring/measuring equipment not calibrated; reference solutions/pH buffers well past expiry dates
	Procedure for periodically evaluating legal compliance	▶ Some organisations believe that, by maintaining a register of legislation, they are legally compliant. ▶ This is often overlooked within the EMS and organisations find it difficult to demonstrate legal compliance during certification. ▶ Legal documents are not available or have been mislaid, or it is not thought necessary to make them available for the assessment.
4.5.2	Procedures for investigating non-conformance and instigating corrective and preventative action(s)	▶ Preventative actions often overlooked ▶ Actions not always documented
	Evidence of corrective and preventative actions required	
4.5.3	Procedures for the identification, maintenance and disposal of environmental records	▶ Misunderstanding of the meaning of environmental records; therefore not all records identified
	Evidence that documents are being retained for the specified periods	▶ New staff have disposed of important records (duty of care transfer notes) which were being maintained by a previous employee.
4.5.4	Procedure(s) and programme(s) for periodic EMS audits. Programmes to be based on environmental importance and results of previous audits.	▶ No audit programme or not based on environmental importance ▶ Auditors not suitably trained/competent ▶ Scope of audits not defined ▶ Little supporting evidence in audit reports and records to demonstrate effectiveness of the audit or to provide data that can be validated by the certification body
	Training/competence of auditors	▶ Audits tend to focus on issues such as 'is there a procedure for X?' rather than 'Has the procedure been issued, implemented and adhered to?', etc.
	Evidence that audit process is effective	▶ Identified non-conformances are not actioned. ▶ 'We didn't think we had to do any audits before certification.'
4.6	Evidence that management review(s) has been held	▶ Top management is not involved in the review process. ▶ Results of audits not considered ▶ Policy not considered ▶ Minutes are very brief and do not demonstrate that key issues have been discussed. ▶ Auditee did not understand that the organisation had to hold a review before certification.

(from previous page)

Part 3
USE OF INFORMATION TECHNOLOGY, ISO 14031 AND OTHER TOOLS AND METHODS

8

USING INFORMATION TECHNOLOGY TO AUTOMATE INTEGRATED COMPLIANCE MANAGEMENT

David Harwood
ALSTOM Power, UK

Barry O'Brien
Waterford Crystal, Ireland

Paul F. Monaghan
Q SET–USA

Anne Downey
Q SET–International, Ireland

The experiences of two large businesses in successfully integrating and achieving multi-standard compliance are related here in two case studies.

Waterford Crystal and ALSTOM Power in Newcastle, UK—which is part of the ALSTOM group of companies—have, at first sight, very little in common, but share these vital characteristics:

☐ A progressive management view of the benefits of integrating management systems, and overcoming perceived obstacles to that integration

☐ Willingness to use the power of information technology (IT) to automate that integration

◢ Categorising multi-standard compliance

In safety, health, environment and quality, three categories of compliance are evident: voluntary; legal/mandatory; and corporate (see Fig. 8.1).

Voluntary compliance encompasses compliance with industry-wide international standards such as ISO 9000 (quality management), ISO 14001 (environmental management systems), BS 8800 (health and safety) or OHSAS 18001 (occupational health and safety). There are also industry-specific voluntary standards or guidelines, e.g. safety

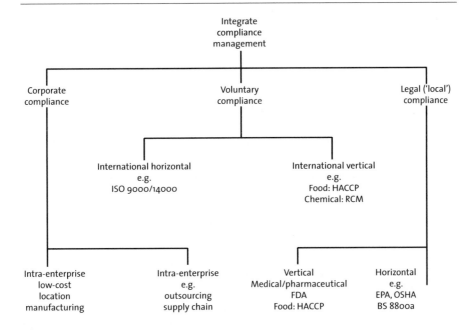

Figure 8.1 **The integrated compliance management chart**

Source: © Q SET 1999

passport schemes in the construction sector. Standards that started out as voluntary may become legal requirements, such as Hazard Analysis Critical Control Point (HACCP) in the food industry.[1]

Legal compliance is often driven by the demands of consumer protection. Environment legislation is enforced by organisations such as the US Environmental Protection Agency. The penalties for non-compliance can range from fines or criminal charges, to plant or line shut-downs. Ireland's Environmental Protection Agency is making links between ISO 14001 and environmental legal compliance.

Corporate compliance with company policy or quality standards becomes increasingly important with globalisation and outsourcing trends, and the general need for corporate knowledge management. Whether a global corporation manufactures products at a number of its sites throughout the world or outsources to third-party manufacturers, it must nevertheless ensure that the new manufacturing sites are aware of existing and changing standards and practices. It must also be able to monitor the sites' compliance with these standards. Some of the international standards such as ISO 9001 and ISO 14001 are becoming prerequisite criteria for inclusion on supplier lists, as demonstrated by the

1   A system developed in 1959 by NASA to assure 100% safety of food to be used in space. In 1979, NASA published and documented the HACCP system in the US. In 1985, the Food and Agricultural Organisation/World Health Organisation cited the system in the Codex. In 1993, European Regulation 93/43/EC promoted the use of the HACCP system for the production of food.

recent announcement that General Motors and Ford will require all their suppliers to be ISO 14001-certified (*IE Professional* 1999).

◢ Benefits of integrating management systems

There are demonstrable efficiencies and benefits in combining the management of all business activities in one system; furthermore, ISO 14001 is the most appealing and logical template on which to model this integration. In a recent survey (Bice *et al.* 1999), US industry experts clearly flagged the way forward:

> The ISO 14001 structure can be used generically for virtually any organisational challenge. This is a standard for change management and has very broad applications within organisations.

ALSTOM Power in Newcastle has found that there is synergy in integrating management systems. Many elements of a mature and structured management system require cross-checking and validation through audit, inspection and management review. Communications coupled with objective- and target-setting are fundamental and essential to continual improvement. It is an old but true adage that any company that fails to continually improve and evolve will lose ground to its competition. Management systems such as ISO 9000, ISO 14001, SMS 8800 (occupational health and safety management system assessment criteria for the application of BS 8800), OHSAS 18001, BS 7799 (information security management) and Investors In People[2] can complement each other. Integrated procedures cut down on paper flow and integrated third-party auditing make savings in time and money.

◢ Obstacles to integrating management systems

Joe Cascio (Bice *et al.* 1999) cites 'politics and competition among specialised staff groups' and 'systems and programmes being developed to address only those issues with which [each] specialist is familiar' as main obstacles. He suggests the following solutions:

- ☐ Merging these groups under one leader with authority over the three areas. ALSTOM Power in Newcastle has one corporate manager with responsibility for quality, health and safety, and environment

---

2   'Investors In People is the national standard which sets the level of good practice for improving an organisation's performance through its people. IIP is based upon common sense: it is about results—not procedures. Everything it calls for has a clear business purpose. The standard provides the basis for continuous improvement of both the organisation and its people and should make your organisation more successful' (Investors In People UK, *How to become an investor in people*).

❑ Management to assign interdisciplinary teams to target potential sources of harm so that hazard analysis can be complete and solutions can be protective of both humans and the environment. At Waterford Crystal, the general manager for strategic projects and quality assurance works closely with the environmental, health and safety manager

Both companies illustrate many areas of financial and business benefits, including improved efficiency, because of proactively dealing with integration issues.

◢ Compliance management inter-enterprise

A brief examination of compliance management interactions presents an outline of the number of players involved, in addition to the multiple sites, divisions and departments of a company itself. These are:

❑ Suppliers

❑ Customers

❑ Auditors

❑ Consultants

❑ Regulators

❑ Public

Suppliers need to be able to get on the approved vendor list. In the ongoing relationship, there are regular audits to ensure compliance and, when things go wrong, the two parties need to interact on supplier corrective actions.

Companies always aspire to satisfied customers, but there needs to be a mechanism so that customers can complain if this becomes necessary. The company has to be able to capture that complaint and not only solve the immediate problem, but set off a chain of improvements or corrective actions to ensure continual improvement and retention of existing customers. In some cases, the company may need to allow audits by its customers.

Auditors and regulators need access to procedures and records. Consultants specialising in helping organisations achieve ISO 14001 certification, legal compliance or business improvement need to be able to help the organisation by carrying out surveillance audits, updating corporations on local, regional or worldwide legislation and monitoring performance in business improvement programmes.

Performance reporting is often a compliance requirement and these reports may need to be submitted to regulators or made public. Public reporting is, in some management systems, a requirement of environmental compliance.

In summary, compliance management in, for example, the supply chain relates to 'business support' or 'integrated management systems', which supplement front-line operational transactions. The multiplier effect in compliance management-related activity across many more areas of business (e.g. customer care, quality, etc.) means that organisations are looking to IT to manage that activity.

◢ IT support in compliance management

The wisdom of harnessing the power and speed of IT to deal with the documentation associated with any management system is evident to those who have had to deal with the sheer volume of paperwork and bureaucracy involved in achieving and then maintaining standards certification. The IT platform needed to support integrated compliance management, particularly for multi-site businesses, has many special requirements:

☐ It must be able to support multiple sites in multiple countries, and mobile users.

☐ Reliable corporate knowledge management is essential. This is the global management and sharing of policies and procedures across departments, sites and functions in one organisation.

☐ There must be an Internet/intranet/extranet environment.

☐ Workflow management, from individuals, to groups and teams, throughout the organisation is vital. Documents must be routed for review and sign off.

☐ There must be powerful security and access-control features.

☐ Many kinds of unstructured information in mixed media must be supported (e.g. text documents, flow-charts, photographs, computer-aided design drawings, attachments, embedded objects, spreadsheets, etc.).

☐ Timetabling and scheduling must be managed, and it must be possible to set alarms to trigger when target dates approach.

☐ It is essential that there are audit trails to track the history of all documents and actions.

Waterford Crystal, having achieved ISO 9001 for its two plants in the early 1990s using a paper-based manual system, was determined to drastically reduce the time and effort spent on documentation management and wanted to automate the management system required for achieving ISO 14001. Similarly, ALSTOM Power's Newcastle operations' priority was to automate its integrated compliance management as quickly as possible. Only intelligent use of IT could achieve the required speed.

To meet these challenges, both companies chose Q SET Groupware—software for integrated compliance management on client–server architecture based on Lotus Domino, Lotus Notes and web browsers. The software consists of eight modules that can be used as a stand-alone tool to manage a specific aspect of compliance, or combined into an integrated total-compliance tool.

Any organisation contemplating certification should consider the attitude of external auditors to integration:

Today, as we enter the world of integrated quality and environmental certification audits, we hear a soft voice from the wings asking, 'What about health and
safety?' (Archie E. Bice, senior lead auditor, DNV Certification) (Cascio 1999).

Automating that integration makes the auditor's task easier, and keeps costs down. With
the appropriate security, it is attractive to perform the document part of the audit from
a remote location. ALSTOM Power utilised remote auditing very effectively from its
Newcastle head office. Another corporation, Sita (Sydney Network Operations), using
Q SET Groupware, recently had a successful Lloyds Register Quality Assurance audit
performed on its site in Sydney, Australia, from an office in London, UK. The auditor
commented on how good it was to see company objectives interpreted and acted upon
right through the organisation (Q SET 1999). Remote auditing is particularly attractive to
multinational or multi-site companies, where a single individual is able to interpret
standards and guidelines in a uniform way for all sites worldwide.

At Waterford Crystal, ISO 14001 certification was achieved in February 1999. At ALSTOM
Power's Newcastle operations, automation of the environmental management system
was achieved in under three months and in time for its triennial audit. The auditor noted
that the entire ISO 14001 system is now concise, effective and user-friendly (Harwood and
Monaghan 1999).

Waterford Crystal's experience

Initially, Waterford Crystal focused on customer care, ISO 9000 and ISO 14001—all
interrelated because effective implementation requires good change management.

Waterford Crystal has a worldwide reputation for the beauty of its crystal ware and has,
in the past ten years, extended the brand to include china, holiday heirlooms, linen,
writing instruments and cutlery. The quality assurance department develops, agrees and
communicates quality standards for home-sourced and outsourced products, auditing
adherence to these standards and administering and developing ISO in all areas. The
customer care group, which operates within the customer service department, is
responsible for processing complaints from consumers and trade customers, and for
ensuring that the company's policies in respect of its 'no-quibble' guarantee is carried out.

Critical issues

Waterford Crystal wanted an IT platform to support compliance management in the
supply chain. Having doubled its business in three years, grown its portfolio into the
luxury gift business, outsourced up to 40% of its products and made the move to third-
party warehousing and distribution, there was an enormous responsibility on the
company to further improve its IT support systems and, particularly, its customer care
strategy.

ISO 9001 had been achieved but had to be maintained; ISO 14001 certification was a
target to be achieved in 1999. The company was determined to employ more effective
methods of document control in its application for ISO 14001 registration, and achieve
integration of its quality systems in Waterford, Ireland, and New Jersey, USA.

Due to an increase in both outsourced crystal and brand extensions, there was increased focus on supplier development, customer care and establishing the organisational structure required to support the needs of a changing portfolio of products. (Waterford's total product portfolio is sourced from 38 companies in 17 countries on three continents.) It also needed standard methods for processing customer care issues and giving feedback to sales and marketing teams throughout the organisation. The customer care department needed a global system for consumer fault analysis, trade fault analysis, information gathering, corrective action processing, feedback to complaint originator, consistent policies and reporting, and online documentation.

With regard to the international standards, ISO 14001 needed an electronic system and certification to avoid the high maintenance costs experienced with ISO 9001 and existing ISO 9001 documentation needed converting to a new multi-standard system.

Implementation

A key component of the successful implementation was the pre-installation planning days and training supplied by Q SET, and defining and supporting the needs of the user group in the US operation, which represents approximately 70% of Waterford Crystal's sales revenue.

The software was remotely installed in New Jersey by electronic communication from the Irish site. The system was then configured for data transfer by Q SET staff in one day, from Ireland. Waterford staff travelled to the US office to provide Lotus Notes training and Q SET Groupware training. The software was implemented in customer care in the US after two days' general training of six customer service employees, and a further day of training with two of the six who would act as 'power users' in the US, with a follow-up visit to review the US operation of the system.

Result

ISO 14001 certification was achieved in February 1999. Waterford Crystal is now connected to its outsourced logistics company Banta Global Turnkey, Texas, USA, and to sister company Stuart Crystal (UK). The customer services department is well placed to support the growth of the business, with a clearer picture of customer complaints and corrective actions for dealing with them.

Q SET Groupware customer care will be rolled out to the rest of the company's world markets and integrated with the new products development system—Project Phoenix. There is now one channel of communication on quality issues. When appropriate, corrective actions requests are raised and tracked through the system until they are closed off and, importantly, their US colleagues can monitor the progress and results of the corrective actions requests.

The process improvement team, customer complaint working group and the materials review board also continually monitor fault analysis outputs from Q SET Groupware—their reports form the basis for the monthly Waterford Crystal quality review meeting, chaired by the chief executive officer. Additional Q SET Groupware modules have been applied: for example, the plant maintenance department uses the calibration module. The IT department stores its non-quality-related documents (procedures, controlled documents) in the software.

The benefits of the system include the avoidance of additional long-term overheads to support the control of ISO 14001 and the development of the growth of the business. This has resulted in the saving of the recruitment of two employees at approximately £40,000–£50,000 per year, representing a payback of one year.

ALSTOM *Power's experience*

UK-based ABB ALSTOM Power in Newcastle specialises in turnkey project management and supply of equipment and services to the UK power industry. This includes design, procurement, installation and commissioning of power stations plus ongoing operation and maintenance

The company was formed as a joint venture between NEI and ABB in 1990 and was called NEI ABB Gas Turbines Ltd, with fewer than ten employees. In 1992, ABB bought out NEI and became a wholly owned ABB company operating as ABB Power Generation Ltd. More recently, ABB Power Generation Ltd has merged with ALSTOM to form the ALSTOM Power Group. The company now employs 100 people in the Newcastle operation. Turnover has increased to more than £200 million.

The company has two other areas of activity. In Staines, Middlesex, ABB Environmental Systems specialises in the supply and installation of major plant components for power plant, incinerators and filtration plant, and in industrial steam turbine, servicing and re-commissioning. In Bolton, Lancashire, Flowsystems is a world leader in the installation and maintenance of district and community heating schemes.

The company achieved certification to ISO 9001 in 1992 and ISO 14001 in 1996 using manual documentation management processes. A paper-based system was maintained until recently and the second ISO 9001 triennial audit was completed in July 1998. The triennial audit for ISO 14001 was scheduled for June 1999. There is a coherent approach to managing the three disciplines of quality, health and safety, and environmental management, led by the corporate manager for these functions and the quality engineer. Working with the senior IT engineer, the team wanted to automate their compliance management process as quickly as possible, going online in March 1999.

Critical issues

ALSTOM Power wanted a fully integrated quality, environment, and health and safety software system running on Lotus Notes to support ISO 9000, ISO 14000 and, eventually, SMS 8800/OHSAS 18001, and to eliminate duplication of documents in each of the three areas. A multi-site, multi-standard system was needed to remove the concept of individual geographic sites. Support was needed for 200 users at five sites: Newcastle (headquarters), Enfield power station, Shoreham power station, Environmental Systems in Staines and Flowsystems in Bolton.

ALSTOM Power also wanted to be able to link all locations, interchange information, and retrieve documents electronically, instantly, while maintaining security and control of documentation access. It needed a uniform and coherent look and feel for the documentation in each of the environment, quality, and health and safety systems. To ensure independence from consultants, facilitate implementation of upgrades, etc., and be cost-effective, no or minimal software customisation was wanted, but the system had to be configurable to the business's needs. It was essential that it would be fast and easy to use, ensuring 'buy-in' from the 200 users, and yet would satisfy senior management by making a sound business case and give a quick return on capital invested.

Implementation

ALSTOM and Q SET's UK operation worked closely together on the project plan to ensure a successful implementation. Together they performed the initial Q SET Groupware database configuration and data population, and within two days the software was operational on the Newcastle hub server and on one of the spoke servers. Subsequent installations were then carried out on the remaining spoke servers, completing the technical aspects of the implementation.

The project was started during March and document transfer was completed on schedule, ready for the June audit. Because of the configurable nature of Q SET Groupware, customised programming was not necessary to meet ALSTOM Power's requirements, and there then followed a rapid and successful roll-out of four modules: documentation; audits; corrective action reports; and suppliers. The company chose to concentrate on the documentation module initially, in order to facilitate electronic document review at the forthcoming ISO 14001 audit.

Q SET trained and supervised a team to enter the documentation as quickly as possible. Training requirements were found to be minimal due to the simplicity and ease of use of the software, and end-users were trained by ALSTOM Power's own Q SET Groupware administrators, after having received a small amount of training themselves.

Result

ALSTOM Power passed the ISO 14001 audit on 16 June 1999. Three auditors were used at different locations throughout the company, and ALSTOM Power project managed the audit with a team at Flowsystems, the Enfield and Shoreham sites, and Newcastle head office. Progress was tracked from head office. The auditors were able to conduct document reviews from Newcastle and from computer terminals at the other locations, using the company's Lotus Domino/Notes network. There were also site inspections, interviewing staff and seeking objective evidence of compliance to the standard from existing records. The addition of Flowsystems and Shoreham power station to the portfolio has been successful. In October 1999, ALSTOM Power in Newcastle successfully passed third-party assessment by Lloyds Register to the joint health and safety standards of SMS 8800 and OHSAS 18001. This was the first time that this dual accolade had been achieved. This health and safety standard is now fully integrated with ISO 14001.

Bob Hill, ALSTOM Power's managing director in Newcastle, said:

> An integrated approach to the development of management systems is a core component within our business strategy. The disciplines involved in good quality, health and safety, and environmental management make their combination within a single system a natural fit. It is my belief that electronic distribution and control of documentation is the way forward and that the new software has already begun to prove itself.

Future

ALSTOM believes that the electronic control of business management systems saves time, money and effort. Value is added to the company because of the ease of access to documentation. One-stop auditing of quality, health and safety, and environmental management systems will be possible in future. The company is using a model consisting of a top-tier health, safety and environmental management system manual, conforming to ISO 14001 and OHSAS 18001. Quality management will be integrated when the ISO 9001/2000 standard is released. Second-tier documents consist of site quality plans, site construction health and safety plans and an environmental plan. Procedures are already being integrated and those that address management review, auditing, corrective action, communication and registers of legislation etc. are common. Integration of the management systems will continue, with the objective of creating a succinct and effective total management system.

◢ Conclusion

The future plans of ALSTOM and Waterford Crystal echo the experts' opinions:

> The future direction for ISO 14001 and the various quality standards entails integration (Marilyn R. Block, president, MRB Associates) (Bice *et al.* 1999: 28-32).

There is a recognition of the need to harmonise and stop the proliferation of standards:

> I would expect the next revision following the publication of ISO 9001/2000 would be an integrated management standard including the ISO 14001 series. This would be an iterative step in the standards development process (R. Dan Reid, manager supplier quality development, General Motors).

In the US, observers are forecasting adoption of integration at government level. The new Department of Energy (DOE)'s *Quality Assurance Management Guide* provides requirements for an integrated safety management system which would have shared attributes with the quality assurance management system.

> This change in DOE policy reflects the [American Society for Quality's] contention that quality, environment, health and safety management systems may be integrated for improved and more cost-effective implementation and could represent a trend in government programmes (Gary L. Johnson, US Environmental Protection Agency) (Johnson 1999: 5-7).

This points to an increase in the legal/mandatory category of compliance and should influence those organisations that are not yet integrating their management systems to follow the lead set by ALSTOM and Waterford Crystal in their future global compliance management planning.

9

ISO 14031 USED AS A TOOL IN ISO 14001 OR AS AN ALTERNATIVE FOR A SIMPLE EMS

Kristian Eg Løkkegaard
Ernst & Young, Denmark

Environmental performance evaluation (EPE) is an internal management process and tool designed to provide management with reliable and verifiable information on an ongoing basis. ISO 14031[1] and ISO 14001 both adopt the 'plan–do–check–act' model as their general management approach. The relationships between ISO 14031 and ISO 14001 are shown in Figure 9.1.

The planning phase of ISO 14031 and ISO 14001 is quite similar in practice, except that ISO 14031 prescribes that the organisation selects a proper set of indicators before any data is collected, with the focus on performance measures. The 'doing' phase of the two standards is different, however. ISO 14031 focuses on how to measure, manage and report the performance of the selected environmental aspects, whereas ISO 14001 shifts the focus from managing the environmental aspects to describing how to set up the organisational elements. The ISO 14031 and ISO 14001 approaches to the 'check' and 'act' phases are similar. The outcome, however, is different because of the different approaches in the 'doing' phase. The check and act activities in ISO 14001 lead to improvements of the environmental management system (EMS) and its processes. ISO 14031 review leads to decisions on how to reduce environmental impacts, how to modify the scope and how to focus the performance evaluation process.

◢ Experience from the marketplace

This chapter is based on experience gained from 17 international examples (ISO 1999) and nine Danish examples (Løkkegaard 1999a, 1999b). The Malaysian example (Bakti

---

1   The full ISO 14031 standard was published on 15 November 1999.

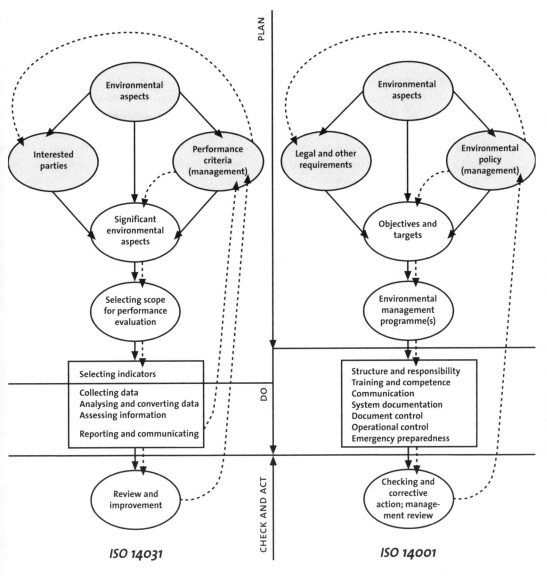

Figure 9.1 **Relationship between ISO 14031 and ISO 14001**

and Shyan 1999) will be used to illustrate and support the analysis and conclusions drawn by the author.

Introduction to the Malaysian rubber glove producer

Perusahaan Pelindung Getah (M) Sdn Bhd (PPG) is a small private limited company established in 1988 and located in the state of Negeri Sembilan, Malaysia. The PPG factory is located on a river, upstream of a public water supply intake. The waste-water from the PPG factory is treated on-site in a waste-water treatment plant before being discharged to the river.

The factory produces approximately eight million pieces of medical examination gloves per month. It has three production lines operating 24 hours a day. The total number of employees at PPG is approximately 100. The management of PPG evaluated its environmental performance following the principles of ISO 14031. PPG had neither an environmental policy nor an EMS when the evaluation began. The choice of ISO 14031 as the basis for the environmental protection work was heavily influenced by the Malaysian Rubber Board as part of a United Nations programme for improving environment protection in the manufacturing sectors.

The planning phase

The management of PPG decided to plan their EPE based on the environmental aspects related to the company's activities, the views of selected interested parties and a set of selected environmental performance criteria. The most important environmental aspects of the company's products and activities were identified (see Table 9.1). After reviewing public statements, minutes of meetings and discussions with interested parties, the PPG management identified the important interested parties (see Table 9.2).

The management then selected the following performance criteria:

☐ Total compliance with regulations

☐ Zero public complaints regarding its operations

☐ Minimal adverse environmental effects

☐ Maintaining the number of pieces of gloves rejected at less than 5% of the total pieces produced, in accordance with product specifications

☐ Maintaining the level of extractable protein in gloves at less than or equal to 0.3 mg extractable protein per gram of rubber

PPG management planned to implement the following environmental management programmes to address its environmental performance:

☐ Reduction of extractable protein level in gloves

☐ Improvements in effluent treatment plant efficiency

☐ Waste minimisation through process modification

☐ Monitoring of surface water quality upstream and downstream from the plant

These decisions strictly reflect the use of ISO 14031. Comparing the Malaysian example to the requirements of ISO 14001 reveals that substantial input to subclause 4.3.1: 'environmental aspects', to subclause 4.3.3: 'objectives and targets' and to subclause 4.3.4: 'environmental management programme' has been achieved. In practice, PPG has the components in place to meet the requirements of ISO 14001 for these clauses, except for the documentation elements of the standard. It would, however, be straightforward for

Product/activity	Environmental aspect	Potential impact/effect
Rubber glove	▶ Disposal of rejected gloves (i.e. those not meeting product specifications)	▶ Soil and groundwater contamination through land application and air pollution through open burning
Latex compounding	▶ Addition of chemicals (e.g. stabilisers, curatives, protective agents, pigments, defoamers) in latex compounding ▶ Discharge of residual latex containing toxic chemicals ▶ Mixing of ammonia-preserved latex in open tanks and emission of ammonia vapour ▶ Addition of sulphur powder during latex compounding and emission of sulphur dust ▶ Washing of latex mixing and storage tanks and generation of hazardous liquid waste with high concentrations of Zn and COD	▶ Soil and groundwater contamination through land application ▶ Water pollution ▶ Health-related problems for workers
Leaching of gloves with water	▶ Discharge of effluent from leaching tanks and generation of hazardous liquid waste with high concentrations of Zn and COD	▶ Water pollution

Table 9.1 **Important environmental aspects of PPG**

Table 9.2 **The views of interested parties**

Interested parties	Expected view
Department of the Environment	▶ Treated effluent shall comply with regulatory requirements.
Export market (e.g. US Food and Drug Administration)	▶ Level of extractable protein in rubber gloves shall be less than or equal to 0.3 mg extractable protein per gram of rubber.
Public water treatment plant operator	▶ Quality of river water at the intake that may be affected by the effluent discharged from the PPG factory
PPG top management	▶ Cost-effectiveness of environmental control measures
Local community	▶ PPG's operations shall not cause any nuisance.

PPG to document the process and describe the elements in accordance with ISO 14001 requirements for system documentation and procedures in subclauses 4.3.1, 4.3.3 and 4.3.4.

PPG management has achieved credible identification of the relevant environmental aspects, reflected on the criteria for significance and, on the basis of these, agreed a set of environmental aspects to be managed.

Selecting indicators

PPG management established a project plan for each programme including the objectives and targets to be achieved within a specified time-frame. Each project plan lists the activities to be carried out, the time-frame, the resources, and the responsibilities associated with each activity.

PPG decided to use indicators reflecting the objectives and targets to measure the performance of each project plan. The indicators provide information on management efforts, performance of its operations and the condition of the environment as a direct consequence of the implementation of the environmental management programme.

The indicators selected to reflect the environmental performance criteria are presented in Table 9.3, which also contains information relating the performance measures to the environmental aspects to be managed. This information is the core input to be used for elaborating the operational control system (ISO 14001: 4.4.6).

Using data and information

Some of PPG's indicators require raw data collection on a regular basis, analysis of the collected data and conversion of the data into indicators. For example, the indicator on the quantity of zinc discharged to a watercourse per month requires regular measurements of effluent flow rates and zinc concentrations in the effluent.

PPG management uses commercial software to enable the collected data to be stored and managed. The computer software has the capability to display the analysed data in a graphical form and to show the trends of the various indicators over time. The information can be incorporated in a report for communication to interested parties on a regular basis.[2]

ISO 14031 prescribes a 'control loop' to be established for each environmental aspect comprising: collecting data; analysing and converting data; assessing information; and reporting and communicating the results.

Using the same information as in the PPG example, Table 9.3 provides an excellent platform for describing and setting up the operational control loop, including working procedures and the required system for measuring, monitoring and filing the information as environmental records corresponding to the requirements of ISO 14001, subclause 4.4.6: 'operational control', 4.5.1: 'monitoring and measurement' and 4.5.3: 'records'.

---

2   The information is also available on the Internet at www5.jaring.my/careplus/page5.html.

Indicators for EPE	Basis for selection of the indicator
Management performance indicators	*The rationale*
▸ Annual total cost of implementing environmental programmes	▸ Evaluation of management commitment (i.e. useful public relations material)
▸ Number of environmentally related complaints received by PPG per year	▸ Evaluation against the environmental performance criterion on zero public complaint
▸ Number of effluent samples analysed monthly not complying with regulatory standards	▸ Evaluation against the environmental performance criterion on total compliance with regulations
Operational performance indicators	
▸ Number of pieces of gloves rejected in relation to the total number of pieces of gloves produced per month	▸ Evaluation against the environmental performance criterion on controlling rejects in order to reduce wastes
▸ Extractable protein level of glove measured in milligrams of extractable protein per grams of rubber	▸ Evaluation against the environmental performance criterion on eliminating the potential cause of protein allergy (this information is useful to the US FDA)
▸ Quantity of zinc in kilograms discharged to the receiving watercourse per month	▸ Evaluation against the environmental performance criterion on minimising wastes
▸ COD load in kilograms discharged to the receiving watercourse per month	▸ Evaluation against the environmental performance criterion on minimising wastes
▸ Quantity of dried sludge in kilograms produced per month	▸ Evaluation against the environmental performance criterion on minimising wastes
Environmental condition indicators	
▸ Incidence of protein allergy associated with the use of rubber gloves by sensitised individuals (number of official reports/year)	▸ Evaluation against the environmental performance criterion on eliminating the potential cause of protein allergy
▸ Changes in the quality of surface water upstream and downstream of the factory's effluent discharge point. Measurement by tests for inhibition of oxygen consumption by the activated sludge carried out in accordance with ISO 8192. The specific indicator is the percentage of change in EC 50.	▸ Evaluation against the environmental performance criterion on ensuring the environment is not adversely affected by PPG's operations (this information will be useful to the water treatment plant operator)

Table 9.3 **Selected indicators for EPE**

Review and improvement

Six months after starting the EPE, PPG management reviewed the indicators and decided to modify several of them in order for the EPE to be more effective. These changes are summarised in Table 9.4.

PPG considered the revised indicators in Table 9.4 on compliance with the regulatory standards to be superior to the existing indicators, being more specific and addressing the major parameters of concern more effectively. It might seem surprising that PPG did not choose these indicators in the first place. However, PPG had to undergo a learning process. Like many companies, they had no focus on regulated environmental aspects. The revised indicators enabled PPG to demonstrate that it could act responsibly as a result of the new information it acquired on its operations.

Figure 9.2 shows the percentage of effluent samples analysed monthly that comply with the regulatory standard for biochemical oxygen demand (BOD). This indicator was found to be useful in providing the focus for PPG to work on improving its waste-water treatment plant. It is interesting to observe that a compliance measure can be used for measuring the performance of a waste-water treatment plant. It implies that the performance of the treatment facility has become a management concern whereas previously this had not been considered an issue.

For the indicator on the number of pieces of gloves rejected, PPG considered that the percentage of defective gloves produced per month is a better indicator. Figure 9.3 shows the trend of this indicator in 1998. The company faced no difficulties in meeting the environmental performance criterion of 5% for this indicator, while the criterion for the percentage of rejects was revised from 5% to 3%.

Water-extractable protein levels (see Fig. 9.4) were generally below the limit set by PPG. On some of the occasions when the protein level seemed to exceed the limit due to water

Table 9.4 **Improved indicators for EPE**

Old indicators	New Indicators
▶ Number of effluent samples analysed monthly not complying with regulatory standards	▶ Percentage of effluent samples analysed monthly complying with the regulatory standard for BOD
	▶ Percentage of effluent samples analysed monthly complying with the regulatory standard for COD
	▶ Percentage of effluent samples analysed monthly complying with the regulatory standard for suspended solids
	▶ Percentage of effluent samples analysed monthly complying with the regulatory standard for zinc
▶ Number of pieces of gloves rejected in relation to the total number of pieces of gloves produced/month	▶ Percentage of defective gloves produced per month

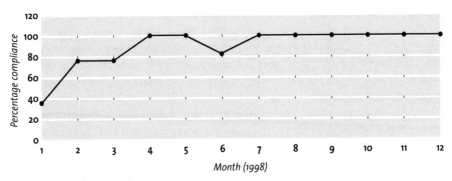

Figure 9.2 **Percentage of effluent samples analysed monthly complying with the regulatory standard for BOD**

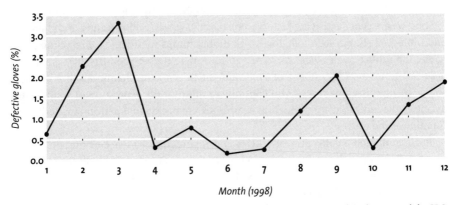

Figure 9.3 **Percentage of defective gloves produced per month by PPG**

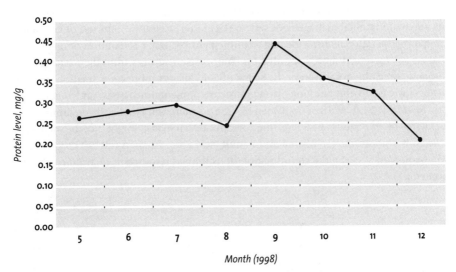

Figure 9.4 **Water-extractable protein levels in the PPG gloves**

shortage, PPG was able to overcome the problem by improving the leaching operation. For the lines with no post-leaching tank (used to remove the water-extractable protein), PPG sold gloves not meeting the specification for extractable protein to another factory which did have the facility to remove the protein. PPG is, however, planning to extend the post-leaching stage to all the lines to reduce the dependency on other factories to buy its off-specification gloves.

PPG realised the indicators requiring measurement of effluent flow—namely, quantity of zinc (kg) discharged to the receiving watercourse per month and chemical oxygen demand (COD) load (kg) discharged per month—were not reliable. This was due to the limitation in flow measurement. PPG will find ways to improve on the data collection.

The indicator on annual total cost of implementing environmental programmes could not be assessed because the EPE had just started. Also, PPG did not receive any environmentally related complaint in 1998, but this indicator would be maintained for evaluation against the environmental performance criterion of zero public complaints.

Solid wastes generated at the factory were: rejected gloves, rubber lumps, and chemical and biological sludge. Rejected gloves and rubber lumps were sent to a recycling plant where the rubber wastes were converted to low-grade rubber products. PPG is seeking approval from the Department of Environment to send the chemical and biological sludge to a fertiliser plant. PPG will continue to monitor the generation of solid wastes as one of the indicators for evaluation against the environmental performance criterion on minimising wastes.

PPG maintained a collection of articles and reports on incidence of protein allergy associated with the use of natural rubber gloves by sensitised individuals, but had not reviewed this indicator. As PPG had just started monitoring changes in the quality of surface water upstream and downstream of the factory's effluent discharge point, the data collected was insufficient for review.

PPG may consider adding more indicators: for example, on the consumption of toxic chemicals, energy and water. The company's management will also consider implementing an environmental management system (ISO 14001) to improve the use of EPE in the company. The rationale for choosing to implement ISO 14001 is that the company feels that an ISO 14001 certificate is needed for competitive reasons within their business. At the same time, the expansion in the scope of EPE calls for more co-ordination because of the increase in the amount of ongoing environmental activities, and this can be provided by ISO 14001. The established ISO 14031 system can handle the environmental elements of ISO 14001; however, the 'organisational parts' might not be managed efficiently without the establishment of a full ISO 14001 system. A full ISO 14001 system will be needed at PPG if the co-ordination of its limited resources is to avoid reaching a bottleneck.

◢ Conclusions

The review and improvement process performed by PPG management follows the guidance of ISO 14031. We recognise that PPG has improved the evaluation process by introducing better indicators and expanding the scope of its performance evaluation. Furthermore, PPG is planning to improve the physical installation, and revamp the leaching facilities and the waste-water treatment plant. The PPG management review fully covers the specifications of ISO 14001 except for the documentation requirements.

We can conclude that PPG has established an EMS using the principles of ISO 14031. The management of PPG states that it recognises the need for environmental performance evaluation as an internal management tool.

Comparing the PPG system to the ISO 14001 specification leads to the conclusion that the 'environmental elements' of ISO 14001 can be generated using the guidance of ISO 14031—environmental aspects, objectives and targets, environmental management programme, operational control, records, monitoring and measurement, and management review.

The experience gained from the PPG example is typical of other examples. Combining these experiences, we can conclude that the use of the ISO 14031 guidelines (Bakti and Shyan 1999; ISO 1999; Løkkegaard 1999a, 1999b) leads to the establishment of simple EMSs focusing on:

- ☐ Few environmental aspects and the criteria for their choice

- ☐ Re-use of data and development of a common data pool

- ☐ Conversion of selected data to useful indicators

- ☐ Visualising the performance trends over time using environmental performance indicators

- ☐ Simple assessment and effective reporting using indicators

The characteristics of simple EMS systems are:

- ☐ Focus on 'control loops' for selected environmental aspects

- ☐ Environmental work managed by action programmes

- ☐ Uncomplicated expansion of simple EMS following the ISO 14001 model

- ☐ Simple EMSs depend on one or only a few persons.

- ☐ System documentation is rudimentary.

- ☐ Auditing of simple EMSs may not be performed.

- ☐ Commitment of management might be low.

- ☐ Involvement of more employees might be limited.

It should be emphasised that the ISO 14031 route leads to highly effective systems that focus on actions and results. The system typically involves only one person, which might be an advantage for small companies with only have a few environmental aspects and limited people to manage them. But the system will then totally depend on this single person. This might be a major drawback, especially if the documentation is rudimentary, which normally is the case, because, if that person leaves, the information leaves too.

Involving more people or expanding the scope of EPE requires the co-ordination of ongoing activities. The environmental work must then be organised in some way. The company will have to delegate responsibilities, set up rules for communication and so on: i.e. it will have to develop the established ISO 14031 system into an EMS according to ISO 14001 or equivalent standards, such as the EU Eco-management and Audit Scheme (EMAS).

It is a relatively straightforward task to expand the ISO 14031 system in accordance with the ISO 14001 specifications. We believe that this approach will preserve the benefits of ISO 14031 even if the system is being developed into a full ISO 14001 EMS.

INTEGRATION OF BUSINESS STRATEGY IN ESTABLISHING SIGNIFICANT ENVIRONMENTAL ASPECTS*

Enrico Cagno and Paolo Trucco
Politecnico di Milano, Italy

Under the ISO 14004 guidelines, the initial environmental review (IER) is the first step taken by a company in considering, systematically and strategically, all the aspects underlying the complex relationship between its production systems and the ecological and social environments. In early 1998, when an ISO 14001 certification project started, the top management of Mazzucconi SpA, an Italian aluminium foundry, was aware of the crucial role of the IER in defining effective environmental policy and programmes. The company also knew that the IER would demand significant human and financial resources in terms of overall project cost. Therefore, a new multi-criteria assessment model (see Fig. 10.1) was requested and implemented in order to identify significant environmental aspects and allow better integration with other company objectives and strategies, so highlighting the strategic potential of environmental management and ISO 14001 certification.

Mazzucconi is a medium-sized company with 360 employees and an annual income of about €100 million. The production site involved in the ISO 14001 certification project is an aluminium foundry in Northern Italy that produces aluminium alloy castings for automotive engines (cylinder heads, exhaust collectors, etc.) and large mechanical systems (e.g. tank components). The two main processes are sand and shell casting which consume about 4,000 tonnes/year of pure aluminium. The site is 14,494m² (12,154m² of covered area) and is located close to a residential district. Founded in 1955, the installation

* This chapter is an extension of a paper originally published in *The Journal of Environmental Assessment Policy and Management* 4.1 (Imperial College Press, 1999).

  The authors gratefully acknowledge Marta and Emilio Di Cristofaro of Galgano & Associati for their contribution and co-operation in developing and implementing the present methodology, and top management at Mazzucconi for its environmental commitment.

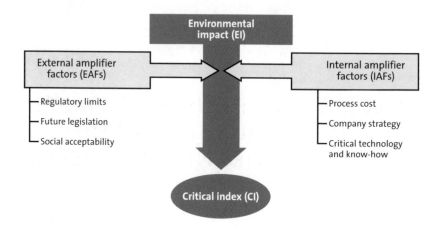

Figure 10.1 **Criteria framework to define the significance of the environmental aspects**

has been greatly modified over the years, increasing production capacity and spreading out over a wider area. The urban settlement near the site has also grown.

As a supplier to the German automotive industry, the company has in recent years been under considerable pressure to adopt specific management systems able to monitor and certify environmental performance improvement.

Hence, there were two main reasons encouraging management to consider an ISO 14001 certification project:

☐ Environment-oriented customer demands

☐ The need to improve relationships with the local community, particularly with regards to the environmental impacts of the site

For the first time, Mazzucconi realised that environmental aspects have a growing impact on company economic systems, affecting profitability (Klassen and McLaughlin 1996) and requiring drastic revisions to management paradigms. Indeed, the conservation of ecological systems and the creation of conditions for sustainable growth already constitute an integral part of the expectations of the large majority of stakeholders. As a result, an increasing number of companies are beginning to look at the environment as one of the potentially most important factors in their long-term competitiveness (Porter and van der Linde 1995; Lawrence *et al.* 1998).

Despite the rapid spread of environmental management systems (EMSs) and ISO 14001 (ISO 1996a), systematic and congruent methodological approaches to the IER have yet to be documented in the literature. Common approaches look at the production site as a **black box** in which the consumption of resources and the undesired output are measured without linking impacts to the processes performed at the site. The most frequently used tools are checklists, questionnaires and databases (ISO 1996c; Rothery 1995).

The top management of Mazzucconi recognised that such an approach presents a number of limitations that have a negative impact on the effectiveness of the EMS:

☐ The static vision of the production system identifies end-of-pipe objectives and measures based on information with short-term validity which is difficult to update as the context changes.

☐ There is little integration with other company objectives, thus reducing the strategic potential of environmental management.

These factors made the IER a critical activity for which methodological development was needed in order to:

☐ Increase the information content of the results of the analysis in support of the subsequent activities of defining environmental management policies, designing and implementing specific measures, and thus establishing an EMS

☐ Rationalise the time and resources needed to carry out the study

◢ A strategy-based methodology for the IER

The basic framework of the proposed methodology to perform IERs is illustrated in Figure 10.2. In the first phase, termed **selection**, the limits of the study are defined (i.e. the breadth of the initial spectrum that defines the group of impact factors to analyse). There follows an initial selection of impacts using general criteria (e.g. industry, geographic location, etc.). In the second phase, termed **inventory**, the main site processes are

Figure 10.2 **Proposed methodological framework of IER**

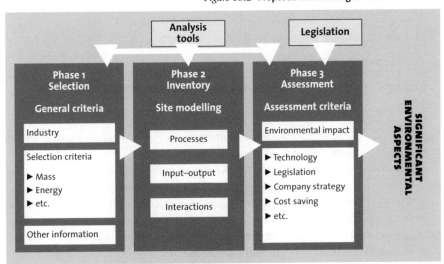

modelled by means of flow charts, highlighting relations between various important process phases and the induced environmental impacts. This is the step in which, with the help of inventory tools (Van Berkel *et al.* 1997), the impacts are quantified and their sources identified. In the third and final phase, **assessment**, the critical environmental factors are evaluated by means of an assessment process based on specific criteria. The relative importance of the latter is defined by management with reference to site conditions, company strategy and objectives.

Below, individual phases of the methodology are described with reference to the Mazzucconi site.

Phase 1: Selection

The first phase aims to select, among all the potential impact factors in the initial spectrum, those that are pertinent to the specific case. A systematic approach to this selection begins by taking account of two principal aspects:

1. The features of the main site processes and activities (industry, technologies, facilities, etc.) including not only the production process, but also all the site utilities

2. The environmental regulations to which the site is subject

The analysis of the production site requires a considerable amount of data and information collection. Close collaboration with other company functions and with existing management systems ensured that in the present case collection times and/or assessment costs were considerably contained. The following were considered:

☐ The waste disposal register

☐ The chemical analysis of gas and liquid emissions

☐ Acoustic measurements outside the site

☐ Data on main products—quantity, mix, costs, etc.

☐ Process and ancillary materials

☐ Safety data sheets of used substances and raw materials

☐ Percentage of discarded and recycled materials

Together, this information provided a starting point for a detailed analysis of the environmental aspects concerning the site.

The main sources of environmental impact were identified by reference to studies and data in the literature (e.g. Yoshiki-Gravelsins *et al.* 1993; Nicodemi and Zoja 1981; EAA 1996; ETH 1994) and to the experience of company management and environmental experts. The most important company processes in terms of environmental impacts are: sand casting, shell casting, maintenance, quality control and plant utilities operations. Each of these is described in depth in the site-modelling phase.

The impacts associated to the selected processes can be traced systematically by defining a process/impact matrix (Table 10.1), where the rows indicate the main site processes and activities and/or other specific phases in the product life-cycle and the columns indicate the environmental impact factors to be considered. The matrix is also the reference framework for the inventory data collection phase (inventory matrix) and the final assessment phase (assessment matrix).

Phase 2: Inventory

As all the impacts generated by the main processes are quantified in this phase, this is the step that absorbs the most resources.

Once the main processes have been defined, the level of detail and the impact factors must be selected for each one. Starting with a full checklist, it is possible to identify criteria (e.g. mass or energy) defining a minimum impact threshold. In the foundry studied, all products with a usage less than approximately 200 kg/year were excluded. This threshold was set by reference to the material safety data sheets (MSDSs) and the experience of local technicians, so as not to overlook highly toxic substances undermining the significance of the analysis.

In order to collect and manage the data dynamically, the site is modelled in flow diagrams for each main process (see Figs. 10.3, 10.4 and 10.5).

The last step in the inventory phase is the processing of the quantitative data for all the impact factors. This produces the inventory matrix (see Table 10.2; cf. Table 10.1). An

Table 10.1 **Process/impact matrix**

PROCESSES		IMPACT CATEGORIES					
		Input			Output		
		Energy	Water	Materials	Air emissions	Waste-water	Solid waste
Input logistics	Activity 1						
	...						
	Activity n						
Production	Activity 1						
	...						
	Activity n						
Output logistics	Activity 1						
	...						
	Activity n						
Product use							
Product disposal							

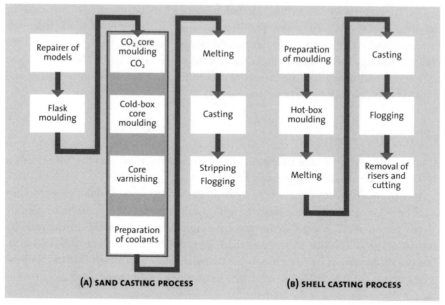

Figure 10.3   **Flow diagrams of the casting processes**

'eco-vector', the components of which represent the individual polluting factors for each specific process, is associated to each cell of the matrix. It is important to underline that the matrix illustrates the distribution of the site's environmental impact in the various processes. In the Mazzucconi foundry, the main impact categories are: materials, energy, waste and emissions.

- ☐ **Materials**. To reduce the consumption of pure aluminium, all discarded production is re-cast. However, due to final product quality requirements, it is not possible to use second-cast aluminium.

Figure 10.4   **Hot-box core moulding**

Figure 10.5   **Shell casting**

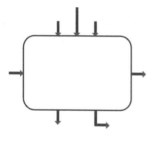

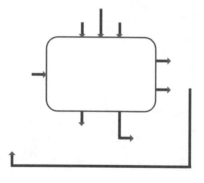

	Materials		Energy		Waste		Waste-water		Air emissions		
	Name	kg/year	Electrical kWh/year	Methane m³/year	Class	kg/year	Substance	mg/litre	Substance	mg/Nm³	mg/h
Shell casting	Varnish	13,920					Aluminium	0.02			
	Nitrogen	3,120					Ammonic nitrogen	0.2	Lead	0.5	1,000
	Boro-titanium	6,000			Sludge containing heavy metals		Nitrose nitrogen	0.07	Aluminium	0.34	9,201
	Kaolin	2,100							Powders	3.4	372,227
	Melting pots	158,400				12,980			VOC	4.1	231,370
	Magnesium	2,760	2,817·10⁶	1,084·10⁶			Nitric nitrogen	2.8			
	Lubricating oils	612					Phosphor	0.8			
	Refractories	1,380					Mineral oils	1			
	Metallic sodium	3,600			Sand and grit		BOD5	6			
	Talc	3,528				1,430,560	COD	28			
Hot-box core moulding	Catalyst	10,000					Materials in suspension	22			
	Paste	3,144			Pollutant waste from melting pots				Furfural alcohol	2	15,600
	Releasing agent	480	1,107·10⁶			13,875			VOC	18	81,000
	Resin	43,000					Total waste	15.887 m³/year			
	Varnish	2,515									

Table 10.2 **Part of the inventory matrix for the aluminium foundry**

☐ **Energy.** The company uses electrical energy and methane gas for production, heating, factory lighting and other utilities. There are no systems to recover energy lost in heat. Consumption is given in Table 10.3.

☐ **Waste.** The types, quantities and relative disposal costs for waste in 1996 are given in Table 10.4. Foundry sand and grit, which cannot be re-used, are the main items.

☐ **Water disposal.** Industrial water is mainly contaminated with aluminium powder and is therefore transported separately to a sediment tank, while water contaminated with penetrating liquids is treated in an active carbon filter and thus has no direct impact on the environment.

☐ **Air emissions.** During cold-box core moulding, SO_2 is released which is removed in humid conditions with automatically fed water and soda. In addition, the mixer used to prepare the mix for CO_2 core moulding produces powders which are passed along a suction tube to a sleeve filter. Traces of

Table 10.3 **Energy consumption of the aluminium foundry**

Processes	Electrical energy (kWh/year)	Methane gas (m³/year)	Use
Sand casting	904,850	67,769	Melting furnaces
Shell casting	2.816,975	1,084,224	Melting furnaces, holding furnaces, core baking burners
Quality control	1,107,275	0	Treatment furnaces, other machines
General services	489,000	280,000	Heaters, lighting, etc.
TOTAL	**5,318,100**	**1,431,993**	

Waste	Quantity (kg/year)	Disposal cost (€/ton)
Exhausted non-de-silvered fixing baths	318	156
Exhausted developing baths	270	156
Basic solutions and mixtures	3,300	370
Mineral and/or synthetic oils	1,538	166
Sludge containing heavy metals	14,580	195
Sludge containing phenols	1,000	195
Foundry sand and grit	2,318,560	21
Hazardous waste	231,25	40
Household waste	8,380	220

Table 10.4 **Classification of waste produced at the aluminium foundry**

furfural and isobutyl alcohol derived from the core moulding and varnishing are also present. The emissions generated by the melting and holding furnaces are rich in lead and aluminium. Other powders derive from the de-gasification, modification, and refining treatments with nitrogen, metallic sodium and boro-titanium, respectively.

Phase 3: Assessment

The last phase in identifying significant environmental impacts is the assessment of the inventory data. Starting from the inventory matrix, the environmental factors are ordered according to their criticality using appropriately chosen assessment criteria. The main criterion is the environmental impact (EI) which is defined as any change to the environment, whether adverse or beneficial, wholly or partially resulting from the company's activities, products or services (ISO 1996a). Although the assessment of criticality and, consequently, the priority of counter-measures, derive mainly from the impact of the specific environmental aspect, this can be considerably modified when related to the strategic objectives. Thus, plant management and operations requirements, together with pressure from internal and external stakeholders, have a considerable effect in determining the criticality of an environmental aspect. Criteria that may amplify the importance of a single aspect have been identified and classified into two categories (cf. Fig. 10.1).

External amplifier factors (EAFs)

☐ **Proximity to regulatory limits (EAF1).** As compliance with legislation is an essential element in environmental management, this criterion assesses the gravity of an environmental impact in terms of the proximity to limits imposed by the law.

☐ **Trend towards more restrictive regulations (EAF2).** The introduction of this criterion is linked to the possibility of early exploitation of medium-term changes in regulations.

☐ **Social acceptability (EAF3)**. This criterion assesses the external perception—by customers, public, media, local communities, etc.—of the environmental impacts generated by the site. At Mazzucconi, this criterion was assessed by company management on the basis of its sensitivity in perceiving the 'voice of stakeholders'.

Internal amplifier factors (IAFs)

☐ **Process costs (IAF1)**. The criterion assesses the incidence of costs induced by the environmental aspect with respect to total process costs.

☐ **Company strategic objectives (IAF2)**. Within the site, the criticality of an environmental impact may be greater or less depending on the strategic importance of the activity by which it is generated.

☐ **Critical technology and know-how (IAF3)**. An impact may be associated with a specific technology or know-how which is considered critical because it is irreplaceable, particularly difficult to manage, or is the main source of the company's competitive advantage.

Each criterion produces for each individual element of the process–impact matrix a qualitative assessment of the impacts that can be transformed into quantitative terms by means of an appropriate scoring system. A possible scale is shown in Table 10.5. For each criterion, a matrix identical in form to the inventory is constructed, in which a points score for each impact is recorded.

Environmental impact (EI). The measure of the environmental impact is defined with reference to the judgement of environmental experts who attribute levels of potential damage to the different impacts (Table 10.6). Since at Mazzucconi little environmental knowledge was available, external experts from a consultancy company were engaged. For the materials category, reference was made to technical characteristics, production processes and MSDSs. For atmospheric emissions, toxicity and the emission factor were considered. The weighting attributed to energy was taken as dependent on consumption by the individual processes. Criticality was associated to waste on the basis of the amount and type of disposal required. Liquid emissions were given a criticality of two in view of the presence of aluminium (albeit at low concentrations), and all processes were given the same values, as only aggregate data for the site was available.

Proximity to regulatory limits (EAF1). For this criterion, reference was made to a quantitative driver (R_L) defined as:

Table 10.5 **Assessment scale with linguistic–numeric equivalents**

1	2	3	4
Hardly important	Modestly important	Reasonably important	Extremely important

COMPANY PROCESSES		IMPACT CATEGORY				
		Input		Output		
		Input materials	Energy	Waste	Liquid emissions	Air emissions
Production	Sand casting	1.00	2.00	4.00	2.00	1.00
	Sand core moulding	3.00	2.00	4.00	2.00	2.00
	Shell casting	2.00	3.00	4.00	2.00	2.00
	Shell core moulding	1.00	3.00	4.00	2.00	1.00
	Quality control	1.00	2.00	4.00	2.00	1.00
Maintenance		2.00	0.00	0.00	2.00	1.00
General services		0.00	1.00	1.00	2.00	1.00

Table 10.6 **Environmental impact matrix**

$$R_L = \frac{\text{emission amount}}{\text{regulatory limit}}$$

Different points scores were given to the different values of R_L as shown in detail in Table 10.7. In cells of the process/impact matrix in which more than one impact factor may be present, the highest value of R_L was taken (Table 10.8).

Trend towards more restrictive legislation (EAF2). Reference was made to a credible, short-to-medium-term legislative scenario within the European Union.

Table 10.7 **Points score for the 'Proximity to regulatory limits' (EAF1) criterion**

Range	Score	Category
No legal limit (R=0)	0	Liquid, atmospheric and sound emissions
$0 < R_L < 0.5$	1	
$0.5 < R_L < 1$	3	
$R_L \geq 1$	4	
Special: municipal waste	1	Waste
Toxic noxious	4	
No regulation	0	Materials
Regulation	4	
No restrictions	0	Energy

COMPANY PROCESSES		IMPACT CATEGORY				
		Input		Output		
		Input materials	Energy	Waste	Liquid emissions	Air emissions
Production	Sand casting	0.00	0.00	1.00	1.00	0.00
	Sand core moulding	0.00	0.00	1.00	1.00	0.00
	Shell casting	0.00	0.00	1.00	1.00	0.00
	Shell core moulding	0.00	0.00	1.00	1.00	0.00
	Quality control	0.00	0.00	1.00	1.00	0.00
Maintenance		0.00	0.00	0.00	1.00	1.00
General services		0.00	0.00	1.00	1.00	0.00

Table 10.8 **'Proximity to regulatory limits' (EAF 1) matrix**

Social acceptability (EAF3). To attribute a points score to the individual impacts, the factors contributing to the definition of criticality must be highlighted. For air emissions, a score of four was attributed to sand core moulding and maintenance, as these are the main cause of complaints by the local community because of the strong smell caused. The level of emissions is, however, well below legal limits.

Process costs (IAF1). This criterion makes reference to an indicator giving the ratio of the environmental cost to the total process cost:

$$R_c \;=\; \frac{\text{environmental cost [\$/unit]}}{\text{total process cost [\$/unit]}}$$

The 'environmental cost' means the sum of the costs sustained by the company for the use of environmental resources.

The 'total process cost' means the total cost sustained to realise an equivalent unit of a single reference product (e.g. 1 kg of cast aluminium alloy).

Company strategic objectives (IAF2). Within the site, the processes that directly influence company competitiveness are identified and these are assigned a points score as a function of their influence. For processes where a criterion is not applicable, a score of zero is given. Mazzucconi is making considerable efforts to improve the quality and efficiency of the shell casting process in order to expand in the European market. For this reason, the shell casting and moulding processes were given a criticality of four.

Critical technology (IAF3). This criterion analyses the inventory matrix by row, thus drawing attention to the processes considered and identifying which use critical technologies. In the present case, the criterion was excluded, as it was deemed irrelevant.

The role of environmental experts, health, safety and environment (HSE) managers and production managers is to estimate objectively the impact of different environmental aspects and to express judgements on the relevance of each external and internal amplifier factor. Environmental management is a competitive lever for the company, so it is top management that must subsequently determine the relative importance of the environmental impact and the internal and external amplifier factors in the light of business strategy, company culture and stakeholder requests. Under these circumstances, the estimate of environmental impact and of the relevance of amplifier factors should be made as objective as possible, whereas the determination of the importance weightings of the criteria is highly subjective. To determine the weightings, the problem is structured as a hierarchy (see Fig. 10.6). Unitary sum weightings were chosen in order to obtain a final points score for criticality (the criticality index [CI]) in line with the scale used for the assessment of each impact factor (e.g. between one and four). The weightings can be calculated in various ways, from pair-wise comparison to assess the relative importance between criteria (Saaty 1980), to direct determination of the weightings.

Figure 10.6 **Hierarchy to determine weightings and actors involved in the assessment phase**

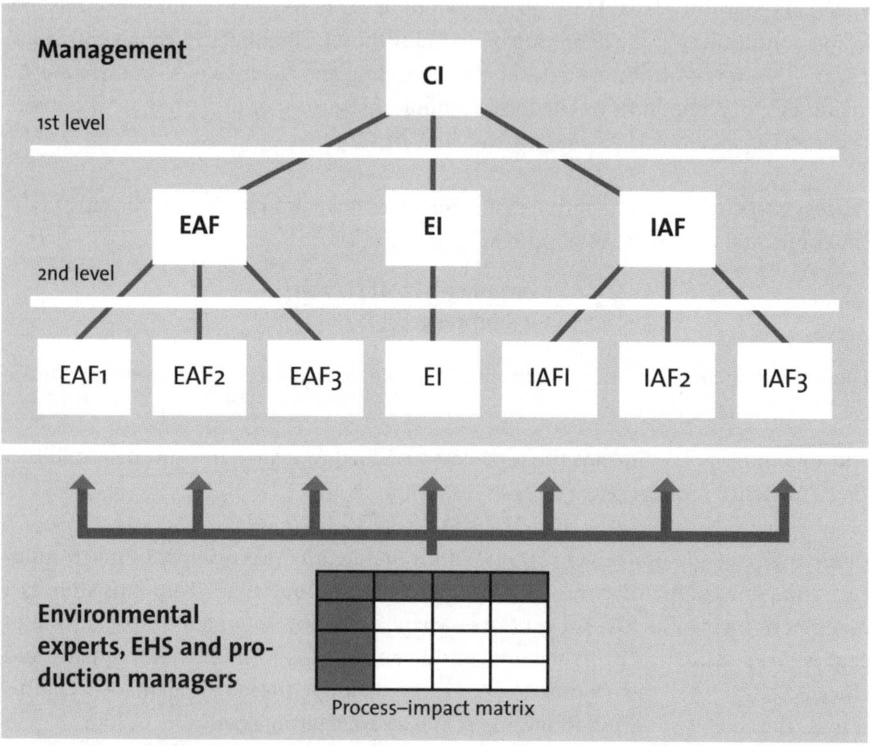

EAF = external amplifier factor; IAF = internal amplifier factor; EI = environmental impact; CI = criticality index

At Mazzucconi, the relative importance assigned to the various criteria categories (Table 10.9, row 1) highlights management's greater sensitivity to external factors (0.4) and, in particular, to the level of social acceptability (EAF3), which contributes 60.1% to the importance of EAF (W_{EAF} = 0.601), generating 24% of the CI for the environmental factor (W^*_{EAF} = 0.240). These judgements are in line with the company's objectives following the introduction of an EMS that is essentially centred on improving the company image and its relations with customers.

Once management's importance weightings have been obtained, environmental experts, HSE and production managers integrate these with the estimates. The process–impact matrix for the environmental impact is multiplied, as is the corresponding weighting, W_{EI} (=W^*_{EI}), to obtain the criticality quota of the factor determined exclusively by its environmental impact. The same operation is performed for the individual amplifier factors, multiplying the corresponding matrix by the weight W^*. The sum of the resulting matrices gives the overall judgement of the criticality (CI) of each factor (Table 10.10). The individual contributions of the environmental impact, the external amplification and the internal amplification are also highlighted (Table 10.11). For example, waste in shell core moulding has a total CI of 2.87, the sum of 1.20 (= 0.3 × 4.00, equal to 41.8% of CI) for environmental impact, 0.61 (= 0.4 × 1.53; 21.3%) for external amplifier factors and 1.06 (= 0.3 × 3.53; 36.9%) for internal amplification.

Impact ranking

The criticality of the environmental impact factors of the site is given by the CI: the higher the points score, the more critical the factor and the greater the importance of the associated measure.

To identify critical impact factors, an assessment scale is proposed which associates a judgement and a possible improvement measure to a given CI. To determine the group of impact factors to be considered in the drafting of an environmental policy, reference is made to the assessment scale given in Table 10.12. The environmental improvement programme—where to intervene, with what aims and with what level of resources—will be a management decision.

The ranking of the impacts can be shown in a target plot graph. Within each circular sector of the graph, the criticality judgements associated to the different processes at the site are shown (see Fig. 10.7). This gives a simple and immediate view for a qualitative assessment of the overall impact of the foundry, showing that the points are mainly

Table 10.9 **Local (bold) and absolute (italic) weightings**

W_{EAF}	**0.4**	W_{EI}	**0.3**	W_{IAF}	**0.3**
W_{EAF1} *W^*_{EAF1}*	**0.324** *0.130*	W_{EAF2} *W^*_{EAF2}*	**0.075** *0.030*	W_{EAF3} *W^*_{EAF3}*	**0.601** *0.240*
W_{IAF1} *W^*_{IAF1}*	**0.533** *0.160*	W_{IAF2} *W^*_{IAF2}*	**0** *0*	W_{IAF3} *W^*_{IAF3}*	**0.467** *0.140*

COMPANY PROCESSES		IMPACT CATEGORY				
		Input		Output		
		Input materials	Energy	Waste	Liquid emissions	Air emissions
Production	Sand casting	0.70	1.41	2.11	0.89	1.08
	Sand core moulding	1.30	1.41	2.11	0.89	1.86
	Shell casting	1.48	2.05	2.87	1.37	1.86
	Shell core moulding	1.18	2.05	2.87	1.37	1.56
	Quality control	0.86	1.29	2.27	1.05	1.24
Maintenance		0.84	0.09	0.62	0.73	1.53
General services		0.24	0.53	1.05	0.73	0.92

Table 10.10 **Criticality index (CI) matrix**

Table 10.11 **Second-level judgements for environmental impact (EI), external (EAF) and internal (IAF) amplification**

COMPANY PROCESSES		IMPACT CATEGORY				
		Input		Output		
		Input materials	Energy	Waste	Liquid emissions	Air emissions
Production	Sand casting	1.00 / 0.53 / 0.60	2.00 / 2.40 / 0.23	4.00 / 1.00 / 1.53	2.00 / 0.53 / 0.32	1.00 / 1.00 / 1.20
	Sand core moulding	3.00 / 0.53 / 0.60	2.00 / 2.40 / 0.23	4.00 / 1.00 / 1.53	2.00 / 0.53 / 0.32	2.00 / 1.00 / 2.41
	Shell casting	2.00 / 2.13 / 0.60	3.00 / 3.53 / 0.23	4.00 / 3.53 / 1.53	2.00 / 2.13 / 0.32	2.00 / 2.60 / 1.20
	Shell core moulding	1.00 / 2.13 / 0.60	3.00 / 3.53 / 0.23	4.00 / 3.53 / 1.53	2.00 / 2.13 / 0.32	1.00 / 2.60 / 1.20
	Quality control	1.00 / 1.07 / 0.60	2.00 / 2.00 / 0.23	4.00 / 1.53 / 1.53	2.00 / 1.07 / 0.32	1.00 / 1.53 / 1.20
Maintenance		2.00 / 0.00 / 0.60	0.00 / 0.00 / 0.23	0.00 / 0.47 / 1.20	2.00 / 0.00 / 0.32	1.00 / 0.47 / 2.73
General services		0.00 / 0.00 / 0.00	1.00 / 0.47 / 0.23	1.00 / 0.47 / 1.53	2.00 / 0.00 / 0.32	1.00 / 0.47 / 1.20

Environmental impact judgement (0.3) Internal amplification judgement (0.3) External amplification judgement (0.4)

Criticality index (CI)	Assessment
0–1	Negligible
1–2	Not critical: monitor
2–3	Critical: measures in the short term
3–4	Extremely critical: immediate measures

Table 10.12 **Assessment scale of environmental impacts**

concentrated on the internal circumferences, meaning that the overall environmental criticality of the site is modest and the processes that are most environmental critical are shell core moulding and casting (in particular in terms of energy consumption and waste production).

With comparisons over time, the target plot can also be used to assess improvements in the site's environmental performance. Comparisons with target values will show the extent to which objectives have been realised.

◢ Implementation results: exploitation of the EMS strategic value

The application of the methodology at Mazzucconi highlighted the strengths and effectiveness of the proposed framework and tools. The methodology traced the main processes and flows at the production site, identified critical impact factors and defined priorities for measures.

For the given size of the company, the overall commitment in terms of time and resources was about five person-months, comparable with that required for similar

Figure 10.7 **Target plot for the aluminium foundry**

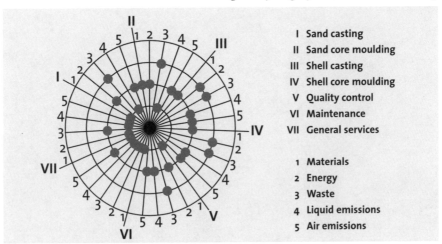

I   Sand casting
II Sand core moulding
III Shell casting
IV Shell core moulding
V   Quality control
VI Maintenance
VII General services

1 Materials
2 Energy
3 Waste
4 Liquid emissions
5 Air emissions

applications. However, the amount and the quality of the information generated were superior in terms of its strategic value, relationship with company production processes and IER documentation. The strengths of the methodological framework can be summarised as follows:

☐ Systematic analysis and effective tools translate into systematic company and non-company data collection and assessment, allowing coherent and effective decisions.

☐ The matrix description of the relationships between processes and environmental impact factors (the process–impact category matrix) supports environmental experts in the identification and assessment of the impact sources.

☐ The assessment phase, particularly the use of a broader set of indicators than merely the environmental impact index, and the elicitation process result in more coherence between company objectives, assessment criteria and IER results.

☐ The use of assessment criteria linked to other company objectives proved to be of help in deploying company strategy, highlighting the strategic role of environmental management (integration).

☐ The systematic and transparent IER model improves the audit process undertaken by the third-party certification body.

☐ The complete development of the methodology, concurrently with its application at Mazzucconi, provided full evidence of the consistency of the proposed approach. Moreover, the proposed assessment model and tools also proved to be suitable for monitoring, auditing and reporting within a certified EMS.

SETTING UP EFFECTIVE ENVIRONMENTAL MANAGEMENT SYSTEMS BASED ON THE CONCEPT OF CLEANER PRODUCTION
Cases from small and medium-sized enterprises*

Johannes Fresner
STENUM GmbH, Austria

The management process determines a company's operations and organisational structure by allocating appropriate resources. Resources can be human working capacity, investment in production means, raw materials and energy. Environmental management is the management of the environmental aspects of a company. The general aim of an environmental management system (EMS) is to develop a strategy to ensure that legal compliance is achieved and materials and energy are used efficiently. The next step is to ensure that this is done by applying appropriate processes, raw materials and energy, and organising human resources effectively.

Schwarz (1999) found from an analysis of Austrian companies with EMSs that most of those that had introduced an EMS according to ISO 14001 were motivated by the expectation of cost reductions. The motivation seems to be slightly different for Austrian companies participating in the EU Eco-management and Audit Scheme (EMAS). These

* The author would like to thank the following: Helmuth Bliem, Günter Kecht and Johann Tanner of Erste Obermurtaler Brauereigenossenschaft; Karel Benes and Pavel Vajcner of Znovin Znojmo; Josef Mair of Eloxieranstalt Heuberger GmbH; Edgar Hauer of Österreichische Kommunalkredit AG; Karl Niederl of the Environmental Office of the City of Graz; Manfred Rupprecht, Environmental Co-ordinator of the Government of Styria; Gerhard Jägerhuber and Wilhelm Himmel of the Government of Styria; Hans Günther Schwarz and Michael Paula of the Austrian Ministry of Science and Transport; Andreas Tschulik of the Austrian Ministry of the Environment; Larry and the team of STENUM.

companies seem to be more motivated by image improvements and better internal and external communication. One has to add, however, that EMAS participation has so far been strongly subsidised in Austria (Schwarz 1999). We conclude that, if EMSs are to be widely accepted among businesses, they must contribute to increased profitability. This means that by the end of each business year there must be a visible positive effect on the balance sheet, through savings in raw materials and energy, reduced costs for environmental compliance, financing and insurance, or through facilitation of internal procedures. In addition, productivity or sales due to a better image of the company and its products should be increased.

STENUM has introduced EMSs in more than 20 companies in Austria, Hungary and the Czech Republic, while focusing on cleaner production as an approach to deal with environmental effects in an active and preventative way. Based on this 'integrated cleaner production and EMS model', effective EMSs with both ecological and economical benefits have been designed.

Typical elements of a cleaner production programme are:

☐ The formation of an environmental team

☐ Input–output analysis providing an overview of the efficiency of the use of material and energy, and classification of waste and emissions

☐ Material and energy flow analyses to show the reasons for waste and emissions

☐ Options for improvement (by product changes, good housekeeping measures, changes in raw materials, technological changes, internal and external recycling)

☐ Feasibility studies to show the environmental and financial benefits of the options

☐ Implementation of these measures and monitoring of their effects

The following examples of three companies show that these elements help to start a process of continuous improvement by providing key tools for the monitoring and control of environmental effects, resulting in quick improvement, the feeling of success, the stimulation of motivation and creating the capacity for autonomous problem-solving.[1]

◢ Case study 1: Znovin Znojmo

Znovin is a medium-sized producer of wine and vermouth, supplying approximately 5% of the Czech market. The company has 90 employees in three locations and has a single majority shareholder. Znovin's competitive advantage is the high quality of its products

---

1   Environmental reports can be obtained from: Erste Obermurtaler Brauereigenossenschaft, Raffaltplatz 19–23, A-8850 Murua, Austria; Eloxieranstalt Heuberger, Lagergasse 135, A-8020 Graz, Austria.

and its main market is the Czech Republic. Five to six thousand tonnes of grapes are processed annually.

The main environmental problems that the company needed to address were water consumption (15,000 m³/year) and emissions of waste-water with high organic content. Another important objective in introducing an EMS was to increase the awareness of all employees towards environmental protection, the impact of their work on the environment, the existence of risks and the possibility of accidents.

The cleaner production project was started in March 1996. The company began with environmental activities such as monitoring the consumption of raw materials, water and energy on a regular basis. Balance figures for water and products were maintained. Consequently, points of losses and inefficient use were identified and measures to reduce the consumption of water and chemicals, and thus cost, were proposed.

A new line for washing bottles was put into operation in August 1996 and a new line for filling bottles started in July 1997. Savings of 25% of total water consumption was achieved in this way as compared to 1995 levels. Considering the increase in production, this means a 50% reduction in water consumption. Other measures included the installation of new jets in the bottle washing machine, reducing the frequency of backwashing of the sand filters in the water treatment plant and the introduction of new moving belts in the bottle plant to reduce the need for lubrication.

Reduction of organic water pollution was achieved through careful separation of the most heavily polluted water in the production plant from other waste-water. Now, water with high biochemical oxygen demand (BOD) is used mainly for irrigation. The resulting level of BOD leaving the company is 25% when compared to the situation prior to these measures. In total, US$50,000 was saved by this measure, with a payback of approximately one year.

For the future, construction of a waste-water cleaning plant in conjunction with the local authorities and the reconstruction of the company's heating system are planned. Substitution of selected materials with environmentally more friendly ones will be implemented through measures such as selecting new suppliers or testing new cleaning agents. Employee training will be done on a regular basis in the future to minimise product losses from cleaning or leakages.

Detailed recording of water consumption and losses will be maintained so the environmental performance of the company is clearly visible and to provide feedback on the improvements. Table 11.1 compares the aqueous emissions of the company to the sewer before and after the project.

Implementation and maintenance of the EMS according to ISO 14001 was a team effort. The team included the managing director, the financial director, the technical director, the environmental consultant, site supervisors, the transportation and maintenance supervisor, the bottling plant supervisor, the main dispatcher, the laboratory manager and the accounts manager.

The main focus was on raising awareness within the company and on defining responsibilities for key activities such as purchasing, production and maintenance. At the start, a team of employees was trained in cleaner production methodology. In the second round of training, all employees were trained in the management of environmental aspects. In the third round, selected employees were trained in auditing.

Parameter	Units	1995	1997
Production	m³	2,344	3,000
Water consumption	m³	21,377	15,000
Waste-water load (BOD)	kg/a	22,800	4,950
BOD concentration	mg/l	1,067	330

Table 11.1 **Aqueous emissions of Znovin before and after the project compared to production**

Znovin's environmental policy and objectives were communicated to the employees by the director and the environmental consultant in a joint meeting of all workers from all sites. Znovin is a small company where employees know each other. This provides good preconditions for collecting employees' ideas and inputs. The company does not have a strict management hierarchy and workers are used to discussing new ideas with their supervisor or even the director. Rapid implementation of good ideas has become the rule.

The awareness of Znovin's employees of environmental protection and the impact of their work on the environment definitely increased. Clear benefits for the employees were perceptible improvements in working conditions. This immediately enhanced staff morale.

The environmental policy is published in a brochure, intended for public distribution, which also includes the company's environmental impacts, methods of problem-solving and the results achieved by using cleaner production strategies. Information about Znovin's ISO 14001 certification in November 1997 was published in the regional and national press. The company is believed to be the first winery in the world to be certified to ISO 14001.

In the future, Znovin will also try to influence its suppliers and customers, and encourage them to improve their attitude towards the environment.

◢ Case study 2: Eloxieranstalt A. Heuberger GmbH

Heuberger is an anodising company with 14 employees in Graz, Austria. Anodising is a galvanic process in which the surface of aluminium is converted to aluminium oxide, which protects the basic material against corrosion and wear. By grinding and polishing, the surface can be prepared in different decorative qualities prior to anodising. The company specialises in processing orders within a very short time. Annually, some 40,000 m² of aluminium sheet, profile and small parts are treated in the plant. Heuberger has participated in the Ecoprofit programme of the City of Graz since 1996 (Baumhakel 1997).

In 1997, the company decided to introduce an EMS according to EMAS. Therefore, a project to introduce an EMS was designed, based on the work done in the Ecoprofit project.

The project started with an initial review using the following information collected during the cleaner production project, as a basis:

☐ Material and energy inputs and outputs as well as options for improvement

☐ Legal compliance

☐ Organisation of the company

From this review, a working programme was drafted, which included:

☐ Development of a project to guarantee compliance with current Austrian waste-water legislation

☐ Evaluation and written documentation of the working conditions at all of the workplaces to fulfil the above legal requirements

☐ Definition of procedures for anodising, analysis of process baths and maintenance

☐ Definition of responsibilities, corrective measures and an auditing procedure

☐ Documentation of the management system

The next step was the introduction of the elements of the cleaner production programme into the daily procedures of the company. Process baths are analysed daily to optimise the quantity of chemicals. The quantities used are recorded and analysed. Changes to the resulting indicators are discussed in meetings of the environmental team which includes the manager, the production supervisor, employees in charge of maintenance and packaging, and the secretary.

Several chemicals were changed because less hazardous alternatives were available. During the process of evaluation of the operators' workplaces, the possibilities of accidents were analysed and documented. Measures for accident prevention were defined.

Hazardous waste in the form of used compressor oil was reduced to a minimum. Non-hazardous waste is separated into categories, i.e. paper, metal, plastic, biodegradable waste and industrial waste. Packaging materials are almost completely re-used for the packaging of products. Returnable packaging systems have been arranged with the most important customers. The annual quantity of industrial waste now amounts to as little as 1,500 kg.

Waste-water mainly results from rinsing parts after pickling and anodising. Longer dripping times were introduced to minimise drag-outs, i.e. the amount of process solutions that are carried from one process bath to the next on the surface of the parts so reducing the need for rinsing. The racks were changed for the same purpose. Spray rinsing was introduced to increase the rinsing effect. A unit to separate solids from waste-water will extend the neutralisation plant for the treatment of waste-water.

Electricity is used for the anodising process and for motors and light. A project to reduce electricity consumption is currently under development.

Gas is used for heating process baths and during the winter for heating the workshop. Measures to reduce gas consumption included the introduction of covers for the baths when they are not in use and a reduction of heating times before production stops at night.

The managing director paid particular attention to formulating a convincing environmental policy. The environmental guidelines are a testimony to the company's commitment to protect the environment. They are very well accepted and the feedback from employees was positive.

The environmental policy includes the statement:

> We try to minimise the effects of our activities on the environment.

This line is explained by a special paragraph to make this point clear to the employees and to illustrate it by referring to actual company activities:

> We know that this is a continuous task consisting of many small steps, which have to be implemented continuously. We do so by improving our racks to optimise the utilisation of the process solutions and to reduce the consumption of water and energy. We minimise dragout by systematically studying dripping and improving our rinsing technology and practice.

The monthly meetings of the environment team form the backbone of the EMS. The team consists of seven members, representing all areas of the company. In the meetings, the following topics are discussed:

- Progress of environmental programme

- Overview of new developments

- Current problems

- Compliance with existing regulations

- Training needs

- Discussion of current indicators of consumption of materials and energy

- Ideas for improvement

The documentation is kept as brief as possible: the meetings are documented in minutes. Current problems and remedies are noted on special forms, printed on red paper. Additionally, there are: audit forms; a form for the control of consumption of water, energy and chemicals; a form for the documentation of environmental effects; and a form for the environmental programme. Checklists have been developed for the key variables of the anodising process, for the adoption of orders and for purchasing. Plans exist for training and continued maintenance.

Each of the employees is trained in first aid. There is ongoing training in the handling of materials and the reduction of the use of chemicals. In spite of doubling its production, the company reduced its water consumption by 50% between 1996 and 1999, representing a cost reduction of US$20,000. The reduction in the use of chemicals (roughly 10%) resulted in annual cost reductions of US$2,000 and the reduction of gas consumption (also 10%) has yielded savings of US$4,000 annually.

The environmental programme for 1999 included measures for a further reduction of water consumption in the compressor cooling plant and by good housekeeping measures. In addition, solids in the waste-water have been further reduced via the filtration plant. Energy has been reduced by reducing peak loads and by good housekeeping measures, and chemical usage has been reduced in the dosage plants by improved production planning.

Despite excellent progress overall, some practical problems occurred which increased the project duration to almost two years:

☐ The authorities were indecisive regarding procedural questions due to changes in legislation, so the company was very cautious about its investments in the waste-water treatment plant.

☐ Environment team members had to work extra hours. Although this work was paid, it reduced the employees' leisure time. There was only partial acceptance of this by the employees.

☐ The compilation of documentation for the management system was originally scheduled to be done by the team. However, this proved to be very time-consuming. In fact, the consultant wrote most of the documentation after discussing the respective topics and procedures with team members. Consequently, it proved difficult for the internal auditors to critically check the management system during the internal audit process.

◢ Case study 3: Erste Obermurtaler Brauereigenossenschaft

Obermurtaler Brauereigenossenschaft is a brewery in the Austrian city of Murau. It was founded in 1495 and has brewed beer at the same site since then. The brewery, which is a co-operative owned by 545 associates, produces approximately two million litres a year of high-quality beer along with some non-alcoholic drinks. Its modern environmental policy, high-quality products and sophisticated niche-marketing policy are the reasons for the company's profitable development over the last few years and for its continuous increases in production.

Between 1990 and 1998 the brewery has increased its production by 50%. During this period the Austrian market for beer was stagnant. Contrary to the trend of falling prices, the brewery could maintain the (high) prices for its products. Today the company has 80 employees.

In 1994, a systematic analysis of the company's weak points was done through its participation in the Styrian Prepare project (Fresner 1998a). In this project, 13 companies analysed their emissions prevention potential following an input–output analysis.

Materials and energy flows were analysed and prioritised. The results of this cleaner production project were a good starting point for the following activities.

In 1995, the quality management system was certified to ISO 9001. After this, the management immediately wanted to introduce into the company's management system elements of ISO 14001 and to participate in EMAS in order to document the innovative position of the company in an environmental statement.

The director of sales and the director of production are responsible for making the decisions and providing the resources necessary for the implementation of the company's environmental policy and programme. They also conduct the management review, checking periodically how the management system works and whether objectives are being met.

The tasks of the environmental manager include the introduction of safety and health aspects into the management system. The environmental team consists of eight representatives of management, production, storage, maintenance, purchasing, accounting and controlling. In monthly meetings information is exchanged, environmental projects are designed and the realisation of measures and training is controlled.

In the job descriptions of the team members, attention is paid to the fact that they are organisationally independent. This means they can more easily identify environmental problems and document them, define preventative measures, initiate problem-solving and control the realisation of solutions, check the effectiveness of measures and eliminate problems for the environment and consumers.

The purchasing guidelines define strict rules for the purchasing of raw and auxiliary materials. Raw materials are bought exclusively from integrated and controlled farms. Material origin, farming method, fertilisers used and yield must be documented. There is regular control of raw materials in the brewery and spot checks of the farmers. Since the cleaner production project, only chlorine-free cleaning and disinfecting agents are used.

The company is verified to EMAS and was certified to ISO 14001 in 1996. The internal audits and the certification audits that have been conducted in the meantime show that the management system is 'alive' and the objectives of the quality and environmental policies have been met.

The company promotes returnable packaging, according to the rules of the Austrian environmental label for returnable packages for drinks (Verein für Konsumenteninformation 1998). According to the rules for this label, the brewery must use PVC-free sealings and heavy metal-free inks for labels. The company has also eliminated the use of aluminium film labels on the bottles.

The main objectives of the EMS include:

☐ Preventative problem-solving

☐ Identification of risk and weak points using material flow analysis

☐ Saving materials by reducing water and energy consumption

☐ Green purchasing

☐ Effective internal communication with employees and external communication using the environmental report

☐ Fostering and training employee awareness of quality and environmental issues

☐ Permanent striving for innovative solutions to improve the economical and environmental situation of the company

☐ Compliance with legal regulations

☐ Reduction of environmental impacts

Sixty measures that have been implemented between 1995 and 1998 are described in the brewery's environmental report. These include: measures for training (the training of internal auditors and of the waste manager, external training of the environmental manager and safety training); organisational measures (controlling, analysis of waste-water sources, changes in purchasing and waste separation); and technical measures (optimisation of storage, process optimisation due to material flow analysis, internal recycling, installation of a new bottle-washing machine and the introduction of peak load management).

The water consumption of the brewery was reduced from 6.70 hl/hl in 1995 to 6.06 hl/hl in 1998. Industrial waste has been reduced by 66%. The financial benefits included a 1% lower interest rate and a 30% lower insurance rate. The annual savings total US$300,000.

The environmental programme for 1999 includes 30 activities involving technical measures, e.g. the reduction of leakages of pressurised air, heat recovery from air compressors, the insulation of several steam pipes, additional meters to control steam consumption more effectively, incineration of biogas from waste-water treatment in the boiler and organisational measures, e.g. the introduction of changes in merchandising goods and in packaging.

◢ Cleaner production helps to create effective management systems

Cleaner production is the strategy to reduce the environmental impacts of businesses by systematically applying the principles of prevention. Cleaner production focuses on the sources of waste and emissions and on changing organisation, raw materials and process technology along the product life-cycle with the clear aim of reducing waste and emissions.

Cleaner production projects give a systematic analysis of waste and emissions, which include their evaluation and prioritisation—management knows where the problems are and can invest resources to resolve them effectively. Early successes and financial savings provide the motivation to continue.

The following principles can be the basis of company strategies: active research for the root causes of problems; continuous improvement; and the application of best available technology where appropriate. These are the key principles of success for innovative businesses (Fresner 1998b).

Cleaner production tools such as input–output analyses, material flow analyses and energy flow analyses build the basis of an information system to determine the efficiency of material and energy flows and the effectiveness of measures. This makes them a valuable tool in measuring the actual improvement of environmental performance.

Transparent information on material flows improves awareness. Training can be more effective with clear priorities and practical examples from one's own company. From a cleaner production project, options and measures for improvement are found. Such visible changes save money and provide high motivation to continue the process of improvement.

The management system ensures consistency and continuity. For practical reasons, existing management system elements should be integrated to avoid parallel development.

Essential factors for implementing an active EMS are:

☐ Commitment of the management

☐ Committed environmental policy

☐ An environmental team as a network covering all the organisation and acting as catalyst

☐ Immediate feedback

☐ Increased room for action and quick change

☐ Documentation of relevant data

☐ Information for everybody involved

☐ Allocation of sufficient resources (including time)

A cleaner production project will help to motivate the management as the results help to reduce daily cost. It will add a strategy of prevention to a company's environmental policy, which can be a powerful guideline for employees in the design of products and processes and during operation. Cleaner production will provide practical experience with problem-focused teamwork. Tools for environmental control are created and practically applied. This guarantees a profound understanding of environmental impacts and the ways of resolving them.

◢ Proposed strategy for the implementation of an EMS

To set up a really 'living' EMS, STENUM uses the following approach. The initial review is carried out as a cleaner production project and an environmental team is formed to do the project work within the company. Together with external consultants the environmental effects are defined on a company-wide level using input–output analyses and the evaluation of materials and emissions. Priority areas are defined and investigated in more detail using material and energy flow analyses. The processes are examined for possible improvement. Options are generated, recorded and their feasibility studied. Measures that can be realised immediately are implemented. During this phase, a legal compliance audit and an organisational audit are conducted.

The initial review is followed by the formulation of the environmental policy which must express commitment, address the main environmental effects and motivate and guide the company's employees. The resulting policy must be communicated internally. Then the EMS is set up using already effective elements. These might be working instructions, process procedures, standard operating procedures or an existing quality management system. The result should be a consistent, simple, effective system of responsibilities and procedures covering the whole organisation and all activities that affect the environment.

A phase of additional training will follow, concluded by internal auditing and, finally, external auditing. These steps should be regarded as steps of learning, in which experiences with the management system are collected and interpreted. The goal must be to make the system leaner, more effective and more practical.

The company's employees, and above all its management, should be involved directly in the initial evaluation. Special emphasis is put on the practical aspects of management, leading techniques and communication during the training and the introduction of the management system.

By considering these steps, management systems with continuous systematic improvement of the use of resources, following the principles of prevention, will be created. Significant reductions of emissions will result, as well as reduced costs for production and increased profits, while contributing to a better environment.

PERFORMANCE-BASED ISO 14001 CASE STUDIES FROM TAIWAN

Nonita T. Yap
University of Guelph, Canada

Taiwan is an island the size of Canada's Vancouver Island (c. 36,000 km^2), supporting a population of 21.8 million. The Government's ability to provide this population with a living standard that is among one of the highest in the region has been made possible by its transition from an agricultural to an industrial economy in less than two decades. Industry now contributes 96% to total exports, while agriculture accounts for only 4%. With a real gross domestic product (GDP) growth rate averaging over 8.6% in the last two decades and 1997 GDP of US$294 billion, the island economy is currently the 19th largest in the world, its productive sectors are ranked 18th in terms of competitiveness and its foreign exchange reserve is US$84 billion, the third largest. Per capita income rose from US$2,500 in 1983 to US$15,200 in 1998 (Canadian Trade Office in Taipei 1998).

The environmental impacts of this dramatic and rapid industrial development on such a small land-base have become obvious. The Tam Shui river, which flows through the Taipei metropolis, is severely polluted with untreated municipal sewage. The costs to the economy have also begun to unfold. Heavy metal contamination of the soil from industrial activities around Tao Yuan county led to a ban on agricultural activity in the region (Cheung 1995). There may also be costs in terms of political stability as a culture of protest appears to be emerging over environmental issues. Organised community opposition against two naphtha cracking plants has persisted after five years, leaving the fate of the Pinnan industrial zone uncertain. This is seen to have serious economic implications. One of the proposed naphtha cracking plants is designed to refine 300,000 barrels of crude oil daily and produce 900,000 tonnes of ethylene each year (Chang 1998).[1]

These 'costs' have not been lost on the government. In 1987, the environment was made a priority in the public policy agenda, including that of the Ministry of Economic Affairs (MOEA). Tremendous resources were invested in a strategy combining diverse

---

1   Ethylene is the chemical 'building block' for the petrochemical industry.

policy instruments—education, research and development, standard-setting, procurement of monitoring and enforcement infrastructure, and economic incentives. Improvement in environmental quality in the last five years, even as the manufacturing sector continued to grow, suggests that the strategy is reasonably effective (Cheung 1995).

◢ ISO 14001 in case study firms

In 1997, a grant from the government of Taiwan administered through the Association of Universities and Colleges of Canada was secured to undertake research in Taiwan on business decision criteria with respect to waste management. The research site covered four counties in central Taiwan—Taichung, Miao Li, Chang Hua and Yun Lin—with a total population of slightly over five million. Documents from diverse sources were reviewed and complemented information obtained from site visits and interviews with experts in government, academia and industry.

The research interest was on cleaner production (CP), defined in this chapter as approaches to product design, manufacturing processes and production that emphasise a reduction in raw material and energy inputs; these approaches focus on prevention of pollution through waste avoidance or minimisation rather than on waste treatment and disposal (UNEP 1994). During the site visits, however, it was discovered that, of the 13 firms, five had been certified under ISO 14001 and six were in the process of seeking ISO 14001 certification.

The process

Critics of the environmental management system (EMS) standard ISO 14001 abound (see e.g. Gleckman and Krut 1997; Benchmark Environmental Consulting 1995). The major criticisms are that ISO 14001 is concerned with conformance not performance, with environmental aspects not environmental impacts. It does not require compliance, only a commitment towards compliance and only with national, not international 'regulations'. Finally, it does not ensure public accessibility of the environmental information of certified firms. The process followed among the Taiwanese firms appears significantly different from the process described by critics.

In all cases the ISO 14001 certification drive was based on demonstrating continuing improvement on the basis of measurable performance targets. Targets and implementation schedules were established and responsibilities allocated with regard to:

☐ Reduction in waste generation

☐ Elimination of, or reduction in the use of, hazardous chemicals

☐ Increased efficiency in the use of materials and energy inputs

Equally interesting to note was the openness of company executives in providing the research team with all the information on the management system and manufacturing

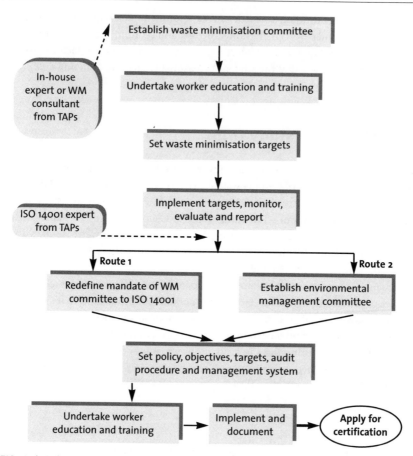

TAP = technical assistance provider   WM = waste minimisation

Figure 12.1 **Process for ISO 14001 certification**

process changes implemented to pursue ISO 14001 certification. At every meeting room, the volumes of EMS-related documents were laid out on the table for the research team to consult. In the four cases described in this chapter, the company executive was assisted at the meetings by the plant or consultant engineer or chemist involved in the ISO 14001 certification drive. They made every effort to respond to all queries and to provide supporting documentation. No question was rejected on the grounds of 'confidentiality'.

There are two different routes as shown in Figure 12.1. Both build on the industrial waste minimisation (IWM) experience of the firm. The certification process, all done through European firms, took between one to two years, with the cost ranging from NT$470 000 to NT$800,000.[2] Details are given in the next section for four of the five certified firms. All four are located in Taichung county, home to 14,221 factories, mostly small and medium-sized (SMEs).

2   NT$1 = US$0.031.

Performance-based ISO 14001: why, what, the benefits and the difficulties

San Yang manufactures integrated circuit boards for both domestic and export market. A branch plant of a multinational, this facility has 750 employees.

The decision to apply for ISO 14001 certification was made by the parent company in Japan, reportedly out of its commitment to the Montreal Protocol. ISO 14001 certification did not pose difficulties for the Taiwan facility since it had already established total quality management and total quality control.

As part of the ISO 14001 certification drive, several CP changes were introduced that cost the company NT$2 million in capital equipment and NT$500,000 in maintenance. Trichloroethylene was replaced with a re-usable non-chlorine-based solvent, energy consumption was reduced by 13%, water consumption by 37%, gas (hydrogen) by 17% and chemicals by 63%. Achieving these changes required retraining of some key technical personnel in the headquarters in Japan and involvement of the rest of the workers through the quality circles. All these CP changes reportedly resulted in savings totalling NT$10 million. This more than compensated for the cost of ISO 14001 certification.

Taiwanese owned firm Hsien Chi custom dyes textiles for local clients. Its annual gross revenues total NT$300 million and it employs 184 workers. CP is seen as important for reducing production costs and improving its corporate image, while ISO 14001 certification was seen to be very important in terms of its plan to go public and expand its operations outside the country. Until 1997 it generated 2,000 tonnes a day of waste-water, with chemical oxygen demand (COD) of 7,000 mg/l and between one and two tonnes of solid waste a month, mostly plastic and paper. In working towards its ISO 14001 certification, the company eliminated the use of azo dyes, installed a secondary treatment facility and a water recycling system. Its water usage of 22 litres per yard of cloth dyed has been reduced by nearly half. The COD of its effluent is now at 200–250 mg/l. The total capital cost for the changes was NT$10 million. The company is experimenting with a tertiary waste-water treatment system and expects to fully recycle its water and have a zero discharge when this is fully operational in 2002. The firm pays approximately NT$2.5 million a month for waste-water disposal.

Worker participation is encouraged through regular workshops on environmental issues as well as financial incentives. Solid wastes, for example, are systematically segregated, sold to a recycling company and the receipts go to the workers as part of a corporate policy to motivate workers to implement some of the conservation measures they learn at the company's environmental workshops.

SOLASIA is a small company with an initial investment of NT$6 million and ten workers on the production line. It produces solar panels mostly for export to southern Europe and north African countries, with annual sales worth NT$42 million. The operations of concern are the plating (mostly nickel and chromium), cutting and finishing of metal parts. Assembly is done in another facility.

Driven by a desire to improve product quality, the company initiated a documentation process for ISO 14001 with financial support from the Industrial Development Bureau of the MOEA. The owner quickly realised that quality control is more effectively achieved by ISO 9002 certification drive rather than ISO 14001; hence he changed the focus of the documentation to product quality objectives. The company obtained ISO 9002 certification first and then went back to seek and successfully obtain ISO 14001 certification.

ISO 14001 certification was pursued because it was seen as an important symbol of corporate responsibility in the export market. The certification was not difficult to obtain since CP changes had already been instituted through the assistance of a local consultant so the paper trail was easy to establish. Lead was eliminated from soldering operations and cyanide from plating processes. Nickel and chromium are profitably recovered from the drag-out, waste-water is recirculated, wood pallets are re-used, energy consumption has been reduced by 15% and sludge is neutralised and detoxified before being sent for disposal. The investment on the heavy metal recovery system alone was recovered in 21.6 months. Both process changes and equipment redesign are documented carefully.

Ta Tung is a Taiwanese-owned printing and dyeing company with 400 employees. Annual sales total NT$0.9 billion on an initial capital investment of NT$1.1 billion. According to managing director Chen Huo-Yuan, 'No carcinogenic dyes are used in the plant.' The firm uses about 2.5–3 tonnes of water per 100 yards of fabric processed, re-uses 3.5% of the total volume used and generates 30 tonnes of sludge a month. Waste-water treatment costs the company NT$15 per tonne and sludge disposal costs NT$2,500 per tonne.

The company achieved ISO 9002 certification in 1997 and ISO 14001 in April 1999. It financially rewards the work team that reaches the CP goal best but also fines those that violate company environmental policy. The combination of 'carrot' and 'stick' seems to have the net effect of motivating workers to create a more efficient production system and safer workplace. Chen Huo-Yuan comments:

> International demand for ISO 14001 does not affect us because we sell to the local market, but we saw how ISO 9002 really brought about an improvement in product quality. We initially pursued ISO 9002 certification just to follow the trend but our reject rate went down from 4.5% in 1997 to 3.5% in 1999. ISO certification costs money but if you do CP you will make money so we put the two together.

After receiving ISO 9002 certification, the management conducted an in-house waste and energy audit and introduced changes in both production process and energy use patterns. The changes reduced the use of reaction chemicals by 80%, dye chemicals by 30%, dispersion chemicals by 10% and resin contamination of waste-water from 6% to 2%. The savings from the CP changes more than paid for the ISO 14001 certification. Operations became 'significantly more profitable' as environmental impacts were reduced.

◢ Discussion

How representative are these observations?

The evidence described for the case study firms is anecdotal. The picture obtained, however, is fully consistent with a survey conducted by the MOEA of 408 certified firms.

Table 12.1 shows the top ten reasons for EMS certification identified by 225 survey respondents.

It is interesting to compare the survey findings with those reported for Japanese firms as described by Kurasaka (1997). Two of the three factors that Kurasaka indicates as explanatory with regard to the Japanese business response to ISO 14001, specifically the importance of exports to the economy and what he calls 'government supervision and "do-as-the-neighbours-do"' would, at first glance, apply to Taiwan. All the experts interviewed for this chapter and the survey results shown in Table 12.1 indicate that the export interest is not the most important driver for ISO 14001 certification in Taiwan. It is, however, indicated to be important enough to contradict the speculation by Cheung (1995) that government policy of encouraging the relocation of Taiwanese industry to other Southeast Asian countries, enunciated in 1994, would exert a countervailing influence on CP promotion. Overseas expansion plans appear to motivate firms to pursue ISO 14001 certification. In the drive for certification, most introduce CP changes in order to recover the cost of certification.

Table 12.2 lists the major benefits from ISO 14001 certification as perceived by MOEA survey respondents. The drive for ISO 14001 certification has reportedly improved business/government relations because of the following:

☐ Explicit commitment to compliance with regulations

☐ Involvement of top-level management in the process

☐ The requirement for continuous improvement

The government is said to be closely monitoring the performance of certified firms and considering granting 'regulatory flexibility' to certified firms if it is satisfied with the results (MOEA 1999: 13).

The MOEA survey did not report on the difficulties encountered in ISO 14001 certification. The experts interviewed for this chapter cited the following as the main difficulties:

Table 12.1 **Drivers for ISO 14001 certification**

Source: MOEA 1999

Rank	Reason
1	To improve corporate image
2	To achieve development in a sustainable manner
3	To be compatible with international trends
4	To promote environmental awareness among employees
5	To strive for compliance with domestic environmental regulations
6	To integrate and improve management systems
7	To improve manufacturing efficiency, reduce waste and pollution
8	To extend ISO 9000 efforts to solving environmental problems
9	To reduce investors' concerns
10	To expand product markets

Rank	Benefit
1	Improved effectiveness of solid waste management
2	Enhanced employees' environmental awareness and participation
3	Improved communication with customers on company's environmental issues
4	Enhanced communication within company
5	Improved control and management of water pollution
6	Enhanced confidence from customers; expansion of product markets
7	Improved health and safety conditions of company
8	Improved control and management of air pollution
9	Improved document flows within the company
10	Improved control and management of noise pollution

Table 12.2 **Major benefits to the firm from ISO 14001**

Source: MOEA 1999.

☐ Time demands of the documentation process

☐ Expertise demand of the documentation process is hard, particularly for SMEs.

One industry executive mentioned the 'poor attitudes of workers in relation to the documentation process'. A government expert indicated that space limitations can be a constraint where CP changes had spatial implications. The cost of certification was never mentioned as a barrier.

Who are the important agents of change?

Central government

The ISO 14000 series of environmental management standards was introduced in Taiwan around 1994. The promotion of ISO 14001 was entrusted to the Policy Guiding Group for Global Environmental Change, later replaced by the National Council for Sustainable Development. The Industrial Development Bureau (IDB) of the MOEA was assigned the responsibility for co-ordinating the work on ISO 14001. Table 12.3 lays out the current division of responsibilities on ISO 14001 and Table 12.4 lists some of the initiatives.

By April 1999, 652 firms had achieved ISO 14001 certification, the fifth-highest figure in the world. What is, perhaps, unique about this is that the government strongly encourages that ISO 14001 certification be preceded by industrial waste minimisation (IWM).

In 1989 the executive of Tao Yuan county declared IWM to be the key to solving environmental problems. The MOEA and the Environmental Protection Administration (EPA) set up a Joint Waste Reduction Task Force. The IWM programme was formally established in 1990. Several technical assistance providers (TAPs) were contracted to provide public education, training, waste audits and technical assistance to industry. Other institutions were funded to conduct IWM technology research development and demonstration.

Central agency	Responsibilities
National Science Council	Implement research and international academic exchange
Environmental Protection Administration	Review and revise current environmental policies and regulations to promote coherence with ISO 14001 Establish eco-labelling system and promote green consumerism
Ministry of Economic Affairs	
Bureau of Standards, Metrology and Inspection	Develop national standards consistent with international standards Formulate environmental standards for 'green' products
Department of Industrial Technology	Undertake R&D on tolls and databases for EMS implementation, environmental audits, environmental performance evaluation and life-cycle analysis
Bureau of Foreign Trade	Collect pertinent information from foreign sources Assess impacts on trade of ISO 14001
National Accreditation Board	Establish national accreditation system
Industrial Development Bureau	Provide overall co-ordination of ISO 14001 programmes in Taiwan

Table 12.3 **Distribution of responsibilities for promoting ISO 14000**

Source: MOEA 1999

Table 12.4 **Government strategy to promote ISO 14001**

Source: MOEA 1999

Components	Some initiatives
Persuasion/exhortation	Encouragement of large firms to employ existing 'corporate synergy systems', currently used to promote industrial waste minimisation, to help suppliers and distributors establish EMS
Education and training	Over 170 outreach workshops delivered with 10,000 participants
Research and development	Financial support for technical assistance provided to industry by technical assistance providers, e.g. ▸ *Industrial Waste Pollution Control Technical Service* ▸ *Industrial Waste Minimisation Technical Service* ▸ *Industrial Technology Research Institute* ▸ *China Technical Consultants* ▸ *Foundation of Taiwan Industry Service*
Information dissemination	Publication of a monthly ISO 14000 newsletter with a circulation of 2,500 Videos, manuals and sector-specific technical manuals; simplified versions for SMEs A website established to provide technical and management information
Financial incentives	115 firms from 28 industrial sectors awarded subsidy for between 40% (large firms) to 60% (SMEs) of the cost for preparation for certification (maximum: US$12,000)

The initiatives on ISO 14001 are rarely described or analysed in Taiwan, independent of IWM initiatives (see e.g. Hsieh and Chen 1998; Chang 1998). Some IWM TAPs reportedly guarantee to their clients that CP changes would ensure certification on the grounds that CP reduces raw material and energy inputs and prevents pollution through waste avoidance or minimisation. Thus CP changes can improve, if not guarantee, a company's ability to comply with national environmental regulations. The process of setting the performance targets and documenting the process changes required to achieve the targets facilitates the task of establishing a feasible and credible EMS.

Local government

Many of the staff, functions and resources of government agencies such as the EPA and MOEA are decentralised to county and city level. So, for government outreach programmes on CP and ISO 9002 and 14001, the county- and city-level industrial promotion and investment agencies play a critical role. For example, in 1998 the Taichung County Industrial Promotion and Investment Agency organised 80 training workshops for industry, including 15–20 on CP and ISO 14001. About 4,500 local industries, mostly SMEs, participate in these workshops annually.

Technical assistance providers (TAPs)

These are for-profit as well as non-profit organisations, staffed with scientists and engineers, mostly sector specialists. Industries competing for government subsidies for ISO 14001 certification need to be paired with a registered TAP to qualify. The criteria for registration as EMS professional include completing 130 hours of IDB-certified training on EMS.[3]

The non-profit TAPs (see Table 12.4) were initially established to deal with pollution control, then redirected and retrained to focus on IWM (Lee and Lee 1998; MOEA 1999). When the IDB started its drive to promote ISO 14001, professionals associated with many of the IWM TAPs were provided further training to become EMS TAPs. A recent evaluation conducted by the MOEA of 33 registered EMS TAPs indicates that those trained in IWM outperform those without the IWM training. The MOEA has concluded that IWM is needed by firms to achieve continual improvement (MOEA 1999).

◢ Conclusion

The extraordinary success of the government in promoting performance-based ISO 14001 is clearly an outcome of the ability of government institutions to recognise the profitability enhancement potential of CP approaches and to link CP firmly and systematically to the process of ISO certification. The government is effectively using private-sector profitability objectives to serve public interest in environmental protection deploying a 'carrot-

---

3   As of April 1999, more than 850 individuals have taken such an IDB course, of whom 743 have successfully passed the examination.

and-stick' approach, argued by Yap to be the most effective strategy to promote CP (1988). The EPA is given resources to establish and enforce high environmental standards and the IDB has the resources to enable industries to comply.

The centrality of research and development and information sharing in promoting industry innovation and competitiveness is recognised. Institutional mandates and programmes of state-supported institutions are evaluated for mutual coherence, minimal redundancy and continuing responsiveness; and are revised or restructured where necessary.

The Taiwan case studies suggest several lessons for proponents and practitioners of ISO 14001. One is that integrating measurable environmental performance targets in establishing ISO 14001 is desirable and technically feasible. It is desirable because it would enhance the credibility of the ISO standard with the environmental advocacy community. Second, where the performance targets are primarily achieved through CP (i.e. improved housekeeping practices, process changes and equipment redesign to minimise, if not avoid, the generation of energy and material waste), the resulting reduction in production costs allows the company to recover the large consultancy fees associated with ISO 14001 certification. In many cases the CP changes translate into greater profitability. CP-based ISO 14001 certification thus provides a 'win–win' opportunity for industry and the environment.

Part 4
COMMUNICATION, TRAINING, EMPOWERMENT AND CULTURAL ISSUES

13

ISO 14001 AS AN OPPORTUNITY FOR ENGAGING SMEs IN POLAND'S ENVIRONMENTAL REFORMS

Rafal Serafin
Polish Environmental
Partnership Foundation

Gill Tatum
Groundwork, UK

Wojciech Heydel
BP Amoco, Poland

On the fast track to joining the EU, the Polish government has embarked on large-scale economic, legal and institutional reform aimed at moving more rapidly towards a market economy and trade liberalisation. There is growing pressure on the private sector to share not only in the direct costs of these reforms, but also an expectation that companies will play a more active role through investment programmes.

Pressure to compete in European markets is already changing the Polish marketplace and this competition will increase still further. In this context, implementation of environmental management systems (EMSs) has come to be recognised by large companies as only a matter of time. But for Poland's 2.3 million small and medium-sized companies (SMEs) the situation is less clear (Dzierzanowski 1998; Piasecki *et al.* 1998). As yet, the Polish government has done little to motivate the private sector to take on a more active role in securing environmental improvements and applying EU standards.[1]

This chapter examines to what extent ISO 14001 certification can help the private sector in Poland contribute more effectively to economic and environmental reforms, which seek to accelerate Poland's accession to EU membership.

◢ European Union accession

EU accession will mean that tighter environmental, health and safety regulations will become the norm, rather than the exception they are today. Yet Poland, in line with other

---

1   Regular Report from the Commission on Progress Towards Accession: Poland—13 October 1999, European Commission DG 1A Enlargement, europa.eu.int/comm/enlargement/poland.

candidates, has indicated that it will seek transition periods for over 20 EU environmental laws, maintaining that the country will be ready to join the EU on 1 January 2003.[2] European Commission president, Romano Prodi, has responded that accession countries, including Poland, must accept and also fulfil the Union's environmental standards, noting that none of the accession countries has made significant headway in applying environmental laws (ENDS 1999).[3]

In practical terms, accelerating EU accession means that the Polish government must find ways of developing further the private sector through privatisation of state industry, reducing subsidies to unprofitable industries and opening up Polish markets to international competition in order to ensure continued economic growth. At the same time, Poland must make greater efforts to meet environmental requirements. One approach to dealing with this situation is to make environmental action a business development issue.

◢ The environmental challenge

According to the World Bank (1999), meeting EU environmental requirements will cost Poland as much as €30 billion. This means that at current rates of environmental spending, it will take more than 20 years to achieve EU standards. Investment is needed in sewage plants, water treatment facilities and air pollution control. Additionally, stricter environmental legislation must be introduced and enforcement mechanisms made more effective. With current annual expenditures running at about €2 billion, environmental investment must be increased significantly.

The challenge lies in achieving this by introducing economic instruments and management systems that will serve not only to enhance private-sector development, but also increase the scale and impact of private-sector environmental investment. Practically, this means finding ways of getting the private sector to see the prospect of tougher environmental regulations and need for environmental investment as important opportunities for business development—not additional costs or bureaucratic obstacles (Baczko and Bobinska 1999).

In Poland, there are currently few legal, institutional or economic incentives in place to encourage companies to implement ISO 14001. No tax or other benefits are currently being considered for companies with ISO 14001 in the current round of public finance reforms. Yet a growing number of companies are seeking certification. ABB Zamech was the first company in Poland to receive ISO 14001 certification in March 1997 having earlier implemented the BS 7750 as part of a global commitment by the ABB Group. By 1999, 36 companies had been awarded ISO 14001 certification with 100 or more engaged in

2 Ministry of Environmental Protection, Natural Resources and Forestry, 'Informacja prasowa: stanowisko RP w obszarze "srodowisko naturalne" ' (Press release on the position of the Polish Republic on environment in EU accession), 6 October 1999 (Polish language).
3 See footnote 1.

implementation. As many as 11 certification companies are now actively co-operating with the National Centre for Research and Certification and the Polish Ship Register, with a growing number of consulting firms offering ISO 14001 (*Problemy Ocensrodowiskowych* 1998; Environmental Information Centre 1999).

Implementing EMSs is now largely a matter of time in large companies; but the issue is not so clear in SMEs which are coming to be recognised more widely by the Polish government and European Commission, as well as inward investors, as the engine of continued economic growth and reform. If the private sector is to really make a significant contribution to accelerating Polish environmental reforms as part of the EU accession process, it is the SME sector that must be motivated to recognise EMSs as a business opportunity. Without greater awareness and involvement of SMEs, larger companies will also lose motivation to undertake ISO 14001 certification, as maintaining such systems with complex SME-dominated supply chains is likely to prove both costly and problematic.

◢ Corporate responsibility

As one of the world's largest global corporations, BP is committed to providing energy and petrochemical products and services without endangering the environment, and to contributing towards sustainable development in its countries of operation. BP has identified a Group-wide target for implementing ISO 14001 across the organisation. By the end of 2001, all major operating sites will have their EMSs certified to the ISO 14001 standard and should be producing verified site environmental reports. Critical to the successful achievement of BP targets is that of ensuring similar environmental standards throughout the company's supply chain. The corporation is tracking progress towards this target and reports performance in annual environmental and social reports published each spring (BP Amoco 1999).

In developing its business operations in Poland, BP established an integrated health, safety and EMS at the outset. Having completed a preliminary audit of BP headquarters, selected retail sites, liquid propane gas (LPG) terminals and a bitumen plant designed to help develop a dedicated EMS, BP has set out to implement an ISO 14001 EMS in its own operations by 2001, in line with the Group-wide target. For BP Poland, the ISO 14001 implementation process is part of a broader strategy to work proactively with non-governmental organisations (NGOs) and smaller companies to promote a move towards environmental sustainability across the country as a whole. Teaming up with two NGOs, Groundwork Blackburn from the UK and the Polish Environmental Partnership Foundation, BP launched a programme to improve environmental performance of Polish SMEs—the Czysty Biznes (literally 'clean business') programme (see Box 13.1). Based on the widely acclaimed Business Environment Association (BEA) programme developed by Groundwork Blackburn in the UK, Czysty Biznes provides BP with a mechanism for sharing its own health, safety and environmental management experience and expertise with Polish SMEs.

THE POLISH ENVIRONMENTAL PARTNERSHIP FOUNDATION, ESTABLISHED IN 1997, is a not-for-profit organisation supporting environmental problem-solving through building partnerships between local government, public agencies, community organisations, universities and businesses, and ensuring active citizen participation.

Groundwork Blackburn is part of a UK-wide network of 44 trusts that collectively form the country's largest environmental organisation. Operating with partners from the public, private and voluntary sectors, Groundwork seeks to make a continuing and significant contribution to social, economic and environmental regeneration. Since the early 1990s, Groundwork Blackburn has pioneered ways of helping companies in north-west England improve their business performance by reducing costs and securing jobs through improved environmental performance. The experience of Groundwork Blackburn's programme in the UK is being applied to developing a national Czysty Biznes programme in Poland.

BP is a leading multinational energy company active in Poland. By the end of 1999, the company operated a national network of more than 125 service stations and had a 20% share in Poland's LPG market. As well as being a major sponsor of the Czysty Biznes programme, BP is using its own business links and encouraging employees to implement the programme objectives.

Box 13.1 **Partners in the Czysty Biznes programme**

The Czysty Biznes programme was launched in 1998, with a US$2.3 million commitment from BP over a seven-year period. It is designed to ensure environmental considerations are given due regard in economic reforms as Poland accedes to the EU. Philanthropic foundations concerned with mobilising the private sector for community action, such as the German Marshall Fund of the US, Rockefeller Brothers Fund, the C.S. Mott Foundation and Stefan Batory Foundation are also contributing, as are the EU PHARE programme and the UK Know How Fund with their concern for supporting the EU accession process. The Czysty Biznes programme identifies practical opportunities for business and NGOs to work together to improve both environmental performance in business operations and environmental quality in the community. The idea is not only to design and implement specific businesses and community-based initiatives, but also to contribute to decreasing bureaucracy, accelerating economic reforms and fostering policy development at the national level. The motivation is to contribute to a new culture of corporate responsibility, in which larger companies recognise environmental improvement as an opportunity for supporting the development of the SME sector.

◢ Motivating SMEs

The Czysty Biznes programme seeks to engage SMEs in environmental action by getting them to join a 'Czysty Biznes' club. By August 2000, 206 companies had joined clubs operating in six cities in southern Poland: Kraków, Nowy Sacz, Tarnów, Bielsko Biata, Knurów and Gorlice. By joining and paying a nominal annual fee, companies make a commitment to taking practical steps to improve the environment and so make their business more competitive. Thanks to their membership, companies can access relevant expertise and identify opportunities for reducing operating costs through improved environmental performance. They are also assisted in developing an environmental policy and introducing other elements of a formal management system.

The premise is that introduction of a formal EMS, such as ISO 14001, is not necessarily appropriate or even feasible in every case. This stems from a conviction that a working EMS must be well timed in the sense that implementation must be part of a broader process of making the company more competitive in the marketplace. In small companies, the need is first to build awareness of environmental action as a business opportunity and a process of continuous improvement that brings tangible benefits in the short as well as the long term. Involvement in a Czysty Biznes club takes a company on a journey from awareness to action to achievement (Fig. 13.1) by providing access to a package of services, which include:

Figure 13.1 **Steps to integrating environment in business activities through the Czysty Biznes model**

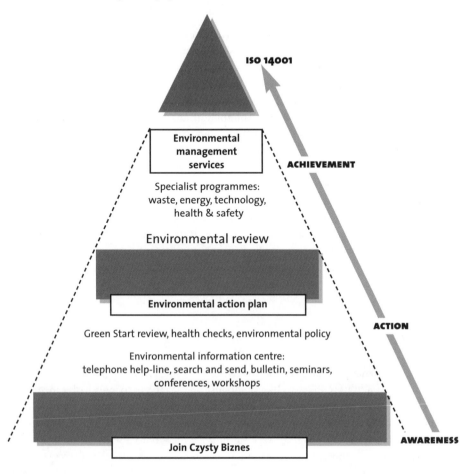

☐ Regular environmental health checks and audits

☐ Advice on implementing environmental problem-solving

☐ Information on the latest technology and changes in legislative requirements

☐ Regular training and seminars

☐ Contact with environmental authorities and other companies committed to environmental improvement

The emphasis is on self-help rather than expensive consultancy, which SMEs can rarely afford. A key message of the programme is that improvements can best be achieved through a company's own employees and better use of resources already available, so creating a culture of good environmental practice on a day-to-day basis that goes beyond the factory gate to benefit the wider community. The overall motivation for the programme is thus to build a bottom-up pressure for, and interest in, EMSs in Poland in a way that responds directly to local needs and circumstances.

Thanks to the programme, two member companies have moved from awareness to action and have chosen to implement a formal integrated quality and environmental management system by seeking ISO 9001 and ISO 14001 certification. One is a boiler manufacturer and environmental engineering company called ABM Solid located in Tarnów in southern Poland. The other is Poland's first hospital to operate in part on a commercial basis, the St John Grande Merciful Brothers' Hospital in Kraków. In contrast to companies that have achieved ISO 14001 certification in Poland, neither of these two companies is associated with a major multinational nor especially motivated by an interest in attracting inward investment or pressure to compete in the international marketplace. It is thus worth examining the two cases in more detail and considering to what extent the experience can be replicated among Poland's SME sector.

ABM Solid

Founded in 1991, ABM Solid is a manufacturer of fluidised-bed boilers and operates as an environmental technology consultant. The company was one of the first to join the Tarnów Czysty Biznes club in September 1998. The club now numbers 35 member firms. The company employs 160 people—nearly 140 of them in a boiler and steel construction elements manufacturing plant. As the Polish representative of the Belgian Seghers Better Technology Group, the company was making plans to implement an ISO 9000 system, as most companies in the construction sector have quality certification and there is a growing tendency among general contracting companies to require such certification from subcontractors.

Involvement in the Czysty Biznes programme, however, provided the opportunity for key ABM Solid managers to learn about the ISO 14001 system, which is not yet common in Poland. They were also able to visit several medium-sized companies with ISO 14001 systems in Lancashire in the UK, active in Groundwork Blackburn's BEA programme. The visit, coupled with interaction with other companies in the Czysty Biznes club, persuaded

ABM Solid management to modify their earlier plans and implement an integrated quality and environmental management system.

As yet there is little pressure on companies in Poland to demonstrate compliance with environmental regulations and so little incentive to implement EMSs. In fact, in contrast to quality management requirements, no ABM Solid client or contractor had ever raised environmental criteria as an issue. Local environmental regulators and municipal authorities had also never exerted any pressure in this regard. Thus, in the case of ABM Solid, the motivation to implement an integrated quality and environmental management system included:

☐ A wish to cultivate the company image as one associated with a concern for the environment and the local community within which the company operates

☐ A need to develop new marketing tools for developing the company's environmental design consultancy, especially in the wider European marketplace

☐ Consolidation of the company's operations to reduce costs and develop a strategy for technology development

The supply chain pressures associated with the development of certified EMSs in Poland are not as advanced as in the UK. The ABM Solid decision to implement an integrated management system for quality and environment is thus a bold one, considering that few companies in the UK are as yet implementing such systems. For ABM Solid, which had no formalised management methods or procedures for either management system, the opportunity was to adopt a holistic approach to consolidating company operations as a whole.

The integrated management system operates with a single control point for all systems documentation. The management system is structured so that the requirements of the ISO 9001 and ISO 14001 standards are fulfilled in an integrated fashion. The system is designed to allow continual environmental and quality management improvements to be made, which is possible through the use of a single set of company objectives and targets and a single improvement programme. The improvement programme is allocated to different staff in the company, but are monitored and reviewed on a regular basis by the senior management. In this way, the company is developing a single set of systems and operational procedures. Many of these procedures, such as document control and internal systems auditing, are single procedures, which fulfil requirements for both the quality and environmental standards. Some of the procedures are only relevant to the separate management of quality or environmental features or operations of the company. This is where there is only a requirement to control that feature within one of the standards.

As a result of work completed to date jointly by trained Czysty Biznes advisors and Groundwork staff, ABM Solid has developed an environmental policy and has taken steps to monitor and reduce energy costs. An emergency response procedure is being developed, along with greater emphasis on health and safety. Environmental impacts of company operations were found to be of little overall significance, but their consideration in the context of a management system has helped the company improve its overall management and planning with considerable success in raising staff morale. Staff are now regularly consulted on health and safety issues, for example, and are able to make suggestions to improve their working conditions. The introduction of new emergency procedures has also helped workers feel they are now having a positive impact on company performance. A direct outcome has been to make the company a leader in the Tarnów community—a small town of 150,000 far from Poland's main business centres.

The company won a regional award for quality and its managing director, Marek Pawlik, has been recognised as 'manager of the year' in Kraków Province. The company is now one of the most active members in the Tarnów Chamber of Commerce with regard to environmental and community issues. In fact, the process of implementing an integrated management system has also led to a greater awareness that a major opportunity for business development lies in the field of environmental technology.

Merciful Brothers' Hospital

The Hospital of the Merciful Brothers in Kraków is one of Poland's first to operate partly as a private organisation. According to the hospital director, Marek Krobicki, medical establishments have not been much interested in their environmental impacts. For the Merciful Brothers' Hospital, the motivation to join the Czysty Biznes club lay more in finding ways of engaging with the local community in which the hospital is seeking to build a profile and constituency for its services.

Founded in 1609, the hospital was moved to its current location in Kraków in 1812. A new building was added in 1906. Nationalised after World War II by the communist authorities, the hospital was returned to its owners, the Merciful Brothers, in 1997. The Order continues to operate the hospital on the basis of a public service contract. With a staff of 134 and 136 beds, services include: general surgery; internal surgery; intensive care and emergency services; laboratory and diagnostic services; ultrasound; endoscopy; and an outpatients' 'one-day' surgery.

Prior to implementing the management system, no formal documentation or procedures were in place. National health and safety, environment and other regulations provided the basis for operations. No customer-oriented or local procedures had been adopted. Thus, the initial motivation and focus on the part of hospital management was to develop a procedure for 'routing' a patient smoothly and effectively throughout his or her treatment at the hospital—from registration to discharge. In practice, this translated into a desire to blur the dividing line between the hospital environment and the outside world so as to make the hospital less threatening.

Located in Kraków's historic Kazimierz district, which is part of a major urban revitalisation programme, the hospital's management saw formal management systems as an opportunity for initiating practical projects to revitalise public spaces in and around the hospital and so to build bridges with the local community and public authorities. A community involvement programme has been developed to make the process of restoring public spaces in areas around the hospital for patients and local residents a participative process led by a newly established community organisation—Friends of the Merciful Brothers' Hospital.

The decision to move to a formal management system was thus motivated by a need to improve patient care by motivating staff to take on a more positive and human-oriented approach to healthcare. This was extremely important for hospital management as they recognised customer care had been virtually wiped out during the communist period. Decentralisation and privatisation of the health sector in Poland bodes also greater competition among those delivering health services and a need to build a strong and positive constituency of support within the area served by the hospital.

The decision of the hospital management to seek not just certification for a quality management system, but also environmental management certification, emerged through participation in seminars and other meetings organised by the Czysty Biznes club in Kraków. The decision to seek certification for an integrated quality and management system was a brave one, considering Poland's health system is currently being decentralised and reorganised as part of sweeping economic and institutional reforms. Moreover, there is virtually no experience with quality and environmental management systems in the Polish health sector, which is plagued by underfunding and growing labour unrest. A national nurses' strike disrupted health reforms in early 1999 for several weeks.

The main benefits arising from adopting an integrated quality and environmental management system as seen by hospital management include:

☐ Establishing a basis for long-term and systematic development planning

☐ Raising the capability and professional skills of hospital staff, especially in the field of patient relations

☐ Integrating economic thinking into hospital operations in day-to-day operations

☐ Providing transparency with respect to the fees-for-service system that has been introduced as part of reform in public healthcare financing

☐ Dealing with hospital waste effectively, as part of overall management activities

☐ Establishing links with other hospitals as part of a process of continuous improvement

☐ Engaging staff and local residents in making the hospital and its surroundings a friendlier place through revitalisation of local public spaces

The hospital will be ready for certification in the summer of 2000, and the process of implementing the quality/environmental management system is to be highlighted at Poland's exhibits at the Expo 2000 World Fair in Hannover. Other hospitals in Kraków are now also interested in EMSs.

◢ Conclusions

An important opportunity for accelerating Polish environmental reforms lies in making the environment a business issue—an issue of jobs, trade, innovation, technology transfer, investment, competitiveness and market development. In this respect, Poland's 2.3 million SMEs offer a special opportunity if they can be motivated to adopt more formal EMSs. This is because helping SMEs become more competitive has proven to be one of the most effective ways of promoting economic development and market-oriented reforms. Experience from EU countries suggests that helping SMEs recognise environmental action as an opportunity for business development rather than a barrier or cost is also an effective way of accelerating environmental improvement.

Experience from ABM Solid and the Merciful Brothers' Hospital suggests that EMSs are of interest to Polish SMEs. The two cases described are typical of Polish SMEs in many ways. Neither had extensive international contacts nor any special interest in environment. In both cases, the organisations were in the process of restructuring and cost reduction, including laying off staff, as they had to respond to increasing market competition and a rapidly changing legislative framework. In common with many SMEs, the prospect of trading with larger companies, such as BP, and becoming part of their supply chain is an important motivating factor. In both cases, decisions to proceed to a formal system were made once management recognised that certification was not a matter of paperwork, but an opportunity to improve day-to-day management and initiate longer-term planning.

In fact, in both cases, the decisions followed a period of six months or so of interaction and awareness-raising, made possible through the Czysty Biznes programme. Participation in monthly seminars, ongoing contacts with other companies and environmental advisors, and initial environmental reviews all helped in identifying opportunities for practical action. In the Hospital, for example, mercury thermometers were replaced by re-usable ones as both a cost and environmental saving. Mercury from broken thermometers is therefore no longer a danger. In ABM Solid, a health and safety campaign in the boiler-making facility helped build staff morale and prepare for emergency situations.

These small steps helped build not just environmental awareness, but also a confidence to take on the far more ambitious challenge of implementing a formal management system and seeking certification.

In Poland, larger companies with strong international links have an interest in ISO 14001 certification due to group corporate policy as in the case of BP, ABB or Philips Lighting, as do Polish companies with an interest in attracting an inward private investor. This is the case in the Gdansk Oil Refinery or Jelcz Truck Factory. For smaller companies rooted in the Polish marketplace, such as ABM Solid or the Merciful Brothers' Hospital, the interest lies primarily with quality management systems and ISO 9001 which provides an opportunity for integration with environmental management. In fact, neither company would have undertaken ISO 14001 without the quality management dimension. For SMEs in Poland, the future clearly lies in integrated quality and environmental management systems. Attempts to promote ISO 14001 alone are unlikely to meet with widespread interest among smaller companies but will remain the domain of large international companies.

The bottom-up approach used by the Czysty Biznes programme has helped build an ongoing relationship between environmental advisors and ABM Solid and the Merciful Brothers' Hospital over the past year, which is now characterised by a feeling of mutual trust. A related result of this is appreciation for the role of an intermediary business support organisation, such as Groundwork or the Polish Environmental Partnership, but also for the ways larger companies, such as BP, can be engaged in working for the community.

The approach has helped build confidence in both the Hospital and ABM Solid to take charge of their future development. The move to ISO 9001/14001 certification is an expression of this self-confidence and a sense that responsibility for business development lies primarily with the company, its owners, management and staff.

As yet such recognition remains the exception in Poland. This is because the post-war period of central planning, which collapsed only ten years ago, promoted a cultural and institutional system of the state undertaking action 'for and on behalf of citizens'. There was little place for individual accountability or local responsibility. Few identified with their place of work and even less thought in economic terms.

One legacy of this 40-year history is that awareness of the significance of local accountability and responsibility for business development must be nurtured, while at the same time new institutional and legal frameworks must be designed to encourage individuals, companies and other organisations to act on their own behalf. In practical terms, this means that macro-level reforms initiated by national government and those demanded by the European Commission will probably only prove effective if local companies, voluntary groups and local governments start working together to shape the future of their own communities.

To the extent that ISO 9001/14001 becomes a tool for enhancing and formalising this needs-driven bottom-up approach, SMEs will choose whether to adopt formal certification in their business development activities. But if certification comes to be seen as an additional hurdle imposed on suppliers by larger companies or by top-down national government directives, SME interest in moving to certification is likely to remain low.

A final conclusion relates to the issue of costs. In the case of ABM Solid, the Czysty Biznes programme is covering 50% of the management systems costs and, in the case of the Hospital, 80%. These costs were contributed in the form of consulting services and not direct payments or grants. In both cases, the companies have had to mobilise human and other resources and allocate them to the project. They are also aware that maintaining the management systems will mean continued resourcing on their part.

Experience from these and other companies in the Czysty Biznes programme suggests that the direct costs of implementing management systems is not the most important barrier. In fact, five Czysty Biznes companies have now opted to implement ISO 9001/14001 at full cost. The principal barrier is access to advisory and consulting services that recognise and respond to the needs and circumstances of the company. The motivation for contributing resources to the two companies was to treat them as partners in developing procedures and an implementation approach adapted to the needs and circumstances of Polish SMEs. In this sense, the costs of implementing the two integrated management systems are seen by all concerned primarily as a social investment in the Czysty Biznes programme as a whole. As a result, both ABM Solid and Hospital staff are actively involved in sharing their experience with other companies active in the Czysty Biznes programme and are contributing significantly to its further development. A pool of locally available expertise is being developed within the companies active in Czysty Biznes, which can be further enhanced by expertise from the Groundwork network in the UK and from across BP and other larger companies that choose to participate.

What is significant is that this expertise can be mobilised in response to identified needs and circumstances. The overall effect of this approach of 'linking people to people at the grass roots' and giving them the opportunity to share their experience and best practice is that the costs of implementing formal quality and environmental management systems can be significantly reduced for SMEs, effectively engaging a whole sector that has hitherto been left out of Poland's environmental reform process.

Larger companies, however, will continue to opt for professional consultancy services on a commercial basis as they will require more customised systems.

IMPLEMENTATION OF EMSs IN SEASONAL HOTELS
Assuring stability

Natalia Anguera, Silvia Ayuso and Pere Fullana
Randa Group SA, Spain

The travel and tourism sector has become the world's leading economic activity and one of the industries that is experiencing the most spectacular growth worldwide. Globally, tourism represents over 11% of GDP, accounts for annual revenues of around US$3.5 trillion and generates more than 200 million jobs.[1] Spain is one of the world's most important tourist countries, ranking second in terms of visitor numbers behind France.[2] Visited by over 43 million tourists each year, Spain has a hotel infrastructure capable of offering 170 million overnight stays (MEH and MIMA 1999). This sector has tended to concentrate mainly on the Mediterranean Sea coast and the Balearic and Canary Islands. Hence, the dominant tourist market is the so-called 'sun and sea' tourism with seasonality as its characteristic feature.

As tourism expands, its environmental impacts have become a major concern. Since the early 1990s, a series of concepts have been put forward in an attempt to establish some basic principles of sustainability, all based on the search for compatibility between conservation and development. The application of the concept of sustainable tourism is tackled in different ways, according to whether the matter is one of mature coastal destinations, development of emerging destinations, or tourism in historical cities. Within all possible approaches, the tourist enterprises, particularly hotels, play a very important role. On the one hand they consume natural resources while on the other they need an attractive setting to attract custom. As a result, the tourist industry is being encouraged to adopt measures to enhance its environmental performance.

---

1 World Travel and Tourism Council (1999): www.wttc.org
2 World Tourism Organisation (1999): www.world-tourism.org

◢ Environmental management for hotels

At present, there exist different tools for hotel environmental management. Local and regional eco-label schemes are becoming successful in the tourist industry as they can help tourism entrepreneurs identify critical issues, speed up the implementation of eco-efficient solutions, and lead to effective ways of monitoring and reporting on environmental performance (UNEP 1998). In Spain, different eco-labels for hotels (*Distintiu Ecoturístic Alcúdia* in the Balearic Islands; *Biohoteles* in the Canary Islands; *Distintiu de garantia de qualitat ambiental* in Catalonia) and for camping sites and youth hostels have been developed. More structured and systematic instruments include environmental auditing, environmental reporting and environmental management systems (EMSs). Through a variety of initiatives, Spanish tourist companies have begun introducing EMS in accordance with the international EMS standard ISO 14001 and the EU Eco-management and Audit Scheme (EMAS).

One of the first, flagship, measures to be put forward by the authorities was the *Ecología y Turismo* (ECOTUR) programme, developed by the government of the Balearic Islands a few years ago (ECOTUR 1997). This initiative seeks to be an umbrella programme for the environmental improvement of the tourist sector. It is broken down according to its different target areas: facilities, destinations, promotion and applications. 'ECOTUR facilities' (*ECOTUR instal·lacions* in Catalan) aims at enhancing the environmental quality of tourist enterprises through a voluntary environmental management and audit system. By means of a decree, the regional authorities opened the way to apply EMAS to tourist facilities (*BOCAIB* 1997). In collaboration with the EU LIFE programme, subsidies were granted to 30 tourist facilities for implementing EMSs: 25 hotels and tourist apartments, four marinas and one golf course (*BOCAIB* 1998). Additionally, promotion and training activities were carried out and various 'Guidelines for good environmental practices in hotel and tourist facilities' have been published. The public administration of Catalonia[3] and the Spanish Ministry of Economy[4] have followed the Balearic initiative and are promoting the implementation of EMS in tourist facilities.

◢ Planning the EMS project

Randa Group is assessing eight holiday hotel installations, which all except one received funding from the ECOTUR programme to implement an EMS (see Table 14.1), and it is currently working with six hotels within the Catalan programme.[5] The first stage of the project was to decide the implementation timetable and the human resource require-

---

3   Order of 8 April 1999 for funding implementation of voluntary EMSs (*DOGC* 1999).
4   1 July 1998, Sustainable Tourism Action within the co-operation framework of the Ministry of Economy and the Ministry of Environment for developing a sustainable tourism programme.
5   Hotel Meliá Confort Apolo, Hotel Meliá Confort Girona, Hotel Meliá Barcelona, Hotel Meliá Gran Sitges, Hotel Caçadors, Hotel Levant.

Hotel	Opening period	Employee number during high season	Implementation stage (April 2000)
SOL Élite Gavilanes	May–October	125	EMAS-registered
SOL Pinet Playa	February–October	80	EMAS-registered
SOL Cala D'Or	May–October	32	EMAS-registered
RIU Festival	All year	80	EMS implementation
RIU Bravo	All year	70	EMS implementation
Pollentia Club Resort (Maris and Village)	February–November	200	In verification process
Bon Sol	February–November	75	EMS design

Table 14.1 **Seasonal hotels in Balearic Islands assessed by Randa Group within ECOTUR**

ments. Generally, the top management wished to implement the whole EMS during one summer season, to encourage understanding and motivation among all employees. As the hotels have different opening periods, the project calendar needed to be adapted to these circumstances with parallel running of some EMS stages, e.g. design of documentation and training activities. At the same time, it was necessary to consider the possible integration of the environmental and quality management systems. Recently, the Spanish Institute for Hotel Quality (ICHE) has developed specific standards for service quality in vacational and urban hotels (ICHE 1998). This voluntary quality system is based on the international quality standard ISO 9001 and includes some environmental issues relevant to top management.

Environmental impact of hotel activities and services

The daily operation of a hotel involves numerous activities that are clearly distributed between the hotel's departments, with the final purpose of assuring the customer's satisfaction. Due to the seasonal opening period, work is heavily concentrated in the summer months—while the autumn and winter months are usually dedicated to repairs and construction. There is, therefore, a wide spectrum of activities and services to consider when identifying environmental aspects. The standard set of activities and their main associated environmental aspects are shown in Table 14.2.

SERVICE/ ACTIVITY	DESCRIPTION	MAIN ENVIRONMENTAL ASPECTS
Administration	▶ Hotel management ▶ Reception of clients	▶ Energy, water and raw materials (mainly paper) consumption ▶ Generation of municipal waste (huge amounts of paper) and hazardous waste (e.g. toner cartridges)
Technical services	▶ Equipment for producing hot water and heating ▶ Air conditioning ▶ Lighting ▶ Lifts ▶ Swimming pools ▶ Green areas ▶ Mice and insect termination ▶ Reparations and maintenance	▶ Energy and water consumption ▶ Consumption of a wide range of hazardous products ▶ In some cases, use of CFCs and HCFCs ▶ Air and soil emissions ▶ Generation of a wide range of hazardous waste types ▶ Generation of waste-water
Restaurant/bar	▶ Breakfast, dinner, lunch ▶ Beverages and snacks	▶ Energy, water and raw materials consumption ▶ Generation of significant amounts of packaging waste
Kitchen	▶ Food conservation ▶ Food preparation ▶ Dish washing	▶ Important consumption of energy and water ▶ Generation of significant amounts of packaging waste ▶ Generation of vegetable oil waste ▶ Generation of significant amounts of organic waste ▶ Generation of odours
Room use	▶ Use by guests ▶ Products for guests' use ▶ Housekeeping	▶ Energy, water and raw materials consumption ▶ Use of a wide range of hazardous products ▶ Generation of waste packaging and small amounts of municipal waste ▶ Generation of waste-water
Laundry	▶ Washing and ironing of guests' clothes ▶ Washing and ironing of hotel's linen	▶ Important consumption of energy and water ▶ Use of hazardous products ▶ Generation of waste-water
Purchasing	▶ Selection of products and suppliers ▶ Storage of products	▶ Generation of packaging waste ▶ Hazardous substance leakages
Activities	▶ Indoor activities ▶ Outdoor activities	▶ Energy, water and raw materials consumption ▶ Local impacts on ecosystems ▶ Noise ▶ Generation of municipal waste
Transport	▶ Transport of guests ▶ Transport of employees ▶ Transport of suppliers	▶ Energy (petrol) consumption ▶ Air emissions
Additional services	e.g. medical services, supermarkets, souvenir shop, hairdresser, etc.	▶ Energy, water and raw materials consumption ▶ Generation of municipal waste and some specific hazardous waste types (e.g. sanitary waste)
Building and construction	▶ Construction of new areas or services ▶ Repair of existing areas or services	▶ Energy and water consumption ▶ Significant consumption of raw materials and hazardous products ▶ Significant generation of construction waste ▶ Generation of hazardous waste

Table 14.2 **Hotel services and activities and their main environmental aspects**

Once the environmental aspects have been identified and characterised, the hotel has to assess their significance in order to establish objectives and control measures. This task is usually performed exclusively by the environmental co-ordinator and reviewed by the hotel manager. The assessment methodology at this stage should be based on clear questions that do not require a deep scientific knowledge in order to answer them, but rather the standard knowledge of an environmentally aware citizen. In the case studies presented here, four criteria were used in the assessment and the aspect would be evaluated as significant if at least one of the following criteria was found to be relevant:

❑ Environmental impact of the aspect

❑ Legal considerations

❑ Economic considerations

❑ Interested parties

In order to evaluate the environmental impact of the aspect, supporting data is required. Unfortunately there is little publicly available data about water consumption, energy consumption or waste production in seasonal hotels, although some international hotel chains and regional hotel associations have published handbooks containing bench-marking data (Inter-Continental Hotels and Resorts 1996; DEHOGA 1997).

The criterion on legal considerations is based on the possibility of a hotel not meeting the existing legislative requirements (e.g. if emission parameters are very near to the legal limit) or failing to meet them in the near future (e.g. standards that are currently being discussed and will soon be approved as legally binding).

The economic criterion considers not only whether significant savings could be obtained by improving the environmental aspect (this is typically the case for minimising energy, water and raw materials consumption), but also what future costs are likely to be incurred by failing to deal with the aspect (e.g. pollution or a poor company image).

Finally, the assessor takes into consideration opinions about the aspect among the different stakeholders: employees, clients, neighbours, public administration, media, banks and insurance companies, competitors, etc.

The process for selecting the objectives and targets for the EMS should involve all the heads of the hotel departments, but it is often very difficult for all the departmental heads to meet at the same time for a reasonable length of time. It is therefore advisable that the environmental co-ordinator and/or the hotel manager use techniques that can generate as many ideas and as much information as possible in the shortest possible time, e.g. brainstorming.

In general, the case study hotels presented in this paper have addressed their environmental actions towards energy and water saving, minimising waste, appropriate disposal of the several waste types, appropriate storage and management of hazardous materials, personnel training and guest information.

Human resources

Management models for EMSs in the tourist sector are based on the fact that the hotel manager and/or the environmental co-ordinator are rarely technical specialists. As the environment is an inter-disciplinary topic, it is necessary to combine the know-how and experience of the key personnel in the hotel, for which basically two models have arisen from the case studies in discussion (see Fig. 14.1). At the same time, a team of environmentally aware and well-trained people is also necessary for assuring the stability of the management of the EMS despite staff rotation, which frequently affects managers and heads of departments.

On the one hand, the 'environmental management triangle' is more suitable for small hotels, where the hotel manager is the environmental co-ordinator and is supported by the head of administration (key person for employees and guests matters) and the head of maintenance (key person for technical matters). On the other hand, the 'environmental committee' model is characteristic of bigger organisations (shown in Fig. 14.1), where the hotel manager appoints an environmental co-ordinator (usually the head of administration) as leader of the heads of department; this model has the additional advantage of facilitating communication among the hotel's employees.

As already mentioned, rotation of staff is a key topic when dealing with seasonal hotels, not only in a negative, but also in a positive way. One positive aspect of rotation arises mainly in extensive hotel chains, where managers and heads of departments often change their workplace, and thus contribute their experience and know-how to the 'environmentalisation' of further hotels. On the other hand, rotation has a negative effect on training of personnel, as it requires solutions that guarantee the continual training of each new worker in the organisation—this is usually performed by means of easily understandable documentation and through the training tasks of the heads of departments themselves. As most of the environmental practices in a hotel do not differ much from domestic environmental practices (see Box 14.1), they are well accepted by the employees, who may also pass on information to other employees and even guests.

Figure 14.1 **Environmental management models**

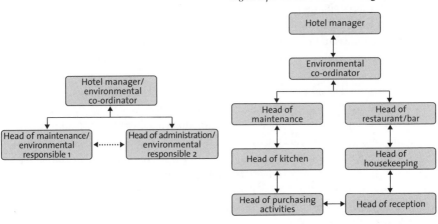

THE ENVIRONMENTAL MANAGEMENT TRIANGLE   **THE ENVIRONMENTAL COMMITTEE**

SOME ENVIRONMENTAL PRACTICES AT A HOTEL ALSO APPLYING TO DOMESTIC USE:

☐ Open fridge and freezer doors as few times as possible, and indicate where the products are located, in order to find them as rapidly as possible.

☐ Use washing machines only when they are full, and with the lowest water temperature that gives satisfactory results.

☐ Use fully biodegradable liquid detergents instead of powdered detergents.

☐ Put a brick into the cistern of each toilet (which can save approximately 1,34 l of water per flush).

☐ Buy locally where possible to support the local community and reduce transportation impacts and costs.

☐ Ensure used frying oil is collected by authorised waste handlers.

Box 14.1 **Environmental practices also applying to domestic use**

A very interesting initiative for promoting hotel staff training is currently being developed by the Directorate for Environmental Planning and the Centre for Cleaner Production Initiatives of the Autonomous Government of Catalonia. With the support of experts from Randa Group, the Directorate has produced basic information on best practice for hotels on: waste management, energy saving, water saving and green purchasing. These kinds of easily understandable guide, which can be developed by the public sector, but also by private companies, can be used either as a specific communication and awareness-raising tool, or can be incorporated into a wider training programme.

Communication and dissemination

As the service end-user of the hotel, the guest is in direct contact with the service provider, so communication and dissemination are important issues. Not only do the organisation's employees have to be informed about the environmental policy and objectives, but also the clients have to be addressed to gain their understanding and collaboration. Due to the unstable situation of personnel within seasonal hotels, the hotel guests might even play a key role in achieving environmental targets. Thus, the success of many environmental measures directly depends on the behaviour of the guests. Therefore, the case study hotels included environmental initiatives that require guests' acceptance or participation (see Box 14.2).

For this reason, it is important to communicate the environmental aims, practices and progress by means of a document such as the public environmental statement. EMAS does not specify the format of a company's environmental statement but instead specifies its minimum contents. Therefore, the challenge is to define the target audience and design an environmental statement that meets its needs. For instance, a highly detailed report may be appropriate for government authorities, tour operators and environmental pressure groups. Otherwise, a brief description of the hotel's environmental achievements, presented in a user-friendly brochure, is more likely to meet the information requirements of hotel guests.

SOME ENVIRONMENTAL ACTIONS THAT DEPEND ON THE ACCEPTANCE OR participation of guests:

☐ Avoid individually packaged portions; use bulk products

☐ Use returnable glass drink bottles

☐ Sort waste, e.g. glass, cardboard, paper, batteries

☐ Reduce water consumption by changing towels only if necessary; take showers instead of baths

☐ Save energy by switching off lights, air conditioning, etc. when not needed

☐ Use gel/shampoo dispensers in bathrooms

☐ Use recycled paper for toilet paper, etc.

☐ Participate in environmentally friendly activity programmes and sports

☐ Use bicycles and public transport in the vicinity

☐ Prefer local dishes and organic pesticide-free products

Box 14.2 **Environmental actions that require hotel guests' collaboration**

Internal auditing

Assuring the auditor's competence and objectivity are two main issues when planning and performing internal audits. There are several possibilities for addressing these issues, depending on whether the hotel is independent or belongs to a chain or group.

The first possibility is to get at least two members of the hotel team qualified as internal auditors, one of whom should normally be the environmental co-ordinator. In this way, all the matters directly driven by the environmental co-ordinator would be audited by the second auditor.

The second possibility is to contract external environmental auditors to perform the audits either on their own or working in conjunction with the hotel's internal auditors.

In the case of hotel chains, a pool of internal auditors can be created, capitalising on the know-how gained by the environmental co-ordinators in designing, implementing and maintaining the EMS in their own hotels. This possibility is most appropriate for hotel chains at an early stage of their environmental programmes.

Finally, hotel chains with a significant number of hotels certified to ISO 14001 or verified to EMAS, or in the process of signing up to these standards, should consider the possibility of creating a specific department for environmental audits or incorporate environmental auditing into other departments (e.g. quality or health and safety).

◢ Drivers and motivations

In comparison with other industrial sectors, hotels are usually perceived as having low environmental impacts. Nevertheless, some large German and Scandinavian tour operators are beginning to include environmental measures in their contracts. For example,

Hotel Sol Élite Gavilanes, the first EMAS-registered hotel in the Balearic Islands

Left: Sorting glass as part of routine practice in the hotel Sol Élite Gavilanes
Right: Hotel guest participation: a battery recycling project in the hotel Sol Élite Gavilanes

Touristik Union International (TUI) asks hotels, clubs and holiday apartments to fill in an annual environmental checklist, informs the contracting managers about the results of that evaluation, and states the environmentally sound practices in its brochures.

But what is really motivating hotels to put in place a full EMS according to ISO 14001 or EMAS? The key drivers appear to be a desire to improve the internal management and public image of the hotel, along with the potential to gain new, environmentally conscious European market segments. Another motivation is cost savings. However, it is significant that there are few statements about quantification of cost savings or material benefits and, in most of the cases, tourism entrepreneurs point out that the main driver for them is their personal environmental awareness.

Stakeholders such as consultants, regulatory authorities, verifiers and accreditation bodies also list image improvement as a main driver along with competitive advantage, meeting customer requirements, managing the environmental aspects and compliance with environmental legislation. Finally, one important factor seems to be the current possibility of acquiring funds for implementation of an EMS.[6]

◢ Conclusions

EMSs are an important tool for improving the relationship of tourist enterprises with their environment, and can bring decisive benefits. In light of the seasonal nature of the hotel industry, there are some key issues to consider when implementing an EMS. There is a wide spectrum of activities to cover when identifying the environmental aspects of a hotel, from large-scale domestic activities (e.g. laundry, housekeeping) to industrial installations (e.g. boilers and gas oil tanks) and even building and construction. Therefore, it is necessary to consider not only environmental impacts, but also legal, economic and stakeholder criteria. Of special importance in this case are the existing environmental indicators for hotels with similar characteristics (number of beds, opening periods, etc.) and the perception of clients.

The environmental co-ordinator should be supported by the heads of departments who have important knowledge about their specific tasks—creating an environmental committee for the hotel can usually help with this. Such support staff should also be involved in the continual training process in order to assure that all the knowledge about the EMS is not concentrated in a single person, which could disrupt the continuity of the system from one season to the next. Staff training, as another requirement for EMS stability, should be supported by the development of simple communication, awareness-raising and training tools. Due to the necessity of communicating with guests about environmental matters, it is also advisable to design an environmental report, which at the same time can serve as an environmental statement according to EMAS. That means

---

6   These statements are based on interviews conducted during the European project EMPOST-NET (*The Emerging Paradigm of Sustainable Tourism: A Network Perspective*), December 1998–May 2000, in which Randa Group participated as the Spanish partner.

that the main difference between ISO 14001 and EMAS, the requirement of a public environmental statement, becomes less important in the case of those hotels who wish to communicate their environmental performance, regardless. However, due to the higher acceptance of EMAS in Germany and the fact that many Mediterranean tourists come from this country, the EU Eco-management and Audit Scheme seems to be more attractive for Spanish hotels in this territory.

ISO 14001 AND THE AMERICAN INDIAN RESERVATION

Pamela S. Evers
Stephen F. Austin State University, USA

During the past century, industrialisation and the effects of other human activities have increasingly impacted on the natural environment of the American Indians, frequently resulting in environmental degradation.[1] As sovereign political entities, American Indian tribal governments have the authority to enact and enforce regulations within their homeland to protect their environment. American Indian nations have the collateral responsibility to comply with the environmental regulatory regime of the United States.[2] Therefore, American Indian nations are beginning to look to environmental management systems (EMSs) as a mechanism to help protect their irreplaceable natural environment as well as achieve compliance with a complex web of environmental regulations. This case study describes one American Indian tribal government engaged in developing an EMS consistent with ISO 14001.

◢ Background

To better understand the tribal perspective on ISO 14001, some background about the status of American Indians in the US is helpful. American Indians and Alaskan Natives,

---

1 Environmental degradation by non-Indians within the American Indian reservation is well documented (see Churchill 1993; Grinde and Johansen 1994; Weaver 1996). However, Indian scholars caution that the image of the 'noble savage' in harmony with nature is ethnocentric romanticism (see Churchill 1993: 16-17; Grinde and Johansen 1994: 1-55). Some scholars (see Krech 1999) dispute the general view that Indians have always been in harmony with their natural environment.

2 The word 'nation' rather than 'tribe' is used to emphasise the political status of the American Indian peoples. The words 'tribe' and 'tribal' may be used when referring to American Indian society or government.

as the indigenous peoples of North America, comprise a small minority population in the US.[3] Unlike other minorities, however, American Indians are members of sovereign polities distinct from, but contractually linked to, the US government in accordance with treaties. As part of the political contract or treaty, the majority of American Indian nations possess a limited geographical homeland, known as a reservation, within which tribal members may live.[4] Tribal membership embodies the benefits and responsibilities of collective property rights, such as shared land ownership in the reservation land-base and shared stewardship of resources. In addition, the members of most Indian nations have treaty rights to engage in the subsistence activities of hunting, gathering, and fishing in the reservation.

The political contracts or treaties between American Indian nations and the US undoubtedly provide tribal members with valuable property rights and the right to maintain a unique culture. Nevertheless, the boundaries of the reservation homeland are immobile. If the natural environment of the reservation is degraded or destroyed, tribal culture and the subsistence way of life are concurrently destroyed. In other words, when environmental harm impacts the American Indian reservation, the harm is not only to the physical health and tangible property of a minority population, but also to the intangible and priceless heritage of American Indian culture. Now limited to 310 reservations within the US, American Indians struggle to protect their lands and culture from encroaching industrialisation.

Through various legal devices, the US government has recognised that Indian nations have the right of inherent sovereign authority to govern tribal territory, tribal affairs and tribal members.[5] Notwithstanding their status as sovereigns, the federal government has taken action during the past two centuries to limit the sovereign authority of Indian nations. One particularly egregious act of the federal government was to allot small parcels of the reservation land-base to the remaining Indian population and sell the surplus lands to non-Indians.[6] The legacy that the allotment policy left on most American Indian reservations is a 'chequerboard' pattern of land ownership in which non-Indian-owned lands are located within the boundaries of an American Indian reservation and adjoin Indian lands. The result is a regulatory nightmare in which tribal, federal, state, county and municipal governments each attempt to regulate the reservation environment.

---

3 In the 1990 US census, 1.959 million persons (0.08% of the US population) self-identified as American Indian (see Bureau of Census, US Department of Commerce 1993).

4 About half of the American Indian population lives on or next to a reservation, but not every Indian nation possesses a reservation land-base reserved by treaty with the US. For example, the Lumbee Tribe of North Carolina is the ninth-largest Indian population, but has no reservation (see Getches *et al.* 1991: 12).

5 Inherent sovereignty or sovereign authority refers to a nation's right to self-governance or self-determination, and the right and responsibility to protect and care for its citizens. Sovereign authority is demonstrated by a nation's power to enact laws, rules or other precepts designed to protect the health, welfare and economic security of the people (see Cohen 1982).

6 The General Allotment Act (1887), and subsequent amendments, was a major policy directive that transferred more than 60% of the 1887 tribal land-base into non-Indian ownership by the end of the policy in 1934 (see Wilkins 1997: 81-97; Conference of Western Attorneys General 1993: 16-20).

To rectify past environmental degradation and protect the future of American Indian nations, many major US environmental laws enacted or amended within the past two decades specifically acknowledge the authority of American Indian nations to develop, enact and enforce tribal environmental regulations.[7] Consequently, most American Indian nations with a significant land-base have developed, or are in the process of developing, tribal environmental codes to better protect their environment.[8] The process of enacting and enforcing a tribal environmental code is an arduous task, however, because there is limited funding and the regulatory conflicts have a chilling effect on the legislative process.[9]

To mitigate some of the burden, the US Environmental Protection Agency (EPA) offers support and assistance to Indian nations in protecting their unique reservation environment. As part of a national effort to encourage private industry and local government to adopt EMSs, the EPA has provided funding to one Indian nation as a pilot project to implement an EMS consistent with ISO 14001. The remainder of this article will focus on the pilot development and implementation of ISO 14001 by the Bad River Band of the Lake Superior Tribe of Chippewa Indians.[10]

◢ The American Indian reservation environment

American Indian reservations are scattered across the continental US, ranging in size from a few to thousands of acres and located in rural as well as urban environments. Therefore, American Indian reservations are widely diverse with regard to landscape and the type and degree of impact that US society may have on the natural environment of the reservation. Despite popular myth, there is no 'typical' American Indian culture. Nevertheless, the Bad River Band is representative of the majority of American Indian nations with regard to tribal government structure, reservation attributes and environmental protection goals.

Located along the southern shore of Lake Superior, the Bad River Band reservation is a remarkably beautiful landscape blessed with two large rivers, numerous tributaries, countless wetlands, and bountiful wild rice beds that become heavy with grain in

7   For example, the US Clean Air Act (1990) specifically acknowledges the authority of Indian nations to develop and enforce air quality standards over reservation lands that are consistent with or more protective than the federal air quality standards.

8   A tribal environmental code helps to establish regulatory authority over the reservation environment for the tribal government rather than the state government (see Suagee and Parenteau 1997).

9   Most industrialised nations have developed laws and regulations over centuries, but American Indian nations have had the opportunity to develop environmental codes for only a couple decades. Consequently, the financial and operational burden placed on tribal governments to achieve this task is monumental (see Gover and Williams 1994).

10   Herein, the Indian nation will be referred to as the Bad River Band. Information for the case study is drawn from the author's personal experience as well as personal conversations with Bad River Band government officials, especially Ervin Soulier, Manager, Natural Resources Department.

autumn. The reservation provides habitat for abundant wildlife, including black bear, white-tailed deer, otter, migratory birds, substantial fisheries, and the endangered bald eagle and timber wolf. Within the reservation boundaries, approximately 1,000 tribal members live and work, often relying on the landscape to provide a subsistence lifestyle or supplement income with the sale of fish or forest products, such as balsam for Christmas wreaths or birch bark for decorative containers. To the members of the Bad River Band, the water, land, air, plants and animals are not merely resources, but are vital to tribal subsistence and economy, spirituality and culture.[11] Therefore, environmental harm to the natural environment affects the health and economic welfare of every tribal member.

Protecting the reservation environment

Environmental harm to the reservation takes many forms: air and water pollution from industrial and residential areas, poor methods of timber harvesting or farming that destroy streams and wildlife habitat, or indiscriminate harvesting of fish and deer by the non-Indian population living within reservation boundaries or trespassing on Indian lands. To protect their environment, the Bad River Band enacted an environmental code during the 1980s to prevent Indians and non-Indians alike from causing harm to the natural environment. The Bad River Band's Natural Resources Department is instrumental in monitoring the impact of human activity to the reservation environment. Tribal law enforcement officers and the tribal court system enforce the tribal environmental code. However, as a result of the allotment policy, the Bad River Band reservation is a chequerboard reservation in which Indian lands adjoin non-Indian-owned lands. This pattern of land ownership often creates jurisdictional conflict. To minimise regulatory conflict, the Bad River Band has strengthened the tribal environmental code and enforcement procedures to assert non-discriminatory jurisdictional authority over all human activities affecting the natural environment. Additionally, it has entered into agreements with federal, state, and county law enforcement authorities to enforce environmental and natural resources regulations at all levels of government.

Given the jurisdictional conflicts inherent in a chequerboard reservation, the Bad River Band tribal government realised that it must go above and beyond minimum requirements to protect the natural environment. To this end, the Bad River Band developed an integrated resources management plan (IRMP) during the 1990s to co-ordinate and manage human activities that may impact on the reservation's natural environment, such as forestry, mining, hunting, fishing, agriculture and residential and commercial activities. The latest initiative is to develop and implement an EMS consistent with ISO 14001.

11 The Chippewa, or Anishinabe, people have been in the Great Lakes region of the United States for centuries and continue to enjoy a thriving tribal culture based on subsistence as well as other economic and commercial means of support (see Satz 1991).

Overview of the tribal EMS process

Recognising the logical relationship between the IRMP and an EMS, the Bad River Band Natural Resources Department initiated the process of developing and implementing the tribal environmental management system (TEMS). With advice and support from the EPA, the first task was to educate and inform tribal government officials about the reasons for, and process of, implementing the TEMS. The process of educating officials and citizens is a task faced by most governments implementing a major project such as an EMS. Unlike the typical governmental body, however, strong clan or familial relationships that naturally influence group dynamics and the balance of power in organisational meetings distinguish most American Indian nations. Accordingly, implementing the TEMS may be equated with the process of implementing an EMS in a closely held family business or small town or village.[12] More noteworthy, given the long history of repression or outright assaults from non-Indian society, tribal members understandably might be dubious about projects advocated by the US government.

The constitution of the Bad River Band, like the majority of American Indian tribal constitutions, delegates both legislative and executive functions of government to a relatively small Tribal Council, not unlike a corporate board of directors. Consequently, a major project will not be executed until the majority of tribal government officials either support or are unopposed to the project. The Bad River Band IRMP process, for example, took several years of development before it became approved tribal policy. Nonetheless, once there is support for a tribal project, the commitment of tribal government and membership is remarkably strong.

Wisely, Bad River Band government officials and tribal members understand that an EMS is entirely consistent with tribal goals and efforts concerning environmental stewardship. Despite such comprehension, the EPA funding for the TEMS was available for almost two years before the TEMS project had gained enough tangible support from tribal government officials to allow the Natural Resources Department to form a project team, retain a consultant, and begin work on the environmental policy statement. Once committed to the project, tribal officials decided that a TEMS was an internal matter, limiting implementation of the TEMS to within tribal governmental units. The decision eliminated a potential delay in implementation because it obviated the need to obtain the approval of tribal members. However, to ensure that the interests of the Bad River Band would be satisfied throughout the development and implementation process, representatives from many departments of tribal government comprise the project team, and these are advised by the retained consultant.

12 Tribal government and society are by no means static, since the membership of the tribal council and government departments changes over time. In addition, tribal members may, of course, move outside the reservation or be uninterested in tribal government. Nonetheless, the reservation remains a tribal member's homeland as long as he or she remains a tribal member; thus tribal members are stakeholders with regard to their reservation for life.

The environmental policy statement

The primary decision during the development of the environmental policy statement was whether the statement should resemble the concise statements espoused by most corporations or declare a definitive tribal vision. After almost six months of development, the Bad River Band environmental policy statement reflects the unique character of the American Indian nation:

> Looking forward seven generations, the Bad River Band of the Lake Superior Tribe of Chippewa Indians is committed to ensuring a clean and healthy environment within the Reservation. We will:
>
> - Comply with all applicable laws and regulations and other requirements to which we subscribe. We are committed to continual improvement of our environmental management system and pollution prevention.
>
> - Reduce consumption of natural resources and material goods. Reuse and recycle natural resources and material goods whenever possible.
>
> - Manage land, water, air, timber, and other resources in a responsible manner.
>
> - Strive to manage natural resources so that proper natural resource functions are maintained and no longer threatened by negative human impacts.
>
> - Strive to achieve a community in which all individuals and institutions value the gifts of mother nature and willingly choose to act in a manner which ensures achievement of sustainable environmental and economic goals.
>
> - Develop a community in which every Bad River member, young and old, shares in the benefits of a healthy environment.
>
> - Make the protection of the Bad River Reservation environment, its natural resource base, and the functions of the natural systems on which all life depends a priority in planning.
>
> - Maintain the traditional cultural values necessary to live harmoniously with the natural world and to demonstrate respect for all living things.

Few for-profit firms implementing ISO 14001 would state that they look forward seven generations or strive to protect mother nature or traditional cultural values, because such goals are neither concrete nor easily achieved. However, the Bad River Band environmental policy statement provides an excellent foundation for a TEMS that satisfies the desires of the Bad River Band tribal government and tribal membership.

Identification of environmental impacts and legal requirements

Focusing only on the operations of the tribal government, the project team identified 26 environmental impacts or aspects. Each government department described two or three major impacts, such as energy and paper consumption, and solid waste. Specific environmental impacts were noted for a few tribal operations, such as the recycling centre (recycled plastics and metals), health department (clinical waste) and gaming casino (waste and car park run-off). After identifying environmental impacts, the project team determined three or four legislative compliance issues of key importance. For example, in the recycling centre and tribal government garage, the Bad River Band must comply with federal environmental laws that regulate the handling and storage of hazardous waste materials.

◢ The next steps

The Bad River Band has only just begun to develop and implement the ISO 14001-compliant EMS. The TEMS manual was recently completed and another round of audits is under way to identify and resolve audit deficiencies. Once these are resolved, the TEMS procedures will be presented to the Bad River Band tribal council for approval to begin system implementation. So far, the most serious problem in developing the TEMS has been that the tribal employees responsible for its development have endured a substantially increased workload. In general, however, Bad River Band government officials are pleased with the progress of the implementation process, especially when compared to the long incubation period of the IRMP.

As the first American Indian nation to pursue implementation of such a complex management system, the Bad River Band is gaining publicity and has been sharing its experience with other Indian nations. Although the Bad River Band's consultant recommends certification to ISO 14001 and tribal officials have discussed certification, whether a tribal government would receive tangible benefits from certification is open to debate. However, certification was never the point of the process. Rather, it was to protect a precious homeland, and the ISO 14001 standard provides a solid framework on which to build a unique TEMS.[13] Undoubtedly, since understanding and prudently managing internal organisational processes is always judicious, implementing an EMS consistent with ISO 14001 will be beneficial to the tribal government, tribal members and reservation environment.

◢ Implications of the Bad River Band case study

The primary lesson from the Bad River Band case study is that an EMS is applicable and adaptable to any organisation, regardless of organisational size, purpose, or location. Further, the ISO 14001 framework may benefit innumerable indigenous organisations endeavouring to protect their environment. Specifically, international discourse addresses discriminatory effects of environmental hazards in the global environment by articulating the rights of indigenous peoples to develop, control and conserve their environ-

---

13   The flexibility of the ISO 14001 standard allows any organisation the opportunity to develop a unique EMS that is socially responsible (see Evers 1997).

ment.[14] Following the example of the Bad River Band, indigenous peoples or advocacy groups could implement the ISO 14001 framework for the sustainable development of their particular natural environment and culture. By setting an example for environmental protection, the indigenous organisations would educate surrounding communities with regard to sustainable development and environmental protection. Additionally, firms experienced in ISO 14001 have an extraordinary opportunity to undertake socially responsible programmes that support indigenous efforts to use an EMS for environmental protection.

14   See draft UN Declaration on the Rights of Indigenous Peoples (1994). Although currently non-binding under international treaty or customary law, the Declaration demonstrates a convergence of environmental and human rights issues with regard to indigenous groups worldwide, and the consensus of opinion may influence future treaties or conventions (see Jaimes 1992; Williams 1990).

Part 5
INVOLVING STAKEHOLDERS: CONTRACTORS, SUPPLIERS, CUSTOMERS AND OTHER STAKEHOLDERS

ANTICIPATING GREENER SUPPLY CHAIN DEMANDS
One Singapore company's journey to ISO 14001*

Michael W. Toffel
Jebsen & Jessen (SEA) Pte Ltd, Singapore

A leading designer and manufacturer of moulded foam packaging in Southeast Asia, the Jebsen & Jessen Packaging group is one of the seven core businesses of the Singapore-based Jebsen & Jessen Group of Companies (South East Asia) (JJSEA). The Packaging group manufactures custom-designed packaging using expandable polystyrene, expandable polypropylene and expandable polyethylene. In addition, the Jebsen & Jessen Packaging group designs and produces moulded foam products for the building and construction industries for such applications as void forming, roofing and insulation, and is one of the largest stockists of insulation materials in Singapore and Malaysia.

The group's original and largest plant, Jebsen & Jessen Packaging Pte Ltd (JJPS), is located in Singapore and focuses on the nation-state's many multinational companies in the high-tech electronics industry. Situated in Tuas, an industrial zone consisting of factories and warehouses, JJPS is close to the causeway leading to peninsular Malaysia.

Along with two factories in Malaysia, JJPS operates round-the-clock production, synchronising computer-aided scheduling with customers to offer 'just-in-time' delivery. One of the first companies in Southeast Asia to receive ISO 9002 certification, its commitment to providing quality, reliability, value, and customer service have been instrumental to its success.

With three shifts operating six days a week, the company's 160 employees produce and sell 2,400 tonnes of packaging per year for over 100 customers, generating over S$25 million in revenue.

* The author would like to thank Loo Tiong Kok for reviewing a draft of this chapter.

◢ Why implement ISO 14001?

Since the launch of ISO 14001 in Singapore in 1996, JJPS management has observed a growing trend toward certification by the local operations of multinationals. In addition, consistent with its active industrial policy to encourage competitiveness, the Singapore government had been encouraging local small and medium-sized enterprises (SMEs) to become certified to ISO 14001 by providing an incentive scheme that paid a large proportion of consulting and certification fees. By late 1999, over 80 companies in Singapore were certified to ISO 14001, with the large majority being American, Japanese, and European-based multinationals but very few local SMEs such as JJPS—despite the government incentive programme.

Several of JJPS's key customers within the electronics industry had begun implementing environmental management systems (EMSs) to meet the ISO 14001 standard. Some of these companies indicated that, in the future, those suppliers that also became certified to this standard would be favoured, as this issue would be included as a criterion in their quarterly business reviews. A few years earlier, customers had encouraged JJPS and other suppliers to adopt the ISO 9002 quality management standard, and this eventually became the norm.

Sensing that a similar situation with regard to the environment would emerge, management of JJPS began to believe that implementing ISO 14001 would become a customer expectation. The 1997 Asian economic crisis had significantly reduced local demand for consumer electronic products—a key customer base for foam packaging manufacturers. Thus, a surplus mounted in the packaging manufacturing capacity. JJPS management was therefore particularly keen to pursue opportunities to gain competitive advantages over other packaging suppliers. Implementing ISO 14001 was considered to have potential to offer such an advantage by improving the company's ability to meet customer demands.

Management also recognised the synergies between the managing of quality and environment, health and safety (EHS) issues, as both seek to ensure predictable and reliable operations. Indeed, since the inception of EHS management at JJPS in 1995, the company's quality manager had been assigned both areas of responsibility. Further encouragement to implement a formal EHS management system that met ISO 14001 standards was provided by JJSEA's corporate EHS department which was convinced that implementation would lead to improvements in EHS commitment, training and performance.

Due to these numerous factors, in late 1998, JJPS management decided to formalise its ongoing EHS programme into an EHS management system that would be certified to the ISO 14001 standard. Quality manager Loo Tiong Kok, already the management representative for the company's ISO 9002 programme and responsible for the company's informal EHS management system, was appointed to head the ISO 14001 initiative.

◢ Assembling the team

Management assigned the EHS committee, which was already meeting monthly to implement the company's informal EHS management programme, to create a formal management system that would meet ISO 14001 standards. Both the corporate EHS department and JJPS management sought to continue the integrated management of environmental issues alongside occupational health and safety. Therefore, the EHS committee was challenged to incorporate occupational health and safety management into the new formal management system. The committee consisted of the following individuals:

- ☐ General manager: Han Hong Juan
- ☐ Factory manager: Lim Gim Boh
- ☐ Quality manager/EHS committee chair: Loo Tiong Kok
- ☐ Plant engineer: Lim Ban Aik
- ☐ Financial manager: Susan Leong Fong Leng
- ☐ Administration and human resources manager: Rolern Ng
- ☐ Confidential secretary: Chris Yip

While not a formal committee member, the corporate EHS Director for environment, health and safety, Mike Toffel, participated in many ISO 14001 meetings to monitor the committee's progress and provide support. In addition, Chui Tau Siong, the Regional Managing Director of the Jebsen & Jessen Packaging group, monitored the committee's progress and provided support as needed.

Similar to its approach to implementing ISO 9002, JJPS management sought outside support to guide its implementation of an EHS management system that met ISO 14001 requirements. Two service providers were approached: the local office of a large multinational consulting firm that specialised in helping companies achieve ISO 14001 standards, and a small quality management consultancy that had helped JJPS prepare for ISO 9002 certification. The latter was chosen due to the established positive working relationships and for its use of a highly structured approach similar to its ISO 9002 approach. Furthermore, due to the consultant's limited experience with ISO 14001, it was agreed that the work would be performed at a particularly competitive price.

◢ Establishing a policy

When JJSEA launched a corporate-wide initiative in 1995 to strengthen EHS management within all of its companies, JJPS developed an EHS policy that assigned EHS management responsibilities and established the company's first EHS standards. Now, after learning that ISO 14001 required all employees to know and understand the EHS policy and that the policy must be made available to outside stakeholders, the EHS committee sought to simplify the EHS policy and incorporate the company's experience in the years since the original policy was drafted. The committee also sought to ensure that the policy was broad enough to become the standard for all three companies within the Packaging group. Supported by the Packaging group's senior management and JJSEA's corporate EHS department, the committee reduced the EHS policy to eight core principles that were meant to provide the foundation for the Packaging group's entire EHS management system (see Box 16.1).

This policy was attached to all employees' identity badges, sent to customers, suppliers and neighbouring facilities, and has been made available to the general public. In addition, it has been posted throughout the facility in English, Bahasa Malaysia and Chinese.

◢ Legal review

With the assistance of JJSEA's corporate EHS department, all Singapore EHS laws and regulations were gathered and organised into the following categories:

Box 16.1 **EHS policy**

JEBSEN & JESSEN PACKAGING IS COMMITTED TO ESTABLISHING EXCELLENCE IN the environmental and occupational health and safety aspects of its operations. The company will actively promote environmentally responsible behaviour at all levels of our organisation and among our customers, suppliers and principals. Our vision is to become a company that promotes environmentally superior products and services that are produced in an environmentally superior manner. We are therefore committed to the following principles:

1   To establish and operate an environment, health and safety management system that promotes continuous improvement

2   To maintain an organisational culture that fosters keen awareness of environmental and occupational health and safety aspects of our operations and that encourages broad participation in managing them

3   To comply with environmental, health and safety laws and regulations in the countries where we operate

4   To prioritise source reduction and pollution prevention over proper waste management, and to maximise the use of recycled and recyclable materials

5   To give significant consideration to environmental and occupational health and safety criteria in our procurement practices

6   To promote our environmental, health and safety management by educating, training and communicating to all employees in the organisation

7   To increase environmental awareness by making available this policy to all company stakeholders, including employees, customers, suppliers, principals, neighbours and the general public

8   To establish environmental objectives and targets in accordance with our policy and ensure effective implementation

☐ Air pollution

☐ Water pollution

☐ Solid waste management

☐ Hazardous substances

☐ Noise pollution

☐ Occupational health

☐ Safety

☐ Fire safety

☐ Land development

☐ Emerging issues

Regulations are managed online in a Lotus Notes database and are updated periodically by the corporate EHS department (see example in Table 16.1).

The management representative identifies the regulatory requirements relating to the company's operations, and learns of updates from the corporate EHS department, a newsletter published by Singapore's Productivity and Standards Board (PSB), and Singapore's packaging industry association. The management representative led discussions with the EHS committee to develop a common understanding of how each regulation applied to the company's operations. This information was documented in

Table 16.1 **EHS laws and regulations database**

▼ 01. Country overview
▼ Overview information
Overview of Singapore's Legal System (S01)
▼ 02. Air pollution control
▼ Emissions from motor vehicles
Road Traffic Act and Regulations and EPC (Vehicular Emissions) Regulations (S07)
▼ Emissions from premises
Clean Air (Standards) Regulations 1972 (S05)
Emissions from Industrial or Trace Premises (S02)
Environmental Pollution Control Act 1999 (S03)
Environmental Pollution Control (Prohibition on the Use of Open Fires) Order 1999 (S04)
Environmental Public Health (Burning of Joss Sticks and Candles) Regulations 1999 (S06)
National Emission Standards for Air Pollution (S10)
▼ Indoor air
Smoking (Prohibition in Certain Places) Act 1992 Smoking (Prohibition in Certain Places) Notification 1994 Guidelines to Good Indoor Air Quality in Office Premises (S09)

the company's legal register (see Table 16.2), which followed the same categorisation as the EHS laws and regulations database.

The management representative worked with the administration and human resources manager to ensure that legislative requirements were communicated to relevant personnel based on their job functions. In some cases, this was done through formal training. The management representative was given responsibility for ensuring that objectives, targets, management programmes, procedures, and instructions would be modified should they be affected by new or amended legislation. Finally, the management representative also became responsible for keeping records and documents illustrating the active tracking of legal requirements and changes.

◢ Identifying aspects and impacts

The committee's next step was to learn the concepts of EHS aspects and impacts, and then to identify all aspects across the company's operations. JJPS also consulted its legal registry to ensure that EHS aspects included all EHS-related issues that were subject to regulations. As required by the ISO 14001 standard, each aspect was categorised as to whether it would occur in normal, abnormal or emergency circumstances, and the company defined these

Table 16.2 **Legal registry [*excerpt*]**

Legislation	Implication for JJPS
5. Water pollution 5.1 Pollution of inland waters	
Environmental Pollution Control Act 1999 (Part V)	
Section 15. Licence for the discharge of trade effluent, oil, chemical, sewage or other polluting matters	Licence required for the discharge of trade effluent
Environmental Pollution Control (Trade Effluent) Regulations 1999	
Section 5. Control mechanism for discharge of trade effluent	Requires sampling test points and recording periodically. (Refer to schematic diagram/floor plan.)
Section 8. Nature and type of trade effluent to be discharged	Temperature at point of entry into public sewer or watercourse shall not exceed 450°C. pH value shall not be less than 6 or more than 9 and caustic alkalinity shall not be more than 2,000 mg of calcium carbonate per litre.
Section 9. Trade effluent to be free of certain substances	JJPS does not discharge any listed substance.
Section 10. Maximum concentrations of certain substances	Refer to Section 10 for the discharge limits

terms as part of its documentation. A 'normal' operating condition was defined as relating to daily or routine events, such as combusting fuel oil to produce steam. An 'abnormal' operating condition relates to events that are expected to occur once in a week or month, such as the maintenance of equipment or machinery, process start-up or shut-down. An 'emergency' operating condition relates to occurrences that are not expected to occur, but could happen nonetheless, such as accidents, injuries, or fire.

Once all aspects were identified, each was linked to the resulting EHS impact. Table 16.3 illustrates a few of the aspects and impacts that were identified.

◢ Prioritising impacts

Once the committee identified all aspects and impacts, they developed a methodology to evaluate the significance of the impacts. The management representative worked with the corporate EHS department to develop a prioritisation matrix that incorporated the following concerns:

☐ Upstream issues, including the environmental impacts of raw materials and natural resources

Table 16.3 **EHS aspect/impact inventory [*excerpt*]**

Area	Activity, product, service	EHS aspect	EHS impact	Condition
Boiler room	Boiler operation	▶ Emission from fuel oil combustion	▶ Air pollution	Normal
		▶ Use of fresh-water to fill boiler	▶ Use of renewable resource	Normal
		▶ Boiler blowdown (water discharge from boiler)	▶ Water pollution	Normal
		▶ Use of fuel oil	▶ Use of non-renewable resource	Normal
		▶ Generation of noise	▶ Worker hearing loss ▶ Boundary noise pollution	Normal
		▶ Possibility of spillage while refilling fuel oil into underground storage tank	▶ Land and water pollution	Emergency
		▶ Possibility of oil leakage from underground storage tank	▶ Land and water pollution	Emergency
		▶ Possible worker injury from contact with hot boiler	▶ Worker injury	Emergency
	Annual boiler cleaning	▶ Discharge of effluent	▶ Water pollution	Abnormal
		▶ Possibility of worker injury in handling chemical	▶ Worker injury	Emergency

☐ Downstream issues, including the environmental impacts of emissions, effluents and solid waste disposal

☐ The EHS impacts of emergency situations

☐ The seriousness of potential health and safety impairments

Natural resources and raw materials that contribute to serious upstream environmental damage were deemed to be 'highly significant'. Non-renewable natural resources and raw materials with no recycled content were considered to be 'moderately significant'. The only upstream issues that were considered to be of 'low significance' were renewable resources that were not associated with adverse environmental impacts and non-renewable resources with at least partial recycled content.

Next, the downstream impacts of the company's wastes were considered. To assess their significance, Singapore's regulations and standards were consulted. Should any of the company's emissions or effluents exceed 85% of the value of any regulatory limit or standard, the emission or effluent would be considered 'highly significant': for example, if the standard for a particular effluent parameter is 100 ppm, then its impact was deemed to be high if test results showed the effluent to contain 85 ppm or more of the parameter. On the other hand, if all tested parameters of an emission or effluent demonstrated that each was at most 50% of the standard, the emission or effluent would be of 'low significance'. Those emissions or effluents that were in between these two situations, whereby the closest parameter to the limit was above 50% but below 85% of the standard, were deemed to be of 'moderate significance'.

Most solid waste in Singapore is incinerated, increasingly so in electricity-generating waste-to-energy facilities, and the resulting ash is landfilled. With continuing pressure on its very limited land resources, Singapore recently opened Asia's first offshore landfill facility. To incorporate the scarcity of landfill space and air pollution generated by waste incinerators situated near Singapore's dense population, no wastes that require disposal were considered as 'low significance'. Wastes with low thermal potential, and thus limited capacity to promote the offsetting benefit of electricity generation, were deemed 'highly significant'. Those wastes with high thermal potential were deemed 'moderately significant' due to their potential to reduce some combustion of fossil fuels to produce the same amount of electricity at a power station. Furthermore, all hazardous wastes were classified as 'highly significant' because of their additional threats posed to the environment and public safety.

To assess the significance of boundary noise, ranges were established for the measurement of noise in decibels during daytime, evening and night periods based on local regulations. Any measurement in excess of the regulatory limit was considered to be 'highly significant'. Any noise within five decibels[1] below the limit was deemed 'moder-

---

1 Decibels and dBA are similar—dBA means decibels weighted on the A scale. This adjustment is made to measure impact of noise on human hearing. This is standard practice for regulatory limits, industrial noise assessment, and measuring hearing. Decibels are more typically used when discussing nuisance noise, such as noise levels at a site's boundary.

ately significant', and any noise levels measuring more than five decibels below the regulatory limits were considered of 'low significance'.

Emergency and other typical situations were considered next. It was decided that situations with the potential for lasting or serious EHS impairment were 'highly significant', while those with the potential for temporary or minimal EHS impact were 'moderately significant'.

Finally, health and safety issues were addressed by weighing the permanence and seriousness of potential injuries and health impairments. Those situations with the potential for permanent injury or health impairment were deemed 'highly significant'. Situations that would result in temporary injury or health impairment were considered 'moderately significant'. Because noise levels can be easily measured objectively, specific guidelines were provided: areas with average noise levels above 85 dBA over an eight-hour period—a generally accepted international standard—were classified 'highly significant', while areas with 80–85 dBA were considered 'moderately significant'. Areas with less noise were considered to be of 'low significance'.

If any issue was addressed by more than one of these areas, a precautionary principle was adopted: the category that took precedence was the one where the issue was considered to be more highly significant. This methodology to prioritise EHS impacts is summarised in Table 16.4.

◢ Documenting procedures and work instructions

Once all aspects and impacts were identified and prioritised, the committee began the large task of ensuring that all highly significant—in addition to many moderately significant—aspects and impacts were managed according to documented procedures.

After studying the requirements of the standard in detail, committee members anticipated that implementing ISO 14001 would require substantial documentation of existing procedures and work instructions, as well as the creation of many new ones.

To begin, the committee reviewed the company's existing documentation and training materials and set an aggressive schedule to document procedures and work instructions to manage all environmental aspects that had been identified. A number of opportunities were recognised where the committee could rely on the existing ISO 9002 documentation, with minor or no modifications, to fulfil some ISO 14001 documentation requirements. The overlap areas included the following:

- ❑ Data control

- ❑ Document control

- ❑ Purchasing control

- ❑ Equipment calibration

- ❑ Record control

	Highly significant impact if . . .	Moderately significant impact if . . .	Low significant impact if . . .
Upstream (materials)			
Impact of raw materials and natural resources	Contributor to a serious environmental concern	Non-renewable resources with 100% virgin content	Renewable resources; also, non-renewable resources with some recycled content.
Downstream (wastes)			
Impact of effluent	If any parameter of an effluent exceeds 85% of the applicable legal standard (pH, total suspended solids, etc.)	If any parameter of an effluent is between 50% and 85% of the applicable legal standard	If all parameters of an effluent are below 50% of the applicable legal standard
Impact of emissions	If any parameter of an emission exceeds 85% of the applicable legal standard (opacity, solid particles, etc.) or permissible exposure limit	If any parameter of an emission is between 50% and 85% of the applicable legal standard or permissible exposure limit	If all parameters of an emission are below 50% of the applicable legal standard or permissible exposure limit
Impact of landfilled solid wastes	Hazardous materials	Non-hazardous materials	Not applicable
Impact of incinerated solid wastes	Low thermal potential	High thermal potential (this enables the waste to generate electricity in a waste-to-energy incinerator)	Not applicable
Boundary noise			
Impact of boundary noise	If boundary noise exceeds legal limit (75 decibels during day, 70 during evening, or 65 during night)	If boundary noise is within 5 decibels of legal limit (between 70 and 75 decibels during day, 65–70 decibels during evening and 60–65 decibels during night)	If boundary noise is more than 5 decibels below the legal limit (70 decibels during day, 65 decibels during evening and 60 decibels during night)
Emergencies			
Issue not part of typical everyday operations	Potential for lasting or serious EHS damage	Potential for temporary or minor EHS damage	Not applicable
Health and safety			
Seriousness and likelihood of injury or health impairment	If permanent injury or health impairment is possible OR the work environment noise levels are above legal limit ($L_{Aeq,8h} > 85$ dBA)	If injury or health impairment is possible, but not permanent OR the work environment noise levels are within 5 decibels of the legal limit (80 dBA $< L_{Aeq,8h} < 85$ dBA)	If injury or health impairment is possible but is very unlikely due to machine guarding or insulation OR the work environment noise levels are more than 5 decibels below the legal limit ($L_{Aeq,8h} < 80$ dBA)

Table 16.4 **Methodology to prioritise EHS impacts**

☐ EMS audit

☐ Corrective actions

☐ Preventative actions

☐ Training

As a result of many hours of work by managers and supervisors across the company, the following procedures and work instructions were developed (see Box 16.2).

Box 16.2 **EHS procedures and work instructions**

EHS PROCEDURES

☐ Aspects and impacts
☐ Legal requirements
☐ Environmental objectives, targets and management programme
☐ Communication
☐ Management of waste
☐ Management of atmospheric emissions
☐ Management of waste-water discharge
☐ Noise pollution control
☐ Supplier/contractor control
☐ Emergency preparedness and response
☐ Monitoring and measurement
☐ EMS audit
☐ Management review of environmental system

EHS WORK INSTRUCTIONS

☐ Handling and storage of materials
☐ Spillage containment instructions
☐ Handling and storage of liquid petroleum gas
☐ Workshop standing order
☐ Factory standing orders
☐ Canteen standing order
☐ Guardhouse standing order
☐ Product sample control
☐ General housekeeping instructions
☐ Handling and storage of fuel oil
☐ Moulding machine maintenance instructions
☐ Pre-expander maintenance instructions
☐ Cooling tower maintenance instructions
☐ Steam boiler maintenance instructions
☐ Air compressor maintenance instructions
☐ Maintenance instructions for equipment in die cut department
☐ Maintenance instructions for equipment in block and trade division
☐ Conveyor belt maintenance instructions
☐ Forklift maintenance instructions
☐ Delivery truck maintenance instructions
☐ Sprinkler and alarm system maintenance instructions
☐ Crushing operation control
☐ Re-use of foam products
☐ Water pool cleaning
☐ Changing and disposal of dust bag

◢ Training

The EHS committee realised that a great deal of formal training would be required for the 160 staff members. Since nearly all training was being done on the job in an ad hoc manner, significant time would be required both to develop training materials and to conduct formal training. Training would need to be provided for the EHS procedures and work instructions listed in Box 16.2, and refresher training was provided for those procedures from the company's ISO 9002 quality management system that were modified so they could be shared by the ISO 14001 EHS management system.

Developing the training material and conducting training would be particularly challenging as:

☐ Workers' education level ranged from elementary to technical college.

☐ Many staff members spoke only one of three languages (English, Mandarin or Bahasa Malaysia).

☐ The plant operated 24 hours a day.

☐ The staff was split among three shifts.

As a result, while training materials were developed in English, training sessions were conducted separately in English, Mandarin and Bahasa Malaysia. Because of tight production schedules, many training sessions were held outside normal working hours. In total, 32 hours of training were provided to the company's managers, supervisors and staff, which resulted in over 750 staff-hours of training. The training incurred over S$7,000 in labour costs, largely comprised of paid overtime.

◢ Establishing objectives and targets

To establish its objectives, the EHS committee considered the company's EHS policy, the operation's EHS impacts deemed to be of high and moderate significance, and the legal review that was conducted. A performance indicator was developed to correspond with every target, and a manager was assigned responsibility to achieve each one. Table 16.5 illustrates a few of the objectives and targets that were established.

◢ Certification

While a number of ISO 14001 certification bodies compete in Singapore, the market is dominated by the government-linked PSB which has handled 47 certifications, representing nearly 60% of Singapore's ISO 14001 certifications. Multinational companies includ-

Policy/commitment	Objective	Target	Performance indicator	Responsibility
To prioritise source reduction and pollution prevention	To increase fuel oil efficiency	Improve fuel oil efficiency by at least 1% over the average 1999 level by 31 December 2000	Monthly fuel oil ratio expressed in litres per kilograms as: *Fuel oil consumed per month ÷ Goods produced per month*	Factory manager
To maximise the use of recycled and recyclable materials	To increase recycled content in expandable polystyrene products, wherever technically and commercially practical	Increase recycled content in expandable polystyrene products to 5% (by weight) by 31 December 2000	Monthly percentage calculated using kilograms of expandable polystyrene material (EPS) as: *Recycled EPS used per month ÷ Total EPS used per month*	Factory manager
To promote safety by educating, training and communicating	To ensure all relevant employees are trained to promote their safety	Establish proper operating procedure for cutting and slicing machines by 31 October 2000	Operating procedures	Engineering manager

Table 16.5 **Objectives and targets [*excerpt*]**

ing Bureau Veritas Quality International (BVQI), Lloyds Register Quality Assurance (LRQA), Société Générale de Surveillance (SGS) and TÜV Rheinland have a modest share, each having conducted six or seven ISO 14001 certifications in Singapore. Four additional companies compete, but together they account for only 10% of the market.

JJPS chose PSB for two main reasons. First, they were already familiar with their staff as PSB had certified JJPS's ISO 9002 quality management system and had subsequently conducted surveillance audits. Second, PSB was priced competitively. The initial two-day preliminary audit resulted in several findings, including the need to:

☐ Review the aspect/impact record to ensure its comprehensiveness

☐ Review the procedure to evaluate EHS impacts to ensure it could be used for assessing the significance of boundary noise

☐ Clarify the definitions for normal, abnormal and emergency operating conditions

☐ Clarify the procedures used by the EHS committee to determine which aspects and impacts to focus on when establishing objectives and targets

Within two weeks of the preliminary audit, the management representative wrote to PSB explaining how each audit finding had been addressed. He explained the immediate fixes made to the specific findings and, importantly, described the changes made to the management system to ensure these situations would not be repeated.

The subsequent two-day pre-award audit resulted in only one observation and two minor non-conformances. The observation related to a company document that reported the annual emerging evacuation drill, where the EHS committee noted the duration was too long. While the company conducted a second drill shortly thereafter, there were no records indicating whether the performance had improved to the satisfaction of the EHS committee.

One minor non-conformance issue involved the company's need to re-test its boundary noise to ensure that it met with Singapore's legal standards. In fact, Singapore's Ministry of the Environment does not require companies to test their boundary noise; it simply requires compliance with prescribed limits. However, as part of the ISO 14001 process, JJPS was required to demonstrate compliance, which meant conducting the test to illustrate that the results are within the standards. While JJPS had already identified this issue in its legal review, the test had not yet been conducted.

The second minor non-conformance issue involved the need to clarify a procedure. At issue was the need for the EHS committee to demonstrate and document the rationale it used when establishing the company's objectives and targets.

The management representative replied to the certification team on all pre-award audit findings within two weeks. The company was certified in May 2000.

◢ Costs

In building its management system, JJPS incurred several one-time costs, including S$22,800 for the consultant and S$6,900 for the initial certification. As mentioned earlier, the labour costs associated with training managers, supervisors and all staff totalled over S$7,000.

Ongoing costs associated with implementing the EHS management system include periodic environmental testing, a strengthened employee health-monitoring programme, as well as S$3,000 for two surveillance audits per year.

Over the course of implementing the EHS management system, JJPS has made additional investments in equipment and engineering projects that will both improve EHS performance and process efficiency.

◢ Using Lotus Notes as a document management system

Just as JJPS was finalising the implementation of ISO 14001, a corporate-wide installation of Lotus Notes was launched. This provided the management representative with an opportunity to create a Lotus Notes database to maintain and disseminate all ISO 14001 documentation online, and eliminated the need to print hard copies (see Table 16.6). The system also provided much more effective and efficient document control. Initial concerns that users could print documents from their workstations were addressed by implementing a policy that only those hard copies that had been stamped by the management representative were to be considered official controlled documents.

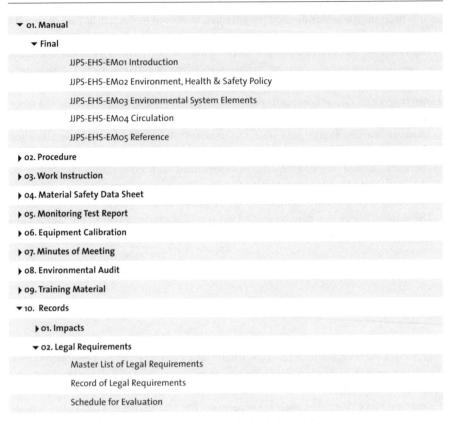

▼ 01. Manual

  ▼ Final

        JJPS-EHS-EM01 Introduction

        JJPS-EHS-EM02 Environment, Health & Safety Policy

        JJPS-EHS-EM03 Environmental System Elements

        JJPS-EHS-EM04 Circulation

        JJPS-EHS-EM05 Reference

  ▶ 02. Procedure

  ▶ 03. Work Instruction

  ▶ 04. Material Safety Data Sheet

  ▶ 05. Monitoring Test Report

  ▶ 06. Equipment Calibration

  ▶ 07. Minutes of Meeting

  ▶ 08. Environmental Audit

  ▶ 09. Training Material

  ▼ 10. Records

    ▶ 01. Impacts

    ▼ 02. Legal Requirements

        Master List of Legal Requirements

        Record of Legal Requirements

        Schedule for Evaluation

Table 16.6 **ISO 14001 'documentation' on a customised Lotus Notes database**

◢ Lessons learned

The ISO 14001 process resulted in several improvements that will be very useful to strengthen the EHS management in the other Jebsen & Jessen Packaging companies. For example, many procedures and work instructions that were largely passed on via word of mouth are now formally documented, and many improvements were made to these during the documentation process. Similarly, much of the pre-ISO 14001 training provided to operational staff had been conducted on the job, risking wide variability in the amount and quality of the training actually delivered. As part of the ISO 14001 process, all training needs were identified, documented training materials were produced and training records were formalised. All of this will be applied in the Packaging group's other companies.

JJPS management gained a great deal of insight on how best to implement an EHSMS, and these lessons will help the other Packaging companies implement their management systems. Explanations by various managers of the company's activities and ongoing programmes, procedures and work instructions dominated the first ten weekly meetings with the consultant. In future implementations, the management representative should take more time—before the committee begins to meet weekly—to ensure that the consultant gains this understanding through thorough one-on-one discussions with the appropriate managers and supervisors. This will also serve to improve the accuracy of the implementation time-line developed by the management representative and consultant.

After every committee meeting, the consultant and management representative learned to work together more efficiently. They began to draft the agenda for the next meeting and determine which managers and supervisors needed to attend. Not only did this reduce the number of managers and supervisors attending meetings where the topics did not relate to their responsibilities, but it also enhanced their enthusiasm for the ISO 14001 process, as most meetings they did attend required their active participation.

The consultant's initial explanation of EHS aspects and impacts did not provide the committee with a clear understanding of the terms and their distinction. As the identification of EHS aspects lays the foundation for the entire EHS management system, it is one of the most important steps in the implementation process. Therefore, in future implementations, particular care should be taken to ensure that the committee is provided with a clear explanation and guidance. When identifying and prioritising impacts, the consultant should emphasise the important distinction between impacts that can be controlled (e.g. emissions), influenced (e.g. raw material composition in some cases) and not controlled (e.g. upstream impacts of water consumption if only one source is available). In addition, the consultant should assist the committee in develop-ing a methodology to prioritise impacts by sharing methods of how other companies have done this—particularly methods used by companies that have already been certified to ISO 14001.

Given the context of many companies operating in Southeast Asia, the implemen-tation timetable should provide a significant amount of time for the committee to become familiar with local EHS regulations. In many cases, there are regulations that have not been enforced, or have been enforced sporadically, that a company may not be aware of. Not only will this promote the respective department's legal compliance, but it will also help all the committee members understand why these impacts are rated as highly significant. In many of these countries, there are periodic training courses offered by regulators, industry associations and consultants that seek to educate company managers about ongoing legal requirements. Attending such a course could be an excellent first step for the management representative, even before the implementation process for ISO 14001 begins.

◢ Conclusions

One major benefit of JJPS's implementation of ISO 14001 is that it acquired a third-party 'seal of approval' that will be used in its marketing efforts to meet the growing environmental concern of its customers within the electronics industry. However, earning the full value of this benefit may still be years away. According to JJPS General Manager

Han Hong Juan, thus far it has usually been American-based multinationals that have expressed interest in whether their suppliers are certified to ISO 14001, typically discussed in the quarterly business reviews they conduct with their suppliers. However, Han believes price, service and the relationship will remain the main factors in securing orders, and that the environmental performance of suppliers will remain a preference rather than a requirement. He observes:

> We do not have any customers dictating that we must be ISO 14001-certified yet and I don't see it coming within the next three years or so. Like the ISO 9000 quality management standard, ISO 14001 will become the norm instead of the exception.

Chui Tau Siong, Regional Managing Director of the Jebsen & Jessen Packaging group, believes that certification to the ISO 14001 standard may bring value to other business relationships:

> I see value when we are trying to obtain a new agency or partner. When we say we are ISO 14001-certified, it will certainly enhance our image and demonstrate our care for the environment.

Many other benefits were realised by implementing an ISO 14001-certified EHS management system. Every JJPS manager and supervisor has gained a thorough understanding of EHS laws and regulations, which has enabled the company to strengthen its regulatory compliance at the same time that Singapore's Ministry of Environment and Ministry of Manpower is increasing its enforcement stringency. This may yet provide advantages if competitors are less effective in compliance and, as a result, regulators take action.

Comprehensive staff training has increased participation in the company's ongoing recycling and energy conservation initiatives, and has focused attention on preventative actions to reduce risks. For example, machine guarding was installed in additional equipment where it could improve worker safety, well beyond just those machines where the manufacturer had already designed this feature. Across all departments, EHS procedures and work instructions were documented and clarified, and, recognising additional potential health impacts of machine noise and chemicals used in production, a more extensive health-monitoring programme was initiated.

Implementing ISO 14001 has therefore enabled the company to improve EHS management across all departments and has ensured that tasks are assigned and accomplished in a much more systematic manner. In particular, management's periodic review and establishment of EHS objectives and targets based on EHS impacts—a new feature of the company's management system—ensures continuous improvement in the most relevant areas.

◢ Future plans

JJPS plans to promote its ISO 14001 experience to its customers and suppliers to encourage their participation. In the coming months, the Jebsen & Jessen Packaging group plans to implement EHS management systems that comply with ISO 14001 requirements in all of its other factories, which are currently implementing quality management systems to meet the ISO 9002 standard. Each company will begin implementing its EHS management system immediately following certification to ISO 9002—expected in late 2000 or early 2001.

In addition, as the Jebsen & Jessen Packaging group is planning to broaden its activity level by expanding its product platform and regional coverage, it will probably implement ISO 14001-certified EHS management systems in any new companies it begins operating.

INTEGRATING QUALITY, ENVIRONMENT, HEALTH AND SAFETY SYSTEMS WITH CUSTOMERS AND CONTRACTORS

Adrian Carter
Amec Process & Energy, UK

Amec Process & Energy[1] (referred to in this chapter as Amec) is probably the largest company specialising in the management of integrated service contracts to oil and gas operators in the North Sea. Its scope of services encompasses design, procurement, construction and maintenance of onshore (oil and gas terminals) and offshore (oil and gas platforms) assets. Future contracts may also encompass decommissioning/recommissioning of platforms. The company employs approximately 4,000 people. Over the last 20 years, Amec has provided services to most of the major oil and gas operators in this region.

Contract lifetimes frequently extend for several years and the nature of Amec's work activities mean that environmental, health, safety and quality issues all attract a high profile within company operations. Amec recently achieved registration to the ISO 14001 standard for a number of business units, including the offshore division, an organisation split between two sites (Aberdeen and Great Yarmouth, UK) separated by a distance of several hundred kilometres.

Amec's offshore division operates an integrated quality/environment/health and safety management system. Amec currently maintains a number of linked management systems under a single certificate, covering the two corporate sites and approximately ten major contracts. In most cases, contract arrangements include a documented interface with client integrated management systems, either health, safety, environment and quality (HSEQ) or health safety and the environment (HSE), with quality being considered separately. Some of the client management systems are also ISO 14001- or EMAS (EU Eco-management and Audit System)-approved.

---

1 Since this chapter was written, Amec Process & Energy has changed its name to Amec Offshore Services.

In this chapter an attempt will be made to show how Amec's environmental management systems (EMSs) have been established and integrated with other management systems, and how interfacing with a variety of client management systems has been addressed.

Why integrate our management systems?

A number of reasons why companies might wish to integrate their approach to management have been identified within literature on the subject (Stares 1997). These include:

☐ Synthesis of diverse evidence for different management areas to provide a 'big picture' of company performance

☐ Reducing duplication of effort in terms of hazard identification, development and maintenance of controls required, auditing, etc.

☐ Employment of a consistent approach across disciplines

The significance of these benefits has been appreciated by a number of oil and gas companies, in line with Harte's (1997) observation that any potential for improvement is worthy of consideration in an industry where management performance in terms of HSEQ was widely seen to have reached a plateau. The need for Amec to stay in touch with new management system developments within the industry was a further imperative for the company's senior management in considering the way forward. This was particularly because management excellence has a key role to play in Amec's performance as a contractor, and a major feature of contractor management is the high degree of interfacing with clients (and subcontractors) and the need to match or lead them in sophistication of management systems.

How did we establish and maintain an integrated system?

The development of the EMS in both sites occurred in what could be described as four distinct phases:

1. **Informal development stage**: ad hoc consideration of environmentally related issues during process

2. **Review stage**: undertaking of environmental reviews of workscope and establishment of a number of environmental improvements and awareness-raising initiatives

3. **Implementation stage**: development, issue and implementation of EMS controls (modification of HSEQ manual and procedures, objectives and targets register) towards registration to ISO 14001

4. **Post-audit maturation**

Informal development stage

Prior to 1996, environmental management at Amec essentially consisted of informal arrangements for waste disposal and clean-up of spillages, although environmental issues were considered on an ad hoc basis throughout the business process. In 1996 however, responsibility for initiating development of a formal environmental management system, aligned to a recognised standard, was delegated—a decision catalysed by the development of the British environmental management system standard BS 7750 (BSI 1992).

Review stage

Amec's EMSs developed from a series of environmental reviews, undertaken in some cases by students in support of an environmental management MSc qualification at the University of East Anglia, with which Amec had already established a number of links. Their involvement, along with specialists from other disciplines, marked the beginning of the second phase of implementation. Initially, environmental advisers tended to work fairly independently of quality and safety advisers, although operating within the same department. At this early stage, management system development tended to consist of tasks that were environmentally specific, such as the establishment of a waste paper recycling scheme, offshore reviews of waste management practice, investigations into ways of improving energy use on-site and awareness-raising.

Implementation stage

With the requirement to formally document and audit the various elements of the EMS, greater collaboration developed with the quality management advisers. In fact, this stage of implementation was considerably facilitated by the existence of an ISO 9001 system on which to build—areas such as document control and management review were already in existence as part of the ISO 9001 system. This existing structure meant that the process of formal management system development was effectively confined to:

- ☐ Distillation of environmental review findings into impacts/aspects registers
- ☐ Establishment of a corporate HSE legislation register
- ☐ Environmental training
- ☐ Identification and documentation of improvement objectives and targets
- ☐ Refinement of the environmental auditing approach
- ☐ Review and modification of procedures and HSEQ signposting documents
- ☐ Establishment and implementation of a strategy for the improvement of supply chain environmental performance

It has been in the area of the last three issues that quality and environment have most tended to dovetail. Environmental management benefited particularly from the existing expertise with ISO 9001 because the implementation team was largely made up of environmental specialists who were not initially familiar with the intricacies of management systems aligned to ISO standards. Key lessons learned from quality management included the need to ensure that procedures were not too prescriptive and understanding the value of involving the workforce widely during implementation. Quality management in turn benefited from the general review of procedures undertaken by staff. This process has helped to reinforce the message that it is staff themselves, rather than quality/environmental managers, who are the owners of company operating procedures.

The experience of health and safety management within Amec has been a further valuable source of learning on which to build. In fact, with respect to some business areas, the review of environmental controls largely followed the dictum that 'anywhere in the procedures where safety is addressed, environment needs to be considered also'. For example, where safety issues were identified in risk assessments, environmental hazards such as potential emissions to air, drains or land were also identified and built in. Moreover, the scope of safety awareness raising activities and safety audits has been extended to consider HSE: for example, an environmental training module has been added to Amec's safety training course.

Collaboration over EMS development between the two corporate sites also tended to increase over time, as communication between the two implementation teams increased. The geographic distance (approximately 850 km) between sites meant that close co-operation over aspects of EMS development was inhibited to some extent. One of the clear successes of the implementation as a whole was the development of 'new ways of working', including improved networking and information exchange throughout the business on environmental and—by proxy to some extent—health, safety and quality affairs. The development by advisers of a three-year strategy for environmental management within Amec, nomination of focal points for particular environmental issues and greater peer review of documentation are all examples of this new way of working. Peer review has been particularly valuable in spreading best practice between advisers, for example in sharing approaches to documenting environmental aspects and impacts and commenting on newly developed procedures and guidance.

Post-audit maturation

At the time of writing (November 1999), the management system is awaiting its first surveillance audit from the assessors. Work undertaken since the previous audit has concentrated on three main areas:

☐ Improvement of areas of weakness

☐ Implementation of a fully ISO 14001-aligned EMS on other contracts

☐ Development of closely linked environmental management systems with clients

This post-audit maturation phase has not been distinguished by further integration between disciplines. The reason for this is, primarily, because the short time since the audit has not been sufficient for such integration to take place. At present, few advisers are fully competent in more than one discipline. Moreover, environmental management system advisers currently have an additional supporting role to play within engineering design, unlike their health and safety counterparts. However, it is envisaged that HSEQ advisers, while maintaining a core competency in a specialised discipline, will begin to expand duties into related disciplines, particularly with respect to low-level audits and the provision of relatively non-specialised advice. It is also anticipated that future integration will include joint ISO 9001/ISO 14001 audits by assessors, as well as approval to a future international health and safety standard (ISO 18001).

While disciplines currently remain mainly the preserve of specialists, activities carried out by company personnel are often conducted using a combination of factors from different disciplines. For example, level-four audits (site inspections) undertaken by site supervisors cover HSE and quality aspects, while task-based risk assessments cover HSE elements. Contract plans, operational controls, training and competency systems, document control systems, subcontractor audits and management review meetings all integrate HSEQ considerations.

How have we approached linking EMSs across Amec?

Given the difficulty of resourcing implementation across the entire company's operations in one phase, an approach was agreed with Amec's third-party assessors, LRQA, whereby initial implementation would focus on the two corporate site facilities, as well as four key contracts. In addition, the approach by which implementation would be extended to other contracts was audited. The approach taken was essentially to develop a set of corporate template procedures covering all aspects of environmental management. Having been developed, these would be implemented initially in the four contracts. They would then be applied to EMSs covering other contracts on a rolling basis.

This approach was adopted to uphold the principle that the entire company should be included within the certificate, rather than simply named contracts, enhancing the status of the approval. Moreover, the approach meant that the certificate would not require amending during successive visits, a process that involves a cost of several hundred pounds each time for the award of a new certificate as new contracts are 'rolled on'. While this approach was broadly acceptable to the assessors, it was stipulated that, as a minimum, a commitment to legal compliance had to be demonstrated across all contracts. This has been addressed in practice through a procedure for reviewing legislative compliance across contracts. It is also worth noting the inevitable risk associated with this approach: that, by holding a single certificate across so many management systems, a non-conformance in any part of the system would lead to loss of the entire certificate. This has been considered an acceptable risk, however, particularly given that the same arrangements have been in place for ISO 9001.

In achieving ISO 14001 registration, one of the primary challenges faced by the implementation team was to achieve a consistent approach to management across Amec. This problem is obviously not uncommon in larger companies. In our case, the key difficulties were posed by implementation of EMSs occurring out of phase with each other, compounded by problems of communication between the two corporate sites.

The approach of developing a corporate EMS that could then be implemented onto contracts proved difficult in areas where corporate development lagged behind development work on contracts. This tended not to occur in areas where completely new controls were required, such as the development of a procedure for identification of environmental impacts/aspects or management of compliance to environmental legislation. However, establishing consistent environmental controls within existing business processes, such as design and supply chain management was initially more difficult.

A typical problem was posed by the need to review and modify controls for a particular task where controls for that task existed corporately and on contracts. Differences in the style of the existing procedures covering the same task in different parts of the business made consistency difficult to achieve. In fact, the consequence of such problems was to drive increased communication between implementation team members.

With the benefit of hindsight, while the philosophy of developing a corporate management system and rolling this out onto contracts was generally adopted, the approach of developing effective, field-tested procedures on contracts and adopting these corporately was seen, in some cases, to be more appropriate. This was undertaken, for example, in developing a procedure for environmental hazard identification in design.

A feature of Amec's implementation process has been the latitude allowed to individual environmental advisers in undertaking implementation. For example, different ways of structuring registers of environmental aspects/impacts have been undertaken on different contracts. Advisers have also differed on the level of prescriptive detail required for the EMS controls within their contract. These differences typically reflect the differing nature of the contracts on which they operate and the management systems of the client, as well as the preferences of the individual adviser. Importantly, however, the principle remains that, while a framework exists for establishing an environmental management system, and a broadly consistent approach is adopted, there is no single 'right' way to undertake all aspects of the implementation.

This issue has been important in shaping the approach advisers take towards evaluating the integrity of each others' management systems, through cross-auditing. Amec's audit schedules include provision for the audit of the whole management system (level-two audit), a task that is essentially the same as that undertaken by the assessors themselves. The value of auditing each others' management systems has been of general benefit to advisers and has helped to enhance an understanding of what the standard itself is about: achieving a consistent and effective set of arrangements appropriate to Amec's workscope.

◢ How did we approach interfacing with client systems?

Establishing the arrangements for interfacing with client and subcontractor management systems within contracts has been an important feature of the EMS implementation process within Amec. Safety management system interfacing within the oil and gas industry tends to follow the guidelines set by the United Kingdom Offshore Operators'

Association (UKOOA) (1993). These guidelines have been revised very recently but current arrangements reflect 1993 guidelines.

The guidelines emphasise the need, first, for effective management to be in place within both parties; second, that interfacing arrangements have been jointly planned and agreed between parties; and, third, that they are comprehensive enough to meet the full scope of interfacing arrangements.

As would be expected, the 1993 guidelines did not fully address the needs of ISO 14001; for example, the need to clarify issues such as responsibility for identification of legislation and legal compliance monitoring were weakly addressed. In addition, potential incompatibilities of systems, such as differences in the way different systems evaluate significance of hazards (aspects) was not covered. The current guidelines offer more detailed guidance and explicitly acknowledge the relevance of this guidance to environmental management system interfacing, although support for an ISO 14001 system is not their main aim.

Effective interfacing of management systems is particularly important for Amec because of the increasing complexity of working arrangements with clients. In many contracts, integrated teams of company (and company subcontractors) and client personnel are deployed. In the past, these were normally controlled by client procedures. More recently, however, integration has increased to the point where contractor personnel are responsible for supervising client staff (see Fig. 17.1). This inevitably complicates the question of who controls and influences particular activities. For the purposes of management system integrity, control within such integrated teams has been considered to belong to the client wherever client procedures are being adhered to (since these are owned by the client). This solution clarifies the interface between management systems but, in doing so, downgrades the principle of a jointly controlled process. Control and influence in such situations needs to be properly clarified in management system documentation.

Figure 17.1 **Overlap of management systems on one contract**

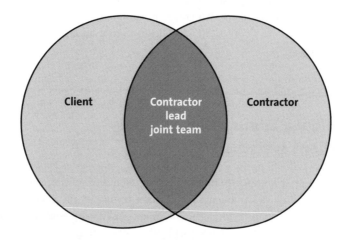

Another difficulty presented by close working relationships with the client has been the need for the contractor to review any weaknesses in the client system to which the contractor is working. For example, if Amec undertakes work to its own procedures—supported by client procedures for risk assessment, site inspections and incident reporting—which inadequately address environmental issues, what action should be taken? The answer would seem to be that the contractor is responsible for, at the very least, communicating concerns over client procedures where an influence is exerted. Where integrity is seriously threatened, and contractor influence is strong, we are responsible for ensuring that additional contractor arrangements are in place to address shortcomings in client arrangements (e.g. a separate environmental risk assessment to be undertaken), although this may have to be undertaken at the contractor's own expense. Inevitably, the problem of duplication of procedures arises in this situation. On the author's contract this issue is currently being addressed with a complete review of risk assessment arrangements by the client to minimise duplication.

The issue is also not always straightforward with respect to interfacing with Amec's subcontractors. Where our management system exerts influence, we are required to insist on certain levels of control among our subcontractors, but we can only do so in situations where we clearly have control. If a long-standing contract exists with the subcontractor, amendments to the contract might be required to ensure that their management control is fully aligned with that of Amec, with the business consequences that this entails. In this case, a long-term programme of amendments to subcontractor contracts, in line with business requirements, is being used to address this issue.

The value of sharing responsibility for the maintenance of management system integrity between client and subcontractor is particularly clear in the offshore sector where, for example, employing a single individual to look at more than one management system can reduce the cost of auditing compliance offshore. In fact, the cost of travelling offshore (approximately £300 per flight) is such that Amec is exploring the potential for collaborating on management responsibilities with companies with whom it has no direct contractual relationship. This sort of relationship is currently informal and restricted to particular issues where Amec has some involvement. Nevertheless, the trend for greater sharing of management duties between companies within the sector is growing and it is here that some of the greatest potential for co-operation exists. Joint-venture agreements are likely to be the norm in future for the industry and EMS arrangements will have to continue to adapt to ensure cost-effectiveness as well as integrity.

◢ Conclusions

The experience Amec has gained in integrating its management disciplines has provided the company with a number of benefits, including the provision of a 'big picture' of company performance. It is anticipated that further integration will lead to efficiency improvements; the adoption and further alignment of all three ISO standards will provide further consistency to the existing approach across disciplines.

The process of development of the EMS to ISO 14001 approval within Amec was strongly influenced by a number a factors, including: the background experience of the implementation team; communication between team members; input to the implementation process from quality and health and safety management; the contract nature of the company's business; the integrated nature of interfaces with clients; and the high level of influence exerted over relatively large numbers of subcontractors.

In providing a summary of lessons learned for the benefit of other companies undergoing a similar implementation process, it is recognised that management processes differ between companies and that there is no 'right way' to implement a management system. Nevertheless, based on our own experiences, a number of concluding observations are made below.

What value can integrated management systems bring to large, complex businesses?

Large businesses often deploy linked management systems covering 'corporate', 'contract' and/or 'departmental' functions. In such organisations, exchange of information between the different business areas is often a problem. Amec has found that an integrated management system, with integrated management reviews, audits, training programmes, etc., does provide important benefits. The difficulty most frequently encountered is that posed by the dissimilarities of HSEQ disciplines, which can, on occasion, result in 'muddy' messages being generated. Care in message presentation should be an important feature of integrated management systems.

How can EMS development benefit from existing quality and health and safety management?

Depending on a company's management structure, quality and health and safety advisers may reside in the same or different departments. Desired levels of integration will again differ, but Amec's experience is that real benefits do exist in terms of cross-learning between HSEQ advisers. The need to develop a strategy to harness this potential should, perhaps, be a consideration for most large businesses. Strong links with other key departments, particularly (if relevant) human resources, purchasing, design and site management are also very likely to smooth the implementation process.

What is the ideal background experience of EMS implementation team members?

EMS implementation requires skills from a number of disciplines, including a knowledge of environmental issues, particularly a knowledge of environmental hazard identification and improvements and environmental legislation. It also requires a knowledge of the business and an understanding of management processes. Amec's implementation team was strongly biased towards environmental expertise and, as such, found that easy access to company staff able and willing to provide active support in the other areas was invaluable. Based on our experience (as well as those of some of our clients), a mixture of backgrounds among implementers would seem desirable.

How can communication between team members be optimised?

In large organisations, management system implementation may be spread between responsible individuals located in separate departments, or business units located in different towns or even countries. If cross-learning and consistency of approach are to be optimised, frequent meetings, heavy use of e-mail and video and telephone conferences are essential and are also more environmentally friendly than visits. A structured updating process is important. Peer review of work is also a 'must' and cross-auditing between facilities can play a very valuable role in the process.

What are the key problems posed by interfaces with clients and subcontractors?

Interfacing with clients and subcontractors is a particularly challenging issue for environmental management and should be addressed earlier rather than later in the implementation process. Well-defined interfaces, clarity over control and influence of activities, clear communication of standards of acceptable working behaviour to suppliers and subcontractors, including methods for communicating issues to occasional site visitors, are all issues familiar to safety advisers. Once again, cross-learning between disciplines can provide benefits.

In summary, we have found that the management of a number of difficulties faced during EMS development to ISO 14001 registration in complex businesses can be improved where integration with quality and health and safety is also a key objective. Degrees of integration may vary between different management activities and, in some areas, integration may best be considered a longer-term goal. However, valuable experience on many common problems facing EMS advisers may be readily available where health, safety and quality support already exists; indeed, we have found that benefits can work in both directions. This chapter has emphasised two of the most important ingredients for success of integrated management system development: clarity over plans of action and areas of ambiguity, and strong lines of communication between key individuals.

ENVIRONMENTAL MANAGEMENT SYSTEMS AND STAKEHOLDERS
The case of the Belgian electricity sector*

Jean-Pierre Tack

Tractebel Development Engineering and
the Catholic University of Louvain, Belgium

EMSs are increasingly being implemented in industrial companies. After a period of observation, Belgian companies have recently understood that ISO 14001 can bring them several advantages, e.g. in terms of public relationships, competition and risk management.

Belgium exports the majority of its goods worldwide, so the perception of the general quality of products and services is very important. However, there is still a relatively small number of companies certified to ISO 14001 and even fewer registered to EMAS. On 1 September 1999, 130 sites were ISO 14001-certified and only nine verified to EMAS, compared to total EU figures of 5,351 and 3,005 respectively.[1] This low rate of uptake is somewhat surprising. However, it seems from discussions with industrialists that the certification rate should increase in the next few months. The large difference between ISO 14001 and EMAS-registered sites in Belgium can probably be explained by its exporting activities. EMAS is an EU regulation which is still largely unknown and unrecognised outside the EU, even though it is perceived in Europe as more stringent than ISO 14001. Major Belgian chemical exporters have already claimed that they consider ISO 14001 as an increasingly necessary certificate, but that EMAS offers little added value to their competitiveness.

* Special thanks to Sandrine Dixson-Declève, international consultant involved in the preparation of the EMS in the Tihange nuclear power site and training sessions to the personnel, who
kindly reviewed this chapter and added elements from her experience.
1 R. Peglau, www.ecology.or.jp/isoworld/english/iso_14k.htm (1999).

Electrabel, a privately owned company, is the Belgian leader in electricity production, transport and distribution.[2] In 1996, Electrabel went beyond the usual statement on integrating the environment into its activities, with its first environmental report emphasising the importance of the environment in its daily activities, together with a proactive approach. The report further points out the main environmental tools used: ecological planning, voluntary measures, environmental agreements with public authorities and an environmental policy. This policy intends to integrate electricity, economy and environment (Electrabel's '3E' policy) and was first used for raising management's environmental awareness.

Since this initial environmental report, the situation has evolved to take into account the very important fact that, under EU law, electricity markets have been liberalised.[3] Therefore, competition will be a major challenge for the next few years. In order to address this issue, the company has undertaken a fundamental review of its structure and management. Consequently, and together with management optimisation, Electrabel considers environmental protection and a proactive environmental approach to be a means of achieving its objective of becoming a key player in Europe's electricity market. The company does not intend poor environmental performance to affect its competitiveness.

Moreover, as a power producer, Electrabel is concerned about current environmental debates, in particular the need to curb greenhouse gas emissions (such as CO_2, CH_4[4] and SF_6), the use of PCBs (polychlorinated biphenyls) in transformers and condensers and pressures to develop and support renewable energy sources. Therefore, environment has become not only a public relations issue, but also a challenging and essential element in the overall economic development and management policy of the company.

There are two major nuclear power production sites in Belgium, one at Doel on the River Schelle, the other at Tihange on the River Meuse. Nuclear sites have always been subject to criticism from environmental groups. A more recent driver is the request from the Green Party (newly entered in the Belgian government) to phase out, as soon as possible, nuclear power production.[5] Electrabel has found that EMS is the tool for organising the incorporation of environmental issues into the daily activities of its production sites.

In 1994, after the adoption of the EMAS regulation,[6] Electrabel decided to launch a feasibility study on the implementation of EMSs in two fossil fuel-fired power plants. In 1995, the EMS implementation process began at those sites as well as at the Doel nuclear

2   Electrabel produces about 90% of electricity in Belgium, at about 15 major production sites. SPE, a publicly owned company, is the second-largest producer and has also implemented ISO 14001 for two of its production sites.

3   Since this liberalisation, the price for electricity was established and frequently reviewed in a national committee comprising producers, unions and the authorities. In Belgium, as in other countries, the selling price is different for industrial clients and households.

4   In some parts of the country, Electrabel is in charge of providing natural gas to households through an underground pipeline network.

5   Their attitude is somewhat different from their German colleagues, as they do not claim a 25-year-term ban on nuclear production; they ask that 40-year-old plants are closed instead of prolonging their life.

6   EU Regulation 1836/93.

power site. These were followed, in 1996, with the Tihange site which is the largest electricity production site in the country. Other fossil fuel-fired power plants began the ISO 14001 process in 1997.

With several years' experience in implementing EMSs in nuclear as well as in 'classic' fossil fuel power production sites, we can learn from our experiences and answer these fundamental questions: Why choose EMAS versus ISO 14001? How effective is an EMS as a communication tool with stakeholders? What are the differences in EMS implementation between nuclear and fossil fuel-fired stations?

◢ Why EMAS or ISO 14001?

Nuclear production—concentrated essentially on two sites—represents about two-thirds of the power production in Belgium. Each site contains three (Tihange) or four (Doel) individual plants. Several fossil fuel-fired power plants complete the production network. Electrabel is involved in a comprehensive programme focused on the 'repowering'[7] of existing plants, the construction of new plants or units and plant decommissioning, usually those using coal and/or fuel with a low installed power. Recently, a number of combined heat and power plants have been built on large industrial sites. A few projects concern renewable energy sources, such as wind power.

In its 1996 environmental report, Electrabel indicated that it intended to extend EMS implementation to plants expected to operate beyond 2000. It was also decided that the two Electrabel nuclear sites would install an EMAS system, with ISO 14001 implemented in the fossil fuel plants.

Electrabel management considers that obtaining an ISO 14001 certificate is sufficient for most of its activities, as the environmental concerns of the public and authorities with regard to fossil fuel plants is rather moderate. Moreover, ISO 14001 is more widely used than EMAS among industry and is perceived as a particularly appropriate first step for upgrading to EMAS at a later date.

Where public concern is more acute, however, there is a need to demonstrate good environmental performance through the EMAS process. This is the case for nuclear power because it generates greater public concern than fossil fuels.

◢ EMAS in a nuclear power plant

Nuclear power sites, by their very nature, are subject to stringent controls. A safety report, in which radiological consequences for surrounding populations are calculated, supports

7   Repowering programmes consist of refitting existing plants with new, more efficient equipment and increasing their power production; environmental investments can be made at the same time (e.g. flue gas desulphuration and denitrification).

the operator's licence application. The consequences for the population are compared to international standards for radioactive effluents and radiological exposures. The environment is also considered, although mainly as a vector for transferring radioactivity to humans. A few years ago, modifications were made to Belgian law to incorporate the mandatory assessment of radiological consequences to the environment (fauna and flora) as well as to humans.[8]

The safety assessment process exerts a feedback on plant design during the project acceptance process by competent authorities. According to international regulations, the 'as low as reasonably achievable' (ALARA) principle is applied to radiological consequences and plant safety.

Nuclear plants are subject to regular external inspections, such as informal peer reviews between neighbouring countries' operators, as well as the more formal Operational Safety Review Team[9] system. In the EU, inspectors from the European Commission and national inspectors also conduct Euratom audits. A few years ago, a peer review and information exchange system was set up among operators worldwide, under the auspices of the World Association of Nuclear Operators.

Quality assurance (QA) systems have been implemented at Belgian sites since the mid-1980s and these are subject to regular internal visits and enquiries. The QA system implemented at nuclear sites does not follow the ISO 9000 series but was inspired by US nuclear standards.

Today, Belgian nuclear plants have a comprehensive set of procedures for safety, production, control, general organisation, administration, industrial security, QA, etc. All personnel receive comprehensive training in numerous aspects of the plant's operation and on the written procedures and instructions. Indeed, some of the employees say that paper became, after electricity, the most important product on-site. This 'procedure culture' exists in most nuclear sites around the world.

Environmental objectives related to radiological issues have been part of general management procedures for many years. With an increasing amount of laws, regulations and, of course, public concern over the environment, the necessity to comprehensively manage all environmental issues on-site (extending to non-radiological issues) appeared essential in order to maintain a high level of protection for employees and the neighbouring population.

The plant management is very concerned about legal compliance, and EMAS implementation was considered particularly appropriate for checking site conformity with all applicable laws and regulations. Moreover, Electrabel decided to enhance public information provision about its nuclear activities and their environmental impacts. With this openness toward the public and the existing management structure, EMAS was considered more appropriate and stringent than ISO 14001 because it requires the production of a public environmental statement.

---

8   Belgium was condemned by the European Court of Justice for incomplete implementation of the 1985 EIA Directive, as nuclear sites were excluded from the scope of Belgian implementation texts. This was rectified in 1993.

9   Organised under the auspices of the International Atomic Energy Authority.

Finally, nuclear sites implemented ISO 14001-specific requirements as well. Experience shows that the international standard gives more precise instructions than EMAS for the preparation of the EMS components, which are, in any case, highly compatible with the core EMAS requirements.

◢ ISO 14001 in fossil fuel-fired power plants

By comparison with a nuclear power production plant, a classic power plant burning fossil fuel is more like any other medium-sized industrial installation in terms of the processes involved, operation team organisation and management.

In Flanders, the northern region of Belgium, a decree dated April 1995 (Flemish Parliament 1995) obliges large companies to designate an environmental co-ordinator and carry out regular environmental audits by external environmental verifiers. The decree is explicitly inspired by the EMAS regulation and renders some of its components mandatory in this region of Belgium, such as those relating to control, monitoring and internal reporting.

According to these new regulatory obligations, Electrabel designated environmental co-ordinators for the whole country, with responsibility for environmental management for each production zone (a zone is a geographical group of plants). Since this law came into force, these co-ordinators have usually dealt with land use and operating permits, EIA and monitoring, as well as waste management.

Classic plants face much less public concern about environmental issues than their nuclear counterparts. Nevertheless, EMSs have been implemented since 1995 in the first two plants according to the British Standard BS 7750 (BSI 1994). After the release of the international standard in 1996, BS 7750 was abandoned in favour of ISO 14001. From the nuclear sites' experience with EMAS, classic sites were considered by Electrabel's management to be less prepared for the EMAS process. As mentioned previously, personnel at nuclear sites are used to procedures and specific working instructions, which is not the case in classic power production sites. Moreover, the EMAS administrative process proved to be very slow in the case of the Doel nuclear power site,[10] principally because public authorities and administrations are involved in the registration process.

Electrabel considered that ISO 14001 fulfilled its EMS needs. In addition, the Flemish provisions on environmental management were covered by ISO 14001 requirements. On this basis, the company decided to use ISO 14001 instead of EMAS for classic power production sites.

10   The combined certification/registration audit was made in April 1997, quickly followed by the auditor agreement for granting the ISO 14001 certificate. Up to September 1999, the formal EMAS registration had not been made.

◢ The communication issue

It is well known that the public views industrial activities with much concern and doubt; the nuclear sector has a negative image because related risks are believed to be uncontrollable, involuntary and not well known (Petts 1994). Sometimes, industrial sites organise 'open-door' events at which they claim to be the cause of only limited environmental problems. They also try to be good local citizens by participating financially in local activities. In Tihange, Electrabel has to pay huge taxes as a counterbalance to the risks posed by the site for the area.

It is increasingly clear that, as public concern for health and environmental issues has risen in Belgium, so have efforts by authorities to effectively control industrial activities. This development has obviously had a direct impact on the environmental awareness of companies across Belgium, who now view environmental issues either as an advantage or a burden for their competitiveness and public acceptance.

Many industries are now aware that communication on environmental issues is essential for facilitating and enhancing their relationship with neighbours, local authorities and technical administrations in charge of their control and inspection. A no-communication policy usually leads to confrontation, e.g. under the form of appeals on licence applications, trials for permit non-compliance and media campaigns.

Contrary to this new communication culture in the environmental arena, the nuclear power sector was convinced that environmental issues were managed efficiently (Western 1994) and considered that it was not necessary to communicate actively on these issues. The radiological environmental aspects of nuclear sites in Belgium are usually handled properly, due to the weight of regulations, frequent controls and a strong safety culture. However, experience in environmental reviews in Belgium and abroad (Kemp and Free 1994) shows that this confident picture cannot be reproduced for non-radiological issues.

Surprisingly, as if they were confirming the no-communication culture perceived by the public, nuclear sites have released environmental information only recently. Experience shows that Belgian nuclear sites have very good environmental performance for nuclear aspects, as they reach only 1% or 2% of their authorised limit for radioactive releases in the air or water. This data has been recently published for the Tihange nuclear power site (Rorive 1997) after the EMAS initial environmental review was carried out in March 1997, but is also reported for other sites, e.g. in the UK (Kemp and Free 1994). Effluents are usually limited to their lowest practicable level for both environmental and cost reasons.

For years, the Tihange site has managed its radioactive wastes with the primary objective of drastically reducing its volume. Admittedly, this is predominantly a cost issue rather than an environmental one as external treatment and storage costs have risen considerably over the years and the definitive storage of radioactive waste remains a difficult debate in Belgium, as in other countries.

In Belgium, communication of environmental performance for nuclear plants still focuses on the issue of radioactive wastes, highlighted by environmental groups such as Greenpeace. Even employees at Tihange have requested more information and communication on this subject. Therefore, it is clear that the communication of detailed environmental performance is necessary to enhance the activities' transparency and provide objective information to workers and the public.

In 1997, the Tihange site began to communicate on radiological and non-radiological issues with local authorities, competent administrations, staff and the public. The site issued a brochure in the spring of 1997 in which detailed information is given on the site's environmental policy, its environmental aspects and principles for environmental management, as well as some objectives for the future. In addition, other forms of communication and public information were set up, such as 'green visits' for the public to the site: as there is a high percentage of land devoted to trees and shrubs, visitors can walk through the site like a park.

As with any important industrial site, Tihange regularly applies for new permits (e.g. building, waste-water discharges) and therefore needs acceptance of its activities by the local community. All the communication initiatives, eased by the existence of an EMS, are aimed at facilitating the development of production activities. In this light, meetings held with local and regional administrations on the EMS implementation were positively welcomed.

Internal communication is an important objective as well. In such a rigorously managed sector, there is little room for individual non-concerted initiative. In addition, the complexity of radiological issues makes it difficult for lay people to understand the associated environmental issues and managers, unfortunately, have little time for advice or communication on environmentally related questions. Fortunately, EMAS implementation and personnel training has allowed the development of individual ideas for improving environmental performance and has filtered information throughout the management structure from bottom to top, and vice versa.

It is clear that environmental issues are a source of motivation for staff. Training sessions have shown that employees are the most valuable resource for identifying problems, proposing solutions and implementing the entire system once adequate means are mobilised. Empowering people is essential, otherwise the EMS remains only an additional obligation and constraint to everyday work.

This communication issue does not appear as important for classic plants. They will often have communicated with their neighbours during EIA procedures and they do not face the same opposition or, even, fear from the public. In fact, there is little concern about accidents in classic plants, compared to nuclear sites. Therefore, even if ISO 14001 can bring more confidence in the operator from the public, certification is not seen as a particular means of gaining better acceptance, as it is for nuclear plants.

◢ Knowledge difference between nuclear and fossil fuel-fired sites

As discussed earlier, the personnel at nuclear sites are usually more aware of safety and security issues, and are more trained and familiar with written procedures than those in classic power sites. Based on this, we could assume an easier implementation of an EMS in a nuclear power production site than in a classic one. Experience so far suggests this is not the case, however. What are the reasons for this? The answer lies in the intrinsic differences between nuclear and classic plants.

At the beginning of the EMS implementation process at the Tihange nuclear power site, it was clear that the site had a great deal of experience with the need for detailed documentation and the management of radioactive environmental aspects under a QA system, and had integrated all of this into a safety culture. But, as mentioned earlier, the amount of daily paper-pushing by most personnel had created some animosity toward such a heavily documented system and would later cause difficulty in incorporating the formal EMS into the general management system. This situation illustrates one of the limits of procedural management systems, i.e. when dealing with written instructions and paperwork can exceed work in the field. In this case, instead of a challenging programme, EMS implementation first appeared to many at Tihange as simply additional instructions and paper workload.

To assuage this opposition, the training sessions aimed at introducing the EMS were modified to focus on information exchange between trainers[11] and personnel, with brainstorming sessions on possible environmental actions. In this case, the training sessions became the main means of explaining that EMS preparation was essentially a formalisation of existing processes and procedures under EMAS. Over time, and with the corrective actions made to the EMS after the internal audit, a good level of acceptance by the personnel was achieved.

With acceptance at all levels and the integration of an internal culture of communication and discussion within the existing procedural culture, it is believed that the site will easily integrate new elements into its environmental management and even enhance the efficiency of pre-existing systems or elements. Since the launch of the EMS in early 1998, many strategic and technical ideas have been implemented which have directly increased the global environmental performance of the site. With the system clearly functional and its environmental performance increasing, the site easily passed its registration verification in October 1999.

At the classic power plants, little of the initial difficulties found at the nuclear site were encountered. Employees on these sites are used to working with operation notices but not with health and safety, quality or environmental procedures. These procedures tend to be handled through the usual work relationships between colleagues or through the hierarchical management chain. Therefore, a well-prepared EMS was welcomed by the staff, as it was quickly understood that environmental performance would improve, as would general site efficiency. Nonetheless, the learning curve on these sites was much steeper than at the nuclear site as the personnel were discovering a completely new way of management. In comparison with the nuclear site, training was focused on the basics of the management system and, in particular, the importance of environmental procedures and the contents of the environmental manual. During the training sessions, the

11   The trainers, from Tractebel Development Engineering, participated in the preparation of EMS elements. They were perceived as a third party between personnel and hierarchy.

employees proposed some adjustments and even suggested specific working instructions that would help manage operations with a high degree of environmental concern. In this case, the personnel truly helped in the implementation of the system from the outset, by finding ways to make the system evolve, instead of reacting against it.

◢ Conclusions

The implementation of EMSs was initiated in the power production sector in 1995, when EMAS was still seen as a curiosity by industry. Electrabel, one of the most important companies in Belgium and the country's leading electricity supplier, operates large (nuclear power plants) as well as smaller production sites that could be considered to operate as small and medium-sized enterprises, as they have sometimes less than 30 employees (e.g. combined gas and vapour turbines plants). After initially implementing BS 7750, Electrabel quickly switched choice of standard to ISO 14001 for classic power production sites and EMAS for nuclear ones. We have seen that this choice was based on a variety of issues, such as public perception of the environmental impacts of production sites, personnel competence and training and the need to communicate environmental performance to enhance public acceptance.

The first lesson from this experience is that, in both nuclear and non-nuclear sites, the installation of an EMAS or an ISO 14001 system has led to an in-depth examination of the sites' environmental aspects and applicable legal obligations. For nuclear sites, the EMAS process was the occasion to check non-radiological environmental issues and fine-tune the necessary environmental links to radiological issues. The latter have been very well managed for years due to health, safety and security concerns. Non-conformities, usually minor, were found during the process and dealt with.[12]

In this process, employees found a source of personal motivation and critical analysis over their own daily activities. Personnel at all sites, both nuclear and classic, felt empowered by the EMS and agreed to participate in the implementation of a formalised EMS. However, they also complained about the amount of written procedures and instructions. This was especially the case at the nuclear site. The new EMS system, like most new management systems, was perceived as creating additional constraints and work and, initially, it proved very difficult to get it accepted. This is a fundamental point, which needs be taken into account when preparing and implementing an EMS in similar conditions.

It is also important to note that a positive interaction with other management systems is not always easy to achieve, in particular if the existing load of procedures is already coming under criticism by staff, which was the case in the nuclear power production sites.

---

12 It appears from our experience that the ISO 14001 or EMAS process is usually not started before heavy environmental problems are solved or rendered inoffensive: industrialists see these management references as high-quality practices for environmental protection, so they rarely use the EMS implementation process for handling difficult environmental issues.

The training process can be a useful tool to help the personnel accept and take ownership of the system. A variety of issues, not always pertinent to the EMS, were raised during the training sessions. These issues were often important indicators of potential problems with staff acceptance of a management system, and allowed the on- and off-site EMS team to take into account staff concerns throughout the implementation process. In addition, the training sessions were occasions for personnel to propose ideas for the further enhancement of the management system and environmental performance.

The implementation of EMAS at the Tihange nuclear power site has added a variety of communication and management tools which will further its environmental performance goals and its relationships with its major stakeholders. This can only be beneficial to its position in a new liberalised electricity market, to public perception of the site and, very importantly, to employee motivation.

Although the ISO 14001 system does not push the public communication and openness elements as such, it is clear that the classic power sites will also gain from an increased openness towards the public and most importantly, as in the case of the Tihange nuclear site, will result in better-managed sites from an environmental perspective.

19

UNCO-OPERATIVE STAKEHOLDERS
ISO 14001 as a means to co-ordinate efforts

Quentin Farmar-Bowers
Star Eight Consulting, Australia

This case study shows how environmental management systems (EMSs) complying with the requirements of ISO 14001, may help a particular group of stakeholders deal with biodiversity issues on road corridors in a similar if not co-ordinated way. These stakeholders are the larger organisations involved with roads and, collectively, they influence or actually carry out much of the work that impacts biodiversity. However, they total only a few hundred of the many thousands of stakeholders involved throughout Australia.

Specific guidelines have been drafted to help these larger stakeholders develop co-ordinated EMSs. Co-ordination now, when the process is just starting in earnest, will help this group later when they have to co-operate with others on the complex problem of biodiversity maintenance. Co-operation will be difficult to achieve, but is essential if biodiversity is to be maintained in perpetuity. The focus on biodiversity as opposed to other environmental issues is in response to the obligation to maintain biodiversity for future generations, and the importance of road corridors in this endeavour.

◢ Biodiversity on Australia's road reserves

One of the most familiar kinds of public reserve in Australia is the land between the road's running surface and the adjacent property boundary. This land is referred to as the 'road reserve'.

In urban and suburban areas, road reserves are usually fully paved and sometimes planted with formal street trees, but elsewhere in Australia road reserves are less well tended and provide space for wild plants and animals. Much of Australia's 800,000 km of road still supports remnants of pre-European ecosystems, which are sometimes the only remnants of the original vegetation in the region (Saunders *et al.* 1987, 1991). But the details of this biodiversity are not known and it will take many decades of meticulous work to get a clear picture.

In addition to supporting biodiversity, road reserves transect the landscape and incorporate a strip of every natural ecosystem they cross. Because of this, road reserves provide a unique 'living map' of the original distribution of Australia's biodiversity. Road drainage systems are also significant for biodiversity, but negatively, as sediment and pollution from the road is washed directly into watercourses, thus impacting downstream aquatic habitats.

Road reserves occupy a special place in the Australian psyche because maintaining the natural heritage of the countryside provides a sense of place, pride and belonging, and 'the bush' seen most frequently is that on the side of the road.

Disappearing biodiversity

Road reserves were set aside for transport purposes and are still extremely valuable economically as transport corridors. Improvements to the road pavement and its appurtenances, as well as other structures such as electricity lines, pipelines and telephone cables, increasingly encroach on the road reserves.

Road reserves are also used for firebreaks, grazing, landscape planting, and even cropping. All these uses are expanding and taking over the space needed for biodiversity maintenance. The reserves are also being invaded by exotic vegetation and various environmental stresses are making native plants more vulnerable to a range of diseases. The result is that the bush on the road reserves is under threat and disappearing fast.

The dilemma is between continuing to expand the current economic uses of road reserves to provide short-term benefit or finding ways of using road reserves that maintain biodiversity and so benefit future generations (de-Shalit 1995). Changing decisions on biodiversity from destruction to maintenance will depend on whether Australians are prepared to implement the sustainable development objectives of inter-generational equity and the protection of biodiversity (COAG 1992a), take heed of national and state biodiversity conservation strategies (CoA 1996; NRE 1997) and inter-governmental agreements (COAG 1992b).

There are many laws and regulations relevant to road reserves, but the task is about complying with the spirit rather than merely the letter of the law (Bates 1999). However, complying with these sentiments requires a significant change in work practices, as many of the activities that impact biodiversity are small-scale and routine.

Choosing to overcome difficulties in maintaining biodiversity

There are technical and economic issues that make the task of maintaining biodiversity on road reserves difficult:

☐ **Technical issues**. Their long narrow shape means that the surviving native flora and fauna is vulnerable to invasion by exotic species and to physical damage from adjacent land uses and highway maintenance activities. This narrowness also makes it harder to prevent drainage water from damaging adjacent aquatic habitats. There is little reliable expertise available to help stakeholders overcome these difficulties.

☐ **Economic issues**. Biodiversity maintenance will increase costs for organisations using the road reserves, and the pattern of expenditure will be different. Systematic biodiversity surveys, information systems and management research will require long-term budget allocations which is quite different from the current pattern of project-oriented environmental expenditure (e.g. environmental impact statements).

These difficulties can be overcome but possibly the hardest problem will be organising the huge number of independent people and organisations that have a stake in road reserves and the biodiversity issue. These stakeholders can be divided into three groups. The largest group is those with an interest in specific sites. Site-specific stakeholders include thousands of adjacent landholders and maintenance contractors, hundreds of local government authorities and country fire brigades, handfuls of utility and telephone companies, and eight state and territory road authorities. Each of these has the power to destroy a site's biodiversity, but, because so many different stakeholders can access the same site, none has the individual power to protect native plants and animals. For example, an electricity company may decide to place its power line on cleared farmland to protect native grassland on the road reserve, only to see the local fire brigade or farmer plough up the reserve the next day to create a firebreak. So the power of these site-specific stakeholders is asymmetric—they can easily destroy but have difficulty protecting. Site-specific stakeholders also include conservationists and natural resource and environmental protection agencies. These stakeholders can provide information about biodiversity and undertake specific research projects.

In addition to the site-specific stakeholders, there are two other groups of stakeholders. The second group includes organisations and associations such as road associations, local government associations, universities and professional associations that provide industry services. These industry stakeholders can influence their members and can also support site-specific stakeholders by disseminating information and commissioning studies. State and federal governments are the third group of stakeholders. These government stakeholders can raise or submerge the biodiversity issue through strategies, regulations, codes and laws, and through funding allocations.

Some stakeholders (particularly government agencies) can function in all three roles. For instance, a state road agency can be responsible for site-specific work, give advice to a local government authority about local roads and also be instrumental in formulating government policy.

◢ Action by Austroads: an industry stakeholder

In 1994, the Commonwealth Government of Australia released a draft strategy for the conservation of Australia's biodiversity (CoA 1996). This stimulated Austroads (the national association of Australian road authorities and Transit New Zealand) to commission a study on how biodiversity could be maintained on road reserves. The Austroads study recommended that a co-operative approach involving all stakeholders be developed and that every stakeholder work within this system.

The Austroads system was called the National Protocol System (NPS). It included primary and operational objectives and described a management process that stressed the value of each stakeholder's contribution and their collective responsibility to operate the system (Farmar-Bowers 1997, 1998a, 1999a). The essential elements of the NPS are given in Box 19.1. Austroads commissioned studies to support the NPS including environmental law (Bates 1999), road drainage (McRobert 1997; McRobert and Sheridan 1999) and decision systems (Humphries 1996), and funded a trial in Tasmania.

A co-operative approach to road reserve management based on the NPS was trialled for a 60 km section of highway in Tasmania in 1998. The Tasmanian state road authority managed the trial and established a committee of stakeholder representatives, undertook biological surveys, ran workshops, organised stakeholder meetings, produced 11 newsletters and published interim and final reports (Farmar-Bowers 1999b).

The programme did not, however, lead to the hoped-for co-operation. The long-term commitment of resources and degree of co-operation and openness recommended by the NPS disconcerted some stakeholder representatives. Others wanted to see better biodiversity protection but on the basis of individual action.

The trial showed that commitment to biodiversity was not strong enough to overcome reluctance to address the need for change, particularly the need for co-operation. This reluctance was exacerbated because moving from an individual to a co-operative system is a political change that most stakeholder representatives do not have the authority to make.

This authority problem may be partly circumvented by changing the focus from co-operative biodiversity maintenance to considering existing stakeholder objectives.

◢ Stakeholder objectives

Stakeholders may agree to protect biodiversity because they can achieve some other pre-existing objective by doing so, such as secure political power, make money, ensure future work or improve their public image. A short cut to understanding what these other objectives may be comes from cultural theory (also known as grid/group theory). This distinguishes four 'ways-of-life' (Thompson *et al.* 1990) (see Table 19.1). Road reserve stakeholders seem to fit into three of the four ways-of-life (fatalism is not relevant). 'Grid' refers to social norms, modes of behaviour, rules and so on. Convention and rules of

THE NPS IS A FRAMEWORK TO ESTABLISH CO-OPERATION BETWEEN ALL stakeholders to maintain biodiversity on road reserves. There are four 'actions':

ACTION 1
All stakeholders adopt the following objectives; this is the core of the NPS.

Principal objective
Protection of biological diversity and maintenance of ecological processes on road reserves and in adjacent natural ecosystems, including adjacent waterways.

Operational objectives
1   Devise and implement a co-operative management system
2   Develop and disseminate knowledge through the co-operative management system
   2.1   *Document roadside biodiversity*
   2.2   *Document threatening processes*
   2.3   *Improve management information*
3   Involve all stakeholders in biodiversity management decisions
4   Establish independent stakeholder review systems

ACTION 2
Every stakeholder decides to undertake a specific programme and prepares an outline called a protocol chapter. The protocol chapter is a public document vetted through independent review to ensure it will help achieve the core objectives. Implementation in the field is also audited to ensure work complies with the protocol chapter.

ACTION 3
Establish, by agreement between stakeholders, an independent review system (operational objective 4) that reviews protocol chapters and their implementation. Each review group would relate to some geographic area and may coincide with bio-geographic or political regions.

ACTION 4
Establish a system of communication and participation that ensures the NPS is democratically administered on a regional basis but linked nationally and that stakeholder participation is adequate but not supererogatory.

Each stakeholder carries out their work programme within the co-ordinating process of the NPS but has an overall responsibility to actively improve co-operation whenever possible. For example, with regard to information, the stakeholders have the following three tasks:
1   Identify biodiversity and share this information with all stakeholders
2   Record current management practices and seek more appropriate practices, and share this information with all stakeholders
3   Identify other stakeholders and make sure they are aware of their responsibilities and involved in the NPS

The efficient implementation of the NPS will depend on good use of networked information that relates to a specific site, such as: which stakeholders are interested in a specific stretch of road; the current management of the reserves; existing biodiversity; research requirements; restoration and maintenance options; and proposed developments.

Box 19.1 **National Protocol System (NPS)**

	Low group	High group
High grid	**Fatalist** People with little control over their situation and resources; they live by coping: e.g. pensioners, unemployed. They would play no part in deciding biodiversity use.	**Hierarchy** People working in large businesses and government agencies (tend to believe that current situation is satisfactory and biodiversity will be protected if not grossly over-used).
Low grid	**Individual/business owner** Farmers, maintenance contractors (tend to believe that human actions cause no harm to biodiversity).	**Voluntary conservation group** (tend to believe biodiversity is in danger and should be protected at every opportunity).

Table 19.1 **Grid/group of cultural theory**

behaviour are very important for stakeholders in government service (road and conservation agencies, local government, fire brigades, etc.) and so they have a high-grid way-of-life. Other stakeholders (individual land-owners, farmers and conservation group members) are less constrained by rules and procedures and so have a low-grid way-of-life. 'Group' refers to the importance of groups in one's way-of-life. A farmer or person running a road contracting business has a low-group way-of-life, whereas group membership is very important to public servants and conservation group members, so they have a high-group way-of-life.

People in the same way-of-life tend to have the same kinds of problem and the same kinds of motivation.

Hierarchy way-of-life

In order for public servants to stay as public servants they must work in a way that maintains the hierarchy. (The same applies to employees of large firms.) This includes delegating authority through management positions, using standard operating procedures and obtaining management control over activities. Their objective is to implement a system that protects biodiversity rather than to maintain biodiversity because the former secures the authority and future of the hierarchy. An EMS that complies with the requirements of ISO 14001 would confirm the legitimacy of the hierarchy way-of-life (within a department or corporation) and so strengthen its management position.

Voluntary conservation group way-of-life

Conservation groups have to find issues that maintain their members' interest and loyalty. Maintaining a strong ethical position is important for loyalty and recruitment of other like-minded people. Groups may co-operate to maintain biodiversity if this demonstrates the ethical stance of the group and reflects members' interests. Some of the

Photo credit: Quentin Farmar-Bowers

Tasmania: grading has irreparably damaged this narrow road reserve which is known to support rare plants.

Photo credit: Quentin Farmar-Bowers

Western Australia: the road reserve supports the last three trees in a once extensive forest.

Photo credit: Quentin Farmar-Bowers

Victoria: the trees are native but the grass is introduced pasture.

Photo credit: Quentin Farmar-Bowers

Tasmania: Tasmanian devils' habit of eating road kills makes them vulnerable to road death too.

voluntary conservation groups in Tasmania have sufficient income to run offices with staff but tend not to have hierarchical management and so may not be interested in using EMSs.

Individual/business owner way-of-life

Farmers and business operators have the primary objective of staying in business. Maintaining biodiversity is not relevant to this as it relates to moral issues of inter-generational equity and distributive justice (Rawls 1972). Motivation to conserve bio-diversity for business people is mainly linked to money (Young et al. 1996). But there could also be other motivations such as a moral obligation to conserve biodiversity for future generations, personal interest, pride in the natural landscape and a desire to work with other people.

Construction and maintenance contractors will tend to co-operate to maintain biodiversity if they are required to do so by the contract letting agency. Letting agencies may require this routinely if biodiversity maintenance is policy and if they insist that their contractors have an EMS.

Overall, cultural theory suggests that EMSs are pertinent for hierarchies but would not be relevant for other stakeholders, except for contractors who would use EMSs to stay in business. It also indicates that biodiversity maintenance may be viewed by most stake-holders as a means to an end and not the final objective. The final objective for the hierarchical organisations is preserving management control and power, and for contrac-tors it is getting contracts. Approaches other than EMSs would be required to secure the positive involvement of adjacent land-owners and conservation groups. These approaches are not dealt with in this chapter.

◢ EMS as a co-ordinating tool

Some stakeholders (such as the Tasmanian electricity distribution companies) have already developed EMSs under ISO 14001, and other large stakeholders are planning to follow suit. Contractors to these organisations are under pressure to develop comple-mentary EMSs. These EMSs do not yet include co-operative biodiversity maintenance on road reserves, but stakeholders may voluntarily include this issue in deference to the growing public interest in biodiversity and because of its relevance to the accepted responsibility of protecting endangered species. Once senior management has accepted the need to conserve biodiversity, the necessary practices can be developed and applied routinely in an EMS.

As part of the final report of the Tasmanian trial, a draft guideline for an EMS on maintaining biodiversity on road reserves was prepared using ISO 14001 as a template (Farmar-Bowers 1998b). Using the draft guideline would help individual stakeholders and their contractors maintain their autonomy yet develop EMSs that have similar core features in relation to road reserve management. Thus, an EMS became a co-ordinating device. Compatibility is highly desirable for the future (assuming that current stakeholder objections to dealing with biodiversity maintenance will eventually be overcome), as many of the issues that individual stakeholders will have to deal with overlap, both geographically and by subject matter. Economies may also become possible if agencies have compatible data and geographic information systems and are willing to share or sell information.

Once compatible systems are operating, the positive grass-roots feedback from the thousands of individual stakeholders may reinforce the advantages of developing compatible systems and co-operation, especially as there is no competitive advantage for any of the stakeholders involved in maintaining biodiversity. (Maintenance contractors could compete with each other on the basis of their biodiversity management knowledge and diligence.) The value of the road reserves as a living map of biodiversity distribution is dependent on being able to aggregate knowledge from different stakeholders. Thus, co-ordination of information is vital to achieve full benefit from this work.

◢ Stakeholders working together?

Although people with different ways-of-life can achieve a community objective (such as biodiversity maintenance), by working towards their own personal objectives, their efforts may interfere with each other and the lack of direct focus on the community objective may lead ultimately to failure. For example, techniques that strengthen the position of hierarchies such as an EMS might alienate other stakeholders and exclude them from participation. Paradoxically, an EMS that gives good management control to an agency and its contractors may eventually hinder the essential participation of other stakeholders.

If biodiversity maintenance is accepted as a long-term community objective, and not exclusively an agency objective, then the EMS should be renegotiated as soon as the other two stakeholder groups (conservation groups and individual/business owners) consistently fail to participate effectively.

Public debate

Biodiversity is essentially a public good that will deliver most of its value to future generations. This makes it a contentious issue today as people have different feelings about what obligations they have to adjust their current behaviours for the benefit of future generations. Information on policy intentions and existing management arrangements could come from EMSs. Honest public debate needs to be encouraged. And the debate, if supportive of biodiversity maintenance, could encourage the inclusion of biodiversity maintenance as an improvement to individual EMSs under ISO 14001 and so help bring about co-ordination between reluctant stakeholders for the benefit of present and future Australians. Thus, EMSs could have an important role in protecting biodiversity.

◢ Conclusions

Effective protection of Australia's biodiversity must include the maintenance of the remnants of native ecosystems that survive on road reserves and the protection of aquatic habitats that are damaged by sediment and pollution from road drainage systems. But biodiversity on the road reserves can only be maintained through the collaboration of all stakeholders. Most stakeholders are independent operators and their co-operation has to be achieved voluntarily.

Although EMS use is starting among the larger stakeholders, including biodiversity maintenance as an objective in an EMS is a further step. While not mandatory, biodiversity maintenance does have the status of an objective in state and federal government policy and the Tasmanian State government is developing a biodiversity strategy to be released in late 2000.

In planning an EMS for road reserves, most individual stakeholders can legitimately claim that their degree of control on changing flora and fauna is small and therefore biodiversity maintenance need not be included in their EMSs. Collectively, however, they have a major role and responsibility. The certification/registration process of ISO 14001 provides an opportunity to influence and encourage stakeholders to include biodiversity maintenance in their EMSs. Developing a guideline such as the draft prepared for this Austroads study would be a diplomatic way to ensure that individual EMSs contain at least similar core features. Having similar geographic information systems, disclosure provisions and definitions would facilitate co-operation between stakeholders, although nothing can force it.

The overall achievement of biodiversity maintenance is dependent on all stakeholders becoming well informed and actively co-operating. The management objective to maintain or destroy biodiversity on these public land reserves should be guided by honest public debate. The use of co-ordinated EMSs by large stakeholders is likely to increase biodiversity maintenance and may also encourage the other stakeholders such as adjacent land-owners to co-operate. In the long term, however, strong control by the larger stakeholders may inhibit community debate and the essential participation of the other stakeholders.

Part 6
INCORPORATING PRODUCTS, DESIGN AND TECHNOLOGY

TECHNICAL AND DESIGN TOOLS
The Integration of ISO 14001, life-cycle development, environmental design and cost accounting*

Matthew M. Mehalik
University of Virginia, USA

This chapter presents a case in which environmental life-cycle design tools were used extensively during the development of a new textile fabric for office interiors. The case exemplifies the spirit of several frameworks for ISO 14001, life-cycle assessment (LCA) and life-cycle development (LCD) (Keoleian *et al.* 1995; Keoleian and Menerey 1993). It illustrates the role of having a design protocol at the beginning of the design process. The LCD strategy used a priority assignment system for optimisation. The ISO 14001-based environmental management system (EMS) and an environmental financial accounting system were integrated with the product redesign efforts.

The aim of this chapter is to show how these tools complement one another. A detailed case history has been published separately (Gorman *et al.* 2000; Mehalik 2000; Mehalik *et al.* 1996, 1997a, 1997b, 1998a, 1998b).

◢ Operating in the absence of life-cycle design tools

Susan Lyons, vice-president of design at DesignTex, a firm specialising in the design and manufacture of textiles for commercial interiors, wanted her next design to be a major

* Support for this project was provided by the Ethics and Values Programme of the National Science Foundation through Michael E. Gorman, William Scherer, and Patricia Werhane of the University of Virginia. Additional support came from the School of Engineering and Applied Science and the Colgate Darden School of Graduate Business Administration. The conclusions are the responsibility of the author and do not reflect the views of the Foundation. The author wishes to thank William McDonough of the University of Virginia, Michael Braungart, Alain Rivière, and Jens Soth of the EPEA, Susan Lyons of DesignTex and Albin Kälin of Rohner Textil for willingly providing the information necessary for this chapter.

breakthrough, focusing on environmental sustainability. She wanted to maintain Design-Tex's leadership in the commercial fabrics design market.

To launch her project, Lyons began by surveying the trade literature, by contacting yarn spinners who claimed to be environmentally responsible, and by paying attention to competitors who were attempting to enter this market. She contacted some of the 40 different mills that supplied DesignTex under contract.

In December of 1992 she became interested in a sample of a fabric product line called Climatex. Albin Kälin, managing director of Rohner Textil AG, a mill located in Switzerland, sent Lyons a sample. He and Rohner Textil had been pursuing an environmental agenda of their own, and he was willing to team up with Lyons and DesignTex in developing a new product based on Climatex (Mehalik *et al.* 1996).

With only 30 employees, Rohner Textil is the smallest unit of a much larger enterprise, Forster-Rohner, a privately held company that consists of five European textile mills producing a range of products from socks to jerseys and embroidery. In order for such a small company to remain useful to the larger enterprise and be competitive in the high-end speciality interiors market, it needed to remain at the cutting edge, providing the most creative and high-quality upholstery fabrics. The mill needed to be able to customise quickly to the demands of customers who wanted small quantities of unique upholstery designs. It also needed to remain price-competitive and profitable and, at the same time, to increase production and market share.

Kälin was sensitive to environmental issues because of the high cost of disposing of waste trimmings. As the fabric came off the loom, the edges were cut to a uniform length. Some of the trimmings were burned in the regional incinerator to generate electricity. The air pollutants were scrubbed before being released into the environment. Overall, the waste trimmings consisted of about 30% of the total environmental costs at Rohner Textil.

Rohner Textil dyes much of the yarn in its own dye facilities and therefore has to treat and dispose of the resulting waste-water, which is a costly procedure in Switzerland, as elsewhere. If not properly treated, the waste-water poses a potential threat to the Rhine river, just yards away, and Lake Constance, a few miles downstream. So, in 1989, Kälin decided to pursue a more environmentally sustainable agenda.

By late 1992 the mill's processes for producing all of its products, particularly its flag-ship product, Climatex, had been certified by the German-based organisation, Eco-Tex.[1] Having been tested for pH value, content of free and partially releasable formaldehydes, heavy metals, pesticides, pentachlorophenol content, carcinogenic compounds and colour-fastness, Climatex received the Eco-Tex trademark and was certified as 'human ecology'-safe. Although an important step, certification had only slightly reduced disposal cost risks, however, by changing disposal categorisation from hazardous to non-hazardous solid waste. The tests certified against human ecology criteria, not against larger ecosystem considerations that are relevant to product disposal (Mehalik *et al.* 1997a).

---

1   Eco-Tex is a German independent institute, the International Association for Research and Testing in the field of textile ecology.

It was at this time that Susan Lyons of DesignTex proposed the idea of creating an environmentally sustainable fabric. Rohner Textil would supply the woven product to DesignTex which would then market the product to its commercial interior customers. Lyons also inquired about the possibility of recycling Climatex. Kälin mentioned that recycling commercial fabrics was questionable because they were typically glued, which makes recycling difficult. Kälin also explained that the fabric released a large amount of energy when burned in regional incinerators, from which he purchased electricity to operate the mill.

By the middle of 1993 Lyons had several options to consider for an environmental design. The most promising one seemed to be the Climatex fabric from Rohner Textil. She was sceptical because the fabric was not recyclable and because it was difficult to make an eye-catching environmental statement using the little-known Eco-Tex label. She considered using yarn made from polyethylene terephthalate (PET) recycled soda bottles, but was not confident that the vendors could deliver reliably nor of the yarn's aesthetic appeal. These were the same concerns she had about another option, Foxfiber, which had limited colour availability (Mehalik *et al.* 1996). In the absence of meaningful tools for environmental sustainability, both Kälin and Lyons's options for an environmental direction were unclear.

◢ McDonough and Braungart design protocols

The design protocol for this project consisted of a combination of elements from the work of William A. McDonough, former Dean of the School of Architecture at the University of Virginia and designer of buildings and products that incorporate environmental considerations (Gutfield 1989). The protocol also reflected McDonough's partnership with Michael Braungart, founder of the Environmental Protection Encouragement Agency (EPEA) in Hamburg, Germany (Hawken and McDonough 1993).

McDonough and Braungart proposed a series of guidelines for use when designing a new product (McDonough and Braungart 1998; Hawken 1997). The core of these consists of:

☐ Waste equals food

☐ Rely on current solar income

☐ Respect diversity

The guidelines require products to be designed so that their disposal is compatible with natural processes (Braungart and Engelfried 1992; William McDonough Architects 1992; Braungart *et al.* 1993; McDonough 1993).

In August of 1993, Lyons contacted William McDonough, who presented his design philosophy to her. According to Lyons:

> Two key principles hit home really hard: the idea that waste equals food and the idea of a cradle-to-cradle design, not a cradle-to-grave design.

McDonough stated that, in order to meet the waste equals food and cradle-to-cradle design criteria, the product had to be able: to compost completely with no negative environmental impacts, thereby becoming food for other organisms (organic nutrients) or to become raw material for another industrial product (technical nutrients);[2] and to be manufactured without the release of carcinogens, bioaccumulatives, persistent toxic chemicals, mutagens, heavy metals or endocrine disrupters.

This information was passed to Kälin who was struck by the 'waste equals food' principle. He realised that the disposal problem could be eliminated if he pursued McDonough's philosophy of zero emissions. If what was coming out of the factory was suitable as food or raw material, there would be no disposal costs (Mehalik *et al.* 1996).

McDonough's design protocols specified requirements for the design of the fabric that was very different from Lyons's and Kälin's original perceptions of what these requirements should be. It established a clear system for why the requirements were important. Making a recyclable product using PET only made sense if the PET yarn was kept in a technical nutrient cycle. Organic cotton only made sense if it was grown without using pesticides or dyes that were not suitable for food for organisms. The fabric, Climatex, was a blend of wool, ramie and polyester which could not be separated and so could not become 'food' for the organic cycle or the technical cycle. Kälin saw that, in order to eliminate the disposal problem, the waste would have to be suitable either for recycling or for composting (Keoleian *et al.* 1995).

The protocol did not provide guidance on what the final design would be in terms of specific chemical composition or manufacturing process. An LCA was needed to work out what chemicals and processes were required.

◢ EPEA's life-cycle development

LCD is a redesign of established procedures for conducting a LCA (SETAC 1991, 1993a, 1993b, 1994; EPA 1993). EPEA personnel characterise the EPEA LCD as containing: scoping, inventory, impact and improvement stages. Inventory, impact analysis and optimisation decisions are simultaneous. Because design protocol compatible materials are used, little new data is needed. During the investigation, the scope and focus may shift. Analysts set priorities for optimisation by examining quantitative and qualitative impacts of material and energy flows.[3] The EPEA has categorised substances as follows:

A   Fully optimised concerning environmental and health soundness

B   Suitable in principle but needing optimisation along the life-cycle

C   Not optimisable over the life-cycle but tolerable in the short term and to be excluded when alternatives are available

2   The organic and the technical should not be mixed or the end-product cannot be used either as food for organisms or as raw materials for technology.
3   Personal communication with Alain Rivière, 16 January 1997.

X To be excluded because of severe environmental, health and safety problems
and because better alternatives are available [4] (Rivière *et al.* 1997)

The results of this classification are 'positive lists' of substances that are compatible with
the design protocol (EPEA 1996).

An important step was getting parts of the supply chain, such as farmers, yarn spinners,
twisters, dyers and finishers to agree to be evaluated according to the design protocols
and LCD analysis. By the end of January 1994 they had eliminated polyester from Climatex, producing a new blend of ramie and wool called Climatex Lifecycle.

The EPEA conducted its LCD in May 1994 and was able to find 16 out of 1,800 available
dyes that passed the protocol. From these 16 dyes, any colour could be produced except
black (Mehalik *et al.* 1996, Mehalik *et al.* 1997a).

The LCD strategy was applied throughout the supply chain for the manufacturing of
the fabric, from the raw materials up to the point where the product was sold. The LCD
tool was effective in finding the technical solutions needed for the manufacturing of the
fabric product. The LCD did not, however, address issues such as implementing environmental procedures within a firm.

◢ Environmental management systems

Rohner Textil passed its quality system audit in 1994 and received its certificate for quality
management according to ISO 9001. The ISO 9001 certification process also required the
development of a management plan—*The Economy–Ecology Concept 1993–2000*—which
specified responsibility, authority and operational procedures for employees.

The plan contained an emphasis on improving the ecological aspects of Rohner Textil's
products as a natural extension of product quality. In early 1995 there was no approved
standard of environmental quality. However, it was possible to be certified against a draft
of ISO 14001. *The Economy–Ecology Concept 1993–2000* management plan formed the basis
of this certification, which Rohner Textil obtained in April 1996.

An important part of the planning stage for implementing an ISO 14001 system is
identifying a firm's significant environmental aspects. Rohner Textil had in place such an
identification system as part of its *Economy–Ecology* management plan. The firm had also
implemented a strategy called 'eco-controlling' to quantify the environmental aspects in
order to set priorities at the product level. First, a set of impact categories is identified.
Within each impact category a rating is assigned and an overall sum is computed for the
product. The raw score for each product reveals which products need improvement in
their environmental aspects. Rohner Textil then uses the raw score to compute an overall
measure of impact based on a coefficient that reflects each product's percentage of overall
sales (Mehalik *et al.* 1997a).

---

4   Personal communications with Alain Rivière, 16 January 1997 and 23 September 1998.

An EMS was important because it communicated a corporate strategy and a vision, and it supplemented expert judgement. It was also needed to identify important environmental aspects associated with Rohner Textil's operations and its products (Mehalik *et al.* 1997b).

◢ Life-cycle cost accounting

Life-cycle cost accounting attempts to describe all costs associated with the design, production, use and disposal or re-use stages of a product. In this case Kälin was concerned with the ecological impacts of products because he perceived that Swiss environmental regulation would be on the increase. Unforeseen changes in regulations could have a significant impact on Rohner Textil because of long product life-cycles—up to 15 years. In addition, the mill needed new looms and dye equipment to improve productivity. The owners, Forster-Rohner, made it clear that any capital investments would have to be earned by the mill, which put it in a tough position because of already thin operating margins (Mehalik *et al.* 1998a).

◢ Environmental cost controlling

Kälin began from a position typical of many companies in that environmental costs were not allocated according to specific cost functions (Popoff and Buzzelli 1993). So, in 1995, as a first step, Kälin included environmental costs in the end-of-year figures, taking an inventory of environmental costs using specific categories instead of aggregating them as overheads.

Kälin allocated the material environmental cost portion of environmental expenses directly in the calculation of producing each product. This added about 2% to the cost of the net material costs of production. The effect was to distribute the material environmental costs, which constituted 75% of the total calculated environmental costs, across the product lines that generated the material wastes. Climatex Lifecycle, which generated compostable wastes, was excluded from this charge. This method of allocation was nearly activity-based (Cartin 1993). If changing the contents of the product to reduce disposal costs could eliminate disposal costs, the 2% value can be viewed as a savings relative to other product lines.

Climatex Lifecycle trimmings were sent to a felt manufacturer which shredded and combined them into blankets. The blankets were sold in a local gardening shop as gardening blankets placed around plants to initially reduce weed growth. The blankets eventually composted in the garden, becoming garden fertiliser. And so the waste trimmings were converted into a saleable product.

◢ Environmental accounting for investment purposes

The other strategy that Kälin employed was to find a way to free capital for improving productivity. He was able to solve this problem through the canton of St Gallen's tax system, which permitted higher depreciation of environmental investments. Kälin convinced Forster-Rohner to include in the 1993 budget 1% of the total for ecological investments. He invested the money in high-energy-efficiency heating equipment and high-efficiency dye plant facilities. The investment resulted in savings from reduced energy usage.

◢ Conclusion

One outcome of this project was a fabric that was suitable for disposal by composting, that was aesthetically appealing, price-competitive, and that met all industry performance standards. Another outcome was a systematic reduction of emissions and energy usage. Rohner Textil's environmental statements illustrate the combined effects of implementing a range of tools on resource and energy usage, costs and emissions (Kälin 1996, 1998).

One reason for these outcomes was that the tools discussed in this chapter were effectively integrated, thus creating network partnerships that were complementary and that addressed specific product- and system-related environmental concerns (Mehalik 2000).

Rohner Textil occupied a difficult position in the marketplace. Its customers expected the highest quality, combined with unique customised designs. The company had little margin for experimentation and was facing a competitiveness problem because of outdated equipment. Further, it was recognised that current and future environmental costs posed serious constraints on the company's ability to compete. It needed to innovate or perish. The creative solution was to recognise that pursuing a strategy of environmental improvement could be a source of competitive advantage. Kälin positioned the mill to reconcile environmental concerns with economic concerns in the ISO 14001-certified EMS. By using tools such as 'eco-controlling', he was able to gauge environmental problems associated with Rohner Textil's products. The act of attributing environmental problems to the production process was a major step towards controlling the problems.

Kälin also needed to find a way of paying for changes to improve Rohner Textil's environmental problems. Finding tax relief based on environmental criteria permitted the integration of environmental costs in Rohner Textil's accounting system, thus enabling substantial capital investments that resulted in further improvements to the technical and environmental performance of the manufacturing system. The potential to demonstrate environmental cost savings furthered efforts to strengthen the link between accounting and environmental performance. The result was a situation in which Kälin was constantly finding ways to save money through reducing environmentally related expenses and improving long-term stability by avoiding the risk of the high cost of compliance with potential future regulation changes.

The ISO 14001 management system, cost accounting, eco-controlling and tax relief tools served to align several of Rohner Textil's operational functions with a common strategy of achieving competitive advantage by cost and risk reduction through environmental improvement.

But in itself this was not enough. At the time, the most 'environmentally friendly' product was Climatex which was only 'human ecology'-certified. The production of Climatex generated waste in the form of trimmings which had high disposal costs. Nor did the certification appeal sufficiently to customers such as DesignTex. This is where the design protocol tool served as a complementary aid to the members of this project network. McDonough and Braungart provided a clear vision for the project that aligned the tools Kälin was using at Rohner Textil with a strategy of product redesign. The EPEA LCD provided the framework for choosing materials for the product or process changes, but within the strategy of the design protocol and with regard to the operational tools already being implemented at Rohner Textil. The continuous improvement strategy coupled with the protocol and the LCD permitted the project to move beyond the strategy of 'control' to one of optimisation of environmental quality. The eco-controlling system permitted the team to measure progress across various product lines. By introducing environmental costs into the cost of producing products, the team could measure need for improvement at both the process and product level. The result was a reduction in disposal costs once the compostable fabric went into production. Coupled with the cost savings that were accruing due to the installation of capital improvements, such as an improved heating system and dye plant, the integrated tools were having an accumulative effect both in terms of product and process improvements.

Most importantly, however, all of the tools were aligned according to a common vision that was easily and credibly communicable to customers and members of the supply chain. Climatex Lifecycle was able to produce a market sensation that customers responded to positively, and competing firms were unable to offer quick alternatives, giving Rohner Textil and DesignTex a competitive edge in the marketplace.

By eliminating any one of these components, the network had the potential to fall apart. Susan Lyons of DesignTex integrated the network at the beginning and maintained it throughout the process of production to the product's introduction to the marketplace. Aligning the network members according to a common strategy was fundamental to integrating the environmental design tools (Mehalik 2000). This successful alignment may account for the reason why a 30-person textile mill and surrounding supplier and customer network could consider a wide array of environmental tools while some other companies with much greater resources have difficulty implementing any of these tools, piecemeal or otherwise.

Other firms' abilities to meet the challenges of aligning network members and tools around a common strategy will ultimately determine whether the processes described in this chapter are repeatable. This is an empirical question to be worked in practice at different firms that are facing their own sets of contingencies, environmental and competitive challenges.

ISO 14001 AND DESIGN FOR THE ENVIRONMENT
A strategy for proactive design in building design, construction and renovation

Riva Krut
Benchmark Environmental
Consulting, USA

Jim Strycharz
New York City
Transit Authority, USA

This chapter describes the implementation of ISO 14001 at New York City Transit Authority (NYCTA)'s department of Capital Program Management (CPM). CPM designs and manages the construction of some $2 billion in capital projects per annum. The challenge of implementing ISO 14001 was to implement a system designed for a fixed manufacturing facility in a project-based organisation where most of the work is delivered by contractors.

The challenges CPM faced were how to use ISO 14001 as an instrument to implement design for environment (DfE) principles, how to fit the ISO 14001 EMS model into a project-based, public-sector organisation and, finally, how to use the EMS to manage contractors. These three challenges are described in this chapter.

◢ Why implement ISO 14001 at CPM?

The catalyst and promoter of this project throughout was Ajay Singh, chief of internal controls and special projects. Singh's motivation was a mixture of personal conviction and political acuity:

> In my lifetime, I have seen the deleterious impact of industrialization and urbanization on the natural environment. Here at the Transit Authority, we

face a paradox: we are working with an inherently sustainable product—public transportation in New York City. But we don't think of making the process of delivering this product more environmentally sound. The potential for a significant impact on the whole of New York City and all its inhabitants and riders is just huge, and we were not even thinking about it.

What we had are environmental management activities focussed on meeting regulatory requirements. Asbestos abatement was the focus of our environmental management work. We needed an EMS that could provide us with a structure to proactively control environmental issues across the whole life-cycle of our design and construction projects. It was especially crucial that we focus not reactively on abatement, but proactively on environmental issues from the pre-design stage. Such an EMS would allow us to control risks, costs, over-runs and so on. The question was, how could we achieve what was in fact a culture change in CPM, a typical public-sector organization?

In 1998, I saw an opportunity in ISO 14001. Here was a flag that we could put in the ground, something that we could rally troops around, and something that we could implement here at CPM and then roll out through the larger transit organization.

With these motivations, Singh not only named the flag but also waved it. He sold the vision to his manager, the senior vice-president and chief engineer of CPM, Mysore Nagaraja. Nagaraja responded with complete support. He was particularly interested in the implementation of a structured, measurable system to identify and quantify CPM's environmental impacts. He responded with a challenge to Singh and his staff to obtain registration to ISO 14001 within nine months.

Step 1: Implementing DfE through ISO 14001

The first job was to shift the minds of the engineers from technical and regulatory compliance issues to the upstream design phase. One of the key implementers of the EMS was Tom Abdallah, senior engineer in the environmental engineering division (EED):

> When I was first asked to describe the life-cycle of a building and construction project, I said, well, first we dig a hole. Boy, have I—have we—changed our perspective since then. We have realized that our principal environmental impact is at the pre-design and master plan stage. The later in the project life-cycle that we try to manage environmental issues, the more difficult it is to be successful, and the less return you get on your effort.

As Nagaraja emphasises:

> We have to think of ourselves as a *design* and construction *management* operation, not as construction engineers.

Fortunately for the EMS advocates, the concept of emphasising the importance of getting things right at the design stage was, in any case, receiving attention at the highest levels in the organisation. A new CPM procedure on master planning proved to be completely consistent with what the EMS was trying to do. A master plan is created for any large capital project, to define it and set a preliminary budget. It is on the basis of this that design alternatives are proposed, a design selected and budget fixed, and bids put out to architects. CPM's new master plan procedure emphasised that careful thinking was required at the pre-design stage. It also provided an opportunity in the preliminary master plan budget for the master plan manager to project forward the quantitative and qualitative benefits of the facility *in use*. This provided an opportunity to make environmental performance issues a consideration in the selection of design alternatives. We were able to show how implementing the EMS was completely consistent with the master plan procedure—to show the organisation that we were not introducing something new, but implementing with the EMS as a key existing strategic objective. This integration was stressed at all EMS training, and all training in the new procedure had a short session on the EMS.

What does DfE mean in design and construction? This issue is increasingly coming under discussion in the US and, particularly, in New York City as it enters the 21st century. Two helpful developments to CPM were, first, the development by the US Green Building Council of a certification system called LEED—Leadership in Energy and Environmental Design (LEED 1999). This provides a system to certify a building that has been designed and built to a level that exceeds those required by the best regulations in the US (state or federal). The advantage of this for CPM is that a facility can apply for a LEED medal that could be placed on a building that recognises design and construction, rather than improved environmental performance for the users. The second development was the production of a workbook, *High Performance Building Guidelines* (City of New York 1999), by the City of New York Office of Sustainable Design and Construction. Copies of this were circulated to environmental engineers and key other managers; Hilary Brown, assistant commissioner at the Office of Sustainable Design and Construction, briefed the EED.

CPM spent time learning about these initiatives and broadcasting this knowledge through the organisation in its intensive training programme for environmental engineers as well as master plan, design and construction managers.

Step 2: Fitting ISO 14001 into a project-based, public-sector organisation

One of the biggest challenges of implementing ISO 14001 at CPM was that there was not an immediate fit between CPM's operation and the organisational assumptions of the standard. Although the text of ISO 14001 notes that the standard was written for all sorts of organisations, it assumes that the EMS is being implemented in a fixed facility such as a manufacturing operation. The assumption is that the facility controls most of its operations—and consequently its environmental impacts. In contrast, CPM is a project-based, service organisation. Most of the projects are delivered through third parties—architects and building contractors—who are subcontracted to do some of the design and all of the building. A typical CPM project might be a bus station design-and-build project in the Bronx, a project that could take five years, cost some $50 million, and involve both internal professionals and contracted specialists and service providers, e.g. an architect and the builder.

At CPM, we do not believe that our organisation is an old-fashioned public-sector organisation. On the contrary, more and more organisations in the developed world are service- and project-based (Allenby 1999). These organisations cannot manage environmental issues only by managing issues within their facilities. We have to look upstream to design issues and downstream to supplier and contractor management. In doing so, CPM had to move way beyond the structure of ISO 14001. We believe that we have created a state-of-the-art, highly effective and creative EMS that may have lessons for project-based, supplier-dependent, private- or public-sector entities. We used ISO as a backbone, but built a unique EMS organisation.

The new CPM EMS organisation was, from the start, managed by a core team, strongly supported by a cross-functional team (CFT) of managers from within and outside of CPM, including the NYCTA legal counsel, senior staff from the Office of System Safety (OSS), and programme, design and construction managers. The CFT was critical in getting the message out about ISO 14001 and the CPM EMS, and winning support from groups that our EMS depends on for success. The EMS has also clearly defined the work of a cadre of environmental specialists within EED (see Fig. 21.1).

Figure 21.1 **The CPM EMS structure and organisation**
Source: NYCTA, Department of Capital Programs Management

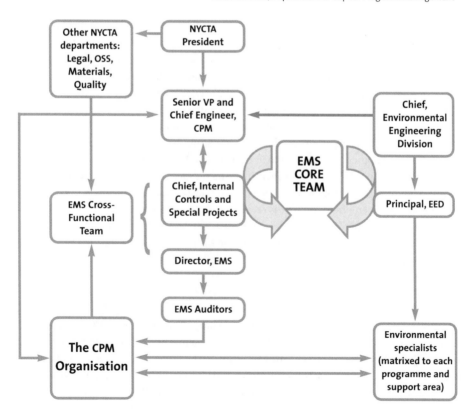

A key to project-based organisations is to understand that internal specialists move between projects and are required to trade their expertise and exercise influence without having line authority. In organisations that combine project and line structures, such as CPM, there can be conflict between project specialists and the line. At CPM, there was already a structure that 'matrixed' quality specialists to projects for the purposes of integrating quality. The EMS organisation we created made use of a model for integrating line and project functions through the use of in-house consultants that we called 'environmental specialists'. Engineers from the EED already performed a variety of tasks such as investigating projects at pre-design stage to see what regulatory obligations it might have—in relation to natural resources, community disruption and air quality—and investigating whether a formal environmental impact assessment (EIA) was required by law. They also provided various support services to the construction manager once building had begun. This nascent structure was built on to create a unique role for environmental specialists within the CPM EMS organisation.

Tasks have been defined for environmental specialists at all stages along the life-cycle of a project. The CPM EMS now provides a procedure that requires environmental special-ists to exercise their influence before and at the master plan stage. The job of environ-mental specialists now includes a number of specific tasks at the master plan stage (see Box 21.1). EED has invested in training, not just of our own staff on process and technical skills, but on awareness training of the master plan and design and construction managers.

Another issue that quickly surfaced was how to show the environmental value of the EMS. Most of the value of an EMS as applied to building design and construction will be felt in the *use* of the building (reduced energy costs, better indoor air quality, and so on). But CPM is not involved in the use of the facility and reaps no benefits from the better environmental performance of the building in use. As we discovered in the process of EMS implementation, this is a dilemma frequently faced in public-sector and other organisations that are organised along strictly functional lines. Once a new programme has been developed for users not in the originating department, it moves under the management of others, and the originators are cut off from programme implementation and from enjoying the benefits of their investment. Over time, this builds in disincen-tives to initiative and thinking 'out of the box'. It is also a standard problem in real estate development, where the developer is creating value for the tenant. In the world of real estate, if this additional value is reflected in additional capital costs, it is difficult to find buyers or renters willing to pay the premium on the selling or rental price of the unit. At the NYCTA, we were concerned that environmentally sound design would not necessarily result in users doing things in a more environmentally friendly way.

When we started putting the EMS in place, there was no incentive for CPM to deliver an environmentally efficient building. Nor, because NYCTA is a public-sector organisa-tion, does CPM measure or try to reduce the quantity of energy it uses. This issue will be partly addressed through the work of the environmental specialists at the master plan stage, where they have an opportunity to estimate the environmental costs of different design decisions and materials specifications. This change cannot be expected to happen overnight, as environmental accounting is a difficult job, and the subject is new to CPM.

At the Master Plan stage, it is the job of the Environmental Specialist to support the Master Plan Manager with the following:

1. **Recognition of environmental issues** through a report on potential environmental issues, and a judgement about whether an Environmental Impact Assessment (EIA) is legally required. This report should be provided in a timely manner to the Master Plan Manger, Program Managers, Chief, EED, and EMS Coordinator. It should take into account:

   ☐ Legal and Other Requirements Database (first preliminary draft)

   ☐ Aspects and Impacts Identification (first preliminary draft)

   ☐ Ideas on the prevention of pollution and Design for Environment (DfE)

   ☐ EMS criteria in Consultant and Contractor selection

2. **Prepare and submit an EIA, if required**, in a timely manner to the Master Plan Manager, the Design Manager, the Chief, EED, and the EMS Coordinator.

3. **Provide the Master Plan Manager with the following services and technical advice:**

   ☐ Methods to understand the environmental and economic impact of various design alternatives.

   ☐ Methods to understand basic assumptions about Asset Useful Life and the lifespan of materials or substances under consideration for the project

   ☐ Identify responsible parties, schedule, and methods for addressing external agency considerations. Items to be discussed/listed include: special approval and permits; environmental impact statements; historic preservation; community relations; access for the disabled.

   ☐ Working with the Field Services Representative, calculate the cost of proposed environmental-related materials, standards, codes or construction techniques; or the environmental cost of these. Supply enough environmental information so that design costing can be made accurately.

   ☐ Working with the Field Services Representative, provide information so that the financial impacts of environmental investments can be realized, and *vice versa* (the environmental impacts of financial investments). For example, reduced energy costs because of design efficiency.

   ☐ Provide information so that the non-financial environmental benefits of each project can be realized and a dollar value attributed. For example, improved airflow in a station could result in less requirement for heating and cooling technologies.

Box 21.1 **Environmental specialists: responsibilities at the master plan stage [*extract*]**

However, the ideas of the EMS have had a gratifying reception from some key players at all points in the organisation.

John Payyapilli is a design manager from the electrical programmes area, who was not involved in the EMS until after ISO registration in March 1999. Since then, he has become an enthusiastic advocate. He comments:

> We [design managers] have been dealing with 'environmental' issues for years, but it was not until the EMS was introduced and broadcast through the organization that we started to think about green design, the concept of a high-performance building, and environmentally friendly technologies. We are

looking at these aspects in projects going forward. We are presently looking at the CPM design guidelines to see how these can be modified to support DfE and the EMS.

Step 3: Managing contractors

A third issue that was complex for the integration of ISO 14001 into CPM was that most of CPM's work is undertaken by third parties—consultants and contractors. ISO 14001 makes only passing reference to suppliers and contractors. We had to decide early on how to deal with this issue. Placing environmental conditions on contractors could not be done casually: CPM is the largest construction contractor in the New York City area and any message it sent would ripple through the construction community. As a public-sector organisation, there were a myriad of legal issues to consider in altering procurement practices and the rules of competition. On the other hand, if it was the right message it could have a positive impact on building in the city.

There were several hurdles to overcome in this area, and in the end this was easily done. First was to get the agreement of the procurement department to the alteration of procurement conditions. This is currently in progress and we anticipate completion during 2000. We found support in a new NYCTA policy that came from the OSS which is a separate department from CPM. It manages safety across the organisation, not only in construction projects but also passenger safety. At the end of 1998, it published a new policy/instruction (P/I) called *TA P/I 8.3.2: Environmental Management Program* (EMP). Ajay Singh notes:

> One of the new issues the EMP directs the whole Transit Authority to address is that of putting environmental issues into procurement and contracting decisions. As this OSS policy is applicable throughout the Transit Authority, CPM, a junior partner to OSS, was able to ride behind this initiative and claim that we were implementing what was now a requirement from OSS. A first step towards contractor environmental management was achieved with the drafting of a letter to contractors in June 1999 that informs them of CPM's EMS initiative and encourages them to align their EMSs with ISO 14001 [see Box 21.2].

The letter recommends that contractors align their EMS with ISO 14001.

◢ Early results from ISO 14001 implementation

The CPM EMS manual has been published; CPM achieved registration to ISO 14001 in March 1999 and successfully passed the review audit in September 1999. The auditor, Underwriters' Laboratories, who also audit CPM's ISO 9001 conformance, commented that the degree of improvement and implementation in the six months since the previous audit was highly impressive. Apart from the intensive commitment to the education and training of environmental specialists within the EED, the process of integrating environmental management into the earliest phases of the project is now well under way.

NYCTA–CPM

June 10, 1999

Re: NYC–Capital Program Management–Environmental Policy

Dear Sir or Madam,

The New York City Transit Authority Department of Capital Program Management (CPM) has a longstanding commitment to compliance with applicable environmental laws and regulations. Recently, we have raised the bar and have implemented an Environmental Management System (EMS) that conforms to the September 1996 International Organization for Standardization (ISO) 14001 EMS Standard. This is the sister standard to ISO 9001, the Quality Management Systems Standard to which we have been already certified. Our EMS has been certified as being in conformance with ISO 14001.

ISO 14001 is a voluntary standard that identifies the core elements of a system necessary for an organization to achieve its environmental goals and effectively manage its impacts on the environment. The ultimate objective of the standard is to integrate that system with the organization's overall business processes and systems so that environmental considerations are a routine factor in its business decisions. The ISO 14001 EMS Standard has quickly become recognized as the benchmark of sound industry environmental management practices.

The foundation of our CPM's EMS is our recently issued Environmental Policy Statement, a copy of which is enclosed.

CPM's commitment to environmental leadership includes doing business with suppliers and contractors who fulfill their environmental obligations responsibly. Our contracts with you require that you comply with all applicable environmental laws and regulations when you perform work for CPM, including the provision of services and materials. In the future, as in the past, you will be responsible for conducting necessary environmental training of your personnel and for assuring that they are competent to perform work for CPM. Although this does not affect your ongoing contracts, in future, in order to assure conformance with our new EMS, we will be communicating to you any additional CPM EMS requirements we determine are applicable to your work for CPM.

CPM encourages you to align your EMS with the criteria of ISO 14001 and to pursue registration under this International Standard. In our view, doing so will not only be an act of good corporate citizenship, but also a good business decision.

Should you have any questions regarding CPM's new EMS or ISO 14001, please contact Ajay Singh, Director, Internal Controls and Special Projects, at 718 243 7039.

Sincerely,

Mysore Nagaraja
Senior Vice-President and Chief Engineer

Box 21.2 **CPM letter to contractors informing them of CPM's ISO 14001 registration**

Environmental specialists have begun working to integrate environmental issues into the master plan for several new projects. Managers putting together bids are sending their drafts to the EMS organisation for suggestions and comments. Further downstream, there are opportunities for the integration of environmental technologies into construction. The most obvious is the use of photovoltaic cells as solar energy sources for NYCTA facilities. Discussion of the integration of photovoltaics into two bus station building projects and one subway station rehabilitation are now under way. Most importantly, consultants and contractors now see this as a 'value added' contribution that they can make to NYCTA projects, and some of them have made presentations to CPM about their technical resources in this area.

◢ Lessons learned

Several lessons are clear from this experience:

1. **A visionary or champion at the top is crucial.** A senior manager well placed in the organisation is absolutely key to the success of any programme of organisational change. His or her task is to set stretching goals and to garner political support both within and beyond the organisation or division getting registered. Mysore Nagaraja, senior vice-president and chief engineer of CPM, supported by Ajay Singh, chief of internal controls and special projects, played these roles admirably.

2. **Define the EMS organisation carefully and gather allies on whom the success of the EMS will ultimately depend.** Given the rather unique challenges we faced of fitting an EMS designed for a fixed industrial facility onto a project-based, design and contractor management organisation, the structure of the EMS organisation was not obvious. In the case of CPM, the core team was the architect of the EMS organisation. It made careful use of the broader political resources of the cross-functional team. The CFT achieved the political objectives of getting buy-in from users and other departments that could have become obstacles if they had not been involved in the design of the EMS organisation from the start.

3. **Find existing initiatives within the organisation that support the EMS, and ride on their coat-tails.** In order to achieve the CPM EMS, it was important to support the new procedure on master planning, gaining allies in that area and accelerating its acceptance. We were also able to gain support from the OSS's new EMP and its directive that environmental issues should be integrated into procurement. In both cases, we emphasised as often as possible that ISO 14001 was consistent with what was already being promoted in the NYCTA, sometimes by more powerful players than those spearheading the CPM EMS. By emphasising that we were followers rather than leaders, we were able to win support and

push both the other programme and our EMS, more quickly than if we had insisted on going it alone. The EMS structure also used and built on nascent organisational structures—for example, where the environmental specialists 'matrixed' to projects—to create the EMS organisation.

4. **Seek out and use external resources**. We sought out and discovered very helpful external initiatives that were coming out at the perfect time for our needs. In our case, there was a great deal that we could use and learn from, particularly the LEED and the high-performance building design principles. Scouting out and using materials that had already been piloted elsewhere saved time, risk and resources.

5. **Develop a pool of recognised internal technical competence.** The whole-hearted support of the EED to the EMS initiative gave the project hands and feet. It committed significant resources and energy to refining the procedures for inserting environmental issues into CPM projects, from the refinement of the methodology for aspect and impact identification, to starting to allocate environmental specialists to projects at the master plan stage. In addition, it has embarked on a comprehensive training programme, delivered to its own staff of environmental specialists as well as to master plan, design and construction managers.

The combination of the above has borne fruit. In the event, the EMS has become warmly endorsed throughout the NYCTA and there is active discussion about rolling ISO 14001 out in more departments.

◢ Conclusions

The most important enduring lesson for CPM was that it does not perform just an engineering function, but a design and contractor management function too. This understanding has helped it to redefine the focus of its activities from operations and compliance management to DfE and contractor management. In principle, the new emphasis on design made sense to the organisation. It was consistent with the quality management adage of 'get it right first time.' It was consistent with the new guidelines on master planning. And the engineers understood well the logic that it always costs more time and money to have to redo work. But, in practice, proactive environmental management and the introduction of DfE tools would not have happened without the introduction of ISO 14001.

As intended, the implementation of ISO 14001 in the organisation became the rallying 'flag'. Senior management endorsed ISO 14001 and provided resources for the EMS design and implementation. Even though some professionals at first failed to understand the applicability of ISO 14001 to CPM, it was easier to justify the effort by reference to an international EMS standard with status than simply to another consulting or organisational change effort. Gradually, some of the most sceptical managers have become enthusiasts for the EMS and the broader ISO 14001 objectives.

This raises the question of what ISO 14001 itself achieved at CPM. It is clear to us that the particular design and results we have achieved would not necessarily have come about from any implementation of the standard. Other consultants and advocates may have ended up with a different EMS design that could have still achieved registration. In practice, it was absolutely key that we did not implement ISO 14001 by the letter. By doing so, we might have conscientiously created aspects and impacts that met the requirement of the standard but were not of practical use for CPM. For example, we might have simply replicated the existing organisational biases that required work to start by 'digging a hole'. It was vital that we always stopped to reflect on what the standard gave us and, if the process didn't give us results that felt right, we stopped and thought 'out of the box' and then forced this logic back onto the standard. The result was the best kind of use of the ISO 14001 standard—as a language with which we created a fully customised EMS.

Moreover, in an environment where the dominant reaction at the start ranged from lack of interest to antagonism, the fact that we could wave an external standard was essential to our success. The EMS structure that we created, and the management system, will remain crucial to the maintenance and continual improvement of the EMS. We will design performance objectives that relate to DfE, but retain the architecture of our ISO 14001-compliant EMS.

The LEED certificate provides us with a way of achieving our objective of installing DfE by simply specifying at the master plan stage that the project should be designed and built to achieve this. This can then be reflected in the scope of work. How this is accomplished becomes the job of the consultant architect and the contractor (builder). The job of the CPM EMS leadership in the coming period will be to define a management plan that specifies how many LEED certificates should be achieved each year. In time, they will become routine for building and rehabilitation of the large real estate inventory managed by the NYCTA. We also hope that the combination of these requirements for architects and the ensuing requirements of contractors that will come from new design and material specifications, as well as the requirement that they align their EMS with ISO 14001, will have positive results for the residents and riding public of New York City.

ISO 14001 AND THE ADOPTION OF NEW TECHNOLOGY
Evidence from Western Australian companies

Dora Marinova
Murdoch University, Australia

William Altham
Curtin University of Technology, Australia

It has become textbook wisdom these days that sustainable development requires new technologies (Freeman and Soete 1997), commonly described as 'environmentally friendly', 'green', 'clean' or 'eco-efficient'. The academic community agrees that there is a need for this new generation of technologies (Beder 1994; Heaton 1997). Industry and the wider community, however, find the introduction and use of these technological changes difficult or slow because of a series of economic and regulatory impediments.

The formation of the international voluntary group of standards ISO 14000 and, in particular, the adoption in 1996 of ISO 14001 which covers environmental management systems (EMSs) in an integrated way, has given rise to hopes for an increase in the adoption of environmental technology. It has been seen as a powerful tool to improve the management of the environment (i.e. the people and institutions affecting the environment) as well as part of the beginning of a new regulatory era of acceptance of voluntary initiatives and deregulation (Begley 1996; Tibor and Feldman 1996). Companies soon started to learn that environmental and financial benefits can go hand in hand and what is good for the environment is often just as good for their bottom line (Scott 1999).

The ISO 14000 group of voluntary standards has also been strongly criticised. Krut and Gleckman (1998: 1) describe it as an élitist approach 'designed to meet the needs of the most active members of a private club', which has left behind issues such as equity and democracy, broad participation and community involvement in environmental decision-making.

The standard series requires companies to periodically measure and review the significant aspects of their environmental impacts, but not to disclose the results. Explicitly excluded from the scope of the standards are test methods and limit values for pollutants and effluents, setting of environmental performance levels and product standardisation (Hortensius and Barthel 1997: 22). A number of industries worldwide have raised concerns about the use of ISO 14001 as a trade barrier preventing non-certified companies from supplying certified multinationals (Zuckerman 1999).

The adoption of ISO 14001 among countries around the world varies, with Japan, Germany and the UK registering the largest numbers of industrial sites by December 1999 (see Table 22.1) and the US being relatively slow. Sweden, Denmark and Switzerland have the largest number of sites on a per capita basis. With 350 certified sites, Australian companies have responded in a relatively positive way to EMS with a rate of uptake similar to Japan, Germany and the UK.

In 1999, we conducted a number of case studies among Western Australian companies, focusing on the introduction of new technologies. We left aside questions relating to the nature and purpose of ISO 14001 as we wanted to find out whether EMS has contributed to the implementation and transfer of environmental technologies. This area has not been addressed before, and it was highly interesting to discover differences in the uptake of new technologies among certified and non-certified companies. The rest of the chapter examines the results from these case studies.

In the next section, evidence from the interviews is presented. This is followed by a discussion on the role certification plays for companies in the implementation and dispersion of environmental technologies. The chapter concludes with a positive assessment of the contribution ISO 14001 has made, so far, for the introduction of these technologies in Western Australian companies.

◢ The case studies

Western Australian-based companies with sites that are certified to ISO 14001 (referred to as EMS companies) were interviewed first. We then matched these with companies from

Table 22.1   **ISO 14001 certified sites by country, 31 December 1999**

Source: Calculated from www.ecology.or.jp/isoworld/english/analy14k.htm and
www.census.gov/ftp/pub/ipc/www/idbprint.html

Country	Registered sites	Number of sites per 1 million persons
Japan	2,773	22
Germany	1,800	22
UK	1,014	17
Sweden	850	95
US	711	3
Taiwan	652	29
Netherlands	530	34
Korea	463	10
France	442	7
Switzerland	413	57
Australia	350	19
Denmark	350	65

Industry	Number of EMS companies	Number of non-EMS companies	Total
Civil engineering	2	2	4
Commercial cleaning and maintenance	1	1	2
Gas supply	1	1	2
Mining	2	4	6
Panel beating and automobile repairs	2	2	4
Pumps manufacturing	1	1	2
Recycling and waste management	1	1	2
Steel fabrication	1	1	2
Waste and waste-water treatment	1	1	2
Total number of companies	12	14	26

EMS = environmental management systems; EMS companies = companies that are ISO 14001-certified; non-EMS companies = non-certified companies

Table 22.2 **Industry sector and number of Western Australian companies covered in the case studies**

the same industry sectors that did not have certified ISO 14001 sites (non-EMS companies). Kemp and Soete (1992) claim that the demand for cleaner production technologies depends mainly on government regulation while the demand for cleaner consumer products arises from the wider environmental concerns of the public. Clark (1999) stresses that the decision to certify for ISO 14001 is a result of a combination of factors, such as customer pressure, peer pressure, stakeholder interests, improved performance and integrated management systems.

The two groups of companies in this study—EMS and non-EMS—are positioned in approximately similar circumstances in respect to all these factors. They have matching products and services, operate in the same regulatory conditions and serve a market with similar consumer preferences.

The case study sample comprises a total of 26 companies, 12 of which are EMS companies and 14 are non-EMS. A breakdown by industry is given in Table 22.2. The EMS companies surveyed represent 100% of non-mining companies and 40% of mining companies with ISO 14001 certification in Western Australia.[1] We have deliberately included in the sample two extra non-certified companies from mining, as this is the main industry sector contributing to the Western Australian economy and exports.

Table 22.3 gives data on the introduction of new technologies, including environmental technologies, since 1996. The adopted working definition for environmental/clean/green technology was: 'the intent of the technology is to reduce overall environmental impact and/or the advantages/benefits of the technology include a significant reduction in environmental impacts of the company's activities'. The focus was on production or process technologies as distinct from environmental/green products. The following ten classes were explicitly used to specify environmental technologies:

☐ Energy conservation technology

☐ Raw material conservation technology

1 Standards Australia JAS-ANZ database, 8 April 1999.

Adopted new technologies	EMS companies	non-EMS companies	per EMS company	per non-EMS company
Environmental	51	41	4.3	2.9
Non-environmental	19	25	1.6	1.8
Total	70	66	5.8	4.7

Table 22.3 **Adoption of new technologies by Western Australian companies, 1996–99**

☐ Water conservation technology

☐ Renewable energy technology

☐ Material recycling technology

☐ Water recycling and re-use technology

☐ Pollution control technology

☐ Waste reduction technology

☐ Waste processing and waste disposal technology

☐ Rehabilitation technology

Examples for such technologies include: closed-loop water collection for water recycling and re-use; photovoltaics for energy generation as a renewable energy technology; systems allowing re-use of air and oil filters as material recycling technologies; biodegradable chemicals as pollution-control technology. A number of technologies fall under more than one category. For example, a new metal-cutting machine could contribute to the conservation of energy and raw materials as well as to waste reduction and pollution control.

The list of environmental technologies is long, but there are a lot of recent and progressive technologies that do not fall into any of these categories. A straightforward example is upgrading of computer systems and we found during the case studies that the majority of companies have invested heavily in such technological developments.

The EMS Western Australian companies appear to be more innovative (Table 22.3) with 5.8 new technologies adopted per company compared with 4.7 for the non-EMS companies (24% more). The fact that the non-EMS companies have adopted fewer new technologies implies that they are probably likely to continue to use older technologies longer; hence, they are potentially more prone to represent an environmental risk.

The two groups appear to be relatively similar when it comes to the introduction of general technologies (1.6 per EMS and 1.8 per non-EMS firm). The difference is when it comes to environmental technologies (4.3 per EMS and 2.9 per non-EMS). The certified companies have adopted 1.5 times more clean technologies than their counterparts. The rate of adoption of environmental technologies by the non-certified companies is actually higher than the introduction of general technologies, which is indicative of certain general positive changes with respect to the environment. They are, however, happening much faster within the EMS group.

Acquisition of new environmental technologies	NOW				IN THE FUTURE			
	EMS firms		Non-EMS firms		EMS firms		Non-EMS firms	
	No	%	No.	%	No.	%	No.	%
Developed in-house	7	58	6	43	8	67	5	36
Developed in collaboration	9	75	9	64	3	25	6	43
Bought from other industries	3	25	6	43	6	50	9	64
No technology introduced/no reply	0	0	3	21	0	0	3	21

Table 22.4 **Sources of new environmental technologies for Western Australian companies, 1996–99**

Collaboration with other organisations is the main source for new environmental technologies for Western Australian companies (Table 22.4). This has been the case for 75% of the EMS and 64% of the non-EMS companies. Fifty-eight per cent of the EMS companies also use their in-house research and development (R&D) capabilities to introduce innovation, which is higher than the current 43% for the non-EMS. In the next five years it is expected that this gap will increase with in-house R&D becoming the main source for EMS and the least-preferred source for non-EMS companies. The importance of technology developed elsewhere and available for purchase is expected to increase for both groups, while there is likely to be less collaboration. A significant share (21%) of the non-EMS companies have not introduced any environmental technology and do not intend to do so in the near future.

The initiative to introduce new technologies comes predominantly from the upper and project management for both groups of companies (Table 22.5). Nevertheless, engineers and ordinary shop-floor workers also appear to have their input in some of the companies. The main difference between the two groups is in relation to regulators. They do not seem to play any role in EMS companies while they are still important for 36% of the non-EMS. EMS companies tend to be ahead of governmental and industry regulations related to the environment while more than a third of the non-EMS companies adopt new technologies in order to comply with existing requirements.

Table 22.5 **Who initiates the introduction of environmental technologies within the Western Australian companies?**

	EMS firms		Non-EMS firms	
	No.	%	No.	%
Upper management	10	83	11	79
Project management	8	67	8	57
Engineers	4	33	6	43
Shop-floor workers	4	33	6	43
Regulators	0	0	5	36
Clients	1	8	1	7

The first exposure to information about environmental technologies varies significantly among the companies. The overall ranking list is presented in Table 22.6. However, the EMS companies appear to be much more versatile in seeking information on new technologies than non-EMS. The average number of sources used is six for EMS companies and five for non-EMS. Only one (9%) EMS company relies on fewer than four sources of information compared with seven (50%) of the non-EMS companies. The top overall source is industry publications, which is used by 76% of companies. This is followed by internal R&D and industry organisations. Information from competitors appears to be the least useful source.

There are important differences between the two groups. The EMS companies have ranked as the highest internal R&D (used by 64%) while non-EMS have indicated information from their peers (50%) to be the most important. In other words, EMS companies rely on their in-house R&D capabilities for solving environmental problems while non-EMS companies seem to follow the leaders and look for already-existing environmental solutions. Collaboration with R&D institutions comes third (after industry publications) for EMS, while it is relatively insignificant for non-EMS.

Active actions (i.e. active search for a solution of identified environmental problem) to solve a problem is the second-most commonly used source for both groups, but it appears to be of average importance. Information from government agencies appears to be less important and is used by only around a third of the companies (36%).

It is clear that the EMS companies have a more proactive attitude towards the introduction of new environmental technologies and consequently are more committed to reducing the impact of their activities on nature, people and human settlements. As a result, they are better informed about the options and existing technical solutions.

Table 22.6 **Exposure of Western Australian companies to information about new environmental technology**

	Overall rank	% firms using	EMS firms		Non-EMS firms	
			Rank	% using	Rank	% using
Industry publications	2.16	76	2.40	91	1.89	64
Internal R&D	2.33	48	1.71	64	3.20	36
Industry organisations	2.77	52	3.86	64	1.50	43
Active actions to solve the problem	3.18	68	3.44	82	2.88	57
Peers	3.38	52	5.50	55	1.57	50
Trade shows	3.75	32	4.25	36	3.25	29
Collaboration with R&D institutions	3.89	36	3.20	45	4.75	29
General publications	3.90	40	4.00	45	3.80	36
Direct sales	4.00	48	5.60	45	2.86	50
Government agencies	4.22	36	3.75	36	4.60	36
Regulators	4.30	40	7.00	27	3.14	50
Other industry	4.70	40	7.40	45	2.00	36
Others (e.g. Internet)	5.00	8	4.00	9	6.00	7
Demonstration projects	5.83	24	8.00	27	3.67	21
Competitors	7.00	24	9.00	27	5.00	21

Companies were permitted to assign the same rank to different sources;
the sample excludes one EMS company.

Another finding from the interviews is that the EMS companies knew much more about the environmental impacts of their businesses, most likely as a result of the environmental review process which is often the first time a comprehensive review of environmental issues has been undertaken at their site(s). They were more aware of the associated problems and were seeking appropriate solutions. Some of the non-EMS companies were reluctant to acknowledge that there was something they could do to avoid existing or possible negative impacts from their main activities. Their attitude was that they comply with regulations and, also, that being in business is so competitive that they cannot risk becoming 'distracted'.

It was also interesting to see how the two different groups of companies perceived the current or possible benefits of the introduction of environmental technologies. The main benefits for the non-EMS group are seen along the lines of energy efficiency, increased productivity and general cost efficiency. They are also driven to change mainly by regulators. Safety issues could also play a part in the decision to introduce new technologies. If the green technologies are at least as good as the others, they could be considered.

The EMS group is not that different from the non-EMS companies in its perceptions of benefits from environmental technologies. Cost reduction, product differentiation, regulatory compliance, energy efficiency, waste reduction and management, reduced toxicity of outputs, improved technical performance, safety and health considerations are major factors in the decision to choose new technologies. However, an important consideration is the way they are perceived by the community, which translates into phrases such as: 'green image', 'good business practices', 'good for the community'. They saw the importance of their image as a tool for improved competitiveness. They also relate environmental technologies to product quality to which non-EMS companies are not fully convinced. One of the EMS companies' managers observed that the 1980s were the time of quality, the 1990s of safety, and the new millennium will be the time for the environment. Nevertheless, only few EMS companies said they are using green technologies because they are good for the environment.

In summary, it becomes apparent from the case studies of the 26 Western Australian companies that the EMS companies outperform the non-EMS ones according to almost all the criteria used. However, the cause–effect situation is not clear: is it because certain companies are more innovative and environmentally oriented that they have certified for ISO 14001, or has the certification become an influencing factor for companies to change the way they do business and look at alternative technologies? Or is it a combination of both?

In order to get some insight into this, we traced the changes in the share of introduced clean technologies to other technologies since the ISO 14001 registration in the case of EMS companies and in the last two years for the non-EMS companies (Table 22.7). Less than half of the companies (46%) have increased this share; however, the increase in the EMS group is 58% compared to 36% for the non-EMS companies. Hence, a significant percentage of the EMS companies have altered their behaviour after ISO 14001 certification. If we make the rough assumption that 36% would have changed anyway (based on the share among the non-certified companies), that still leaves 22% directly assigned to the registration. When considering the impact ISO 14001 has had on technological uptake in Western Australia, this figure is difficult to ignore.

	Increased share of environmental technologies	Unchanged share of environmental technologies
EMS companies		
Number	7	5
%	58	42
Non-EMS companies		
Number	5	9
%	36	64
Total		
Number	11	14
%	46	54

Table 22.7 **Recent dynamics in the introduction of environmental technologies in Western Australian companies, 1999**

◢ ISO 14001 and technology transfer

Kemp and Soete (1992) list three major barriers affecting the decision to adopt or not to adopt a cleaner technology, namely: price and quality of the innovation; lack of information and knowledge; and risk and uncertainty with respect to the economic consequences. The study confirmed that these are major considerations in the case of Western Australian companies. But the EMS companies are better positioned to deal with at least one of these barriers: lack of information and knowledge. They explore wider sources of information and have a better awareness of the environmental impacts of their businesses. The two groups are equally concerned about the price and quality of these technologies as with the associated risk and uncertainty.

Another significant difference between the EMS and non-EMS companies is that only the EMS companies perceive the use of environmental technologies as a feature giving them the competitive edge while for the non-EMS it is still business as usual. The EMS companies use the ISO 14001 certification as an active marketing tool.

The study shows some evidence that the ISO 14001 certification has stimulated technology transfer. This is justified by the large number of adopted environmental technologies by EMS companies, 82% of which have been developed in collaboration with other organisations, such as universities, government research organisations and other companies. There is a big demand for 'over the counter' cleaner technologies but they have to be flexible and easy to adopt to the individual companies' requirements. This demand is even more obvious in the case of non-certified companies.

The sample of companies studied represented a number of industry sectors and, consequently, the new production technologies adopted by them vary. There are different levels of environmental component in the selection of the innovations and in the motivation behind their introduction. Table 22.8 shows examples of technologies adopted by the Western Australian certified companies using Geiser's classification (1994) according to the primacy of environmental motivation and sophistication of technology. As can be seen, all classes of technologies are used by the EMS companies.

		PRIMACY OF ENVIRONMENTAL MOTIVATION	
		Low	High
SOPHISTICATION OF TECHNOLOGY	High	**Appropriate technologies:** water- and low-solvent-based paints, hydrocarbon bunkers, dust filters, replacement of kerosene-type degreasing, hazard prevention equipment, air filter recycling, interception of washdown systems, low-pressure/high-volume paint guns, lime waste for cement manufacture	**'Low-hanging fruit' technologies:** oil spill prevention, oil, oil filters and grease recycling, solid waste recycling, air filter, use of biodegradable chemicals, bioremediation, pit liners, use of worms
	Low	**Business-driven technologies:** energy-efficient metal sheet-cutting machines, caustic recycling, bin measuring equipment in waste collection vehicles, bigger operations to reduce waste, better cleaning equipment, remote control magnet cranes	**Cleaner technologies:** closed-loop water collection and recycling system, hydrocarbon management, plasma water recycling, integrated management system, diesel/LPG substitution, heat weed control, arsenic stabilisation, co-generation

Table 22.8 **Examples of technologies adopted by Western Australian ISO 14001-certified companies**

Source: Adopted from Geiser 1994

One of the early criticisms of ISO 14001 is that 'once again the challenge will be to "beat the inspector" and not to be innovative and adopt new technologies to find long term solutions that lie outside the acceptable boundaries of the inspector' (Kean 1996). The results from this study do not support such fears, as the EMS companies are more innovative. Being a voluntary certification, the standard series does not direct or prescribe the pace of technological change and companies are left to make the choices that suit them.

The EMS companies have pride in their environmental leadership. By being at the forefront of any changes, they are most likely to become part of the process of technology transfer which will spread to other, less environmentally oriented organisations. Steer (1996), for example, claims that there appears to be a number of environmental technological solutions available; however, the old fashioned technology-driven approach to the environment needs to be complemented with improved management practices. This is exactly what the EMS companies are doing. They will be in a position to transfer not only technologies but also environmental management practices.

◢ Conclusion

In summary, the Western Australian EMS companies are more innovative than non-certified companies when it comes to environmental technologies. In-house R&D is becoming more important for certified companies while regulators play an insignificant role. ISO 14001 is seen as a strong marketing tool related to product quality. At least 22% of the companies have changed the rate of adoption of new technologies directly because of the EMS certification. A higher rate of adoption of environmental technologies can realistically be expected to translate to improvements in environmental performance in the longer term because old technologies are being replaced with new and these reduce the environmental impact of production.

There is a broad agreement that EMSs are a crucial tool in progress towards ecologically sustainable development. Even if critics of ISO 14001 say that it is one of many tools (rather than the only tool), this study concludes that the voluntary standard is contributing its fair share.

It is not unreasonable to expect that the trends observed in this study are indicative of general developments resulting from EMS implementation elsewhere. The increased adoption of environmental technologies associated with ISO 14001 certification is a very positive outcome for the companies themselves, for their peers, for setting environmental performance practices and, most importantly, for preserving the natural environment.

Part 7
ENVIRONMENTAL AND ECONOMIC BENEFITS

23

ISO 14001 AND ENVIRONMENTAL PERFORMANCE
The management goal link*

Jason Switzer and John Ehrenfeld
Massachusetts Institute of Technology, USA

Vicki Milledge
University of Massachusetts, USA

ISO 14001 poses a dilemma to the environmental regulator seeking to improve compliance, to the insurer seeking to limit liability, and to the environmental activist looking to identify 'clean' companies. The adoption of the ISO 14001 environmental management system (EMS) could lead to revolutionary gains in environmental performance if—as in the case of the diffusion of the ISO 9000 quality management system series of standards—the leading multinational manufacturers 'green' their operations and require the same from the many thousands of companies that make up their supply chains.[1] Both Ford and General Motors have declared they will require suppliers to obtain ISO 14001 registration.

On the other hand, because the standard lacks minimum environmental performance requirements and does not require full legal compliance as a condition of registration, some companies may use it to garner an 'easy A', while continuing to operate in illegal or irresponsible ways (Gleckman and Krut 1998: 11).

This chapter argues that ISO 14001 registration does stimulate positive changes in an organisation's environmental management goals, making it more likely they will be translated into environmental performance improvements.

* The authors would like to thank Dr Sandra Rothenberg for generously assisting in the research design. A more extensive version of the results presented in this chapter may be found under the title of 'ISO 14001 and Environmental Goal Setting: Promises Kept', in *Environmental Quality Management* 9.2 (Winter 1999): 1-24 (John Wiley & Sons).

1 There is some evidence that this process of greening the supply chain has already begun. Both Ford and General Motors, for example, have declared that they will require their suppliers to obtain ISO 14001 registration. See also, USAEP (United States–Asia Environmental Partnership) 'Global Environmental Management: Candid Views of Fortune 500 companies', available at www.usaep.org/gem/report.htm (1998).

◢ The aims of this study

At its heart, the resolution to this dilemma lies in the impact of the ISO 14001 standard on environmental performance and the means within the standard for assuring that its impact is positive. The purposes of this study, by the Technology, Business and Environment Group at Massachusetts Institute of Technology (MIT), are to:

☐ Demonstrate that an ISO 14001-based EMS provides mechanisms for establishing and attaining environmental management goals

☐ Evaluate the impact of ISO 14001 implementation on environmental management goals in registered organisations, on characteristics such as goal stringency, measurability, transparency and commitment to regulatory compliance

☐ Draw policy recommendations for ensuring positive environmental outcomes, based on the links that this research suggests between ISO 14001 management goals and environmental performance

◢ Many ISO 14001 management goals will lead to action

Management objectives may be characterised as either 'official' or 'operative' (Milledge 1995: 11):

> Official goals are those that are publicly stated by the organisation and are often vague or quite general. Their purpose is often symbolic. Operative goals are specific enough to direct the behaviour of organisational members. They provide cognitive guidance and the basis for operating decisions.

For example, Ford's environmental policy requires 'that its operations, products and services accomplish their functions in a manner that provides responsibly for protection of health and the environment' (Trotman 1996). This goal does not provide a clear description of what constitutes 'responsible' behaviour and, therefore, must be considered 'official' only.

In the Ford example: 'With respect to health and environmental concerns, regulatory compliance represents a minimum' (Trotman 1996: 5). There is no question here—ensuring compliance is an operative goal guiding management practice.

Operative goal establishment and attainment are at the very core of the ISO 14001 standard. Under ISO 14001, a firm's senior management is required to establish an environmental policy, spelling out its 'guiding principles', some of which are goals. It must then convene a cross-functional team to select environmentally 'significant' aspects of its operation, based on the policy statement.

ISO 14001 demands that firms' 'objectives should be specific and targets should be measurable wherever practicable' (ISO 14001 A.3.3), including designation of responsible personnel, timetables, budgets and performance metrics (Martin 1998: 22). Thus, from among those aspects it has chosen as significant, the firm will set meaningful objectives, targets, timetables and metrics—making them operative goals. It must establish a system for monitoring its progress towards its goals and for correcting them to better reflect its growing understanding of its limitations and capabilities, and its changing priorities. Most importantly, the firm must demonstrate to the certifier that it is making progress towards the attainment of its goals, and that the root causes of non-conformances are being corrected (continual improvement). Finally, senior management must periodically review the policy and management system to ensure it continues to be effective and appropriate to the organisation's needs.

What emerges from this analysis is that registered firms or facilities have a strong incentive for achieving those goals they choose to make specific. They must do so, or have a compelling reason for not doing so, in order to satisfy their registrar and maintain registration.[2] For the same reason, firms may have a strong disincentive acting against setting stringent, measurable goals, as they will be held to them by the certifier.

Assuming for the moment that third-party certification is effective and consistent, what is the impact of ISO 14001 registration on environmental management goals? Do they become more specific, more operative in character or do they become less stringent, as companies move from platitudes to more realistic and attainable management objectives?

◢ Criteria for evaluating the impact of ISO 14001 implementation on environmental management goals

What are the criteria by which one could explore the impact of ISO 14001 adoption on management goals and their subsequent effect on environmental performance? First, one could look at changes in the content of the goals themselves, before and after registration, to see if they move in ways that might be environmentally beneficial; placing regulatory compliance as a minimum, for example or reducing emissions (stringency). Second, one could look for changes in the process by which goals are established, to see if it becomes more open to outside stakeholders (participatory), more externally verifiable (transparent) and more comprehensive (see Table 23.1).

---

2 Assuming that third-party registration auditing is effective, which has not been sufficiently tested (see Switzer and Ehrenfeld 1999), in which we find that certain conflicts of interest and scope for interpretation of the ISO 14001 standard's requirements undermine the credibility of the private third-party auditing system.

Content-related goal characteristics	Process-related goal characteristics
▶ Goal stringency ▶ Commitment to regulatory compliance ▶ Comprehensiveness ▶ Specificity ▶ Measurability	▶ Top-level management commitment ▶ Participation in goal-setting ▶ Transparency of goals

Table 23.1 **Desirable characteristics for environmental management goals**

◢ Data, methods and limitations of this study

As part of the study reported here, corporate and facility-level environmental managers in nine ISO 14001-registered organisations and one non-registered small business were contacted and interviewed (see Table 23.2). Each interviewee agreed to participate under the condition that the identity of their corporation be confidential.

An important consideration is that the conclusive power of this study is limited by its methodology and small sample size. It compares goals following ISO 14001 registration to those existing previously, relying largely on subjective opinion and, where possible, documented goal statements. However, the results can be seen as indicative of prevailing trends due to the nature of the companies surveyed—they represent some of the largest multinational firms in each industry sector represented.

Table 23.2 **Interviews with corporate and facility-level managers**

Company	Name	Corporate manager	Facility manager	Description
A	Akoshi	A1	---	MN Asian auto-maker
B	Beta	B1	B2	MN European chemical manufacturing
C	Chips	C1	. . .	MN American aviation company
D	Data	. . .	D2	MN Asian microelectronics manufacturing
E	Epsilon	. . .	E2, E3	MN European microelectronics manufacturing
F	Fido	. . .	F2	MN Asian microelectronics manufacturing
G	Giant	G1	G2, G3, G4	MN US microelectronics manufacturing
H	High	. . .	H2	Small US power generator
I	Impact	I1	. . .	Small US parts manufacturing*

* Considered obtaining registration to ISO 14001, but elected not to pursue it
MN = Multinational enterprise

◢ Summary of results: goals changed in positive ways

Table 23.3 summarises the results of our study. In general, registration had a positive effect on the nature and process by which environmental management goals were established in the organisations surveyed. In the following sections, we will examine the results for each of the characteristics studied.

No change in goal stringency

Will organisations take on greater environmental responsibility following ISO 14001 registration? One measure of an organisation's commitment to environmental management is the stringency of its management objectives. An environmental performance commitment—which can be a policy commitment, or an objective or target—is stringent 'either because compliance requires a significant reduction in [emissions], because

Table 23.3 **Summary of interview results: ISO 14001 registration has a positive impact on the content of environmental management goals and on the process by which they are set.**

	Firm	A	B	C	D	E	F	G	H
Goal content	More **stringent**—demanding a higher level of environmental performance or a lower level of emissions	Yes	No change	. . .	. . .	No change	No change	No change	No change
	A greater **commitment to compliance** with all regulations	Yes	Yes	Yes	. . .	Yes	Yes	Yes	Yes
	The responsibility of **specific** people within the organisation	Yes	Yes	Yes	Yes	Yes	Yes	Yes	Yes
	More **measurable/ quantifiable**	Yes	Yes	Yes	Yes	Yes	Yes	Yes	Yes
	More **comprehensive,** covering a broader range of an organisation's environmental impacts/aspects	Yes	. . .	Yes	. . .	Yes	Yes	Yes	Yes
Goal-setting process	Backed by a commitment from **senior management** and CEO	Yes	Yes	Yes	Yes	Yes	Yes	Yes	Yes
	More **transparent** to external stakeholders	No	No	No	No	Yes	Yes	No	No
	More open to external **participation** by other stakeholders	No	No	No	Yes	No	No	No	No

Yes: Interview comments or related documentation suggest greater presence of this characteristic than prior to registration.
No: Interview comments etc. did not suggest any greater presence of this characteristic.

compliance using existing technology is costly, or because compliance requires a significant technological change' (Ashford 1996: 7-8).

This study relied on the subjective opinions of managers who were asked how the goals established following registration are different from what was in place prior to registration. Will these goals be difficult to achieve?

The results show that the perceived stringency of goals has not changed significantly in the organisations studied. Some goals were made more difficult, others less so; still others were eliminated or replaced with new objectives.

One interpretation of these results is that ISO 14001 has no impact on an organisation's commitment to environmentally preferable ends. Another interpretation is that, as they identify organisational benefits and costs that were previously ignored, registered firms modify their goals in ways that increase their likelihood of attainment. As better data are gathered and linked to quality and financial management systems within the organisation, sometimes organisations may recognise:

☐ That they are actually overspending on some environmental issues and can cut back

☐ That previously established goals are simply unattainable given technological or budgetary constraints

☐ That less stringent goals are needed, reflecting greater sensitivity to organisational and technological constraints and financial goals

Reduce environmental overspending

One certifier we interviewed recounted the experience of a US car-maker which, while improving its information tracking system as a requirement for ISO 14001 registration, identified a location where it was operating a redundant water treatment plant. The primary source of the pollutants in that waste-stream had been closed some time earlier. It realised significant financial benefits by reducing the treatment level.[3]

Set fewer, more attainable goals

A manager at Epsilon noted that the number of goals at her site had actually been diminished following registration, from 29 in 1996, to 13 in 1997 (following registration) to nine in 1998 (E2 in Table 23.2). She noted:

> We needed to reduce the number of objectives so that we could properly manage them using available resources.

This seems to indicate that ISO 14001 registration stimulated a process in Epsilon of rationalising environmental management goals to better reflect organisational realities such as multiple demands on managers' time, technological lock-in, and conflicting objectives.

3   Personal communication with G. Bellen, NSF Strategic Registration, October 1998.

Set more appropriate, less stringent goals

Environmental managers must sell the goals within the organisation, but hard goals are tough to sell. Failure to set achievable goals may block subsequent environmental efforts. A facility manager from Fido electronics (F2 in Table 23.2) stated:

> We don't want to set ourselves up for failure. If we can't meet our targets, we don't want to be penalised.

Furthermore, establishment of overly stringent goals may reflect a lack of understanding of a firm's economic and technological constraints. Through the process of ISO 14001 implementation and operation, a firm may become more aware of these constraints and so set more appropriate goals.

Greater commitment to regulatory compliance

ISO 14001 requires that an organisation's environmental policy 'includes a commitment to comply with relevant environmental legislation and regulations' (ISO 14001, 4.3c). The standard is intended to assist organisations in identifying and correcting the cause of non-conformances, including non-compliance with regulations:

> By correcting the fundamental cause of the non-compliance, companies gain greater assurance of future compliance (Tucker and Kasper 1998: 8).

Indeed, this commitment to compliance is reflected in ISO 14001-registered firms' management goal statements. For example, Akoshi dedicated itself to 'closely adhering to environmental legislation'; while Beta committed itself to 'reduce incidents of reportable non-compliance' and 'have zero notices of violations from [regulatory] inspections'.

One Epsilon facility found that its monitoring of a regulated pollutant stream was done only once a month. If an accident led to a discharge in excess of regulatory requirements at any time other than during that monitoring test, the facility would not detect it. In order to meet its 100% compliance goal, therefore, the facility will be implementing a continuous monitoring system (E2 in Table 23.2).

Increased goal specificity and measurability

> The central tenet of individual level goal setting and task performance theory is that specific, difficult goals result in higher performance on a task than if the individual had no goal or a general goal (Milledge 1995: 4).

Therefore, an important question is whether ISO 14001 encourages firms to set more specific, measurable goals than they might otherwise choose.

All the organisations interviewed established performance-oriented, quantitative targets, with clear designation of responsible personnel. Epsilon, for example, modified its goals to reflect greater measurability:

A previous goal was to reduce H_2SO_4 consumption. Following ISO 14001 registration, we committed to recycle more than 30% of the H_2SO_4 consumed in the manufacturing process in 1998 (E2 in Table 23.2).

Giant noted a similar change. Prior to ISO 14001 implementation and subsequent registration, objectives were stated in terms such as 'let's reduce water consumption'. Now they state:

> We will reduce water consumption, and here are the timetable, metrics and resources to do so. [Goal statements are] more structured now so that objective evidence is in place to demonstrate to [our] registrar that progress is occurring (G1 in Table 23.2).

More comprehensive, area-appropriate goals

An organisation's environmental goals define its perceived scope of responsibility. Does ISO 14001 registration lead an organisation to broaden its notion of environmental responsibility beyond legal requirements?

Interview results suggest that, through the aspects identification and goal selection process mandated by ISO 14001, organisations will indeed take responsibility for a broader array of environmental impacts, such as energy use and noise.

Through ISO 14001 registration, firms are also more likely to prioritise their environmental activities based on region or area-specific needs. Giant has found that, in addition to setting goals for its regulated aspects and common unregulated aspects (e.g. energy consumption, solid waste), its facilities are targeting specific local issues. For example, water consumption is a big issue in California so a California-based facility has set a water use reduction goal that is more stringent than standard corporate policy (G2 in Table 23.2).

Greater senior management commitment

Top management commitment to environmental goals is essential to their attainment. According to a meta-analysis of 70 studies performed by Rodgers and Hunter in 1991, 'when top management commitment [to organisational goals] was high, the average gain in productivity was 56%, but when commitment was low, the average gain was only 6%' (see Milledge 1995: 17).

ISO 14001 registration requires evidence of top-level management commitment (ISO 14001, A.2). Environmental goals will therefore have more senior-level management commitment following ISO 14001 registration. Examples of high-level corporate commitment in our sample group were common. At Beta Chemicals, 'top-level commitment to the environment [is] communicated to all employees,' according to the corporate environmental manager (B1 in Table 23.2). At Fido and at High Power, senior managers were actively involved in the goal-setting processes. These examples indicate a more active commitment towards environmental management from senior personnel.

Broader participation in goal-setting, but no gain in goal transparency

Social psychologists have acknowledged the power of public commitments to drive performance:

> Whenever one takes a stand that is visible to others, there arises a drive to maintain that stand in order to look consistent . . . (Cialdini 1993: 82).

Does ISO 14001 catalyse external participation in internal goal-setting, and does the company communicate its goals, or make them transparent, to external stakeholders?

Goals are not made public

While ISO 14001 requires that organisations 'consider processes for external communication on its significant environmental aspects' (ISO 14001, 4.4.3), the organisation is not required to make substantive public commitments or disclosures. Interviews indicate that firms are not disclosing greater amounts of goal- or performance-related information to the public following ISO 14001 registration.

No additional external participation in the goal-setting process

While it must establish a means for incorporating the views of interested parties into its goal-setting process, the ISO 14001-registered organisation is not required to formally invite them to participate (ISO 14001, 4.3.3).

Interview evidence indicates that firms are not likely to involve outside stakeholders in the ISO goal-setting process unless they were already doing so prior to registration.

Firms do, however, seem to be involving a broader group of participants from within the organisation in the aspects-identification and goal-setting processes. Almost all sites studied made use of cross-functional team efforts to identify aspects and establish goals. As one manager at Giant put it, ISO 14001 'gets environmental management out of the hands of the half-dozen environmental professionals and out to the people who really affect the environment' (G2 in Table 23.2). This was echoed by the facility manager at High Power (H2 in Table 23.2), who noted,

> If the environmental engineer got run over by a car six months ago, we would have been dead. Not anymore. Now, we know who is responsible for each action. [Now, we have a] greater emphasis on procedure, and less on [the] person.

◢ Summary of research

This chapter has presented an assessment of the impact of ISO 14001 registration on the content of environmental management goals, the process by which these goals are established and the likely link between those goals and resulting environmental performance.

While the firms interviewed did not substantially modify the stringency of their environmental goals, they did increase their commitment to goal attainment, as demonstrated by increased senior management commitment, more measurable goals, and more specific designation of roles and responsibilities. Moreover, where stringency was lowered, it may have reflected the greater understanding of organisational and technical constraints that emerged through the ISO 14001 management process.

Almost all of the firms surveyed established compliance assurance-related goals. They set environmental management goals that went beyond regulated substances, and included aspects such as water use and energy efficiency. Furthermore, they indicated enhanced sensitivity to local variations in environmental constraints and community interests.

In terms of process, firms did not increase outside stakeholder involvement in their goal-setting processes, nor were they more likely to disclose their environmental performance goals, but they did appear to broaden internal participation, drawing on cross-functional teams in contrast to leaving environmental management goal-setting to the environmental manager.

Policy prescriptions

How does this analysis translate into recommendations regarding ISO 14001? What should the manager, the regulator, and the environmental activist know about ISO 14001?

First, it appears that the diffusion and adoption of the ISO 14001 EMS standard among companies will help the environment insofar as it helps companies systematically identify areas where environmental performance gains contribute to the organisation's financial bottom line. It is not, as has been stated elsewhere many times, a guarantor of enhanced environmental performance.

Second, management goals are the key to predicting the magnitude and direction of environmental performance change in a registered company. It follows that ISO 14001 can be a useful tool for regulatory reform,[4] provided such initiatives require firms to disclose their goal statements and environmental performance.

In the absence of goal disclosure, registration audits are the primary mechanism through which regulators and other interested stakeholders assure that firms live up to the standard's requirements and their own stated environmental policies. More attention must be focused on the critical role of third-party certifiers, to identify means to enhance their effectiveness, objectivity and broader credibility.

Finally, the ultimate aim of those interested in the contribution ISO 14001 can make to sustainable development should be to open up the goal-setting process to a broader range of stakeholders, whether through modification of the standard, regional environmental regulation or by direct negotiation with registered facilities.

---

4 'Alternative-track' regulatory reform efforts, which typically involve granting regulatory flexibility to participating firms in exchange for adoption of a management system and reporting requirements.

The ISO 14001 aspects identification and goal establishment process is a powerful lever for directing the attention and energies of a firm, and should be harnessed. Stakeholder participation in goal establishment could be used to move firms towards the management of the full range of environmental and social issues upon which they have impact. External participation modes could include:

☐ Region-specific guidance documents, prepared by environmental regulators, laying out local environmental priorities

☐ An Appendix to the ISO 14001 standard referring to international environmental agreements as 'significant' (Rotherham 1998)

☐ Multi-stakeholder dialogues between company representatives, environmentalists, community members and regulators for the establishment of facility-level, area-specific, social and environmental goals

As it is designed today, ISO 14001 helps a firm manage systematically those areas of operation that are regulated for environmental reasons, identify those areas in which it is using resources inefficiently and adjust its focus to be sensitive to local community concerns. However, those who seek to seize the opportunity posed by ISO 14001 to advance the cause of sustainability will pay close attention to whom and what is involved in setting environmental management goals, whether the goals are made public, and how third parties assure that progress is being made in achieving them.

ASSESSMENT OF THE VALUE OF ISO 14001 IN IMPROVING ENVIRONMENTAL PERFORMANCE

Pamela J. Bridgen
Environment International Ltd, USA

Nancy Helm
Environmental Protection Agency, USA

The US Environmental Protection Agency (EPA) Region 10 (Pacific Northwest) is interested in the use of environmental management systems (EMSs) to manage environmental responsibilities and improve overall environmental performance. In particular, EPA Region 10 is interested in how performance relates to ISO 14001.

An ISO 14001 performance study was conducted to identify and evaluate key decisions made during the development of ISO 14001-based EMSs. The seven participating facilities, which represent a cross-section of private and public entities within the Pacific Northwest, utilised the ISO 14001 standard to develop their EMSs. Environment International Ltd (EI) examined and evaluated indicators of improved environmental performance in relation to EMS development, including the incorporation of pollution prevention (P2) activities, measurable improvements in environmental performance, and activities that represented an effort to move beyond regulatory compliance. At the time of the study there were few organisations certified to the ISO 14001 standard within the region, so organisations developing EMSs based on the standard were included in the study.

The study revealed key decisions in EMS implementation and measures of improved environmental performance. Once the decision to implement an ISO 14001-based EMS is made, facilities need to make some critical commitments in order to improve environmental performance. The most important steps that a facility should take to develop an EMS that imbeds P2 into its core activities and leads to measurable improvements in overall environmental performance are included in Box 24.1.

The process of formally identifying aspects and impacts, and establishing and monitoring progress towards goals through an ISO 14001-based EMS, results in improved environmental performance. These results are apparent in both environmental data and approaches to environmental problem-solving: facilities implementing ISO 14001-based

☐ **TOP MANAGEMENT SUPPORT**

Top management commitment to a strong EMS instils in all facility employees a sense of the importance of integrating P2 and continual improvement into day-to-day operations.

☐ **FORMALISATION OF EMS**

The EMS formalisation process transforms an ad hoc procedure to address environmental issues into a structured framework specifically designed to achieve continual environmental improvement.

☐ **DOCUMENTATION OF PROCEDURES**

Documentation facilitates information exchange for improvement of environmental initiatives and informs employees of their individual environmental responsibilities.

☐ **EMPLOYEE INVOLVEMENT AND TRAINING**

Employee involvement and training improves the understanding of both top commitment to environmental performance and potential and actual environmental impacts of day-to-day operations. Employees are more likely to suggest potential environmental improvements.

☐ **ESTABLISHMENT OF FOCUS GROUPS OR P2 TEAMS**

The establishment of focus groups or P2 teams fosters the development of EMS activities and adds perspective from various aspects of the operations on how best to address environmental issues.

☐ **IDENTIFICATION OF ASPECTS AND GOALS**

Formal identification of environmental aspects and establishment of goals and objectives provides direction and specific time-lines for implementation so that environmental initiatives receive appropriate priority.

☐ **IDENTIFICATION OF IMPACTS BEYOND FACILITY OPERATIONS**

Identifying impacts beyond direct facility operations broadens a facility's environmental perspective and responsibility to involve its vendors and suppliers.

☐ **DEVELOPMENT OF COMPREHENSIVE BASELINE DATA**

Evaluating processes that have the potentially largest environmental impact is part of the ISO 14001 implementation process.

☐ **DEVELOPMENT OF INTERNAL AUDITS**

Development of internal audits enables facilities to utilise in-house expertise to identify opportunities for and measure progress toward environmental improvement.

Box 24.1 **Key decisions in ISO 14001-based EMS implementation that lead to improved environmental performance**

EMSs are moving towards hazardous/toxic substance reduction, air pollution reduction, water pollution reduction, improved management of compliance activities, and development of procedures to manage change. Thus, ISO 14001 enhances the ability to tackle environmental issues effectively by providing a structured framework. As a result, facilities develop stronger environmental objectives and work continually to reach their environmental goals.

EPA Region 10 is interested in providing incentives for superior environmental performance and in finding indicators of such performance. The most widely considered incentive has been the concept of a 'performance track' which would reward companies with exceptional environmental performance by providing incentives such as streamlined reporting or extended permits. For regulatory agencies a barrier to implementing performance tracks has frequently been the inability to assess optimal environmental performance. ISO 14001 holds out the possibility that facilities with an EMS that has been certified as meeting the standard are likely to be achieving exceptional environmental performance.

The study was conducted in early 1998, before there was significant evidence regarding the environmental improvements resulting from the implementation of ISO 14001. With this study, EPA Region 10 sought to identify and document links between ISO 14001 certification or other EMS implementation and ongoing superior environmental performance.

◢ The participating facilities

EPA Region 10 identified 15 facilities as potential participants in the ISO 14001 performance study. These facilities were selected because they are some of the first to implement an ISO 14001-based EMS and because they represent a cross-section of the region. The facilities were contacted and seven were selected to participate in the project. These have all utilised the ISO 14001 standard in developing their EMSs although they are not all ISO 14001-certified.

The participants were: Eugene Water and Electric Board (EWEB), Intalco Aluminum Corporation (Intalco), Micron Technology (Micron), Naval Air Station (NAS) Whidbey, Naval Station (NAVSTA) Everett, Oki Semiconductor Manufacturing (OSM), and Rudd Paint Company. These organisations were hopeful that, if the EPA study was able to conclude that environmental improvements resulted from the implementation of an EMS, then the EPA may consider greater regulatory flexibility for facilities that have a functioning EMS in place.

The organisations agreed to participate on the condition that the results of the study would be aggregated and specific information about the facility would not be included in the report without explicit permission from the organisation. In addition, the organisations were provided with feedback during the site visits, the results of the study, and a copy of the final report before it was distributed elsewhere. More information is provided in Table 24.1.

Company name	Location	Product/process	Employees	ISO 14001-certified
EWEB	Eugene, OR	Electricity generation	450	No
Intalco	Ferndale, WA	Aluminium smelting	1,200	Yes
Micron	Boise, ID	Semiconductor manufacturing	8,000	Yes
NAS Whidbey	Oak Harbor, WA	Aircraft maintenance	8,000	No
NAVSTA Everett	Everett, WA	Ship maintenance	6,400	No
OSM	Tualatin, OR	Semiconductor manufacturing	135	Yes
Rudd Company	Seattle, WA	Paint/coatings manufacturing	53	No

Table 24.1 **Characteristics of participating facilities**

The seven facilities are diverse in size and activity, representing both public and private enterprises, and were at different stages of developing and implementing EMSs. Four belonged to commercial corporations, two were federal government facilities and the last was a publicly owned utility. Three had already achieved third-party certification to ISO 14001, some were undertaking gap analyses to identify critical elements in EMS development, while others were using ISO 14001 to assist in improving their management structure. This diversity gave added value to the study.

EPA Region 10 is interested in providing incentives for superior environmental performance and in finding indicators of such performance. In order for EPA Region 10 to determine the value of ISO 14001, it was important to understand why facilities are investing in the standard, why some are hesitant to implement it, and why others decide to use the standard without intending to certify.

◢ Methodology

To minimise impacts on the day-to-day business of the seven facilities, the EI team developed the following simple but effective information collection process to identify critical decision points leading to improved environmental performance:

- ☐ Initiating phone conversations with facilities to discuss the scope of the project, the information collection process, and willingness to participate

- ☐ Developing and faxing a list of preliminary questions to guide facilities in understanding the aims of the study

- ☐ Gathering documentation in preparation for on-site visits

- ☐ Conducting conference calls with key facility personnel

- ☐ Scheduling a date for a one- to four-day on-site visit by two personnel from EI

- ☐ Conducting on-site visits

☐ Drafting on-site visit summaries for facility review

☐ Gathering additional information through follow-up calls

On-site visits consisted of facility tours, interviews with relevant personnel and EMS documentation review. Facility tours provided familiarity with manufacturing/industrial processes. Extensive interviews with employees provided an understanding of roles and responsibilities while an EMS review established an understanding of management structure.

Throughout the process, the team examined and evaluated the facility's incorporation of P2 activities, measurable improvements in environmental performance, and activities that clearly represented efforts to move beyond mere regulatory compliance. Using information gathered during the facility interviews, published information and team members' industry knowledge and experience, the team identified the factors that had the most significant influence on the facilities' decision-making processes during EMS development.

◢ Key decisions in EMS implementation

The key decisions presented in this section are based on the findings regarding the implementation of the EMSs at the facilities visited and discussions with employees at these facilities (see Box 24.1).

An ISO 14001-based EMS can improve environmental performance if a facility makes certain critical commitments. Some facilities may find it difficult to develop and follow through on these commitments without the intent to certify. The most important steps that a facility should take to develop an EMS that imbeds P2 into its core and leads to measurable improvements in overall environmental performance are summarised in Box 24.1 and discussed below.

Top management support

Top management commitment to a strong EMS instils in all employees a sense of the importance of integrating P2 and continual improvement into day-to-day operations. Almost all facilities participating in this study identified this as critical. Although some facilities had been working on developing environmental programmes for years, progress was often delayed by other high-priority activities (changes in production, requirement to write end-of-year reports, etc.). ISO 14001 implementation enabled facilities to support these programmes and provided a robust structure to demonstrate that objectives were met.

Formalisation of EMS

Most facilities believe a major advantage of ISO 14001 is the ability to encourage 'out-of-the-box' environmental management thinking, to integrate systems and to improve environmental quality. The EMS formalisation process transforms an ad hoc procedure into a structured framework, designed to achieve continual environmental improvement systematically. It establishes protocols for developing time-lines, distributing resources and identifying responsibilities so that progress can be tracked. Many facilities stressed that all employees should be accountable for environmental quality improvements—formalisation conveys that all employees are accountable.

Third-party certification furthers the commitment to environmental quality and establishes credibility, although some organisations do not currently perceive either a marketing or regulatory advantage and are unwilling to spend the additional money for third-party certification. Many of the participating facilities, however, believe that an external evaluation of their EMS prompts a higher level of commitment during both the development and the implementation phases. One facility indicated that its third-party certifier acts as the 'conscience of the company'.

Documentation of procedures

Documentation facilitates information exchange on environmental initiatives and informs employees about their individual environmental responsibilities. Management at a number of facilities believed it had developed an ISO-based EMS philosophy prior to implementation but lacked sufficient documentation and training to promote awareness. Documentation can lead to a reduction in the need for individual training and communicate the environmental implications of facility operations to employees. For example, at Micron, documentation is effective because, in part, it helps train individuals about important processes within the company. This helps employees come up to speed more quickly and makes them more effective in performing their job responsibilities. It also reduces the amount of time required for training.

Employee involvement and training

Employee involvement and training improves understanding of both top-level commitment to environmental performance and an awareness of the environmental impacts of day-to-day operations. This increases the likelihood that employees will make suggestions regarding potential environmental improvements.

Under a properly implemented ISO 14001 EMS, employees understand that there is a senior-level commitment to environmental quality. For example, at OSM there is a new three-tiered employee orientation training scheme. First, it is presented by the chief executive, which conveys the importance/relevance of environmental stewardship and ISO 14001 to the company. Second, environmental health and safety staff train new employees on how ISO 14001 is implemented and explain the impacts and risks associated with their work responsibilities. Finally, employees need to pass a competency test on environmental processes and procedures. All of the facilities interviewed are receiving more employee inquiries, such as questions regarding monitoring, permit requirements and waste-water discharge levels as a result of ISO 14001 implementation. A number of facilities believe that greater employee satisfaction results from pride in recycling, reduction of chemical usage and participation and ownership in environmental programmes. Employees trained on the environmental aspects of their jobs can incorporate environmental stewardship into day-to-day operations.

Establishment of focus groups or P2 teams

The establishment of focus groups or P2 teams fosters identification of opportunities to improve environmental performance and adds perspective from all aspects of the operations. Establishing a core team of individuals from different operational areas to review environmental data, identify environmental aspects and impacts, establish goals and objectives and meet ISO 14001-based criteria is a critical decision facilities make to improve environmental performance. In general, facilities that successfully implement an ISO 14001-based EMS hold environmental team meetings at least monthly. Members are often trained in environmental assessments and internal auditing procedures, and take steps to promote employee awareness.

Identification of aspects and goals

Formal identification of environmental aspects and establishment of goals and objectives provides direction and specific time-lines for implementation so that environmental initiatives receive appropriate priority. Once the entire range of environmental aspects has been identified, facilities employ a variety of methods to designate a subset of their environmental aspects as significant.

Regardless of the method, this process ensures a thorough consideration of environmental issues and avoids a narrow focus on only regulatory aspects of the operation. Facilities then establish objectives and targets to improve environmental performance. Monitoring progress towards environmental goals encourages improvements.

Identification of impacts beyond facility operations

It is important that the organisation considers its entire operations when evaluating its environmental aspects and impacts. Identifying impacts beyond direct facility operations broadens a facility's environmental perspective and responsibility to involve vendors and suppliers. In one case, it was determined that the absence of a bus line nearby was an environmental aspect related to commuting practices. Management subsequently met with city officials to discuss the potential for a bus line, initiated a van pool service with other nearby companies and started a car pooling programme.

Such efforts indicate that companies implementing ISO 14001-based EMSs are adopting a broader view of environmental impacts and aspects.

Development of comprehensive baseline data

Development of comprehensive baseline data provides the building blocks for current and future trend analysis that may enable the facility to identify and address potential environmental problems before they arise. This process helps to identify cross-media issues (land to water, air to land), providing management with specific information to help identify new initiatives. Some facilities indicated that this exercise was important because it led to the determination of significant environmental aspects that may not previously have been identified.

Development of internal audits

Development of internal audits enable facilities to utilise their in-house expertise to identify opportunities for, and measure progress towards, environmental improvement that may not be so obvious to someone less familiar with the company's operations. Certified facilities indicated that the loss of ISO 14001 certification would have a significant negative impact on their image both internally and externally, so management established a rigorous review process to avoid such an occurrence.

All the certified facilities believe that the development of the internal audit is one of the most valuable activities associated with the EMS because it focuses on internal scrutiny of environmental management processes. In addition, because facilities cannot be sure of exactly what will be addressed during third-party certification and surveillance audits, they often prepare for the most difficult test by thoroughly ensuring that all EMS policies and procedures are in place.

◢ Improved environmental performance

The process of identifying aspects and impacts, and establishing and monitoring progress towards goals through an ISO 14001-based EMS results in improved environmental performance (see Box 24.2). These results are apparent in both environmental data and approaches to environmental problem-solving. Historically, the approach to environmental problem-solving for many of the participating facilities was less strategic than it is today. Facilities believe they might have missed opportunities for environmental improvement and P2 in the past. ISO 14001 enhances the discipline in tackling environmental issues by providing more structure and formality. As a result, facilities develop more defined environmental initiatives and work continually to reach their goals.

Box 24.2 **Measures of improved environmental performance**

☐ **Hazardous/toxic substance reduction**
☐ **Air pollution reduction**
☐ **Water pollution reduction**
☐ **Improved management of compliance activities**
☐ **Development of procedures to manage change**

Hazardous/toxic substance reduction

An ISO 14001-based EMS requires facilities to evaluate environmental aspects associated with chemicals used in their processes. Continual improvement means that facilities undergo a process of reviewing and monitoring their activities to achieve improvements in overall environmental performance in line with the facility's environmental policy. Some of the following activities represent such continual improvement in reduction in the use or risks associated with hazardous and toxic substances:

☐ **Reduction in resist edgebead remover chemical use.** Specific chemicals used in the photolithography process resulted in volatile organic compound (VOC) emissions during application and generated a hazardous waste. Micron worked with production and the chemical manufacturers to identify alternative chemicals resulting in a substantial reduction in VOC emissions and elimination of the hazardous waste stream.

☐ **Waste accumulation area relocation.** Intalco's satellite waste accumulation areas were moved to an indoor location to consolidate activities, reduce exposure to the elements, and minimise potential storm-water contamination.

☐ **Reduction of isopropyl alcohol (IPA) use.** IPA was commonly used as a cleaning solvent but it generated VOC emissions and hazardous waste. Micron researched alternatives and switched to an aqueous-based ammonium hydroxide cleaning solution.

☐ **Elimination of freon.** Micron anticipated new regulatory controls on freon, phased freon out of its process, and developed alternatives.

Air pollution reduction

A number of facilities were able to reduce the amount of airborne emissions through the identification of aspects and development of objectives and targets:

☐ **Reduction in potline emissions.** Intalco has experienced a reduction in emissions of fluoride from its potlines since the implementation of ISO 14001, due to improved work practices. Emissions were increasing until ISO 14001 implementation in January 1997 when they began to decrease (see Fig. 24.1).

☐ **Reduction of fugitive dust.** For processes causing excessive dust, Intalco is building canopies to reduce exposure to the elements. Intalco is also building a new storage facility to keep spent carbon away from rainwater, a spent potliner storage site, and roofs over the scrap paste area. These activities will minimise storm-water contamination.

☐ **Reduction of airborne particles.** For the pot room, Intalco is in the process of purchasing a device designed to vacuum dust off beams and collect particles instead of blowing dust and adding to fugitive dust and airborne particles.

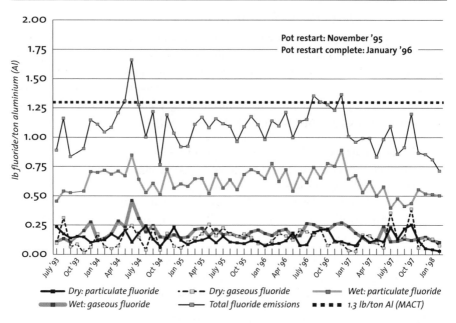

MACT = maximum available control technology

Figure 24.1 **Intalco's potline emissions: example of an environmental improvement**

Water pollution reduction

Some facilities were able to identify activities to reduce the amount of water used in industrial processes or recycle water. These facilities utilised environmental data established as part of their P2 activities and subsequent ISO 14001-based EMS:

☐ **Reduction of the amount of water being drained from the process vacuum pump by 30%.** After realising there was no correlation between production output and water consumption, an OSM team recognised that fewer vacuum pump operating hours (lower vacuum set points) and a reduction in water flow from the pump could reduce water consumption. By re-piping the process vacuum pump and cooling tower, OSM promoted the reclamation of water, so reducing consumption.

☐ **Waste-water area and sanitary lagoon improvements.** Issues at the lagoon include low BOD (biochemical oxygen demand) removal and high algal levels. Intalco is required to remove 65% of BOD entering the lagoon; thus, high BOD inflow levels make this requirement easier to meet. After looking for root causes, Intalco found several sources of dilution water that lowered BOD and made it difficult to meet requirements. Intalco eliminated dilution sources and experienced a 77% reduction in flow.

Improved management of compliance activities

ISO 14001 assumes regulatory compliance with existing environmental laws; however, many regulated organisations encounter challenges in meeting regulatory requirements. It is often difficult to keep track of regulatory changes and to monitor changes in use of chemicals that may exceed regulatory thresholds. Documentation and tracking under an ISO 14001-based EMS can help facilities improve their planning activities and ensure compliance with regulatory requirements. An ISO 14001-based EMS also assists facilities in formalising the tracking of regulations to keep up to date with legal requirements or plan for future changes.

In addition, ISO 14001 may help facilities integrate regulatory activities with the management of P2 and continual improvement. For example, one facility customised a software package to track environmental impacts. This enabled management to develop time-lines, distribute resources, and identify responsibilities so progress could be tracked from both ISO 14001 and regulatory perspectives.

Development of procedures to manage change

A number of participating facilities developed management of change procedures as part of their ISO 14001 EMS. As a result, on consideration of a new process, total resource impacts associated with new chemicals, change in volume of resources or production, changes in coolant water discharge, etc. are addressed. This process enables the facility to be proactive and consider issues before implementation. For example, when a process change results in increases in chemical use, the facility may now have a process to discuss permitting implications prior to implementation. This can save and has saved money because the facility can perform an entire evaluation of impacts and give full consideration to the relevant issues beforehand, thus avoiding increases in chemical use leading to exceedences of regulatory thresholds.

For example, OSM employees in the purchasing department suggested to management that the company receive larger quantities of an oxidiser purchased and transported from Japan in order to save money by buying the oxidiser in bulk. The review process allowed OSM to recognise in advance the lack of sufficient storage space. By preventing mass shipment OSM avoided both storage problems and the increased risk associated with having large amounts of the oxidiser on-site.

Similarly, Micron's 'Chem Req' programme is a computerised rule-driven (Superfund Amendments and Reauthorization Act, Occupational Safety and Health Act) system that enables Micron to evaluate the hazards of bringing new chemicals on-site; the programme predates ISO 14001. If a chemical introduces new environmental impacts, the requester and the suppliers will be queried for options and alternatives that reduce such impacts. Chem Req includes—but is not limited to—analysis of compatibility, hazard evaluation, air emissions, recycling and hazardous waste generation. It reduces impacts to human health and the environment and allows the company to avoid the use of chemicals that are contaminants to semiconductors. The programme helped Micron find a substitute for hydrochlorofluorocarbons.

◢ Conclusion

ISO 14001 is most relevant to companies with pre-existing environmental consciousness, rather than to those attempting to use it as a 'band aid' for poor environmental performance.

Top management commitment to the standard is the single most important factor. Such a commitment shows employees and the public that a strong environmental ethic is a part of the corporate culture. Other key decisions relating to improving environmental performance under an ISO 14001-based EMS are provided in Box 24.1 on page 274.

Third-party certification appears to increase commitment and thoroughness of EMS implementation; however, because none of the seven participating companies in the performance study were self-certified, it is difficult to make a comparison between self-certification and third-party certification. A further study would be necessary that includes facilities that have self-certified to determine whether third-party certification results in a more rigorous EMS than one that is self-certified.

Environmental agencies at the national and state level (including several Region 10 states) are exploring innovative, non-regulatory approaches to improved environmental performance, especially performance that exceeds regulatory requirements. This study has furthered EPA Region 10's knowledge of how EMSs can lead to such improvement. EPA sees the value of EMSs in encouraging organisations to integrate environmental activities with their day-to-day operations.

Although EPA Region 10 has not yet decided to take any specific actions to endorse the implementation of EMSs, the Region has used the information gained in this study in several ways. Several Region 10 states and EPA at the national level have been exploring the use of performance track incentives and Region 10 has been able to use the results of this study to assist with the development of these programmes. The state of Oregon, with EPA support, has begun implementing its 'green permits' programme, which will provide regulatory incentives for the implementation of EMSs and concomitant improvements in environmental performance.

By furthering their understanding of the management systems and decisions that lead to higher levels of performance, the authorities have improved their ability to make decisions about such approaches.

REAL FINANCIAL BENEFITS FROM ISO 14001?
Potential for economic value added through ISO 14001 at Unique Images Ltd*

Andy Hughes

URS Dames & Moore, UK

Vicky Kemp

Loop Environmental Networks, UK

Using Unique Images Ltd as a case study, we discuss how ISO 14001 can impact on economic value added, first considering the standard's effect on profits and, second, on the cost of capital. We examine different financial arguments for seeking ISO 14001 certification and recommend the best approach. Throughout we draw a distinction between adding/creating value through reduced costs or increased revenue, and conserving/protecting value from future losses.

Unique Images Ltd is a wholly owned UK subsidiary of Hallmark, the US greetings card and gift wrap company. Based in Bradford, West Yorkshire, Unique Images prints, packs and distributes 1.3 billion greetings cards and 102 million m^2 of gift wrap per annum, employs over 800 people and has an annual turnover in excess of £70 million. The firm was first alerted to environmental issues in 1998 by an impending piece of regulation and cost-saving opportunities. In the same year, it decided to develop an environmental management system (EMS) in line with ISO 14001 requirements and was certified in January 2000, while in reporting year 1999–2000 it aims to save £0.75 million through operating the EMS.

◢ Can ISO 14001 increase net operating profit after tax?

Can ISO 14001 increase profit through increased sales and/or reduced operating costs? We address this question by looking at Unique Images in three ways.

* The authors are extremely grateful to Ian Bowles, environmental manager, Unique Images, for his help, time and enthusiasm in gathering material for this case study.

☐ Is there increased net operating profit after tax (NOPAT) through more sales as a result of certification?

☐ Disaggregating ISO 14001 requirements, does the way the firm implements ISO 14001 increase NOPAT through more sales and/or reduced operating costs?

☐ Does increased profit support a case to implement an ISO 14001-compliant EMS?

Does certification increase NOPAT through more sales?

Unique Images' corporate customers do not require their suppliers to be certified to ISO 14001, but should that situation change, the firm believes certification will help protect it against loss of business. Neither the firm nor the environmental manager of one of Unique Images' largest corporate customers believe that certification to ISO 14001 will, by itself, lead to increased sales, new supply contracts or new supplier–customer relationships.

Of course, if existing customers come to demand certification and other suppliers do not respond, then Unique Images' would be at an advantage. Buyers' usual approach, however, is exemplified by Ford and Rover, which set their automotive parts suppliers target dates for achieving certification rather than dropping the guillotine overnight. The competitive advantage of a firm having gained certification in advance of the buyer's decision would, therefore, depend on its competitors not meeting their target date.

In summary, certification can protect against loss of business, but can only by itself be responsible for generating business if competitors fail to respond to a new customer requirement for certification.

Disaggregating ISO 14001: does implementing ISO 14001 specifications increase NOPAT through more sales and/or reduced operating costs?

Scrutinising both ISO 14001 and ISO 14004 reveals no requirement or recommendation to make increased profits an objective. Out of both documents, only one clause makes any reference to financial benefits—ISO 14004, 4.3.2.1, *Structure and responsibilities*, suggests: 'organisations develop procedures to track the benefits as well as the costs'. The standard and guidelines offer protection against the possibility of incurring future costs, such as fines or clean-up costs. However, they do not by themselves increase sales or reduce costs unless the firm is currently attracting fines or clean-up costs, or making provisions for such expenditure as an exceptional item in the profit and loss account.

Increased profit can occur from the way a firm implements the specifications. Specifically, this would be how aspects are deemed significant, what supporting objectives, targets and action programmes are put in place and, of course, how they are monitored.

It begins with aspects: if defining 'significance' does not address criteria that aim to increase sales or reduce operating costs, there will only be added value by accident. We illustrate this point in Table 25.1 where we list all 45 entries on Unique Images' aspects register,[1] signifying where reduced operating costs are:

☐ An explicit objective or target

☐ Not targeted explicitly, but there is implicit potential for them

☐ Not apparent from the entry on the aspects register

No entries on Unique Images' aspects register have any explicit or implicit aim to increase sales.

For 22 of the 45 environmental aspects listed in Table 25.1, cost reduction objectives and/or targets are either explicit (16 out of 22) or are implicitly derivable through the action programmes (6 out of 22). However, none is in the top 13 aspects ranked by the scoring model.

To ensure profit increase is addressed, therefore, we suggest a two-step process for determining aspect significance. This is illustrated in Figure 25.1 where there are twin objectives to conserve existing value and create new value. A firm that prioritises aspects on environmental criteria alone can protect value, but limits its opportunities to create it if it does not specifically use a profit increase screen as well. Conversely, a firm that focuses exclusively on profit will not only risk being denied certification through inadequate environmental prioritising, but also risks destroying value with insufficient protection.

Using increased profit to support a case for implementing an ISO 14001-compliant EMS

The foregoing arguments suggest that increasing profit through cost reduction and/or sales increase, cannot be used to support a case to implement an ISO 14001-compliant EMS, since the benefits will not be identifiable until a firm is already into the ISO 14001 process, i.e. prioritising its aspects register. One way over this hurdle may be to identify a pilot environmental issue that can increase profit when addressed, and use it as an example of what could follow by implementing ISO 14001. Unique Images provide an example of this 'pilot' approach in the way it addressed its use of solvents.

Aware of impending legislative requirements[2] on solvents use, Unique Images decided in 1998 to move to water-based inks throughout its flexographic and gravure printing processes. It is believed to be the only gift wrap producer in Western Europe to have done this.

---

1 The firm uses a proprietary rating method to determine the significance of its environmental aspects, which is described in Box 25.1. Table 25.1 includes the score for each aspect up to a maximum of 600. The scoring system ranks environmental aspects and the firm decides significance by what it is feasible to achieve in a set time-scale, e.g. 12 months, starting with the highest scorers and working down. It acknowledges that the aspects register will change over time as new ones are added, as a result of new business processes, and that some significances will change as it addresses each significant aspect.

2 Environmental Protection Act 1990, s.7(2)(a).

Environmental aspect description (Total: 45)	Score*	Profit objective
Trade effluent: water/petrol distillates	550	Not apparent
Contaminated steel drums (envelope department)	470	Not apparent
Contamination: compressor condensate	470	Not apparent
Effluent discharge: Roland 800	450	Not apparent
Special waste: ammonia	450	Not apparent
Engineering department: industrial gear oil waste	420	Not apparent
Goods inwards: deliveries	400	Not apparent
Security: diesel fuel deliveries (contamination)	400	Not apparent
Special waste: absorbent granules	400	Not apparent
Special waste: absorptive granules	400	Not apparent
Trade effluent: developer	350	Not apparent
Trade effluent: water	340	Not apparent
Finishing department: absorbent granules waste	320	Not apparent
Solid waste: card print department	310	**IMPLICIT**
Special waste: film fixer	310	Not apparent
Waste: general waste (print department)	310	**EXPLICIT**
Water treatment plant (effluent)	310	Not apparent
Solvent-contaminated cleaning cloths	300	Not apparent
Special waste: developer/preservative	290	Not apparent
Gas, electricity and water consumption (all site)	270	**IMPLICIT**
Make-ready waste: envelope production	260	**EXPLICIT**
Waste: KLS cardboard	250	**EXPLICIT**
Finishing department: pale envelope waste	240	**EXPLICIT**
Waste: wooden pallets/pallet tops	240	Not apparent
Waste: bobst foil	230	**IMPLICIT**
Finishing department: foiled/non-foiled card waste	220	**EXPLICIT**
Chemical store: solvents, print department	210	**EXPLICIT**
Finishing department: general waste	210	**EXPLICIT**
Finishing department: white envelope waste	210	**EXPLICIT**
Contaminated steel drums (print department)	190	Not apparent
General waste: landfill	190	**EXPLICIT**
Goods inwards: general waste	190	**EXPLICIT**
Solid waste: envelope production	190	**EXPLICIT**
Special waste: envelope adhesive	190	Not apparent
Extraction system anti-set-off spray (air quality)	180	Not apparent
Finishing department: guillotine trim waste	170	**EXPLICIT**
Finishing department: shrink-film/soft plastic waste	170	**EXPLICIT**
Process waste: bobst running waste	170	**IMPLICIT**
Waste: paper reel packaging	170	Not apparent
Energy use: artificial light and heat	160	**EXPLICIT**
Waste: steel banding	130	**IMPLICIT**
Finishing department: light and heat usage	100	**EXPLICIT**
Solvent-based inks: gift-wrap print	30	**IMPLICIT**
Waste: aluminium lithoplates	30	Not apparent
Waste: plastic packaging	30	**EXPLICIT**

* See footnote 1, page 287, and Box 25.2, page 291

Table 25.1 **Unique Images' environmental aspects and increases in NOPAT**

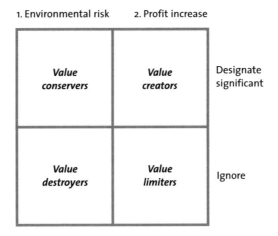

Figure 25.1 **Significant aspects value matrix**

In June 1998, the firm agreed with the local authority to change over completely by September 1998. The firm calculates that switching to water-based inks saves it almost £250,000 annually. In terms of up-front costs, the change was not the cheapest option to deal with the solvent issue, but long-term was deemed to be the most environmentally and cost-effective. The dual benefit from dealing with solvents this way was a persuasive factor in Unique Images deciding to implement an ISO 14001 EMS, on the grounds that other similar cost reduction opportunities might be revealed.

To support a case for implementing ISO 14001, however, there is still an element of speculation that the pilot is not a one-off value creator and, of course, environmental aspects would still need to be prioritised with an explicit profit increase objective.

Box 25.1 **The model for ranking environmental aspects used by Unique Images**

THE MODEL HAS SIX EQUALLY WEIGHTED PARAMETERS, EACH WITH A VARIETY of filter questions, dealing with:

- ☐ Legislative control
- ☐ Danger to humans, wildlife and the natural environment
- ☐ Community concern
- ☐ Financial liability
- ☐ Customer concern
- ☐ Quantity of input and waste material

The maximum score is 600, equally divided between each parameter. The model itself does not set a threshold for 'significance'; users determine their own depending on their individual circumstances.

◢ Can ISO 14001 reduce cost of capital?

> What we call profits, the money left to service equity, is usually not profit at all. Until a business returns a profit that is greater than its cost of capital, it operates at a loss. The enterprise still returns less to the economy than it devours in resources . . . until then it does not create wealth, it destroys it (Ehrbar 1998).

Before examining how ISO 14001 might influence the cost of capital, a little explanation of its significance may be appropriate. The function of the cost of capital is to help determine whether the returns a company gets on investing in itself are higher than the costs of making those investments, and it does this by qualifying NOPAT and the capital employed in the business. The result of this qualification is 'economic value added', which is derived in two ways.

☐ Difference or spread between cost of capital and 'return on capital employed' (ROCE)[3]

☐ NOPAT minus a 'capital charge', being the total capital employed multiplied by cost of capital

These are staple calculations among equity analysts (HSBC James Capel 1997) for determining whether a business adds value and, therefore, whether its shares are under-, fairly or over-valued and so whether shareholders should be advised to buy, hold or sell. The calculations are gaining similar use among companies' financial departments (Spencer and Francis 1998). If NOPAT or ROCE are higher than the capital charge or the cost of capital respectively, the firm should grow its capital creating value, but with the reverse outcome, shrink its asset base rather than grow, since capital costs more than it returns (HSBC James Capel 1997). In any event, the firm should always look for ways to reduce its cost of capital as that will make the spread more favourable to ROCE and decrease the capital charge.

The standard calculation for cost of capital is the 'weighted average cost of capital' (WACC), a combination of the cost of debt and the cost of equity. The cost of debt is the weighted average loan interest rate. The cost of equity is the opportunity cost of not investing elsewhere in the stock market, the most widely used calculation being the capital asset pricing model.[4]

Does implementing ISO 14001 reduce cost of capital?

It is necessary to consider this question looking at each constituent part of the cost of capital, beginning with the cost of debt, followed by the cost of equity.

---

3   NOPAT as a percentage of total capital employed to run the business

4   Risk-free rate* + β(market average rate** – risk-free rate), where β = difference in a given period between variability of a firm's share price and market average variability: market average always = 1, more stable stock <1, more volatile >1 (*e.g. three-month treasury bills; ** e.g. FTSE All Share).

KAISER CARRIED OUT A REGRESSION ANALYSIS OF 330 FIRMS FROM THE USA Standard & Poor 500 Index, covering 1980–87 and 1988–94. It compared β values of the firms with the quality of their environmental management and performance, and found that improvements to the quality of either or both resulted in lower β. Specifically, in a hypothetical example, Kaiser calculated that, for a firm whose cost of equity is 13%,* with a β of 1:

☐ Improve management by 50%, β = 0.915, cost of equity = 12.57%

☐ Improve performance by 50%, β = 0.935, cost of equity = 12.67%

☐ Combined effect, β = 0.868, cost of equity = 12.34%

Kaiser concludes that a firm with improving environmental management and performance achieves a lower cost of equity via less volatile share price (lower β), through growing market confidence. But Kaiser raises a caveat that other statistically significant factors could influence β. One should also note that there may be differences between US and UK equity markets' views of environmental issues, e.g. the more punitive fines in the USA may cause higher environmental sensitivity. However, the last point is moot for our case, as Unique Images is not quoted in the UK, but is a subsidiary of US firm Hallmark.

* Assuming risk-free rate = 8%, market risk premium = 5%; if the latter is higher, expect greater reductions in cost of equity.

Box 25.2 **ICF Kaiser: Improved environmental management and performance can reduce cost of equity**

Can implementing ISO 14001 reduce cost of debt?

Certification to ISO 14001 can suggest reduced environmental risk. However, among lenders there is no systematic or widespread discounting of interest rates, which would reduce the cost of debt on account of reduced environmental risk evidenced by certification, disaggregating ISO 14001 specifications, or by any other means for that matter.[5] Where a bank does consider environmental issues with loan proposals (by no means all do), they are integrated into the overall credit risk assessment and their relative importance determined by individual circumstances. Therefore, if lenders consider ISO 14001 certification or its disaggregated parts, they would do so in concert with all other factors impacting on a proposition; the influence would vary from case to case, but is currently impossible to identify in terms of an interest rate discount.

Can implementing ISO 14001 reduce cost of equity?

Before considering whether certification can have this effect, it is necessary to disaggregate ISO 14001 specifications in the light of findings of ICF Kaiser, a US environmental and engineering consultancy (see Box 25.2) (Feldman *et al.* 1996).

Accepting the caveat that other statistically significant factors could influence β, we need to ask what Kaiser identifies as the ingredients of environmental management and environmental performance which can reduce the cost of equity, and how they relate to ISO 14001 specifications. While Kaiser used its own proprietary scoring system in the research, the published information specifies the key parameters on which they focused attention (see Table 25.2).

5   Survey of UK banks conducted by Andy Hughes as part of research for Prudential Portfolio Managers Ltd.

Kaiser's environmental criteria		ISO 14001 and (ISO 14004) reference	Comments
Management	Performance		
1. Commitment to a policy		4.2	Kaiser criterion matches ISO 14001 specification.
2. Senior corporate official assigned to implement policy		4.4.1, A4.1, 4.3.2.3	ISO 14004 recommends appointing a 'senior person' to implement.
3. Lines of responsibility and accountability identified		4.4.1, 4.3.2.3	Kaiser criterion matches ISO 14001 specification.
4. Defined, measurable goals		4.3.3	Kaiser criterion matches ISO 14001 specification.
5. Adequate resources allocated		4.4.1	Kaiser criterion matches ISO 14001 specification.
6. Environmental accounting		(4.3.3, 4.4.1), 4.3.2.1	While ISO 14001 refers to only having objectives and adequate resources to meet financial requirements, and explicitly does not compel environmental cost accounting (A3.3), ISO 14004 does recommend tracking costs and benefits.
7. Track inputs (materials, etc.)		4.3.1, 4.5.1	Kaiser criterion matches ISO 14001 specification, subject to inclusion in the aspects register.
8. Track emissions, discharges, etc.		4.3.1, 4.5.1	Kaiser criterion matches ISO 14001 specification, subject to inclusion in the aspects register.
9. Employee training to ensure they operate processes correctly and address risks proactively		4.4.2	Kaiser criterion matches ISO 14001 specification.
10. Design for environment on a life-cycle basis		A3.4, 4.2.5	Kaiser criterion matches ISO 14001 specification, but NB this does not mean LCA methodologies.
11. Monitoring to ensure compliance with regulatory requirements		4.3.2, 4.5.1, (4.4.4)	Kaiser criterion matches ISO 14001 specification.
12. Creation of a corporate culture that rewards performance related to environmental issues		4.3.2.4	'Rewarding' is not mentioned explicitly, but ISO 14004 does highlight the importance of 'recognising' employee contributions.
13. Demonstrate reducing pollutants		4.3.1, 4.3.3, (4.4.4)	Kaiser criterion matches ISO 14001 specification, subject to inclusion in the aspects register.
14. Demonstrate minimising liability exposure		4.3.1–4 (4.4.7, 4.5.2)	Kaiser criterion matches ISO 14001 specification, supported by emergency preparedness and corrective actions, subject to inclusion in the aspects register.
15. Data on waste generation, effluent discharge, hazardous spills		4.3.1, 4.5.1, 4.5.3, (4.4.4)	Kaiser criterion matches ISO 14001 specification, subject to inclusion in the aspects register.
16. Set and achieve more stringent goals than those required by law		(4.3.1–3), 4.1.4	14001 does not mention going this far, but 14004 suggests a policy commitment to do so.
17. Obtain independent audits to verify stated performance		4.5.4, A5.4	Kaiser criterion matches ISO 14001 specification.

Table 25.2 **ICF Kaiser's cost of equity improvement criteria and ISO 14001**

The only clauses of ISO 14001 missing from Table 25.2 are 4.4.3–6 (communication, EMS documentation, documentation control and operational control respectively), and 4.6 (management review). Communication, EMS documentation, documentation control and operational control all underpin the successful implementation of any environmental programme, such as that made up by Kaiser's criteria, and the standard explicitly refers to management review as the key driver of continual improvement. Our view is, therefore, that, while not applying to any one Kaiser criterion in particular, clauses 4.4.3–6 and 4.6 are relevant in a holistic sense to an environmental programme that will reduce the cost of equity.

Kaiser also stresses the need for 'strategic environmental communications' to ensure equity markets are kept informed: i.e. communicate relevant, detailed and reliable information on an ongoing, proactive basis externally, not merely what regulations require. While ISO 14001 currently does not make any requirement to communicate externally beyond responding to comment, section 4.4.3 (communication) does suggest 'considering' voluntary communication. Further, section 4.3.3.1 in 14004 in the 'practical help' includes example media such as annual reports, advertising, and industry association publications, all of which mirror Kaiser's recommendations for 'strategic environmental communications'.

Our *prima facie* conclusion is that the environmental improvement parameters that Kaiser concludes can reduce cost of equity are consistent with the specifications of ISO 14001 implemented with the aid of ISO 14004, provided that specific environmental aspects (Table 25.2, criteria 7, 8, 13, 14, 15) are addressed in the aspects register. Thus, implementing ISO 14001 in such a way could itself lead to a fall in the cost of equity, with three qualifications:

1. Providing the firm communicates what it has done with equity markets

2. Accepting Kaiser's caveat that other statistically significant factors could influence β

3. Subject to differences between US and other equity markets

Subject to those qualifications, certification could, therefore, lead to reduced cost of equity by virtue of being a sum of the relevant parts, provided that the firm also communicates with equity markets about the specific environmental aspects which Kaiser highlights (as above), which certification alone would not necessarily do.

◢ Case study:
Unique Images, ISO 14001 and cost of capital

We now apply the foregoing findings to Unique Images' implementation of ISO 14001. We first highlight which of Kaiser's parameters are reflected in Unique Images' objectives, targets and action programmes, and might therefore contribute to reduced cost of capital, by reference to the 45 aspect register entries (Table 25.3). We then examine other parts of

Environmental aspect description (Total: 45)	Score*	Kaiser criteria from Table 25.2
Trade effluent: water/petrol distillates	550	9,13,14
Contaminated steel drums (envelope department)	470	9,14,15
Contamination: compressor condensate	470	13,14
Effluent discharge: Roland 800	450	9,13,14
Special waste: ammonia	450	9,14,15
Engineering department: industrial gear oil waste	420	9,11,14
Goods inwards: deliveries	400	9,11
Security: diesel fuel deliveries (contamination)	400	9,11
Special waste: absorbent granules	400	9,11,14,15
Special waste: absorptive granules	400	9,14,15
Trade effluent: developer	350	9,13,14
Trade effluent: water	340	9,13,14
Finishing department: absorbent granules waste	320	9,11,14,15
Solid waste: card print department	310	14,15
Special waste: film fixer	310	9,15
Waste: general waste (print department)	310	9,15
Water treatment plant (effluent)	310	8,9,11,15
Solvent-contaminated cleaning cloths	300	13
Special waste: developer/preservative	290	9,14,15
Gas, electricity and water consumption (all site)	270	7
Make-ready waste: envelope production	260	9,15
Waste: KLS cardboard	250	6,9,15
Finishing department: pale envelope waste	240	9,15
Waste: wooden pallets/pallet tops	240	9,11,14,15
Waste: bobst foil	230	9
Finishing department: foiled/non-foiled card waste	220	9,15
Chemical store: solvents, print department	210	9,11,13,14
Finishing department: general waste	210	9,15
Finishing department: white envelope waste	210	9,15
Contaminated steel drums (print department)	190	9,14,15
General waste: landfill	190	9,15
Goods inwards: general waste	190	9,15
Solid waste: envelope production	190	9,14,15
Special waste: envelope adhesive	190	9,14,15
Extraction system anti-set-off spray (air quality)	180	
Finishing department: guillotine trim waste	170	9,11,14,15
Finishing department: shrink-film/soft plastic waste	170	9,15
Process waste: bobst running waste	170	11,14,15
Waste: paper reel packaging	170	9,14
Energy use: artificial light and heat	160	7
Waste: steel banding	130	6,9,14,15
Finishing department: light and heat usage	100	7
Solvent-based inks: gift-wrap print	30	7,11,13,16
Waste: aluminium lithoplates	30	11,14,15
Waste: plastic packaging	30	9,11,14,15

* See footnote 1, page 287, and Box 25.2, page 291

Table 25.3 **Unique Images' environmental aspects and cost of capital**

Unique Images' EMS, which may potentially reduce cost of equity through matching Kaiser criteria in Table 25.4.

This time, 44 out of 45 environmental aspects explicitly address at least one of the 17 environmental management and performance criteria Kaiser identifies for reducing the cost of capital, with almost half the criteria addressed across all 44. If we then consider Unique Images' EMS as a whole, the firm meets 16 of the possible 17 Kaiser criteria, missing only criterion 12 (reward). The additional requirement for strategic communication, which Kaiser highlights as vital to enable reduced cost of equity, was not evidenced in our investigations. Unique Images have no guidelines for external reporting, though this requirement is more relevant to Hallmark, as the US parent. Information was not available on Hallmark's external reporting practices or on Unique Images' reporting to Hallmark.

◢ Conclusions

Being certified to ISO 14001 can raise profits through increased sales if customers require certification and competing suppliers do not respond, or fail to meet the target date customers set them. Otherwise, certification does not add to profits. It does, however, protect against loss of business, but even then only where it is a supply chain requirement (for where it is not required any protected loss is speculative).

Table 25.4 **Kaiser criteria covered by other parts of Unique Images' EMS**

ICF Kaiser's criteria from Table 25.2	Unique Images action
1. Commitment to a policy	Policy statement issued by managing director.
2. Senior corporate official assigned to implement policy	Managing director ultimately responsible for programme, environmental manager appointed to implement.
3. Lines of responsibility and accountability identified	Environmental task force—environment, QA, H&S, personnel managers—work with departmental Green Teams to progress some aspects, while departmental managers have responsibility for some, and named individuals take others.
4. Defined, measurable goals	Each registered aspect has associated objectives and targets.
5. Adequate resources allocated	See lines of responsibility.
10. Design for environment on a life-cycle basis	'Design for production' to minimise waste is a current initiative, artwork designers are in-house to facilitate.
12. Creation of a corporate culture that rewards performance related to environmental issues	No employee incentive or encouragement schemes
17. Obtain independent audits to verify stated performance	Intention to audit EMS every three years after certification

Further, disaggregating ISO 14001 specifications reveals no requirement or recommendation to increase sales or reduce costs, either of which would raise profits. Disaggregation does, however, reveal consistency between ISO 14001 specifications and criteria found to be consistent with reduced cost of equity, which adds economic value.

Summing the parts, therefore, suggests certification could add value by reducing the cost of equity, subject to communication with equity markets, including information about specific environmental aspects highlighted in the earlier analysis. But the same does not appear true of the cost of debt where there is no evidence of discounting interest rates on account of reduced environmental risk generally, let alone ISO 14001 certification or disaggregated specifications.

The key to increasing profits is specifically in the way aspects are deemed significant, namely targeting income generation and operating cost reduction explicitly. The two-stage process, outlined in Figure 25.1, facilitates identifying such profit increase opportunities.

These conclusions beg the question, 'How should a firm make a financial case for seeking ISO 14001 certification?' Clearly, where there is a real risk of loss of business because customers require it, the case speaks for itself. Where there is no such requirement, the argument based on sales depends on the firm's appetite for risk and its reading of the market. Unique Images used operating cost reduction opportunities to support the case for implementing an ISO 14001-compliant EMS, taking a pilot aspect, and demonstrating long-term environmental impact and cost reduction. The potential flaw with the pilot approach is the speculative assumption that there will be similar occurrences with other aspects. There will always be a degree of uncertainty over where the specific opportunities for reducing impact and costs lie until the aspects have been identified and evaluated. For publicly listed companies, a more robust case for seeking certification appears to be founded on the cost of equity reduction argument, providing the firm commits to communicate with equity markets about what it is doing. The argument runs as follows:

☐ Environmental criteria have been identified which can lead to lower cost of equity.

☐ ISO 14001 specifications match most of the criteria.

☐ Other criteria that relate to specified environmental impacts can be addressed when prioritising aspects. Since the identities of the specified impacts are known through Kaiser's study, there is no element of speculation over whether or not they will be identified after the ISO 14001 implementation process has begun. The firm knows in advance what it should look to address for the purposes of reducing the cost of equity.

Given that reducing cost of equity adds economic value, our recommendation is that, in a supply chain-neutral scenario, the financial case for ISO 14001 certification be made on the basis of added value through reduced cost of equity.

DRIVERS AND ADVANTAGES OF IMPLEMENTING EMSs
Brazilian cases

Dalia Maimon
Federal University of Rio de Janeiro, Brazil

Up to September 2000, about 196 Brazilian companies had obtained ISO 14001 certification, indicating an increasing interest in the incorporation of environmental compliance into business.

The fast pace in which these companies have become ISO 14001-certified results, mainly, from two tendencies consolidated in Brazilian companies in the 1990s—the movement towards management modernisation and the incorporation of environmental compliance.

Due to the control of inflation, the stabilisation of the Brazilian economy and liberalisation, Brazilian companies have had to reduce costs and improve competitiveness. These factors have caused companies to introduce innovative management practices which have resulted in the implementation of quality programmes and ISO 9000 standards. This was the first step towards the ISO 14001 standard, which presupposes planning and strategic know-how.

With regard to environmental issues, in general, Brazilian companies believe there is a conflict between environmental awareness and business. Environmental responsibility is limited to compliance with pollution control standards and environmental impact reports,[1] the requirements of which vary from state to state. Institutionalisation of the environmental function in big companies occurred in the mid-1980s as a result of the consolidation of environmental legislation.

Environmental responsibility varies in accordance with the industrial sector and the size of the organisations. The main determinants for environmental management are pressure by both the regulating authorities and the local community, and the international links between companies (see Fig. 26.1).

---

1   Since 1988, in order to get an operating licence, new projects have to consider minimising environmental impacts.

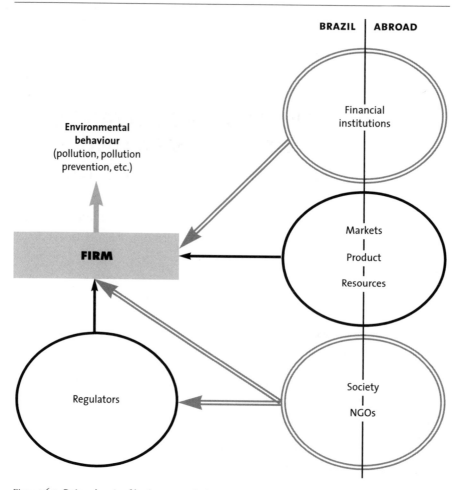

Figure 26.1 **Determinants of business eco-strategy**

In spite of the emphasis placed on the globalisation of ecology, the existing literature on business and environment does not emphasise the role of companies' increasing global presence as an explanation for their respective environmental performance (Tomer 1992).

Maimon's surveys (1996) show that the Brazilian companies with the greatest international transactions also have the greatest environmental responsibility. Included in this group are exporting companies which are often subject to environmental discrimination and pressured to adopt the environmental and ecological standards of the countries to which they export. Companies that depend on international funding from the World Bank have to submit environmental impact reports—and projects to solve negative environmental impacts—in order to receive loans. There are multinational companies which, due to shareholders' and consumers' demands, are forced to improve their environmental performance.

The role of the local population and of the environmental movement in controlling companies' performance has resulted in Brazilian legislation requiring public hearings on the subject. Polluting companies located near major urban centres have been forced to change their relationship with the environment while pressure from the general Brazilian public has helped change the course of the Brazilian nuclear energy programme and the behaviour of companies considered vital to national security such as Petrobras, the state-owned oil company. Pressure from the community was also important in the case of Borregard, a cellulose and paper company located in southern Brazil. Air pollution and pollution of the Guaíba river caused the company to be shut down in 1973.

International non-governmental organisations are also very active in relation to the environmental performance of companies and public enterprises in the Amazon region.

◢ The case studies

The eight case studies presented in this chapter[2] are from companies in different sectors—paper and cellulose, glass, cleaning, automobile, power, textile, chemicals and iron industries—whose productive activities cause different types of environmental impact. Nevertheless, they have something in common; they were the first in their sectors, in Brazil, to obtain the environmental management system (EMS) standard ISO 14001. The history of each of these pioneers can be found below, with more details in Table 26.1.

Almost all of the firms had participated in early discussions on the ISO 14000 series and became thereafter part of GANA (the Brazilian Environmental Standardisation Support Group), a decisive fact for defining the certification process among them.

By introducing different eco-strategies into their activities, these companies became proactive and positioned themselves ahead of their competitors. If their example is followed, impacts from industrial activity will be reduced, benefiting everybody.

Bahia Sul Celulose SA

Bahia Sul, a national cellulose and paper company, was founded in 1990. It is a joint venture between Companhia Suzano de Papel e Celulose and Companhia Vale do Rio Doce, and its stock is now sold on the Brazilian and American stock exchanges. It was the first South American company to be certified for compliance with ISO 14001 standards.

Bahia Sul's installed capacity is for 500,000 tonnes/year of cellulose and 250,000 tonnes/year of paper, with paper weight ranging from 56 g/m^2 to 110 g/m^2. In 1996, Bahia

---

2 The information contained in these case studies was obtained from a survey of 30 companies holding ISO 14001 certificates at January 1999. Additional information can be obtained from the following websites: www.bahiasul.com.br, www.blindex.com.br, www.santaelisa.com.br, www.cetrel.com.br, www.fiat.com.br, www.furnas.com.br, www.hering.com.br and www. samarco.com.br.

FIRM	SECTOR	DRIVERS	LABEL	ADVANTAGES
Bahia Sul	Cellulose/paper	Export market	ISO 14001 BS 7750 ISO 9002	Improvements in international management, in the foreign market and energy saving
Blindex	Glass	Multinational shareholders	ISO 14001, ISO 9002	Image, lower costs with prevention, energy saving
Cetrel	Cleaner pollution	Regulators	ISO 14001 BS 7750	Image, lower costs with prevention, improve internal management
Fiat	Automobile	Multinational	ISO 14001 ISO 9002	Image, lower costs with prevention
Furnas	Hydroelectric	International funding	ISO 14001	Image, lower costs with prevention
Hering	Textile	Export market	ISO 14001 ISO 9002, Ecotex	Image, foreign market
Petroflex	Petrochemical	Privatisation Regulators	ISO 14001, ISO 9002 BS 7750	Image, lower costs with prevention
Samarco	Iron mining and production	Multinational shareholders	ISO 14001 ISO 9002	Image, lower costs with prevention, energy savings

Table 26.1 **Drivers and advantages of implementing EMSs in Brazilian companies**

Sul was responsible for nearly 13% of the Brazilian production of short-fibre bleached cellulose and it accounted for 9% of paper production in Brazil.

Most of the company's production is exported—81% of cellulose and 62% of paper. The major markets for Bahia Sul cellulose exports are Japan and South Korea (52.5%), North America (28%) and Europe (18%). Printing and writing paper exports are shipped mostly to North America (35%) and Europe (28%), but also to Asia (20%), the Middle East (14%), Latin America (2.5%) and Africa (1.5%). Bahia Sul accounts for 14.4% of Brazil's total paper exports.

Bahia Sul achieves high quality and environmental standards, having been granted ISO 9002 in 1995, BS 7750 in 1996 and ISO 14001 (draft) in 1996. Bahia Sul obtained the certifications in order to boost productivity, guarantee customer satisfaction and enhance the company's image. BS 7750 was the basis for the implementation of ISO 14001. Bahia Sul has turned quality and environmental management into an integrated system.

Environmental certification to BS 7750 and ISO 14001 have costs: altogether, US$1 million were invested in the first two years of the standards' implementation; 44% was used for training; 30% for instrument calibration according to Brazilian and international standards; and 18% in consulting services (US$70,000 allocated to environmental issues). The remainder was spent in general expenses.

The ISO 14001 certificate has improved the company's image, since it was achieved two years ahead of its competitors. Bahia Sul estimates yearly gains of US$700,000 as a result of its improved reputation both at home and abroad. This has allowed the company to save about US$50,000/year in advertising and shows that environmental management is not a liability, but rather an investment.[3]

Blindex Vidros de Segurança Ltda.

Blindex Vidros de Segurança Ltda. is a leading company in the safety glass business. It is committed to sustainable development and environmental excellence through continuous improvement in its production processes and products. Founded in 1951, the company was acquired, in 1973, by the British group Pilkington, the world leader in the production of flat glass and by-products. Blindex was the first Latin American company in its sector to obtain ISO 14001 certification for one of its plants.

The Pilkington group's corporate environmental directory sets out the minimum guidelines to be followed by all subsidiaries, independently of local legislation, to secure a minimum standard of environmental conduct.

All of the group's companies submit quarterly reports on their environmental performance and achievements, and monthly statistical data on water and energy consumption, waste generation, gas emissions and other parameters. Environmental audits are conducted every three years, covering health and security aspects. A plan of action is required for any reported deficiencies.

Cetrel SA

Cetrel was founded in 1978 to treat the environmental pollution (air, water and waste) generated by the Camaçari Petrochemical Complex (CPC) in the state of Bahia, north-east of Brazil. Located between two hydrographic basins, close to the coast and in the vicinity of the metropolitan area of Salvador, CPC is the largest industrial complex in South America. Cetrel's task is to treat the effluents and waste produced by the companies located in the complex. Cetrel was the second company in Brazil to obtain environmental certifications to BS 7750 in January 1996 and ISO 14001 in August 1996.

Using an EMS that comprises 600 standardised internal procedures, Cetrel maintains water quality by enforcing effluent discharge standards and removing the main pollutants in its effluent treatment plant.

EMS implementation represented a revolution in Cetrel's general management. All the procedures were changed: strategic planning, objectives, goals and continuously improved policies are now part of the company's routine.[4]

Fiat Automóveis SA

Fiat Automóveis SA is one of the 12 companies in the Fiat group in Brazil. It started its operations in 1973 as a result of an agreement between Fiat SpA (the Italian holding company) and the government of the state of Minas Gerais in south-eastern Brazil.

---

3   www.bahiasul.com.br, 1999
4   www.cetrel.com.br, 1998

Responsible for about 30% of the Brazilian automobile production, Fiat Automóveis is the second-largest car-maker in Brazil. Its products are sold both in the domestic (78%) and foreign markets (22%).

Fiat Automóveis's EMS was implemented in 1996 and, in 1998, it obtained certification to ISO 14001. The main reasons for obtaining the certificate were: compliance with Fiat group's corporate environmental policy and the parent company's determination to turn Fiat Automóveis into the pilot operation for obtaining certification in order to compete effectively in world markets. Fiat Automóveis also obtained the ISO 9002 quality certificate.

EMS implementation increased Fiat Automóveis's employees' environmental awareness, and helped to prevent material and energy losses. Other positive results included: electricity and water consumption, as well as waste generation, were reduced by 37%, 29% and 25%, respectively. Black smoke emissions by diesel vehicles belonging to suppliers were reduced by 55%, thanks to constant monitoring.

In the medium term, Fiat Automóveis will require its suppliers to have environmental licences and, in the long term, to be certified to ISO 14001. The objective is to get the whole production chain environmentally certified.

Furnas Centrais Elétricas SA

Furnas Centrais Elétricas SA is Brazil's largest hydroelectric energy generator. Its commitment to environmental preservation, together with the quality and reliability of its services, made it the first Latin American company in the power industry to obtain, for the Ibiúna power sub-station, ISO 14001.

Furnas was founded in 1957 to meet energy demand in Brazil's south-eastern region. Since then, its operations have been expanded to generate and transmit power to central and western Brazil as well. Furnas supplies energy to 47% of the Brazilian population and to 69% of the country's industries.

Furnas is a public company with a complex power generation and transmission system: nine hydroelectric power plants, two thermoelectric power plants and 22 sub-stations. This system is connected to five other hydroelectric power plants, one nuclear power plant and eight sub-stations belonging to other companies. The power generation installed capacity is 9,080 MW, 93% of which is from a renewable source—hydroelectric power.

Total spending on ISO 14001 certification amounts to US$120,000, of which 69% was spent on consultancy services, 11% on material and equipment purchase, and 20% on training. However, EMS implementation has so far saved US$200,000 by oil recycling. Energy and water consumption were also reduced and employee morale improved—interviews with employees revealed that they were very proud to work in a company with environmental certification.

Hering Têxtil SA

Concern over environmental issues and the quality of life of its surrounding communities has been one of Hering's key business principles throughout its hundred-year existence. It was the first textile company in Brazil and the first fully Brazilian-owned company to obtain ISO 14001 certification from the Brazilian Certification System.

Hering's production of cotton shirts began in 1880 with German immigrants in Blumenau—a city in the state of Santa Catarina. Hering is currently the country's largest clothing manufacturer, accounting for 7% of the Brazilian market. It exports about 10% of its production to Latin America, Europe and the United States. Hering's products are distributed through approximately 250 sales representatives and salespeople, besides 60 Hering stores plus 33 Dzarm stores.

Hering has always been pressured by importers to maintain an environmental policy, and is frequently monitored by them. The company has introduced clean technology and forest conservation programmes. Hering's headquarters is located in a native forest reserve, covering 4,535,000 m^2, which includes several areas of original tropical forest. For each square metre of constructed area, the company has 17 m^2 of 'green' area in the form of preserved forest or planted gardens.

The environmental quality-oriented actions of the company are recognised by Ecotek, the textile industry label, and shown by its ISO 14001 certification—the latter obtained in April 1997.

The company's main reasons for implementing the EMS and obtaining ISO 14001 certification were to show conformance to an international standard of environmental excellence and to provide the firm's products with a competitive advantage in a demanding market. Indeed, this competitive advantage has helped Hering to survive the Brazilian economic recession of the 1980s and '90s. Domestic textile companies were among those most severely affected, having to compete domestically with cut-price Asian producers and being penalised abroad by the overvaluation of the Brazilian currency, the real.

Petroflex Indústria e Comércio SA

Petroflex Indústria e Comércio SA is responsible for processing and commercialising rubber and other chemicals. Its three industrial facilities are certified according to ISO 14001 and all of its procedures are certified to ISO 9002.

Created in 1976 as an affiliated company to Petrobras Química SA (Petroquisa), Petroflex is Brazil's market leader, supplying over 85% of the demand for synthetic rubber.

In 1992, Petroflex became the first company in the Brazilian petrochemical sector to be privatised. Among its new shareholders are Suzano (20.45%), Copene (20.45%) and Unipar (10.22%). Late in 1996, Petroflex acquired the voting capital of COPERBO (Companhia Pernambucana de Borracha Sintética), the second-largest Brazilian synthetic rubber producer.

Petroflex has joined the chemical industry's Responsible Care programme, introduced in Brazil by the Brazilian Chemical Industry Association. All three plants owned by Petroflex have implemented and been certified to ISO 14001 and have shown that the procedures applied have allowed Petroflex to appropriately manage its environmental impacts. Issues such as image improvement and cost reduction have driven the quest for certification.

The need for environmental protection was taken into consideration when planning a petrochemical complex in Triunfo. In 1994, Petroflex started implementing an EMS at its Triunfo plant, according to the ISO 14001 standard, and in 1996 the plant was certified.

Petroflex is now working on systematising its industrial safety and occupational health activities, according to DNV's International Safety Rating System, as well as working on implementing standards compliant with BS 8800.

US$40,000 and US$33,000 were invested in the EMS implementation and ISO 14001 certification for the Triunfo and Cabo de Santo Agostinho plants respectively. A much smaller amount was invested in the Duque de Caxias plant because there the employees themselves implemented the EMS, applying knowledge acquired from the other plants.

Samarco Mineração

Samarco Mineração is a company that operates in the iron ore industry, using itabirite as raw material. Samarco produces iron ore pellets—used in blast furnaces and direct reduction steel-making processes—and concentrated ore fines. It was the first iron ore-mining enterprise in South America to obtain ISO 14001 certification for all phases of its production process.

The result of a joint investment by two large mining groups—Brazil's Belgo-Mineira (51%) and Australia's Broken Hill Proprietary Company, Ltd (49%)—Samarco began mining itabirite in 1977. Until then, the mineral had been rejected due to its low iron content. There are two production units, one in Germano, in the state of Minas Gerais, which includes a processing plant and the Alegria mine, and one in Ponta do Ubu, in the state of Espírito Santo, comprising two palletising units and a marine terminal.

All stages of Samarco's production process—mining, concentration, transport, pelleting and shipping—have been certified to ISO 9002 since 1994. ISO 9002 certification aimed at guaranteeing production quality and promoting the stability and continuous improvement of the company's processes.

The EMS was awarded ISO 14001 certification in 1998 and brought the company several advantages, such as improved image, both in the market and within the community, cost reductions and improved internal organisation.

◢ Conclusion

The eight case studies in this chapter, presented and summarised in Table 26.1, lead us to the conclusion that, in countries such as Brazil where environmental values are not yet widespread among the population and policy-makers, the globalisation of the environment has been an important tool in changing companies' attitudes.

In order to maintain and increase their markets, export companies seek competitive advantage by means of certification to ISO 14001. Today, competitiveness and quality patterns are being reconsidered in the light of sustainable development. The reconciliation of competitiveness with environmental protection is now a major challenge for modern companies such as Hering and Bahia Sul.

In the case of multinationals, pressure from shareholders and consumers has forced them to take on responsibility for the environment—even those firms that, in the 1970s and 1980s, came to Brazil attracted by the lack of environmental regulations. Such companies include Fiat, Samarco and Blindex.

Large public companies, which were considered national security companies and were inspected as such until 1986—the year democracy was reinstated in Brazil—have had to change their behaviour in order to improve their image. The conditions imposed by international financing institutions have played a major role in their change of attitude. This can be seen in the case of Furnas.

Finally, Petroflex is an example of the behaviour by recently privatised companies that inherited large environmental liabilities and are gradually trying to improve their management and performance.

Our survey did not allow for a precise cost–benefit analysis of the introduction of the ISO 14001 standard, but in the two extreme cases of Bahia Sul, where the implementation of the standard cost more than US$1 million, and of Petroflex, where the amounts for the three establishments were around US$100,000, show that investments in the environment can be profitable. According to statements made by Bahia Sul's representatives, return on investment was achieved in the first six months after certification. In the case of Petroflex, the return from pollution control, cost reduction and image improvement have more than compensated for the investment.

Part 8
SUSTAINABILITY
AND ISO 14001

ISO 14001: A TOOL FOR MUNICIPAL GOVERNMENT TO ACHIEVE SUSTAINABILITY

The experiences of Hamilton-Wentworth, Canada

Mark Bekkering
City of Toronto Urban Planning
and Development Services, Canada

David McCallum
M+A Environmental
Consultants, Canada

The value of the ISO 14001 standard to municipal government is very different from its value to a private company. Municipal government is a forum for public policy debate, a regulator and the provider of a number of community services. A defined management system can be used by municipal government to help set priorities for addressing the concerns of its community, plus ensure its services are being delivered following efficient and effective practices. The ISO 14001 standard, or similar standards, can also be used to help municipal government achieve the wider global goal of sustainability as outlined in Agenda 21[1] and by the Brundtland Commission in *Our Common Future* (WCED 1987).

Municipalities around the world are using a structured EMS as a tool for implementing the sustainability agenda. In New Zealand, eight district councils recently supported and participated in the development of a guide to ISO 14001 for local government (Cockrean 1999). The Environmental Protection Agency (EPA) in the US successfully completed a pilot project with seven municipalities, a county and a state prison to test the applicability of ISO 14001 to public administration functions (McGraw-Hill Companies 1999). In the UK, local authorities are using the EU Eco-management and Audit Scheme (EMAS), which is similar to ISO 14001, as a way to implement the requirements for Local Agenda 21 (Riglar 1996). In Australia, ISO 14001 is being used by municipalities to address the requirement for a plan to implement Agenda 21 (City of Manningham 1999).

---

1 Agenda 21, which resulted from the 1992 United Nations Conference on Environment and Development, is a set of guidelines for achieving sustainability.

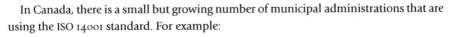

In Canada, there is a small but growing number of municipal administrations that are using the ISO 14001 standard. For example:

☐ The Regional Municipality of Waterloo has registered its solid waste management operations to ISO 14001 (Frisken 1999).

☐ The operator of the water treatment facilities for the Regional Municipality of Peel is registered to ISO 14001.

☐ The Regional Municipality of York has commenced implementation of ISO 14001 for its waste-water treatment operations.

☐ The Province of Ontario, with the participation of three municipalities, is preparing an implementation guide to create an EMS for solid waste management functions (Envirosphere EMC and Gartner Lee Ltd 1999).

☐ The City of Calgary has initiated implementation of ISO 14001.

Many of these municipalities, and those involved in the EPA pilots in the US, have focused their efforts on the delivery of hard services, such as solid waste management or water treatment, and on addressing environmental concerns associated with the delivery of these services. In the North American context, it is rare that an EMS goes beyond the delivery of hard services, particularly to address the goal of sustainable development.

The Regional Environment Department (hereafter referred to as the Department) of the Regional Municipality of Hamilton-Wentworth, Canada, has developed its EMS to broaden its scope and apply the management systems concept to all types of decision-making. The applicability of ISO 14001 to the operations of municipal government is seen through an overview of the experiences of the Department in developing its EMS and how it has been designed to implement the goals of Hamilton-Wentworth's VISION 2020 Sustainable Community Initiative.

◢ The setting

The Regional Municipality of Hamilton-Wentworth, Canada (hereafter referred to as the Region), is the upper tier of a two-tier municipal government structure. With an annual budget of about $500 million (Canadian), it is responsible for providing the 470,000 residents of the area with: water treatment and distribution; waste-water collection and treatment; public transit; regional roads; public health and social services; economic development; solid waste management; police services; and regional land use planning. There are six area municipalities, which are responsible for: parks and recreation; local land use planning; local roads; storm-water management; and solid waste collection.

In 1990, the Region initiated a community-driven effort to implement the concept of sustainable development. A citizens' task force consisting of community leaders representing all major sectors of the community was organised and given the mandate to define a community vision based on the idea of sustainability. Over a two-and-a-half-year period the task force met with over a thousand fellow citizens and came up with a vision statement for the future entitled *VISION 2020: The Sustainable Region* (Regional Chairman's Task Force on Sustainable Development 1993). Regional Council endorsed this vision statement in February 1993 and it has become the goal that all policies, programmes and actions of Council and the administration are trying to achieve (Bekkering and Eyles 1998; Bekkering 1998; Region of Hamilton-Wentworth 1999).

In March 1997, under the general banner of the VISION 2020 Sustainable Community Initiative, the Department initiated a project to develop an EMS and seek registration to the ISO 14001 standard. With an annual budget of $100 million (Canadian) and over 220 employees, the Department is responsible for the delivery of the Region's:

❑ Water treatment and distribution services

❑ Waste-water collection and treatment services

❑ Solid waste disposal and management services

❑ Regional planning and development services

❑ Collection of storm-water in the City of Hamilton

◢ Why an EMS and ISO 14001?

Provincial governments, which are legislatively responsible for municipalities in Canada, have restructured the municipal–provincial relationship with the result that many environmental, financial, planning and social services have become the responsibility of municipal governments. As restructuring is occurring, residents question the quality and type of municipal services they receive and the decision-making of those responsible for the delivery of those services. Municipalities must prove themselves to their business partners, to the political structures to which they are responsible and to the citizens they serve.

In 1996, against this environment of change and under the direction of a new chief administrative officer, the Region went through an organisational restructuring that resulted in the creation of five departments, one of which was environment. Although there were a number of challenges facing senior management with the integration of formerly independent units, the greatest came with the Regional Environment Department and the mandate to establish itself as the lead agency of the municipality for protecting the natural environment. What tools could be used by the Department to fulfil this mandate?

Establishing an EMS and seeking independent certification of the management system was the primary tool selected to achieve the Department's mandate. Independent certification establishes credibility with the community and provides reassurance that issues of concern are being identified and addressed in the delivery of the Department's services. Having a structured decision-making process to demonstrate how and why priorities are being set helps counter the public image that decision-making is short-term and ad hoc as opposed to systematic.

In terms of managing daily operations, an EMS creates a structured mechanism for:

☐ Ensuring compliance with environmental statues and regulations

☐ Providing the evidence of due diligence

☐ Reducing both corporate and employee liabilities

☐ Improving employee health and safety

☐ Increasing employee morale by creating a focused direction for the Department

☐ Spreading environmental responsibility throughout the organisation

☐ Identifying potential operational improvements and efficiencies

☐ Improving the efficiency of service delivery by creating a cycle of continuous improvement

☐ Creating the evidence that environmental issues are being identified and controlled in the delivery of the services

In contrast, managing compliance with regulations primarily motivates most organisations seeking registration to the ISO 14001 standard. Other motivators typically include the opportunity for cost savings, enhanced employee safety and environmental stewardship. These factors were important to the Department but the key motivator was the need to have an effective tool for implementing Council directives and to be able to show that appropriate action was being or had been taken.

◢ Developing the EMS

Before the ISO 14001 initiative began, it was recognised that various types of management process already existed in the Department and many proactive efforts had been and were already being made to address environmental issues. Therefore, the project focused on:

☐ Structuring the existing management processes to meet the requirements of the ISO 14001 standard

☐ Confirming that departmental activities are consistent with existing environmental commitments

☐ Creating the evidence that environmental issues are being addressed by locating and formalising the existing evidence

Development of the EMS must also create the structures for integrating the Department and involving all employees in the achievement of the Department's mandate. Recognising this key priority, the process followed for developing the Department's environmental mission statement, which is one of the first steps to building an EMS, allowed for the involvement of all personnel. This was achieved through a departmental newsletter, 'open houses' for personnel hosted by the Commissioner of the Department, presentations to union officers and other communication tools.

This effort also served as an opportunity to introduce the concept of an EMS to all personnel, involve them in the project and highlight how the EMS will help the Department to achieve VISION 2020. Although some personnel expressed concerns about potential job loss and change, to a large extent most were either supportive or just indifferent to the effort. Initial interest is reflected in that over 10% of personnel (25 people) made suggestions towards the development of the mission statement.

Completed in January 1998, the mission statement confirms the commitment to address the community's environmental concerns as expressed in VISION 2020 and integrates the notion of continuous improvement as required in the ISO 14001 standard. Since completion, the mission statement has been communicated to all personnel through an employee newsletter. As a ongoing reminder, the mission statement was posted in visible locations at all facilities, printed on a mouse pad for all personnel with computers, and included on the back of all business cards.

The environmental mission statement is:

> The Regional Environment Department is committed, within the framework of its assigned mandate, to work towards the achievement of the sustainable community expressed in VISION 2020 and complying with Regional Council's Environment Policy. This includes a commitment to continually improve its environmental performance, to sustain and protect our human and natural community by identifying significant environmental aspects and by enhancing positive effects and reducing negative effects as it delivers its services to the community.

Identifying environmental impacts and legal requirements

The next major component of the project was to identify how services were being delivered and what were the environmental impacts and legal and other requirements associated with them. Two major investigations were carried out to complete this task.

The first was a 'gap analysis' exercise implemented in the spring/summer of 1997. This effort assessed the amount of change required in existing management systems to meet the ISO 14001 standard. To achieve this purpose, eight personnel were trained by the project consultant on the ISO 14001 standard and interview methods. The gap analysis concluded that the Department had about 65% of the requirements of the standard in place with the major gaps being:

☐ Documented standard operating procedures

☐ Well-maintained records to provide the evidence that procedures are being followed and environmental issues are being addressed

☐ A structured management plan to show how environmental issues are considered in setting work plans and budgets

☐ Systematic auditing or review of management systems

Following the findings of the gap analysis, senior management decided to structure the EMS according to the five core businesses of the Department. This made it easier to link operations to the goals of VISION 2020 and, more importantly, allowed for continuity of the management system. For example, all five of the Department's operating units have a role in the delivery of the waste-water collection and treatment service. Structuring the EMS according to the service instead of the operating units ensured that all five units work towards the same goals.

Five staff working groups were organised in autumn 1997. Involving about 30 personnel from all operating units of the Department, these groups were each assigned one of the core businesses. The working groups were asked to identify:

☐ The core functions for the business area

☐ Current responsibilities for delivering the core functions

☐ The positive and negative environmental impacts associated with the core functions

☐ The legal and other requirements that must be met in delivering the core functions

Completed in February 1998, the efforts of the working groups created the foundation for the EMS.

Probably the most challenging aspect of this component of the initiative was establishing a system for defining significant environmental aspects, setting objectives and targets, and keeping that system in line with the goals of VISION 2020. The system that was established starts with the identification of environmental aspects and impacts. Any identified environmental aspects that were, or could, result in an incident of regulatory non-compliance were immediately defined as significant. For all other issues, significance is defined using a simple risk assessment process.

The identified significant environmental aspects were then prioritised according to the goals of VISION 2020. A set of objectives and targets were developed for each significant environmental aspect that related to a goal within VISION 2020. These objectives and targets link the expressed environmental concerns of the community with the environmental impacts identified as being associated with the Department's services and operations. In other words, the objectives are an expression of what contribution the Department will make towards achieving VISION 2020.

Development of these objectives and targets was a touchy issue for the Department. Although all of the identified environmental aspects could be associated to a VISION 2020 goal, it was recognised that the Department could not realistically address *all* of the environmental aspects and, therefore, meet *all* of the VISION 2020 goals. Senior management was uncomfortable with setting priorities that it felt were the responsibility of the elected Council. To address this concern it was decided to develop objectives and targets for all environmental aspects, prioritise them according to significance and present to them to Council as part of the annual budget process. This way, if Council decided that other issues deserved higher priority it could do so during the budget. The EMS became the tool with which senior management could recommend and explain priorities to Council but still leave the final decision-making to Council.

Establishing responsibilities, procedures and records

The next major component of the EMS initiative focused on filling the gaps identified in the gap analysis. The working groups were now asked to:

☐ Review and confirm how the service is delivered, what are the environmental impacts, and what are the legal and other requirements guiding their service

☐ Identify what mechanisms, such as standard operating procedures, technological changes, inspection and monitoring, personnel training and capital improvements, currently exist or are being implemented for controlling the environmental impacts and maintaining regulatory compliance

☐ Structure existing systems where required to meet the requirements of ISO 14001

☐ Develop an environmental management plan to address the defined objectives and targets

The efforts of the implementation groups resulted in the establishment of a cycle of continuous improvement. By going through the process of reviewing the environmental impacts associated with their operations, awareness was increased and a number of quick and easy modifications in procedures were made. In some cases concerns were brought forward that have resulted in the initiation of special studies to investigate the issue and make changes in operations.

Creating systems for regular evaluation and improvement of the management system

The final phase of the EMS initiative involved establishing the systems for completing the cycle of continuous improvement. The major tasks were:

☐ Reviewing the procedures and systems developed by the working groups to ensure they link to the approved objectives and targets

☐ Presenting Council with an action plan, as part of the annual budget process, for achieving the recommended objectives and targets

☐ Training and awareness about the EMS requirements for all personnel

☐ Establishment of an internal management system audit process

☐ Implementation of an annual management review of the overall effectiveness of the EMS

As of September 1999 only the working group for the solid waste management business area had moved into this phase of the initiative. It is planned that, for this business area, the EMS will be complete and operational by December 1999.

Due to a new municipal restructuring process that started in September 1998, the work in the other four business areas has been put on hold. Whether work will begin again on completing the EMS in these areas is questionable, as it is unknown whether the new management will have the same interest towards the development of an EMS. The commitment and interest of senior management in the EMS has been critical to the ongoing development and success of the initiative. Without it, the EMS, no matter how well structured or developed, has failed to be implemented as initially envisioned.

◢ Project resources

The project budget was $166,000 (Canadian) over a two-year period. From this budget, a full-time project assistant was hired for 16 months and two temporary project assistants for six-month periods were hired with the assistance of federal job training programmes. In addition, an independent consultant was hired, to provide:

☐ Strategic advice on structuring the management system to meet the requirements of ISO 14001

☐ Training for personnel on the ISO 14001 and management system auditing techniques

☐ Advice on internal and external communication strategies

In addition to the budget, a full-time project co-ordinator was employed for two years. In August 1998, a second member of staff was assigned to the project on approximately a two-thirds basis, to be responsible for ongoing management of the EMS. The time required for this was estimated at being a half-time position.

Because the development of the EMS was seen as something that must be done in-house, a large number of personnel were involved in the initiative. Personnel conducted preliminary internal audits, identified environmental impacts and legal requirements, and developed operating procedures. The amount of time spent on these tasks, as of September 1999, is estimated to be in the range of 350–400 person-days.

Taking staff away from their daily work activities to participate in the development of the EMS has been the most expensive aspect of the project. Justifying what was seen as a short-term cost for a long-term benefit was a challenging task. Although the majority of staff who participated in the initiative felt it was worthwhile, they struggled with the limitations on their time to complete both daily and assigned EMS development tasks. Naturally, the assigned EMS development tasks always took second precedence. Greater effort and resources should have been found at the outset of the initiative to free up the time of certain key personnel to participate in the development of the EMS.

◢ Conclusions

Different organisations have different reasons for developing an EMS and for seeking registration to the ISO 14001 standard. These reasons determine how the EMS is developed and how it evolves.

The Regional Environment Department judged that an EMS, registered by an independent objective third party, was the preferred tool for creating the structures needed to integrate changing responsibilities, and to plan and allocate resources to address community priorities—in a systematic and defensible manner. The EMS was seen as a tool for ensuring the Department maintains the goals and priorities of VISION 2020. This is very different from many private-sector organisations that see ISO 14001 as a means to investigate their environmental performance and develop ways to control and improve it.

The challenge in Hamilton-Wentworth with its VISION 2020 initiative has been in finding ways to make this vision and its values a reality. The Department chose ISO 14001 as that tool. The EMS explicitly stated that VISION 2020 is the root of the Department's environmental mission statement and the expressed goals of VISION 2020 are the main drivers for the objectives and targets. The EMS is the method of translating the vision statement into action and change.

That, at least, was the intention when the EMS initiative was started in 1997. Changes in senior management and municipal restructuring have resulted in the effort, to a large extent, being put on hold. However, the experiences over the two years of development have provided many insights into the usefulness of ISO 14001 for municipal government.

A major challenge has been the rigour required in ISO 14001 for defining environmental significance, setting objectives and targets, preparing environmental management plans and integrating this with systems for setting annual budgets and annual work planning. The area of greatest concern has been over how the system recognises that staff do not have control of the decision-making process. By placing the recommended objectives and targets within the context of the goals of VISION 2020, it is hoped that they will match the priorities of the Council and that the rigour of the ISO 14001 process will result in credible and accountable recommendations.

The experiences of Hamilton-Wentworth show that, if Agenda 21, or something similar, is a priority for a municipal government, ISO 14001 can assist the organisation in translating those goals and values into daily activities. An EMS will structure the operations of the organisation so that it can show the rationale behind recommended priorities and allocation of resources. Successful development of the EMS, however, depends on the allocation of sufficient resources, the commitment of senior management and the maintenance of an environment that will allow for its development and maturation.

PROYECTO GUADALAJARA
Promoting sustainable development through the adoption of ISO 14001 by small and medium-sized enterprises*

Richard P. Wells and David Galbraith

The Lexington Group, Environmental Management Consultants, Inc., USA

In theory, a company that implements an environmental management system (EMS) such as ISO 14001 should be able to improve its competitiveness and its environmental performance. By integrating environmental considerations in everything it does, a company will identify solutions to environmental problems where they can be most effectively addressed—generally in the design of products and processes rather than at the end-of-pipe. The concept of continual improvement built into EMSs ensures that companies are constantly learning from their past experiences to improve their future environmental performance.

Unfortunately, the promise of EMSs has not been translated into reality—particularly among small companies. Sceptics argue that, because EMSs are management- rather than performance-based, they do not necessarily improve the environmental performance of many companies. A more significant objection is that ISO 14001 and most other EMS models were designed by large companies for use by large companies. An important question follows: Can small companies use EMSs to improve both their environmental and economic performance?

This question is of very real significance for Mexico. The vast majority of employment in Mexico is among micro, small and medium-sized enterprises (SMEs). Moreover, a recent World Bank study demonstrated that, although results vary by standard industrial classification (SIC), in general SMEs generate more pollution per employee than large plants (Dasgupta *et al.* 1998). One reason that SMEs are greater polluters on a per-

* The authors would like to thank the many participants of Proyecto Guadalajara, and especially Kulsum Ahmed and Paul Martin of the World Bank, for their dedication to the project and willingness to try something new.

employee basis than large companies is that they lack environmental management capabilities: a 1996 survey revealed that about 70%–80% of large Mexican and multi-national companies in Mexico had key EMS elements in place, as opposed to about 20% of the surveyed SMEs (see Fig. 28.1). The existence of key EMS elements is one of the best predictors of superior environmental performance (Dasgupta *et al.* 1997).

Proyecto Guadalajara, jointly funded by the World Bank and ten large Mexican and multinational companies with facilities in Guadalajara, was an experiment to determine whether SMEs have the capability to implement EMSs based on ISO 14001, and whether their implementation actually promotes improved environmental awareness and performance.

The project demonstrated that SMEs can indeed implement ISO 14001-based EMSs and that both the SMEs and the environment will benefit. The rest of this chapter describes Proyecto Guadalajara, discusses the significant outcomes, and concludes by addressing the thorny question of how to make EMS implementation—and the resulting benefits—more broad-based and sustainable.

◢ Origins of Proyecto Guadalajara

The idea for Proyecto Guadalajara came during a seminar on ISO 14001 given by Richard Wells of The Lexington Group, an environmental management consulting company based in Massachusetts, USA, to the environmental managers of a number of multinational corporations with facilities in Guadalajara, Mexico. The seminar, which was sponsored by the United States Agency for International Development (US AID), prompted the question of how to improve environmental management in SMEs in Guadalajara. The Lucent Technologies and IBM facilities in Guadalajara did not need US AID-subsidised

Figure 28.1 **Distribution of environmental management capabilities in Mexican industry**

Source: Lexington Group 1997

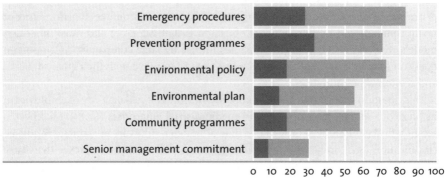

Emergency procedures		
Prevention programmes		
Environmental policy		
Environmental plan		
Community programmes		
Senior management commitment		

0 10 20 30 40 50 60 70 80 90 100

■ Small companies   %

□ Large companies

Note: Large companies in Mexico are much more likely than smaller companies to have implemented key EMS elements

ISO 14001 assistance, but some of their small local suppliers, who mix chemicals or manufacture packaging, did.

Proyecto Guadalajara was developed both to meet this need and to test its premise: that SMEs could benefit both environmentally and economically from implementing ISO 14001-based EMSs.[1] The World Bank agreed to finance one-half of the costs of an SME-oriented project as an innovative research effort. At the urging of bank staff and several local champions of the idea, ten large Mexican and multinational companies agreed to finance the remaining half.

The large companies themselves recruited SMEs for the project: each was allowed to invite from one to three suppliers. Although participation was 'voluntary' on the part of the SMEs, the invitation of a large client in some cases made refusal difficult. This point was confirmed toward the end of the project, when approximately half of the SMEs said that they would not originally have participated in Proyecto Guadalajara if not invited by an important client.

The project was officially inaugurated in November 1996 at a signing ceremony in Mexico City. It provided one year of ISO 14001-based EMS assistance to the SMEs in the form of 'just-in-time' training provided by The Lexington Group and more frequent, on-site assistance from a group of local consultants overseen by The Lexington Group. The large companies were also meant to act as mentors to the SMEs they had invited. A more complete description of the different groups that formed Proyecto Guadalajara and of the chronological sequence of the project is given below.

Participants

The large companies

Ten large companies—four Mexican and six multinational—participated in Proyecto Guadalajara: Acietera La Junta, Casa Cuervo, Cydsa, Cementos Guadalajara, Compañía Siderúrgica de Guadalajara, Honda de México, Lucent Technologies Productos de Consumo de México, Quimikao, SCI Systems, and IBM de México.

The role of these companies was to recruit, motivate and mentor their SME suppliers (or customers, in several cases) in the process of developing EMSs. In addition to helping their suppliers improve their environmental management, the project gave the large companies an opportunity to support publicly a positive environmental initiative, sanctioned by the Mexican environmental authorities.

The SMEs

Each large company invited 1–3 SMEs that met the following criteria:

☐ Each SME had to be a supplier to or customer of its large company sponsor.

☐ Each SME had to be an independent company, not a subsidiary of a larger company.

---

1   It is important to note that the goal was not certification to ISO 14001 per se.

❑ No SME could have more than 250 employees (the upper limit of the official Mexican definition of a medium-sized business).

The participating SMEs ranged in size from 3–230 employees and represented a variety of industries, including construction, chemical manufacturing, automotive parts, environmental services and printing. The actual number of SMEs participating varied from 15–20 over the course of the project, with some dropping out for reasons to be discussed below.

EMS consultants

The Lexington Group was contracted to help co-ordinate the project and to provide training and periodic technical support to SMEs in implementing an ISO 14001-based EMS.

Seventeen affiliates of two universities, the Instituto Tecnológico y de Estudios Superiores de Monterrey and the Universidad de Guadalajara, participated in Proyecto Guadalajara as consultants to individual SMEs. The Lexington Group trained and provided ongoing guidance to these consultants, who had backgrounds in environmental sciences, law and regulation, and/or management. One of the goals of Proyecto Guadalajara was that the university consultants develop the capacity to act as ISO 14001 and EMS consultants on their own.

Mexican environmental authorities

Though they played no formal role in Proyecto Guadalajara, representatives of local and national Mexican environmental authorities attended many sessions of the project as observers. The national environmental agency had particular interest in the project because it was concurrently developing a voluntary environmental management programme for industry.

The World Bank

The World Bank provided part of the funding for Proyecto Guadalajara and also supported a study to measure changes in the culture of the SMEs and in the attitudes of their employees. Representatives of the bank participated in all training and review sessions.

◢ Phases in the project model

Below is a short summary of phases in the project from its commencement in November 1996.

November 1996–May 1997: initial planning sessions

Project participants met in work groups over this period to discuss whether ISO 14001 should be adapted in any way for SMEs and to prepare for several other aspects of EMS implementation. The work groups decided that ISO 14001 was a suitable EMS model for SMEs without adaptations. Representatives of the larger companies also prepared a list of legal requirements potentially applicable to the SMEs.

May 1997: ISO 14001 course (part 1) for SMEs

In May 1997, The Lexington Group gave a two-and-a-half-day training course on the first sections of ISO 14001. Participants were given a broad overview of ISO 14001 and then trained on the policy and planning elements of the ISO 14001 model. The course included a short general session for the chief executive officers (CEOs) of the SMEs.

May–August 1997: SME implementation of ISO 14001 (as presented in part 1)

Before embarking on part 2 of the course, the SMEs were asked to complete the following seven policy and planning tasks, with help from their university consultants and large-company mentors:

- ☐ Perform a self-evaluation

- ☐ Identify the environmental aspects (EAs) of their operations

- ☐ Evaluate their state of compliance with selected Mexican environmental regulations

- ☐ Develop criteria for determining significant environmental aspects (SEAs) and identify SEAs based on these criteria

- ☐ Develop a draft corporate environmental policy

- ☐ Develop realistic objectives and targets for the EMS in conjunction with their environmental policy

- ☐ Prepare an implementation plan (including a timetable, budget and assignment of responsibilities) for achieving the objectives and targets

August 1997: progress review meetings and ISO 14001 course (part 2)

Before the second part of the course, four half-day sessions were conducted to review SME progress in accomplishing the tasks outlined above. An average of five SMEs attended each session. Each described what it had accomplished under each of the seven tasks and identified what had proved difficult and what was helpful during the process.

The Lexington Group then delivered the second part of the EMS course to the SMEs. The course covered the remaining ISO 14001 elements (from implementation to management review).

August–October 1997: SME implementation of ISO 14001 (continued)

During these three months, the SMEs were expected to complete the initial seven tasks and the following six implementation tasks, again with the help of their university consultants and large-company mentors:

- ☐ Conduct a root cause analysis for each SEA identified
- ☐ Determine and establish appropriate operational control procedures
- ☐ Define authority and responsibility for employees *vis-à-vis* the EMS and develop a strategy for internal communication
- ☐ Develop and establish a training and awareness programme
- ☐ Identify baseline environmental performance indicators
- ☐ Plan and establish emergency procedures

October 1997: progress review meetings

A second series of progress review meetings, similar in format to those held in August, was conducted in October 1997. SMEs reported on their progress in achieving the six implementation tasks assigned for the prior period as well as the initial seven policy and planning tasks. Representatives of the World Bank and The Lexington Group also conducted site visits to selected SMEs.

The Lexington Group then held a general session with the SMEs, large companies and university consultants to review the group's overall progress and to lay out additional tasks for the upcoming five-month period.

October 1997–February 1998: SME implementation of ISO 14001 (continued)

In addition to completing the previous implementation tasks, SMEs were asked to:

- ☐ Establish a documentation system for the EMS
- ☐ Conduct a second self-assessment
- ☐ Conduct an EMS audit
- ☐ Establish procedures for correcting non-conformance
- ☐ Conduct a management review of the EMS

Also during this period, The Lexington Group trained the university consultants to audit an EMS.

February 1998: progress review meetings

A third series of progress review meetings, similar in format to the previous two series, was conducted in February 1998. SMEs reported on their progress in achieving the tasks assigned and presented the environmental and economic performance improvements they had realised.

The Lexington Group then conducted a final general session to discuss overall progress, administer a survey, and award certificates to companies and individuals who had participated consistently in the project. The session also provided a forum for the SMEs, large companies and consultants to begin preliminary discussions about sustaining the project without the oversight and support of the World Bank and The Lexington Group.

February 1998–April 1999: continued implementation and two review visits

Following the February meeting, the Guadalajara participants formed a committee to provide leadership to the SMEs in continuing EMS implementation. The SMEs were divided into four groups and a structure was established for providing consultancy and/or mentorship to these groups. Lexington Group staff made two trips to Guadalajara during this period—in August 1998 and April 1999—to review the status of the SMEs.

◢ Results

To our knowledge, Proyecto Guadalajara is unique in providing a diverse group of SMEs in a developing country the opportunity to develop ISO 14001-based EMSs. The findings of the project will therefore carry a great deal of weight as Mexico and other industrialising countries search for effective means of reducing pollution from their SME sector.

At the outset of the project there were three key unknowns:

☐ Do SMEs have the capability to implement an ISO 14001-based EMS?

☐ Will SMEs that implement an ISO 14001-based EMS improve their environmental performance?

☐ Is EMS implementation by SMEs sustainable? In other words, will SMEs continue to improve their environmental performance using an EMS?

In the rest of this section we discuss these questions based on data from Proyecto Guadalajara.

Appropriateness of the ISO 14001 model for SMEs

After reviewing the ISO 14001 model during the first training session, the SMEs, somewhat to our surprise, declared that its implementation was well within their capabilities. They were right. Figure 28.2 shows the results of an 18-question self-evaluation (similar to an ISO 14001 'gap analysis') taken three times over the course of the project. At the start, in May 1997, most SMEs had few EMS elements in place. But, by July 1998, average results were high for all policy, planning and implementation elements, although only a few of

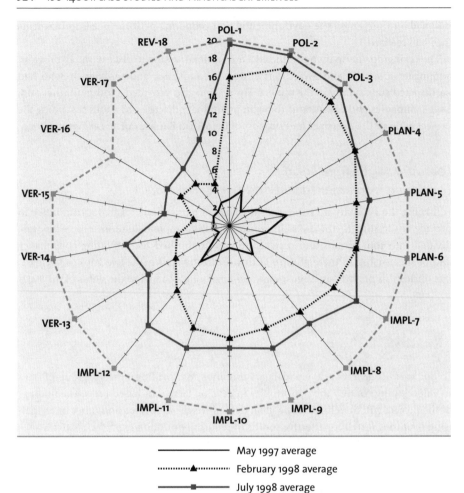

————————— May 1997 average

···········▲··········· February 1998 average

————■————— July 1998 average

– – – –■– – – – Maximum

Note: The 'radar chart' above shows the average scores attained by the 10 SMEs that completed an EMS self-assessment at each of the dates indicated. Each of the self-assessment's 18 questions refers to a specific EMS element (noted below), with potential scores ranging from 0 (no evidence of the element) to 20 (full implementation of the element).

POL-1	Environmental policy exists	IMPL-10	EMS documented
POL-2	Policy appropriate to business	IMPL-11	Operational control procedures
POL-3	Policy includes key commitments	IMPL-12	Emergency procedures exist
PLAN-4	Significant EAs identified	VER-13	Monitoring and measurement
PLAN-5	Process to identify legal requirements	VER-14	Compliance evaluation
PLAN-6	Environmental objectives and targets	VER-15	Non-conformity procedures
IMPL-7	Roles and responsibilities established	VER-16	Records
IMPL-8	Training needs identified	VER-17	EMS audits
IMPL-9	Internal communication process	REV-18	Management review

Figure 28.2 **SMEs' assessment of EMS implementation**

Photo credit: David Galbraith

Two employees from a 20-employee manufacturer of machine parts in Proyecto Guadalajara explain improvements in environmental performance. The company halved its oil use by replacing old seals, and the local government subsequently changed its classification from a hazardous to a non-hazardous waste generator.

the companies had made significant progress on checking and corrective action and management review.

Not only is ISO 14001 technically appropriate for SMEs, as the self-evaluation results demonstrate, in many respects implementation is substantially easier for them than it is for large companies. First, SMEs usually have fewer significant environmental aspects. Corporate bureaucracy is substantially less for SMEs, and training and internal communication are much easier. SMEs may, however, lack experience with procedures and work instructions and with documentation and document control—an ISO 14001 element that is especially significant for SMEs with a high rate of staff turnover (exhibited by many of the Guadalajara SMEs).

Environmental performance improvements

An unequivocal 'yes' is the answer to whether implementing an ISO 14001-based EMS improves an SME's environmental performance. Every SME that attended the review visit in August 1998 reported at least one significant improvement in its environmental performance (see Table 28.1). In some cases, these improvements were achieved at very low cost and yielded relatively significant financial savings. They included 'good housekeeping' measures as well as process changes, and brought substantial reductions in materials and energy use, and in environmental impacts. One of our favourite examples

 # 2: 20-employee custom manufacturer of machine parts
- Oil use halved through better machine maintenance (replacement of old seals)
- Reclassified as non-hazardous waste generator
- Work area cleaner and safer
- Small garden built within facility

 # 4: 12-employee environmental services group specialising in effluent analysis and manufacture of water treatment products
- Improved work environment
- Extraction hood reduced waste of raw material and dust
- Water treatment system improved quality of effluent

 # 5: 100-employee plastic manufacturer
- Reduced energy consumption
- Reduced number of health and safety incidents

 # 6: 100-employee manufacturer of packaging materials
- Reduced VOC emissions by gradual shift from polyurethane using volatile adhesive to moulded polyethylene
- Reduced scrap from 1% to 0.5%

 # 7: 210-employee print shop
- Paper waste cut 30% by buying paper in custom sizes
- Greater use of recycled paper
- Designed waste collection system into new layout
- Contaminated effluent reduced by 90% (from 700 to 60 litres/month) by separation of aqueous hazardous wastes

 # 8: 45-employee construction company, specialising in construction of gas stations
- Increased tarpaulin use and sprinkler application (now required of subcontractors) reduced dust emissions
- Modified construction plan saved several native trees
- Cut wood consumption by 30%

 # 9: 30-employee manufacturer of hot sauce and sangrita
- Vehicles better maintained to reduce emissions
- Change in cleaning process reduced use of iodine-based stainless-steel sanitiser by 11,000 litres per year (overall effluent discharge also reduced)
- Requiring suppliers to use stronger containers reduced raw material waste
- 3,000 lbs of orange juice concentrate (6% of annual use) recovered annually by spraying scooped-out containers with water and using resulting juice

 # 10: 70-employee company that shapes, cuts and prints customer logos on PVC to make safety seals
- Changed the incentive structure in the printing area (to reflect quality as well as quantity) to reduce waste
- Reduced hazardous rag waste (from 5.5 to 1.7 kg of rags per ton of product)
- Significantly reduced machine noise
- Reduced electricity consumption
- Offer used-battery collection programme to employees

 # 11: 10-employee environmental services company, including waste-water analysis and production of chemical products for water treatment
- Separation and proper disposal of hazardous waste
- Reduced evaporation and additional waste of hexane and reduced generation of other gases through changed analytical procedures
- Cut water consumption by 50%

 # 12: 20-employee environmental services company offering laboratory analysis and chemical products for water treatment
- Less effluent generated
- Separation and appropriate disposal of hazardous effluent and waste, including chloroform and hexane
- Precipitation and/or neutralisation of heavy metals

 # 13: 21-employee print shop
- Four 55-gallon containers of paper recycled each week
- Reduced paper consumption by reducing trial runs and using both sides of test paper

 # 14: 8-employee company performing analysis of hazardous industrial waste
- Changed location to improve ability to separate and treat effluent
- Installed carbon filter to improve quality of air discharge

 # 17: 120-employee manufacturer of seat belts and air bags
- All used maintenance oil now treated as hazardous waste
- Reduced consumption of maintenance oil

 # 19: 3-employee mixer and distributor of chemical products such as chlorine
- Use of personal protective equipment
- Reduced transportation risk by purchasing new truck (to take place of family car) to separate chemical drums from each other and from driver
- Reduced number of chemical spills by labelling storage drums and using alternative drums that make it easier to transfer product

 # 21: 45-employee mixer and distributor of concrete
- Cut water consumption 1,800,000 litres/month (40%) by recycling water used to wash out mixers
- Reduced dust emissions

Note: Only data from the 15 SMEs that attended the August 1998 review session is included.

Table 28.1 **SME environmental performance improvements**

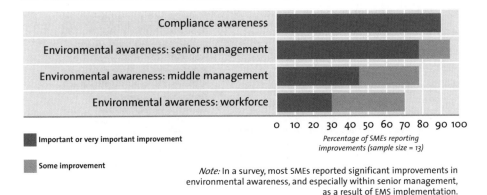

Figure 28.3 **Improvements in environmental and compliance awareness**

was a small salsa and sangrita[2] producer which changed its process for adding orange juice concentrate to the sangrita mix, thus saving US$4,000 a year and reducing the discharge of leftover concentrate to a nearby lake by 3,000 lbs.

Before yielding environmental improvements, an EMS generally must first bring about a transformation in the attitudes of an organisation's senior managers, middle managers and employees. As shown in Figure 28.3, this transformation occurred within the Guadalajara SMEs. Because the project initially targeted senior managers, changes in their attitudes are most evident: two-thirds of the SMEs reported important or very important changes at this level. SMEs embraced formal commitments to environmental improvement by adopting environmental policies (signed by the company's CEO), objectives and targets. As of August 1998, all but one SME had taken these steps.

The actual environmental improvements made by the SMEs are categorised in Figure 28.4. Over three-quarters of the facilities reduced releases to the environment, 70% improved the workplace environment and about two-thirds reduced energy and/or materials use, improved waste handling and improved regulatory compliance.

The environmental performance improvements noted above also led to improvements in economic performance in 80% of the SMEs. Many of these arose from simple, low-cost housekeeping measures that resulted in reduced raw material, energy or water use. Also noteworthy is that the SMEs that were most successful at realising environmental and economic performance improvements generally had a high level of worker participation in their EMSs.

Sustainability of the EMSs

On the question of whether SMEs will maintain ISO 14001-based EMSs over time, the results of Proyecto Guadalajara were somewhat disappointing, although instructive. As

2 Sangrita is a potent mixture of orange juice, tomatoes, chillies, sugar and other ingredients. Mexicans drink it with tequila.

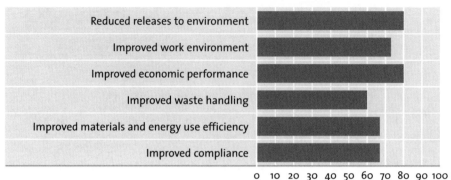

0 10 20 30 40 50 60 70 80 90 100

Percentage of SMEs reporting
improvements (sample size = 15)

Note: In the review sessions, SME representatives reported a variety of performance improvements. The categories above represent our attempt to classify these improvements. For example, if an SME reported implementing an energy-saving measure, that SME would receive a tick in the categories of improved economic performance and improved materials and energy use.

Figure 28.4 **Environmental and economic improvements, by category**

of April 1999 (the date of our last visit to Guadalajara), six SMEs were actively maintaining their EMSs, and several of these were planning to pursue ISO 14001 certification through the Mexican Institute for Normalisation and Certification (IMNC).[3] Four SMEs had 'temporarily suspended' EMS development, but planned to pick it up again, and the rest had simply abandoned their EMSs (although retaining the performance improvements made initially).

The reasons given by the SMEs for suspending or abandoning EMS development included changes in senior management, more pressing priorities (ISO 9000 implementation, for example), lack of staff time and lack of sustained interest on the part of their customers. On the other hand, the SMEs who were maintaining their EMSs saw clear business benefits from having an EMS and certifying to ISO 14001. Several SMEs, suppliers to large multinationals such as IBM, Hewlett-Packard, Microsoft and Lucent Technologies, saw ISO 14001 as a means of demonstrating their commitment to environmental performance to customers who cared. Other SMEs planned to use their ISO 14001 certification as a means of becoming more attractive to selected customers.

It seems clear that SMEs need a clear business incentive to maintain an EMS and, certainly, to certify to ISO 14001. Because SMEs in Guadalajara generally do not face intense pressure from regulators or neighbours to improve environmental performance (and ISO 14001 certification is currently not an accepted response to this sort of pressure, where it exists), the clear business incentive must come from customers.

---

3   The IMNC recently provided a reduced cost preliminary audit to four SMEs. Of these four, two plan to achieve certification in 2000 and one, potentially, in early 2001. The other company, which has just three employees, would like to become ISO 14001-certified and is seeking financial assistance to do so.

The business component of sustainable development has economic, social, and environmental dimensions. Implemented effectively and in the right circumstances, an ISO 14001 EMS can help even a very small business achieve economic efficiency, make environmental improvements and develop better managers. Although most of the participants in Proyecto Guadalajara would agree that they realised these benefits during EMS implementation, in reality it is exceedingly hard for a small business to maintain commitment to an EMS. It is crucial that, in the foreseeable future, larger businesses (themselves subject to customer demands on price and environmental performance) may be in the best position to pressure SMEs into making this commitment. In other words, large companies have an influence on sustainable development that is much wider than their own operations might suggest.

◢ Conclusions

On the consultants' last day in Guadalajara, a Mexican newspaper published the results of a survey in which children were asked what they considered to be the principal problem facing Mexico today. The overwhelming response was environmental pollution (*Reforma* 1999).

These results reflect a significant trend in Latin America: citizens are recognising the close relationship between environmental quality and their own quality of life, and are increasingly unwilling to accept current levels of environmental contamination as the inevitable companion to economic development. Evidence of this trend ranges from community activism in the industrial city of Torreón, Mexico, where lead dust from a smelter has probably caused serious developmental problems in children (Preston 1999), to protests by indigenous groups and local allies over oil and gas exploration and drilling in the upper Amazon.

The realisation that SMEs, which account for the majority of employment in Latin America, often generate more pollution per employee than larger companies implies that improving SME environmental performance is central to sustainable development in the region. This chapter has attempted to answer the question of what ISO 14001 can contribute to improving SME environmental performance. From our experience in Proyecto Guadalajara, and elsewhere in Mexico and Latin America, we draw the following conclusions:

☐ An ISO 14001-based EMS is an effective tool by which SMEs can improve their management systems and environmental performance, thus contributing to sustainable development. Group-based training programmes, supported by local consulting capacity, are effective delivery mechanisms.

☐ Certifying to ISO 14001 is an even more effective means for a given SME to improve environmental performance because certification necessitates sustained commitment to improvement.

☐ Low-cost certification must be available in developing countries such as Mexico, otherwise SMEs will not be able to take advantage of ISO 14001.

☐ In general, SMEs will not undertake ISO 14001 certification unless they perceive a business benefit in doing so. Now, the only business benefit of ISO 14001 certification for SMEs in Latin America is meeting supplier qualifications of selected large companies.

ISO 14001 is a good tool that will support sustainable development under the right conditions, but it cannot create those conditions. For SMEs to use ISO 14001 in developing countries there must be accessible, low-cost training and certification programmes and the right combination of incentives from large customers, government and the public.

ENHANCEMENT OF ISO 14001 AND THE INTEGRATION OF SUSTAINABILITY INTO THE FOOTWEAR SUPPLY CHAIN AT NIKE INC.

Paula Valero
Nike Inc., USA

Naomi Gollogly
Freelance Writer
and Consultant, USA

Mark Curran
The Gauntlett Group, USA

On the evening of 18 June 1999, in the function room of a shoe-manufacturing facility just outside the small town of Fuzhou in southern China, a rather unlikely mix of nationalities kicked up their heels to celebrate a milestone in the history of Nike Inc. Dancing enthusiastically to an eclectic line-up of Chinese disco and traditional Irish folk tunes, the mixed Chinese, Korean, Taiwanese, American and British nationals let off steam at the end of almost 300 person-hours of training on environmental, safety and health management.

This small celebration of the Nike and factory management environment, safety and health (MESH) teams by no means marked the end of a journey. Instead, it was more of a roadside rest stop. The nine workshops just completed over a 12-month period in Nike's subcontracted China footwear factories meant that the drive to greatly enhance environmental, safety and health (ESH) standards in Nike's subcontracted footwear-manufacturing factories was well on its way.

The following presents a case study of how Nike got to the point of practical implementation of an effective management system within the footwear-manufacturing supply chain. The focus of the chapter is on the evolution of traditional ESH management at Nike to the model that is being used today.

◢ From buyer–seller to partnerships

Almost two years before MESH became a reality, round-table discussions were already being held with Nike's six key manufacturers in the form of twice-yearly 'global leadership summits' at Nike's US world headquarters. The purpose of these meetings was to make a transition from a buyer–seller relationship to one where information was shared back and forth. This was part of Nike's new manufacturing philosophy which would measure performance no longer simply on quality, price and delivery of product, but on teamwork, innovation, product leadership, business leadership and integrity (corporate responsibility in social and environmental arenas).

At the first meeting, suppliers eyed each other—and Nike management—with suspicion about the unknown. They were uneasy about the prospect of Nike interfering with their business and sharing information with their competitors. They lacked understanding of what Nike was trying to achieve. However, as they learned that the paradigm shift would provide a forum through which to broach their concerns, improve the industry, gain competitive advantage, benefit society and the environment, and operate more efficiently, they started to come around.

At the second leadership summit, dialogue began to open up between factory groups. By the third summit, joint voices began emerging from the hubbub. From there, it became a partnership, where learning could occur and ideas shared. From these meetings, the new business philosophy was rolled out to Nike's remaining footwear-manufacturing partners.

Once suppliers were part of the business conversations as the transition to a partnership took place, MESH could be introduced. Suppliers already knew that there was a change in Nike's business philosophy and they would be involved in bringing about those changes, as part of the partnership. The stage was set to begin the process of working with factories to implement a management system that would ultimately incorporate all of Nike's corporate responsibility programmes, policies and philosophies—MESH.

◢ The vision

Developed in 1997, MESH represents Nike's commitment to corporate responsibility. In the footwear supply chain, Nike's initial target was to have all subcontracted footwear factories implement an effective management system by 1 June 2001, in order to move them towards sustainability. This effort supports the transition from the buyer–seller relationship to one of partnership. It empowers the factories to internalise Nike's corporate responsibility values, developing and driving their own programme, while still being required to meet Nike requirements. Since the initial target for footwear, Nike has expanded the MESH framework to its own facilities, subsidiaries and apparel supply chain.

The uniqueness of MESH lies in raising the bar of ISO 14001 to include management, safety and health along with environmental issues (see Fig. 29.1). In doing so, the programme allows for better synergies within Nike as well as with its suppliers. MESH is the vehicle for integrating sustainability into the supply chain, thereby supporting Nike's

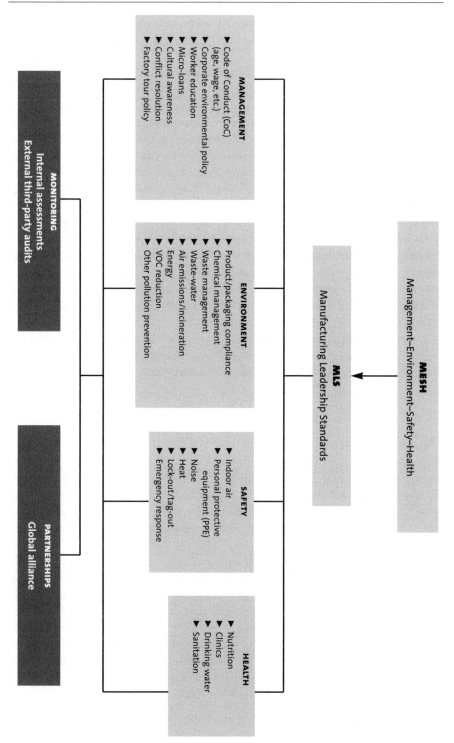

Figure 29.1 **MESH defined**

corporate mission statement.[1] This journey towards sustainability—and all of its accompanying side-roads—might well be one of the biggest challenges faced by Nike in its 28-year history.

However, rather than simply ordering its footwear suppliers to get ISO 14001-certified without providing any assistance, Nike seized the opportunity and developed a 'shared responsibility' with manufacturers to initiate and ensure real progress towards sustainability. Initially, Nike did not include a requirement for ISO 14001 certification in MESH, viewing certification (without controlling the quality) as no guarantee of progress or meaningful long-term improvements, particularly when factories can sometimes get 'certified' even if they are not managing their environmental issues effectively. Nike desired more than a document check—it wanted close scrutiny of practices on the factory floor, leading to accountability, progress, proactive improvements in conditions and reductions of environmental impacts, as well as thorough reviews. Undoubtedly, many factories are seeking certification, so Nike has developed an approved list of certification companies to ensure they receive credible certifications. As of October 1999, approximately 25% of Nike subcontracted footwear factories were ISO 14001-certified. Many of these are located in Thailand where factories had begun to implement environmental management systems before MESH workshops were initiated and are now working to integrate the remaining elements of MESH.

It was an exciting idea which inspired Nike, but it was not going to be achieved overnight—nor without a lot of hard work and determination. Luckily, by this time, some of the crucial foundation work was already well under way.

◢ Nike's culture

Ever since Nike was born on the running tracks of the University of Oregon in 1972, it has invented ways of doing business that have vastly reconfigured the landscape of the marketplace. Bill Bowerman poured rubber into a waffle iron and changed running forever. Phil Knight tested the waters of overseas manufacturing and revolutionised an entire industry.

Nike is a company that takes risks—some succeed and some don't. But if there is one thing the company does well, it is to try to learn from its mistakes—and avoid repeating them. Nike's attempts to improve its reputation in the arena of labour practices stands as an example of what can be done through effective and open communication and dialogue with the company's stakeholders.

Unfortunately, despite the revolutionary, innovative nature of many of Nike's environmental initiatives over the past few years, the company's approach was fundamentally flawed. The free-form structure of the company encouraged not only great creativity and autonomy in its players but also, in many ways, chaos.

---

1   One of Nike's six corporate goals: 'To lead in global corporate citizenship'.

Here's how it worked within the footwear supply chain: ideas came up; somebody took the initiative; the idea was thrown into use—in one or two areas; it lost momentum and was finally abandoned in favour of the next 'new' thing. No matter how innovative or beneficial (long- or short-term), many ideas would fail when it came to communication, understanding, implementation and perpetuation. In short, no framework existed within which to test these ideas and, when proven valuable, ensure their transmission to and application by the intended audience—in this case, the supply chain.

Manufacturers who were aware of the need for some type of corporate responsibility programme often put it in the hands of a factory ESH manager who was far removed from the process. Sharing of best practice among factories was not even on the horizon. Factory managers were also receiving corporate responsibility mandates from Nike in a piece-meal fashion, with short notice, little explanation, no cohesive order and no follow-up plan. Because Nike does not own its manufacturing facilities, its ability to instigate long-term change was even more limited since factory owners were, generally, reluctant to be told how to run their business, especially without a clear identification of deliverables or benefits.

◢ Creation of Nike's corporate responsibility division

In the past, Nike's environmental action team, labour practices and community affairs departments worked in isolation. This needed to change if the long-term goals associated with sustainability were to be achieved. In early 1998, a corporate responsibility division was formed, allowing for synergies between departmental visions, strategies and objectives. Without this unity, departments risked continuing confusion, duplication and inconsistency.

The formalisation of Nike's corporate environmental mission statement[2] took place in late 1998. This helped to solidify the company's commitment to sustainability, both in the supply chain and in its corporate facilities around the globe (see Box 29.1 and Box 29.2).

◢ Bringing it all together

To successfully execute MESH, Nike had to determine an approach that would allow for almost 40 subcontracted footwear factories to develop consistent management systems in all countries in the most cost-effective manner possible. To do this, Nike sought help from two experienced outside consulting firms—The Gauntlett Group, based in Portland,

---

2   Nike's environmental policy mission statement: 'Through the adoption of sustainable busi-
    ness practices, Nike is committed to securing intergenerational quality of life, restoring the
    environment and increasing value for our customers, shareholders and business partners'.

NIKE INC. WAS FOUNDED ON A HANDSHAKE. IMPLICIT IN THAT ACT WAS THE determination that we would build our business with all of our partners based on trust, teamwork, honesty and mutual respect. We expect all of our business partners to operate on the same principles.

At the core of the Nike corporate ethic is the belief that we are a company comprised of many different kinds of people, appreciating individual diversity, and dedicated to equal opportunity for each individual.

Nike designs, manufactures and markets products for sports and fitness consumers. At every step in that process, we are driven to achieve not only what is required, but also what is expected of a leader. We expect our business partners to do the same. Specifically, Nike seeks partners that share our commitment to the promotion of best practices and continuous improvement in:

1   Occupational safety and health, compensation, hours of work and benefits standards

2   Minimising our impact on the environment

3   Management practices that recognise the dignity of the individual, the rights of free association and collective bargaining, and the right to a workplace free of harassment, abuse or corporal punishment

4   The principle that decisions on hiring, salary, benefits, advancement, termination or retirement are based solely on the ability of an individual to do the job. There shall be no discrimination based on race, creed, gender, marital or maternity status, religious or political beliefs, age or sexual orientation

Wherever Nike operates around the globe, we are guided by this code of conduct. We bind our manufacturing partners to these principles. Our manufacturing partners must post this code in all major workspaces, translated into the language of the worker, and must endeavour to train workers on their rights and obligations as defined by this code and applicable labour laws.

While these principles establish the spirit of our partnerships, we also bind these partners to specific standards of conduct. These standards are set forth below:

1   **Forced labour.** The manufacturer does not use forced labour in any form—prison, indentured, bonded or otherwise.

2   **Child labour.** The manufacturer does not employ any person below the age of 18 to produce footwear. The manufacturer does not employ any person below the age of 16 to produce apparel, accessories or equipment. Where local standards are higher, no person under the legal minimum age will be employed.

3   **Compensation.** The manufacturer provides each employee at least the minimum wage, or the prevailing industry wage, whichever is higher; provides each employee with clear, written accounting for every pay period; and does not deduct from worker pay for disciplinary infractions, in accordance with the Nike manufacturing leadership standard on financial penalties.

4   **Benefits.** The manufacturer provides each employee all legally mandated benefits. Benefits vary by country, but may include meals or meal subsidies; transportation or transportation subsidies; other cash allowances; healthcare; child care; emergency, pregnancy or sick leave; vacation, religious, bereavement or holiday leave; and contributions for social security and other insurance, including life, health and worker's compensation.

Box 29.1 **Nike's code of conduct** *(continued over)*

5 **Hours of work/overtime.** The manufacturer complies with legally mandated work hours; uses overtime only when each employee is fully compensated according to local law; informs each employee at the time of hiring if mandatory overtime is a condition of employment; and, on a regularly scheduled basis, provides one day off in seven, and requires no more than 60 hours of work per week, or complies with local limits if they are lower.

6 **Management of environment, safety and health (MESH).** The manufacturer has written health and safety guidelines, including those applying to employee residential facilities, where applicable; has a factory safety committee; complies with Nike's environmental, safety and health standards; limits organic vapour concentrations at or below the permissible exposure limits mandated by the US Occupational Safety and Health Administration; provides personal protective equipment free of charge, and mandates its use; and complies with all applicable local environmental, safety and health regulations.

7 **Documentation and inspection.** The manufacturer maintains on file all documentation needed to demonstrate compliance with this code of conduct; agrees to make these documents available for Nike or its designated auditor to inspect upon request; and agrees to submit to labour practices audits or inspections with or without prior notice.

Box 29.1 (continued)

NIKE WILL ENDEAVOUR TO:

☐ Integrate principles of sustainability into all major business decisions

☐ Scrutinise our environmental impacts in our day-to-day operations and throughout every stage of the product life-cycle

☐ Design and develop product, materials and technologies according to the fundamental principles of sustainability

☐ Promote our practices throughout the supply chain and seek business partnerships with suppliers who operate in a manner consistent with our values

☐ Educate our employees, customers, and business partners to support our goal of achieving sustainability

☐ Turn awareness into action by integrating environmental responsibility into job responsibility

☐ Partner with experts and organisations that contribute to our knowledge about sustainability and stewardship of our outdoor playground

☐ Contribute to quality of life in the communities in which we operate

☐ Monitor, measure and report progress

☐ Strive for continuous improvement in everything we do

☐ Comply with all applicable and relevant regulations wherever in the world we do business

*Box 29.2 **Nike's corporate environmental mission and policy***

Oregon, who worked locally with corporate responsibility staff at Nike headquarters to develop the programme, and Environmental Resources Management (ERM) who brought to the table a local presence and the necessary language skills for each country.

In order to effectively manage two consultancies and ensure seamless execution, a kick-off meeting was held with all parties in June 1998, marking the formal implementation process in Asia.

MESH workshops brought all subcontracted footwear manufacturers in each country together for a series of nine, two-day workshops over a period of 12 months with location rotating among the in-country factories. One to two people from each factory (environmental and employee representatives) were required to attend all nine workshops. However, additional individuals attended when MESH elements were being covered for which they were responsible. This ensured that MESH elements were integrated into the factory operations. Representatives then returned to their factories to face the challenges of implementation. Local ERM staff and Nike corporate responsibility staff were available during and between the workshops to provide ongoing technical support to factories in developing and implementing their management system—serving to further strengthen the partnership.

Designed to guide suppliers through a step-by-step learning process, the workshops were intended to be interactive. Factories reported back on their progress since the previous workshop, exercises were conducted around new MESH elements, and new 'homework' was given to take back to the factory and complete before the next workshop. Templates and tools were provided to assist suppliers. Importantly, the step-by-step implementation process of introducing new MESH elements at each workshop minimised factories' frustrations and feelings of being overwhelmed. The workshop format also provided plenty of room for developing factory-specific programmes, learning from others' experiences, difficulties and successes, internalising MESH concepts and ideas, and initiating better review procedures.

Documents (presentations, tools, etc.), provided in advance of each workshop, helped enhance understanding, particularly where language issues were involved. Accordingly, proper translation of all materials and workshop presentations was both critical and challenging. Sufficient time during workshops for one-to-one homework review helped deepen understanding, particularly when provided in conjunction with written feedback on group presentations. Additionally, exercises conducted during the workshop session needed to be well planned to ensure an appropriate level of difficulty.

While Nike paid for and managed the development of the programme, factories paid one of two workshop fees (US$24,000 or US$32,000). Fees were calculated so that, regardless of factory location or size, each factory paid the same for MESH implementation and the reduced rate was applied to factory groups with multiple factories in one country. The workshop fee covered all costs associated with the programme, including workshop participation, full regulatory review/summaries, gap analysis, technical support, translated materials (Mandarin, Vietnamese, Indonesian Bahasa and Korean) and final preparedness audit (to determine readiness for ISO 14001 should the factory choose to seek certification). In addition, the cost-sharing fee structure encouraged partnership and demonstrated commitment on behalf of all parties involved. All costs need to be calculated carefully; therefore, a contingency fund should be established to cover all unexpected costs that will inevitably arise so there is no need to go back to suppliers and ask for more money above the original workshop fee. Participation in the programme and payment of the workshop fee was non-negotiable since corporate responsibility criteria were now part of the business model and philosophy. It is, however, a partnership, so Nike ensured that all factories understood the objectives and supported them before programme implementation began.

Having Nike co-ordinate the overall project management (workshop logistics, consultants, invoices, etc.) and working with one ERM project leader allowed the factories to focus on learning, development and implementation of MESH. Strong project management (including a clear outline of expectations and responsibilities) by Nike and ERM proved crucial given the extremely large scope of the project.

The first MESH workshops began in China in June 1998, followed by Vietnam, Indonesia and Korea. In total, MESH was introduced to 35 Nike subcontracted footwear factories and two footwear development centres. At the completion of the nine workshops, Nike recognised factories for their hard work and dedication. All participants were awarded a certificate and each factory received a MESH plaque.

In addition to receiving certificates, each factory participant receives a POLE (Pollution Offset Lease for Earth) from the Dream Change Coalition, a US non-profit that accepts donations of $29 per POLE. One POLE keeps one acre of trees standing, offsetting 1.5 tonnes of CO_2 for a year. To date, the forest area has been located in Ecuador. The scheme also provides funding for educational programmes and resources which are invested directly at the local level to forest groups. The emphasis is on teaching about the causes of ecological imbalance and inspiring adults and children to adopt more sustainable ways of living and working. Participants receive a package that includes an explanation of the donation, a special gift from the forest, a Dream Change newsletter, and a certificate which records their participation.

◢ Benefits

By the third MESH workshop in each country, suppliers began to realise how an effective management system would not only make their operation more productive and efficient but would have long-term benefits. This solidified their commitment and encouraged them to became 'champions' of the process.

The amount of team-building and the sharing of information that occurred between suppliers during the workshops was astounding, with the newly formed lines of communication leading to new innovations and problem-solving approaches. MESH has also created a real breakthrough in opening the door for a feedback loop between Nike and its subcontracted footwear manufacturers. The factories are now capable of working with Nike to reduce impacts during the entire life-cycle of a shoe.

MESH has also encouraged manufacturers to get more involved in manufacturing and technological innovations, order management and environmental processes and procedures. In addition, they now understand why Nike sets policies and know they have a chance for input before their implementation. MESH has enabled manufacturers—and Nike—to work together towards sustained improvement through a workshop implementation process that promotes deep understanding, consistent messages and goals, and a sense of shared responsibility.

Jack Chen, Assistant General Manager at Shoetown Footwear Co. Ltd (subcontract footwear factory in Guangzhou, China) says:

> MESH has bridged our ideal and the reality. By setting up a complete and feasible system and standardising its daily implementation, MESH is making a concrete difference that is seen by all. As a result, our factory has achieved a responsible image in the eyes of our workers, our customer, our community as well as the government officials. Factories at different locations have also become more open in sharing experiences, learning and environmental management mind-set. Such benefits, in the meantime, stimulate greater support for MESH from our management team. That is the virtuous circle MESH creates.

◢ Moving forward

Nike is still in the early stages of MESH implementation both in its supply chain as well as in its own operations. There is clearly still a great deal of work to be done. Identifying strengths and weaknesses in the already-completed MESH workshops and developing ways to achieve even greater improvements in operations and performance is an ongoing process. As MESH efforts continue in the footwear supply chain, Nike will focus on expanding the scope and application in all areas of its business. In particular, development of an appropriate strategy for the more complex and challenging apparel supply chain.

The year-long MESH workshop structure in the footwear supply chain, complete with tools, templates and technical support in the local language, supplies the education and information necessary for suppliers to get jump-started on the road towards setting and reaching these higher standards and lessening manufacturing impacts. Factories must continue striving for an increasing working knowledge of MESH, ISO 14001 standards and the supporting documents developed during the workshops and relate them to practical on-site issues. In addition, implementation will need to occur at remaining subcontract footwear factories.

Nike is in the process of developing MESH standards. Prior to MESH, Nike's ESH mandates would appear in spurts that were often not only overwhelming but also lacked explanation or implementation assistance. The necessity for a clear set of Nike's minimum requirements led to the development of Nike's MESH standards so that suppliers can systematically integrate into their management system (legal and other requirements element). Supporting guidelines and tools will be included in the MESH standards package. MESH standards will be integrated into corporate responsibility performance criteria in revised footwear factory evaluations to obtain overall assessment of a supplier's performance, including measurements of price, quality and delivery.

Once the MESH standards are in place, revision of internal and external assessment tools will be necessary. Internal assessments are conducted by Nike and factory representatives. In addition, third-party MESH audit programmes will be conducted as needed. Nike's goal is to develop integrated audit programmes in order to minimise the number of internal and external audits that are conducted.

As facilities continue to make progress toward their objectives and targets, development of tools that capture accurate MESH-related baseline costs from which to measure tangible benefits and savings will be an important element. This is critical so that value to the business can be demonstrated to all levels of management. Early in the management system implementation process, this cost information, combined with the significant impacts determination process, will allow facilities to select the most appropriate issues to address and establish meaningful metrics and indicators.

At the core of Nike's sustainability values are The Natural Step (TNS) system conditions and natural capitalism principles. As facilities achieve successes with their MESH implementation, the challenge will be to continually integrate sustainability criteria into the tools. This needs to be done in a manner that is simple and straightforward and is relevant and meaningful to the various types of operation that use the tools (i.e. inclusion of significance criteria for TNS system conditions in the aspects and impacts identification process). Learning programmes with factories will include sustainability as the foundation/context going forward. In addition, the opposite is being done—integration of appropriate MESH elements (i.e. simple aspects and impacts identification) into other initiatives within Nike.

Invitation to play in the game . . .

While Nike's journey toward sustainability is just getting under way, one thing is certain: the creativity and freedom of the players on the global team will undoubtedly make it an exciting game. Nike invites and encourages all others to participate in the game . . . after all, a sustainable company in an unsustainable world won't make the difference that is truly needed in order for society and the planet to win in the end.

DESIGNING A SUSTAINABILITY MANAGEMENT SYSTEM USING THE NATURAL STEP FRAMEWORK*

Susan Burns
Natural Strategies Inc., USA

How can an environmental management system (EMS) adapt and evolve to address the larger issue of sustainability? How does an EMS change when it is focused on sustainability as a goal? In this chapter, we introduce The Natural Step (TNS) framework as a set of principles that describe sustainability. Then we explore how the framework has been used to enhance the EMSs of a variety of companies.

◢ Why The Natural Step?

As a society, our understanding of sustainability is new and is coming into sharper focus as it is collectively described. So, while many companies are addressing the issue of sustainability, few know how to define it. A recent Arthur D. Little survey of 481 corporate executives reported that sustainability was ranked 'important to their companies' among 95% of executives surveyed (Arthur D. Little 1998). Yet a precise definition is not commonly in use.

Sustainability is said to encompass the 'triple bottom line'—the balance between social, economic, and environmental goals. Describing the domains that sustainability encompasses is important, but what is sustainability itself? Quite literally, it is a state, or a socioeconomic system, that can be 'sustained' over time. The TNS framework describes the minimum, non-overlapping, conditions necessary for such a system. The system conditions help describe and define the goal of sustainability; with this clear definition, we can move more effectively toward it.

* Special thanks goes to Karl-Henrik Robèrt for his review and contribution to this chapter, and for his continuing insight and inspiration.

☐ **Matter and energy cannot be created or destroyed.**

The first law of thermodynamics reminds us of the fact that our waste products do not 'disappear' and that waste 'disposal' is a myth. When we incinerate rubbish, for example, it does not disappear; it is merely transformed into molecules of gaseous waste. Because the Earth is a closed system to matter, there is no 'away'.

☐ **Matter and energy tend to disperse.**

The second law of thermodynamics says that matter and energy in a closed system are always tending toward a state of greater and greater disorder. Only by input of outside energy (the Sun in the case of the Earth) can a system maintain constant or improving levels of order.

☐ **What society consumes is the quality, purity or structure of matter, not its molecules.**

We cannot 'consume' energy or matter—but we can and do consume material quality. If we as a society turn natural resources into dispersed waste faster than nature can reconstitute the waste into resources, then we are becoming collectively poorer.

☐ **Increases in order or net material quality on Earth are produced almost entirely through Sun-driven processes.**

There is only one large-scale source of net increases in material quality on Earth, and that is photosynthesis. Virtually all non-photosynthetic activity (by humans and animals) produces more waste than material quality and requires nature to restore the balance.

Box 30.1 **Scientific principles**

Source: Kranz and Burns 1997

◢ The Natural Step and EMSs

The TNS framework is a strategic planning tool, which helps an organisation identify the risks and opportunities associated with the sustainability challenge. The TNS framework provides a clear vision and scientifically rigorous definition of sustainability, and is also a 'compass' that helps a company move in that direction. However, because TNS is not a prescriptive process, a company gains most benefit from integrating it into a formal management system, such as an EMS. Used together, the TNS framework and an EMS can provide a clear vision of where the business is headed, along with a practical methodology for getting there.

◢ The Natural Step framework: a compass

The Natural Step, a sustainability framework developed in 1989 by Swedish oncologist, Karl-Henrik Robèrt, offers four common-sense 'system conditions' for sustainability, which are based on four scientific principles (see Box 30.1)[1] and a programme designed

---

1 The Natural Step is an international non-profit organisation with affiliate organisations in seven countries. For more information see www.naturalstep.org.

to move an organisation toward sustainability. While these scientific principles are not new, the system conditions they form (see Table 30.1) are a breakthrough in making complex scientific principles understandable and defining the minimum conditions necessary for a sustainable society.

The TNS framework helps us envision sustainability from a systems perspective. Steve Goldfinger, the former director of training for The Natural Step, has said:

> In the simplest terms, sustainability means that we must not turn resources into waste faster than nature can turn waste back into resources.

Mathis Wackernagel, the developer of the Ecological Footprint concept, which measures the area of productive land and water we use for all our resources and waste absorption, created another useful definition of sustainability. Wackernagel illustrates the balance

Table 30.1 **The four system conditions**

Source: The Natural Step (adapted from Robèrt 1999 and Robèrt *et al.* 1996)

In order for society to be sustainable, nature's functions and diversity are not systematically subject to:

SYSTEM CONDITIONS	THIS MEANS	REASON	QUESTION TO ASK
1. Increasing concentrations of substances extracted from the Earth's crust	Fossil fuels, metals and other minerals must not be extracted at a pace faster than their slow re-deposit into the Earth's crust.	Otherwise the concentration of substances in the ecosphere will increase and eventually reach limits—often unknown—beyond which irreversible changes occur.	Does your organisation systematically decrease its economic dependence on underground metals, fuels and other minerals?
2. Increasing concentrations of substances produced by society	Substances must not be produced at a pace faster than that at which they can be broken down and integrated into the cycles of nature or deposited into the Earth's crust.	Otherwise the concentration of substances in the ecosphere will increase and eventually reach limits—often unknown—beyond which irreversible changes occur.	Does your organisation systematically decrease its dependence on persistent unnatural substances?
3. Physical impoverishment by over-harvesting or other forms of ecosystem manipulation	We cannot harvest or manipulate ecosystems in such a way that productive capacity and diversity systematically diminish.	Our health and prosperity depend on the capacity of nature to re-concentrate and restructure wastes into new resources.	Does your organisation systematically decrease its dependence on activities that encroach on productive parts of nature, e.g. over-fishing?
4. Resources are used fairly and efficiently in order to meet basic human needs worldwide	Basic human needs must be met with the most resource-efficient methods possible, and their satisfaction must take precedence over provisions of luxuries.	Humanity must prosper with a resource metabolism meeting system conditions 1–3. This is necessary in order to get the social responsibility and co-operation for achieving the changes in time.	Does your organisation systematically decrease its dependence on using unnecessarily large amounts of resources in relation to added human value?

between social and environmental goals when he defines sustainability as, 'securing people's quality of life within the means of nature'.[2] Wackernagel's definition is compatible with the TNS framework, especially when system condition four is equated with 'securing people's quality of life' and system condition one, two and three with 'the means of nature'.

The triple bottom line

One common question about the system conditions is that, if sustainability is thought of as the integration of social, environmental and economic goals, then does the fourth system condition really address the social dimension adequately? It should be noted that the system conditions are the *minimum* necessary for a sustainable society. Social goals such as labour rights and the end of discrimination, while very important goals to many people, are not minimum socioeconomic conditions for sustainability. In other words, they should be pursued, but they are not incorporated into the four system conditions because they are not *minimum* conditions for sustainability. An opposite criticism is that system condition four goes too far; that a fair and equitable distribution of resources is not something companies can embrace as a goal. Each company needs to determine what the implications of the system conditions are for its own future.

Applying the system conditions

The system conditions are obviously a tall order and cannot be met easily in the current economic system. However, they are not meant to be used as prescriptive rules; rather, they are intended as a tool to help a company envision a future towards which to orient its investments. In this way they act as a compass, helping a company avoid decisions that will have negative environmental and business consequences.

At the strategic planning level, the TNS framework clarifies what is required of business to move from its current resource intensive processes to processes that support a sustainable relationship with nature. Because ecological pressures will increasingly shape the future economy, companies that understand the sustainability challenge are more likely to thrive.

◢ The business case for sustainability

Why focus on sustainability as a business goal? Knowing that the economy and environment are linked, companies are realising that nature's laws create restrictions and limitations with major economic consequences. Significant economic benefit can be gained by learning to operate in a way that does not put the business on a collision course with the immutable laws of nature. We can use the image of a funnel (see Fig. 30.1) to depict the pressures that are exerted on a business today.

2   Personal communication with M. Wackernagel, June 1999.

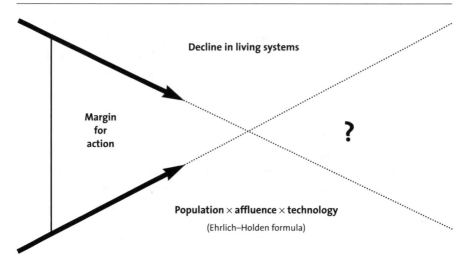

Figure 30.1 **The concept of the funnel**

Source: P. Hawken, K.-H. Robèrt and The Natural Step, 1996

The Earth's capacity to provide resources is systematically decreasing, as illustrated by the top line of Figure 30.1. At the same time, human needs and demands on the biosphere are increasing due to population, affluence and technologies that allow us to extract resources faster.

For a business, the walls of the funnel superimpose themselves more and more into daily economic reality in numerous ways, including customer pressure, regulations and tougher competition from companies that take advantage of ecologically superior business practices (see Fig. 30.2). For a business wanting to make skilful investments, the crucial thing is to direct those investments towards the future market—the opening of the funnel.

Swedish-based Electrolux, the largest appliance manufacturer in the world, states the challenge this way:

> As long as we do not adhere to the system conditions, the walls of the funnel will lean inwards . . . For those companies who seek to act wisely, it is a matter of investing as quickly as possible in moving towards the funnel opening. What it is about is making oneself economically independent of breaking the system conditions (Electrolux 1994).

◢ Strategic planning using The Natural Step framework

The TNS framework also offers a method for strategic planning called 'backcasting'. This method aligns a company's long-term vision with its current actions and plans.

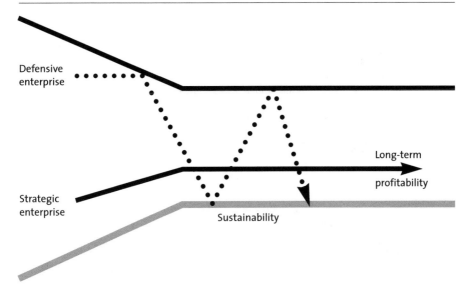

A strategic company adjusts its course in good time since it is impossible to foresee when the surrounding world will force certain changes to occur. The defensive company is forced to implement the same changes at a later stage, at a much higher cost.

Figure 30.2 **Investing for the future**

Source: P. Hawken, K.-H. Robèrt and The Natural Step, 1996

When backcasting, a company takes the following steps (Robèrt 2000):

A   The participants in the planning exercise learn and discuss The Natural Step framework and agree to use it as a shared mental model.

B   The participants analyse the company's current situation in light of the funnel and the four system conditions (see Fig. 30.3). The company examines its current operations, products and services to determine where it is most out of alignment with the principles of sustainability. For example, for system condition one it asks whether the company is dependent on materials from the Earth's crust that accumulate in nature. If so, is the company willing and able to phase out its dependence on this type of activity? This is done for each of the four system conditions.

C   Next, the company envisions an ideal future in which it operates in accordance with the principles of sustainability. This includes imagining how the marketplace of the future will view its products and services and how its core competencies can best be positioned to service that market. This can be a tremendous source of creativity and innovation.

D   Finally, the company designs an action plan that will move it from its current reality to its long-term vision. It takes advantage of 'low-hanging fruit', making

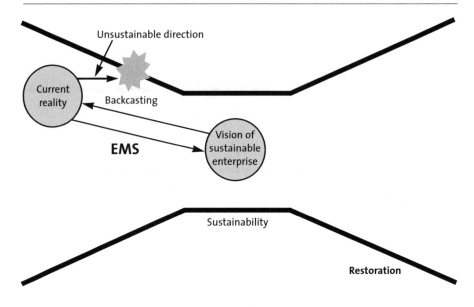

Figure 30.3   **The Natural Step, backcasting and environmental management systems**

sure that each short-term action serves as a platform for longer-term goals that are in alignment with the system conditions. This is necessary to avoid 'dead ends', or solutions that work in the short term, but pose problems in the long term.

This type of long-term strategic planning makes for a stronger EMS, especially when contrasted with the traditional forecasting approach of many companies. During forecasting, a company reviews its current impacts and sets targets that incrementally reduce its impacts year after year. This can lead to incremental improvements in environmental performance, but does not provide the types of leap that are possible from focusing on a longer-term goal. Companies that develop a strong vision of the future align multiple resources and departments toward this unified vision. If they don't, their efforts could potentially move them along a number of different paths, without adding up to a coherent direction with significant improvements.[3]

◢ How The Natural Step enhances EMS

Karl-Henrik Robèrt, the founder of TNS, has compared an EMS to a powerful sailing boat. The boat comes with a detailed instruction manual, describing where the stern and bow

3   Personal communication with Charles McGlashan, a principal with Natural Strategies Inc., June 1999.

are, how to operate the sails, etc. Dr Robèrt adds, however, that building an EMS without a strategic planning tool (such as the TNS framework) is like having no compass or map to guide the boat. The metaphor can be taken further to say that a typical EMS may only support a company sailing along the familiar coastline of regulatory compliance and incremental improvement, but may not guide it in the stormy waters of the global economy and increasing ecological pressures (Kranz and Burns 1997). With the TNS framework providing direction, a company's EMS can move from a focus on compliance and incremental improvement to support goals such as market leadership and improved competitiveness.

Jimmy Sjoblom, former environmental manager of Sånga-Säby Hotel and Conference Centre, notes:

> By using the system conditions, our ISO programme is something we can use on the offensive, rather than just guarding our back . . . We are way beyond incremental improvements or defensive strategies. Defensive activities are not a constructive use of our resources.

Bertil Rosquist of McDonald's, Sweden, adds:

> Since our whole environmental programme is based on the system conditions, incorporating the TNS framework into our new ISO system will be no problem. In fact, ISO will solidify our goals even further.[4]

◢ A sustainability management system

A 'sustainability management system' is similar to a typical EMS, but with two important differences. The TNS framework enhances each step by providing a sharper focus and, in doing so, creates a clearer overall strategic vision both for the EMS and the company. Figure 30.4 depicts the general structure of an ISO 14001 EMS and the enhancement made by integrating the TNS framework. What follows is a detailed explanation of how the TNS framework enhances specific components of an EMS.

Environmental policy

Because TNS provides a framework of sustainability principles, it helps a company articulate a vision of the future that can be reflected in the environmental policy. This defined vision can, in turn, be used both externally and internally to bring clarity and unity to a company's EMS communications.

Oki Semiconductor Manufacturing (OSM), a Portland, Oregon-based semiconductor manufacturer, has integrated the TNS framework into a fully developed EMS (see also Chapter 24 in this volume). Former chief executive officer (CEO) Larry Chalfan led the effort to re-orient the EMS to incorporate TNS principles. One of the first steps was rewrit-

---

4   Personal communication with B. Rosquist, September 1998.

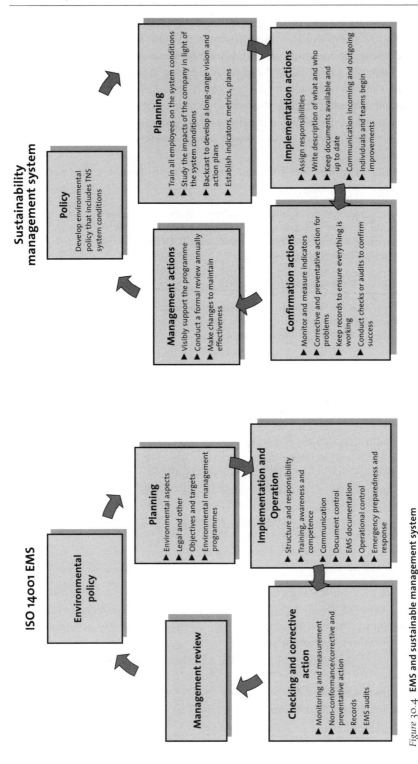

Figure 30.4 **EMS and sustainable management system**

Source: Larry Chalfan, former President and CEO of OKI Semiconductors, Oregon, USA

1. *Include sustainability and TNS conditions in the company's environmental policy.*

2. *Train all employees on the four system conditions; include in the induction process.*

3. *Include TNS principles in the rating and ranking of environmental aspects:*
   ☐ To help determine the significance of impacts to the environment
   ☐ To help ensure objectives chosen are in accordance with sustainability
   ☐ To help ensure resources expended will be balanced towards sustainability
   ☐ Use specific criteria from TNS for evaluation and ranking (in database).

4. *Include TNS analyses in decisions on new materials, products, processes and activities:*
   ☐ New product/process system meeting agendas include TNS analyses.
   ☐ Use ranking analysis sheets for thoroughness.

5. *Include confirmation of effective use of TNS analyses during internal audits:*
   ☐ Records confirming use must be defined and retained as objective evidence.

6. *Include a TNS activities review for effectiveness in management reviews:*
   ☐ Review the records as objective evidence, look for evidence of effectiveness.

Box 30.2 **Integrating The Natural Step and ISO 14001**

ing the environmental policy to incorporate sustainability and the system conditions. Other key integration goals are depicted in Box 30.2.

Planning

Environmental aspects

Completing an inventory of environmental aspects is an important step in understanding how the company's activities impact on the environment. The TNS model can help a cross-functional team to think about their operations' environmental impacts and to see them in a global context. For example, companies may miss ways in which they impact the environment other than those regulated by law. The TNS framework can help them identify all sources of potential impact to the environment—especially ones that may surprise the company in the future or that have a more global effect.

Tom Chapman, former Mitsubishi Electric America vice-president for corporate communications, explains:

> As we study how to combine TNS and ISO 14001, our approach is to use the TNS framework as a way to organise information about our environmental aspects. Before, the aspects were all just data, but using TNS has turned them into objectives. ISO 14001 is the 'what', TNS provides the 'why'. [5]

Larry Chalfan adds:

5   T. Chapman quoted in *Business and the Environment* 1998.

> Our idea of what aspects to include and what their impacts really were was very different after a year of studying TNS. We now look more deeply at our impacts and ask very different questions.

Determining which aspects are significant

When determining which aspects are significant (and are, therefore, the focus of the EMS), the TNS compass adds significant value. Normally, a cross-functional team uses a framework of its own choosing using their best judgement about which aspects pose the highest risks, etc. A common practice is to take a downstream approach to this process, looking at the local risks associated with emissions to air, soil and water. This approach is adequate, but sells the EMS short.

Determining significance from the upstream perspective means that a company takes into account the local and global environment, short- and long-term effects, activities that are not regulated today but may be in the future and, most importantly, the company's long-term goals.

Referring to strategic goals for guidance

One method for determining significance is to focus on the results of the company's backcasting exercise. At the completion of the exercise, a company will have a good idea of where it violates the system conditions most severely, of its vision of itself in the future, and of some of the critical steps needed to get there. From this future vision, it can then set objectives and targets for the company as a whole.

For example, if a company recognises that its use of persistent compounds poses a significant risk (as seen through the lens of the TNS framework), it can set a corporate target of reducing its dependence on these materials. It can then automatically flag these aspects as significant and assign them a facility-specific target and objective in alignment with the company's long-term goals.

IKEA, the Swedish furniture manufacturer, has taken this approach by striving to eliminate all heavy metals and persistent compounds from its products company-wide. This objective is adopted at each of the manufacturing sites. Such a company-wide strategic approach plays a vital role in creating an EMS that is focused on sustainability.

System conditions as indicators of significance

This section describes how each system condition can illuminate the aspects that should be priorities.

System condition one aspects. John Holmberg, a physicist working closely with Dr Robèrt to develop the TNS model, has derived a set of indicators that can help a company prioritise its environmental aspects development (Holmberg 1995).

Holmberg's analysis explains that a material's relative abundance in nature compared with human-created flows will have an impact on its ultimate effect. For example, human-created flows of aluminium are relatively insignificant compared to aluminium's abundance in nature, whereas human-created flows of lead are 12 times that of naturally occurring flows. The following formula may be used to weigh the relative significance of a company's use of metals and minerals:

$$\text{Significance} = \frac{\text{human-made quantity}}{\text{abundance in nature}} \times \text{quantity used by the company}$$

System condition two aspects. System condition two seeks solutions to avoid increasing concentrations in nature of various human-made compounds. As a consequence, most firms systematically phase out persistent and unnatural compounds, because even minimal releases of such compounds are likely to cause increased concentrations. A company should undertake a material inventory looking to reduce its dependence on these materials. These compounds are often substances that have the potential to be regulated in the future. For example, endocrine disrupters—synthetic compounds found in plastics and other materials that tend to mimic hormones in the body—are not regulated at the present time but, because they are suspected to have a role in infertility and certain cancers, they are currently being studied by the US Environmental Protection Agency and other organisations,[6] and the chances are that they will be regulated in the future. System condition two reminds us that the time to think strategically about our use of such compounds is not when everything is known about a chemical, but when we know it is not in accordance with the principles of sustainability.

System condition three aspects. Companies in the mining, forestry, fishing and agricultural industries have obvious system condition three impacts. For many manufacturing facilities, their direct impact on the productive capacity of the biosphere may be less directly visible, but are no less important. A company should consider the environmental effects caused by the extraction of the raw materials it uses in manufacturing. In addition, there are two areas in which an understanding of system condition three may help frame a facility's impacts. The first is the company's raw material use such as water and paper, while the second is the impact of the physical building on the local environment.

System condition four aspects. Inefficiencies in energy use, material use and the transportation of raw materials or the final product may be considered system-condition-four impacts. In addition, a company's impact on communities—both local and global—and the extent to which its products and services meet human needs should be addressed here.

Objectives and targets

The process of setting objectives and targets is one of the areas where the 'compass' adds the most value. Objectives and targets that are in alignment with a company's long-term vision can make an EMS a powerful tool for reaching its goals. Too often, however, a company's targets are set to minimise short-term risks and are incremental. It is preferable that objectives and targets are based on longer-term objectives set within a business

6   US Environmental Protection Agency website, www.epa.gov/edrlupvx/participants.html.

CORPORATE ENVIRONMENTAL TARGETS

Facility level

☐ Reduce energy use by 25% below 1990 level by 2000

☐ Reduce waste disposal by 30% below 1995 level by 2000

☐ Reduce tree-based paper use and purchase by 75% (factor 4) by the end of 1999 and by 90% (factor 10) by the end of 2001

☐ Eliminate the use of old-growth/primary forest products by 1998

☐ Eliminate the use of chlorinated solvents in open systems by the end of 2000

Product level

☐ Increase the use of recycled materials (excluding metals) in products by 30% above 1995 levels by 2000

☐ Reduce packaging materials by 20% under 1995 levels by end 2000

Box 30.3 **Mitsubishi Electric Corporation**

Source: Mitsubishi Electric Corporation

context. These objectives and targets then provide a structure for balancing and integrating both commercial and ecological concerns.

To do this, it is helpful to refer to the company's backcasting exercise. Companies that use the TNS framework start with the assumption that the overriding objective is to systematically phase out activities that contribute to society's violation of the system conditions. During backcasting, this objective is made specific to the company, based on the vision the company has of itself in a sustainable future. Those objectives that represent 'low-hanging fruit' and are solid platforms for future initiatives in alignment with the system conditions are given the highest priority.[7]

Mitsubishi Electric Corporation is an example of a company that integrates its business objectives in its EMS. Its overarching corporate environmental objectives and targets are integrated at the plant level, with the individual plants setting additional objectives and targets (see Box 30.3).

Implementation

Training, awareness and competence

One of the TNS framework's most powerful areas of influence is in employee training. Larry Chalfan explains:

> We tried to get people's hearts and minds engaged when starting our ISO 14001 programme. During employee training, I reviewed the environmental situation, connecting it to our lives and the lives of our children and grandchildren. I explained, however, that I had faith that it could change, if we all do our part.

7   E-mail correspondence with Karl-Henrik Robèrt, November 1999.

This broader perspective helps employees understand personal and company roles in creating a sustainable future and often leads to a stronger commitment to the environmental programme.

This can be contrasted to many employee training programmes that focus on regulatory compliance as something they 'have to' do because 'it's the law'. TNS training creates a framework for defining sustainability and enhances understanding of the company's environmental objectives and vision. This helps to clarify responsibilities, stimulates interaction and employee involvement, and creates a connection between 'day-to-day' activities and the environmental strategy.

Checking and corrective action

Environmental performance measurement

Companies use a variety of indicators to measure environmental performance. Designing good environmental performance indicators (EPIs) is vital, because what gets measured gets managed. Corporate sustainability indicators are created when a company refers to sustainability principles and its own strategic goals and asks the following questions:

☐ What are our biggest impacts (violations of the system conditions)?

☐ What are our current strategies for mitigating these impacts?

☐ What indicators will tell us if we are successful?

The following are examples of three companies that use EPIs to measure sustainability progress.

Electrolux uses a systems approach. Electrolux credits TNS for its holistic approach to environmental management. In its 1997 annual environmental report (see Box 30.4), the company articulates both corporate- and facility-level EPIs that show its systemic approach to sustainability. Its EPIs, in addition to being designed with sustainability goals clearly in focus, are also expressed in business terms such as 'share of total sales' and 'added value' so that they are understandable to senior management for planning purposes.

The first three corporate level indicators relate to Electrolux's products directly. According to the company's own analysis, the biggest environmental impacts occur during product use, not manufacturing. Its strategy, therefore, is to produce the most ecologically superior products on the market (ones with the lowest water and energy use, for example). The indicator: 'share of total sales represented by environmentally leading products' measures the success of this strategy directly and can demonstrate to even sceptical managers the value of the company's investment in its sustainability strategy.

In its 1997 report, the company reported that environmentally leading products were 4% more profitable than other products.

Interface looks at the big picture. Interface, a US$1.3 billion carpeting and textile company, is using this systemic approach. When the CEO, Ray Anderson, began shaping

Corporate level

☐ Share of total sales represented by environmentally leading products

☐ Average annual environmental improvement of product range

☐ Increased recyclability of products

☐ Environmental improvement of manufacturing facilities

Facility level

☐ Energy cost/added value* (%)

☐ Energy consumption/added value* (kWh/US$)

☐ Carbon dioxide emissions/added value* (kg/US$)

☐ Water consumption/added value* (m³/US$)

☐ Energy consumption of heated surface area (kWh/m²)

☐ Direct material efficiency (kg product/kg raw material used)

* Added value is defined as the difference between total manufacturing costs and direct material costs.

Box 30.4 **Electrolux environmental indicators**

Source: Electrolux 1997

the company's vision of sustainability, he asked: 'What is the total quantity of material moving through the company?', 'How much material from the Earth's crust is removed each year due to our operations?', 'How much is deposited in landfills each year?' He calculated that the company is responsible for 1.2 billion lb of petroleum being extracted from the Earth's crust each year. Only one-third is used for raw carpet materials; two-thirds is the energy needed to make the carpet. Over 250 million lb of carpet are produced each year in the US. With an average life of 15 years, most of this material eventually ends up in landfills.

Quantifying these flows can be a very powerful experience; it motivates people because they begin to see the whole picture. This realisation led to the development of a key indicator for company performance—'pounds-of-petroleum per dollar sales'. Interface's vision is to eventually make all carpet from recycled materials and to use totally renewable energy sources. If its strategy succeeds, the indicator will approach zero. Since it started its journey to sustainability, Interface has watched this indicator fall as its sales have risen.

Sånga-Säby designs indicators around the system conditions. A further example of innovative utilisation of sustainability metrics has been adopted by Sånga-Säby, a hotel and conference centre located in central Sweden. The company has utilised the TNS framework in all aspects of its EMS, starting with its environmental policy, and has designed a comprehensive set of EPIs based on the system conditions. The company tracks and publicly reports, in annual environmental reports, its performance as either a positive, neutral or negative trend for each indicator.[8]

8   Sånga-Säby Kurs & Konferens, *Environmental Report*, 1996, available at www.sanga-saby.se.

Management review

The last step in the EMS cycle is the periodic management review. Management reviews the company's progress towards meeting its objectives and targets, reviews the results of EMS audits to determine whether the EMS is functioning effectively, reviews the company's inventory of aspects, and plans for the next cycle. The TNS framework enhances this process by illuminating a vision a company can work towards, year after year. The TNS framework can enhance management's strategic planning sessions so that the EMS is seen in the context of the company's backcasting, action plans, business climate, and the impact of ecological trends on the business. New or revised targets and objectives set in this larger context can then be created during the management review.

◢ Conclusion

Environmental management systems are gaining popularity around the world. They provide structure for the integration of environmental issues into management and day-to-day operations, but they don't provide the vision that guides a company on its voyage to sustainability. Nor are they meant to provide an understanding of what constitutes a sustainable direction.

The TNS framework provides the compass to navigate these new waters. It can help a company 'brainstorm' environmental aspects from a wider perspective, set objectives and targets with a view towards a long-term vision, provide a common framework for employees to understand sustainability, and provide senior management with a tool for understanding how sustainability relates to other business objectives. Once the vision and direction is set, an EMS is a valuable vessel for making the journey, instilling the vision and documenting progress.

BIBLIOGRAPHY

ALGA (Australian Local Government Association) (1996) *Managing the Environment: A Practical Guide for Local Government to Environmental Management Systems and ISO 14001* (Deakin, Australia: ALGA).

Allenby, B. (1999) 'Environmental Management Systems: A Tool Whose Time Has Passed?', *AT&T Environment, Health and Safety, News and Notes*, September 1999, http://att.com/ehs/newsletter/09_99/page_4.html.

Ammenberg, J., and O. Hjelm (1999) 'Joint Environmental Management System at an Industrial District: Environmental Improvements and Commercial Advantages', presented at the *Industrial Ecology and Sustainability* conference, Troyes, France, 22–25 September 1999.

Arthur D. Little (1998) *Realising the Business Value of Sustainable Development* (Cambridge, MA: Arthur D. Little).

Ashford, N. (1996) 'The Influence of Information-Based Initiatives and Negotiated Environmental Agreements on Technological Change', presented at the *International Conference on the Economics and Law of Voluntary Approaches in Environmental Policy*, November 1996.

Baczko, T., and K. Bobinska (1999) *Ochrona Srodowiska w Polskich Przedsiebiorstwach: Komunikat z Badan* (*Environmental Protection in Polish Companies: Report of a Survey*) (Cambridge, MA: Harvard Institute for International Development).

Bakti, N.A.K., and L.K. Shyan (1999) 'Environmental Performance Evaluation of a Rubber Glove Manufacturing Company: A Case Study', *ISO/TC207/SC4 N 295 Document*: 29-33 and *EPE Workshop, 7th Meeting, ISO/TC207*, 1 June 1999, Seoul, Korea.

Bates, G. (1999) *Environmental Law and Road Reserves* (Special Report 55; Vermont South, Victoria, Australia: ARRB Transport Research Ltd, 2nd edn).

Baumhakel, M., D. List, B. Mooshammer, J. Sage and K. Schauer (1997) *Ecoprofit* (Graz, Austria: Umweltamt der Stadt Graz).

Beder, S. (1994) 'The Role of Technology in Sustainable Development', *IEEE Technology and Society Magazine* 13.4 (Winter 1994): 14-18.

Begley, R (1996) 'ISO 14000: A Step toward Industry Self-Regulation', *Environmental Science and Technology* 30.7: 298-302.

Bekkering, M., and J. Eyles (1998) 'Making a Region Sustainable: Governments and Communities in Action in Greater Hamilton, Canada', in M. Hoff (ed.), *Sustainable Community Development: Studies in Economic, Environmental, and Cultural Revitalization* (Washington, DC: Lewis Publishers): 139-62.

Bekkering, M. (1998) 'VISION 2020: Sustainable Community Initiative', in *Local Agenda 21 Model Communities Programme: Case Studies* (Toronto: International Council for Local Environmental Initiatives): 77-104.

Benchmark Environmental Consulting (1995) *ISO 14000: An Uncommon Perspective* (Brussels: European Environment Bureau).

Bice, A.E., M.R. Block, P. Caillibot, J. Cascio, C. DeVries, M.A. Gerber, J.M. Juran, R. Kammer, H. Line, S. Mazza, R.A. Munro, R.D. Reid, D.H. Stamatis and J. West (1999) 'What they're saying about standards', *Quality Progress*, July 1999: 28-32.

BOCAIB (*Boletín Oficial de la Comunidad Autónoma de las Islas Baleares*) (1997) 'Decreto 81/1997 para la implantación de un sistema voluntario de gestión y auditorías medioambientales en los centros turísticos de las Islas Baleares', *BOCAIB* 82 (1 July 1997).

BOCAIB (*Boletín Oficial de la Comunidad Autónoma de las Islas Baleares*) (1998) 'Orden de estableci-miento de subvenciones para la implantación de sistemas de gestión y auditoría medio-ambientales en centros turísticos', *BOCAIB* 110 (27 August 1998).

BP Amoco (1999) *Environmental and Social Report* (London: BP Amoco).

Braungart, M., and J. Engelfried (1992) 'An Intelligent Product System to Replace Waste Manage-ment', *Fresenius Environmental Bulletin* 1: 613-19.

Braungart, M., J. Engelfried and D. Mulhall (1993) 'Criteria for Sustainable Development of Products and Production', *Fresenius Environmental Bulletin* 2: 76-77.

BSI (British Standards Institution) (1992) *Specification for Environmental Management Systems. BS 7750: 1992* (London: BSI).

BSI (British Standards Institution) (1994) *BS 7750: Specifications for Environmental Management Systems* (London: BSI).

Bureau of Census, US Department of Commerce (1993) *We The . . . First Americans* (Washington, DC: Population Division, US Bureau of Census).

Business and the Environment (1998) 'Case Studey: Mitsubishi Electric America Combines ISO 14001 and The Natural Step', *Business and the Environment* (Cutter Information Corp.) 9.2 (February 1998).

Canadian Trade Office in Taipei (1998) *Taiwan: A Briefing Book* (Taipei, Taiwan: The Canadian Trade Office in Taipei).

Cartin, T.J. (1993) *Principles and Practices of TQM* (Milwaukee, WI: ASQC Quality Press).

Cascio, J. (1999) 'Applying ISO 14001 to Health and Safety', *American Society for Quality's Environ-mental and Energy Update* 19.3 (July–September 1999): 2-3.

CEC (Commission of the European Communities) (1996) 'Commission Recommendation of 3 April 1996 Concerning the Definition of Small and Medium-Sized Enterprises', *Official Journal* L107, 30/04/1996: 0004-0009 (Document 396X0280).

Chang, Y.T. (1998) 'Cleaner Production at Hsin-chu Mill of Cheng Loong Corporation, Taiwan, ROC', *Cleaner Production Newsletter* 3.3: 19.

Cheung, P.S. (1995) 'Republic of China', in K. Sakurai (ed.), *Cleaner Production for Green Productivity: Asian Perspectives* (Tokyo: Asian Productivity Organisation): 11-69.

Churchill, W. (1993) *Struggle for the Land* (Monroe, ME: Common Courage Press).

Cialdini, R. (1993) *Influence: The Psychology of Persuasion* (New York: Quill).

City of Manningham (1999) *Environmental Management System for Local Government: A World's First*, www. isems.vic.gov.au/articles.htm.

City of New York (1999) *High Performance Building Guidelines* (New York: City of New York, Department of Design and Construction).

Clark, D. (1999) 'What drives companies to seek ISO 14000 certification?', *Pollution Engineering* 31:7 (Summer 1999): 14-15.

CoA (Commonwealth of Australia) (1996) *The National Strategy for the Conservation of Australia's Biological Diversity* (Canberra: Department of Environment, Sport and Territories).

COAG (Council of Australian Governments) (1992a) *The National Strategy for Ecologically Sustainable Development* (Canberra: Australian Government Publishing Service).

COAG (Council of Australian Governments) (1992b) *Inter-governmental Agreement on the Environment* (Canberra: Australian Government Publishing Service).

Cockrean, B.J. (1999) *A Guide to Environmental Management Systems and ISO 14001 for Local Government: New Zealand* (Auckland: Pattle Delamore Partners).

Cohen, F.S. (1982) *Handbook of Federal Indian Law* (Albuquerque, NM: University of New Mexico Press).

Conference of Western Attorneys General (1993) *American Indian Law Deskbook* (Niwot, CO: University Press of Colorado).

Crowther, A. (1999) 'Methods for Determining the Significance of Environmental Impacts' (MSc thesis; Lancaster, UK: Lancaster University, Department of Geography).

Dasgupta, S., H. Hettige and D. Wheeler (1997) *What Improves Environmental Performance: Evidence from Mexican Industry* (World Bank Policy Research Working Paper Series No. 1877, www. worldbank.org/nipr/work_paper/index.htm).

Dasgupta, S., R.E.B. Lucas and D. Wheeler (1998) *Small Plants, Pollution, and Poverty: New Evidence from Brazil and Mexico* (Washington, DC: World Bank; www.worldbank.org/nipr/work_paper/index.htm).

DEHOGA (Deutscher Hotel und Gaststättenverband eV) (1997) *Greener Management for Hotels and Restaurants* (Stuttgart: Hugo Matthaes Verlag).

De-Shalit, A. (1995) *Why Posterity Matters, Environmental Policies and Future Generations* (London/New York: Routledge).

DOGC (*Diari Oficial de la Generalitat de Catalunya*) (1999) 'Ordre per la qual es fa pública la convocatòria d'ajuts per a actuacions d'adopció i d'implantació de sistemes voluntaris de gestió ambiental', DOGC 2881 (4 May 1999).

Dzierzanowski, W. (ed.) (1998) *Raport o Stanie Sektora malych i sRednich Przedsin Biorstw w Polsce w Latach 1996–97 (Report on the State of Small and Medium-Sized Companies in Poland in the Years 1996–97)* (Report of the EU PHARE and USAID Gemini Small Business Project; Warsaw: Foundation for the Promotion of Small and Medium-Sized Companies).

EA (European Co-operation for Accreditation) (1998) *EA Guidelines for the Accreditation of Certification Bodies for Environmental Management Systems* (EA 7-02; London: UKAS).

EAA (European Aluminium Association) (1996) *Ecological Profile Report for the European Aluminium Industry* (Brussels: EAA).

ECOTUR (Ecología y Turismo) (1997) *Programa para la Integración del Turismo y el Medio Ambiente* (Palma, Mallorca: ECOTUR: Balearic Government, Ministry of the Environment, Territorial Planning and Coastline).

Ehrbar, A. (1998) *EVA: The Real Key to Creating Wealth* (New York/Chichester, UK: John Wiley).

Electrolux (1994) *Environmental Report 1994* (Stockholm: Electrolux).

Electrolux (1997) *Environmental Report 1997* (www.electrolux.se).

ENDS (Environmental Data Services) (1999) 'Environment takes a back seat', ENDS *Environment Daily* (e-news), 14 October 1999.

Environmental Information Centre (1999) *Special Report on ISO 14001 in Poland. Prepared as part of the Czysty Biznes Programme* (Polish language; Kraków: Polish Environmental Partnership Foundation).

Envirosphere EMC Inc. and Gartner Lee Ltd (1999) *Guide to ISO 14001: Implementation in the Municipal Waste Management Sector* (Toronto: Ontario Ministry of Environment).

EPA (US Environmental Protection Agency) (1993) *Product Life-Cycle Assessment: Inventory Guidelines and Principles* (EPA Report Number EPA/600/R-92/036; Cincinatti, OH: EPA).

EPEA (German Environmental Protection Encouragement Agency) (1996) *Profile and Scope of Work* (Hamburg: EPEA).

ETH (Swiss Federal Institute of Technology) (1994) *Energy Version 2: Ökoinventare von Energiesysteme* (Zurich: ETH).

European Commission (1999) *Site Summary Statistics, 19 September 1999* (http://europa.eu.int/comm/dg11/ emas/sitesummarystatistics_1.htm, accessed 3 November 1999).

Evers, P. (1997) 'ISO 14000 and Environmental Protection', *Mississippi Law Journal* 67.2: 463-526.

Farmar-Bowers, Q. (1997) 'Implementing the National Protocol System Down Under: Co-operative Management Device for Biodiversity Conservation on Road Corridors in Australia', in J.R. Williams, J.W. Goodrich-Mahoney, J.R. Wisniewski and J. Wisniewski (eds.), *6th International Symposium, Environmental Concerns in Right-of-Way Management, 24–26 February 1997, New Orleans, USA* (Oxford, UK: Elsevier Science): 375-82.

Farmar-Bowers, Q. (1998a) *The National Protocol System in 1997* (Research Report ARR 317; Vermont South, Victoria, Australia: ARRB Transport Research Ltd).

Farmar-Bowers, Q. (1998b) *Managing the Maintenance of Biodiversity on Road Reserves: Report on the Trail of the National Protocol System, Tasmania 1998* (Report Prepared for Austroads, Department of Transport, Hobart, Tasmania).

Farmar-Bowers, Q. (1999a) 'Co-operative Management of Road Reserves for Biodiversity Maintenance', in A.I. Robertson and R.J. Watts (eds.), *Preserving Rural Landscapes: Issues and Solutions* (Melbourne: CSIRO Publishing).

Farmar-Bowers, Q. (1999b) Biodiversity Protection Objectives: For Motivation or Show? The Case for Road Reserves, *Roads and Transport Research* 8.2: 62-75.

Feldman, S.J., P.A. Soyka and P. Ameer (1996) *Does improving a firm's environmental management system and environmental performance result in a higher stock price?* (Fairfax, VA: ICF Kaiser).

Flemish Parliament (1995) 'Decree completing the decree of 5 April 1995 defining general provisions regarding the environmental policy, by a title on environment protection within industrial companies', *Moniteur Belge* F95-1807: 18773-76.

Freeman, C., and L. Soete (1997) *The Economics of Industrial Innovation* (Cambridge, MA: MIT Press, 3rd edn).

Freider, J. (1997) *Approaching Sustainability: Integrated Environmental Management and New Zealand's Resource Management Act* (Wellington: Ian Axford New Zealand Fellowship in Public Policy): 15-16.

Fresner, J.(1998a) 'Options, Measures, Results: Ecoprofit-Styria-Prepare Two Years after Project End', *Journal of Cleaner Production* 6: 237-45.

Fresner, J. (1998b) 'Cleaner Production as a Means for Effective Environmental Management Systems', *Journal of Cleaner Production* 6: 171-79.

Frisken, A. (1999) 'Region of Waterloo achieves first municipal registration to ISO 14001', *Municipal World* 109.3 (March 1999): 7-8.

Geiser, K. (1994) 'A Study of the Cleaner Production Technology Industry', paper presented at the *UNEP Third Advisory Meeting on Cleaner Production*, Warsaw, 12–15 October 1994.

Getches, D., C. Wilkinson and R. Williams (1991) *Federal Indian Law: Cases and Materials* (St Paul, MN: West Publishing).

Gilbert, M., and R. Gould (1998) Achieving Environmental Standards (London: Pitman Publishing).

Gleckman, H., and R. Krut (1997) 'Neither International nor Standard', in C. Sheldon (ed.), *ISO 14001 and Beyond: Environmental Management Systems in the Real World* (Sheffield, UK: Greenleaf Publishing): 46-59.

Gleckman, H., and R. Krut (1998) *ISO 14000: A Missed Opportunity for Sustainable Global Industrial Development* (London: Earthscan).

Gorman, M.E., M.M. Mehalik and P. Werhane (2000) *Ethical and Environmental Challenges to Engineering* (Upper Saddle River, NJ: Prentice–Hall).

Gover, S., and P.C. Williams (1994) *Report to the National Indian Policy Center: Survey of Tribal Actions to Protect Water Quality and the Implementation of the Tribal Amendments to the Clean Water Act* (Washington, DC: National Indian Policy Center, George Washington University).

Grinde, D., and B. Johansen (1994) *Ecocide of Native America* (Santa Fe, NM: Clear Light Publishers).

Gutfield, R. (1989) 'Will Poland plant a forest to satisfy a US architect?' *Wall Street Journal*, 23 October 1989: 1.

Harte, H. (1997) 'Are senior management getting the big picture from auditing?', *Safety and Environmental Management Systems: Aligned or Integrated?*, Seminar Notes, IBC UK Conferences Ltd.

Harwood, D., and P. Monaghan (1999) 'Three Months to Automate ISO 14001', *Quality World*, August 1999.

Hawken, P. (1997) 'Natural Capitalism', *Mother Jones*, March/April 1997: 40-43.

Hawken, P., and W. McDonough (1993) 'Seven Steps to Doing Good Business', *Inc.*, November 1993: 79-92.

Heaton, G.R., Jr (1997) 'Towards a New Generation of Environmental Technology', *Journal of Industrial Ecology* 1.2: 23-32.

Hillary, R. (1996) 'Environmental Management Standards: What do SMEs think?', in C. Sheldon (ed.), *ISO 14001 and Beyond: Environmental Management Systems in the Real World* (Sheffield, UK: Greenleaf Publishing): 333-55.

Holmberg, J. (1995) *Socio-Ecological Principles and Indicators for Sustainability* (Göteborg: Chalmers University).

Hortensius, D., and M. Barthel (1997) 'Beyond 14001: An Introduction to the ISO 14000 Series', in C. Sheldon (ed.), *ISO 14001 and Beyond: Environmental Management Systems in the Real World* (Sheffield, UK: Greenleaf Publishing): 19-44.

HSBC James Capel (1997) 'Strategy Matters: Winners and Losers in the Battle for Competitive Advantage' (unpublished).

Hsieh, C.S., and C.H. Chen (1998) 'Role of Industrial Waste Minimisation in Implementing the Environmental Management System at President Enterprises Corporation', *Cleaner Production Newsletter* 3.3: 17.

Humphries, S.E. (1996) *Enhancing the Human Element in Environmental Decision Making* (Sustainable Development Series 7; Vermont South, Victoria, Australia: ARRB Transport Research Ltd).

Hunt, C.B., and E.R. Auster (1990) 'Proactive Environmental Management: Avoiding the Toxic Trap', *Sloan Management Review*, Winter 1990: 7-18.

ICHE (Instituto para la Calidad Hotelera Española) (1998) *Normas de Calidad para Hoteles y Apartamentos Turísticos* (Madrid: ICHE).

IE Professional (1999) 'Haley and Aldrich promote Q SET's compliance information management software', *The IE Professional*, 6 October 1999: 1-2 (www.emigrant.ie).

Inter-Continental Hotels and Resorts (1996) *Inter-Continental Hotels and Resorts Environmental Review* (Cambridge, UK: Inter-Continental Hotels and Resorts).

ISO (International Organization for Standardization) (1994) *ISO 9001 Quality Systems: Models for Quality Assurance in Design/Development, Production, Installation and Servicing* (Geneva: ISO).

ISO (International Organization for Standardization) (1996a) *ISO 14001 Environmental Management Systems: Specification with Guidance for Use* (ISO/TC207/SC; Geneva: ISO).

ISO (International Organization for Standardization) (1996b) *BS EN ISO 14011: 1996—Guidelines for Environmental Auditing—Audit Procedures—Auditing of Environmental Management Systems* (Geneva: ISO).

ISO (International Organization for Standardization) (1996c) *ISO 14004 Environmental Management Systems: General Guidelines on Principles, Systems and Supporting Techniques* (ISO/TC207/SC; Geneva: ISO).

ISO (International Organization for Standardization) (1996d) *AS/NZS ISO 14001. Environmental Management Systems: Specification with Guidance for Use* (Wellington: Standards New Zealand).

ISO (International Organization for Standardization) (1997) *ISO/DIS 14031. Environmental Management. Environmental Performance Evaluation: Guidelines* (ISO/TC 207/SC 4 N 248; Geneva: ISO).

ISO (International Organization for Standardization) (1998a) *ISO /IEC Guide 62 for Bodies Operating Assessment and Certification/Registration of Environmental Management Systems* (Geneva: ISO).

ISO (International Organization for Standardization) (1998b) *Environmental Management—Environmental Performance Evaluation. Guidelines: ISO 14031 (Draft) TC 207 SC 4 JWG N 135* (Geneva: ISO).

ISO (International Organization for Standardization) (1999) *ISO TR 14032 Environmental Management: Examples of Environmental Performance Evaluation* (ISO/TC 207/SC4 N295; Geneva: ISO).

Jackson, S. (1997) *The ISO 14001 Implementation Guide* (New York: John Wiley).

Jaimes, M. (ed.) (1992) *The State of Native America* (Boston, MA: South End Press).

Johnson, G.L. (1999) 'Integrated management systems is a growing government trend', *American Society for Quality's Environmental and Energy Update* 19.3 (July–September 1999): 5-7.

Kälin, A. (1996) *Ecological Controlling Report* (Heerbrugg, Switzerland: Rohner Textil AG, 23 January 1996).

Kälin, A. (1998) *Environmental Statement 1998* (Heerbrugg, Switzerland: Rohner Textil AG, October 1998).

Kean, B. (1996) 'Dangers and Weaknesses', *Proceedings of the Conference on ISO 14000: Regulation, Trade and Environment, 2 July 1996* (Canberra: Australian Centre for Environmental Law).

Kemp, N.W., and A.J. Free (1994) 'Nuclear Electric's Approach to Environmental Management Systems', *Energy and Environment* 5.3: 277-84.

Kemp, R., and L. Soete (1992) 'The Greening of Technological Progress', *Future* 24.5 (June 1992): 437-57.

Keoleian, G.A., and D. Menerey (1993) *Life-Cycle Design Guidance Manual* (EPA Report Number EPA/600/R-92/226; Cincinnati, OH: Risk Reduction Engineering Laboratory, US Environmental Protection Agency, January 1993).

Keoleian, G.A., J.E. Koch and D. Menerey (1995) *Life-Cycle Design Framework and Demonstration Projects* (EPA Report Number EPA/600/R-95/107; Cincinnati, OH: Sustainable Technology Division, US Environmental Protection Agency, July 1995).

Klassen, R.D., and C.P. McLaughlin (1996) 'The Impact of Environmental Management on Firm Performance', *Management Science* 42.8: 1199-214.

Kranz, D., and S. Burns (1997) 'Combining The Natural Step and ISO 14001', *Perspectives on Business and Global Change* (World Business Academy) 11.4: 7-16.

Krech III, S. (1999) *The Ecological Indian: Myth and History* (New York: W.W. Norton).

Krut, R., and H. Gleckman (1998) *ISO 14001: A Missed Opportunity for Sustainable Global Industrial Development* (London: Earthscan).

Kurasaka, T. (1997) 'Attitudes and Experiences of the Japanese Business Community vis-à-vis EMS Standards', in C. Sheldon (ed.), *ISO 14001 and Beyond: Environmental Management Systems in the Real World* (Sheffield, UK: Greenleaf Publishing): 156-68.

Lawrence, L., D. Andrews and C. France (1998) 'Alignment and Deployment of Environmental Strategy through Total Quality Management', *The TQM Magazine* 10.4: 238-45.

Lee, S., and C. Lee (1998) 'Taiwan IDB Held Training Workshop for CP Technical Assistance Providers', *Cleaner Production Newsletter* 3.3: 13.

LEED (Leadership in Energy and Environmental Design) (1999) *Green Building Rating System™ 1.0, Pilot Version* (San Francisco: US Green Building Council; www.usgbc.org).

Lexington Group (1997) *Industrial Environmental Management in Mexico: Results of a Survey* (Report to the World Bank; Lexington, MA: The Lexington Group).

Løkkegaard, K. (1999a) *Field Test of ISO 14031: 1999* (Copenhagen: Danish Environmental Protection Agency, October/November 1999, www.mst.dk/200003artikler/00_083.htm).

Løkkegaard, K. (1999b) *Environmental Management in the Electroplating Sector* (Draft; Copenhagen: Danish Environmental Protection Agency, October/November 1999).

Maimon, D. (1996) *Passaporte Verde Gestão Ambiental e Competitividade* (Rio de Janeiro, Brazil: QualityMark Editora).

Martin, R. (1998) *ISO 14001 Guidance Manual* (Technical Report NCEDR/8-06; Oak Ridge National Laboratory, TN: National Centre for Environmental Decision-Making Research).

McDonough, W. (1993) *A Centennial Sermon: Design, Ecology, Ethics and the Making of Things* (New York: The Cathedral of St John the Divine, 7 February 1993).

McDonough, W., and M. Braungart (1998) 'The Next Industrial Revolution', *Atlantic Monthly* 282.4 (October 1998): 89-92.

McGraw–Hill Companies (1999) 'EPA, government organizations complete ISO 14001 pilot', *The Environmental Management Report* 14.8 (August 1999).

McRobert, J. (1997) *Biological Diversity in Transport Corridors, Road Drainage Management* (Research Report ARR 302; Vermont South, Victoria, Australia: ARRB Transport Research Ltd).

McRobert, J., and G. Sheridan (1999) *Road Runoff and Drainage: Environmental Impacts and Management Objectives* (draft manual prepared for Austroads project NTE 9708; Vermont South, Victoria, Australia: ARRB Transport Research Ltd).

MEH (Ministerio de Economía y Hacienda) and MIMA (Ministerio de Medio Ambiente) (1999) *Spain: A Sustainable Tourism* (Madrid: Centro de Publicaciones).

Mehalik, M.M. (2000) 'Sustainable Network Design: A Commercial Fabric Case Study', *Interfaces: Special Edition on Ecologically Sustainable Business Practices* 30.3 (May/June 2000): 180-89.

Mehalik, M.M., M. Gorman and P. Werhane (1996) 'DesignTex Inc. (A)', in *Darden Case Collection* (Charlottesville, VA: University of Virginia Darden School of Graduate Business Administration): 1-31.

Mehalik, M.M., M. Gorman and P. Werhane (1997a) 'Rohner Textil AG (A)', in *Darden Case Collection* (Charlottesville, VA: University of Virginia Darden School of Graduate Business Administration): 1-9.

Mehalik, M.M., M. Gorman and P. Werhane (1997b) 'Rohner Textil AG (C)', in *Darden Case Collection* (Charlottesville, VA: University of Virginia Darden School of Graduate Business Administration): 1-3.

Mehalik, M.M., M. Gorman and P. Werhane (1998a) 'Environmental Protection Encouragement Agency (A)', in *Darden Case Collection* (Charlottesville, VA: University of Virginia Darden School of Graduate Business Administration): 1-19.

Mehalik, M.M., M. Gorman and P. Werhane (1998b) 'Rohner Textil AG (E): Environmental Cost Accounting', in *Darden Case Collection* (Charlottesville, VA: University of Virginia Darden School of Graduate Business Administration): 1-7.

Milledge, V. (1995) 'Goal Setting and Task Performance at the Organisational Level: Studies of Emissions Reductions Goals and Performance' (unpublished doctoral dissertation; Berkeley, CA: University of California).

MOEA (Ministry of Economic Affairs Industrial Development Bureau) (1999) *ISO 14000 in Taiwan* (Taipei, Taiwan: MOEA).

Møller-Jørgensen, A., B.B. Nielsen, H. Niemann and C. Pedersen (1999) *EMAS: A Tool in Sales and Marketing* (Danish language; Copenhagen: Danish Environmental Protection Agency).

New Zealand Ministry for the Environment (1994) *Taking up the Challenge of Agenda 21: A Guide for Local Government* (Wellington: Ministry for the Environment).

Nicodemi, W., and R. Zoja (1981) *Processi ed impianti siderurgici* (Milan: Masson Editori).

Nielsen, B.B., and C. Pedersen (1999) *Maintaining the Momentum: Experiences of an Environmental Management System after the Certifier has Left* (Danish language; Copenhagen: Danish Environmental Protection Agency).

NRE (Department of Natural Resources and Environment) (1997) *Victoria's Biodiversity, Directions in Management* (Melbourne: Department of Natural Resources and Environment).

Peglau, R. (1999) 'Research and Studies: ISO 14001 Implementation by Worldwide Companies' (Berlin: Federal Environmental Agency, www.riet.org/research/index.html, accessed 28 October 1999).

Petts, J. (1994) 'Risk Communication and Environmental Risk Assessment', *Nuclear Energy* 33.2: 95-102.

Piasecki, B., A. Rogut, E. Stawasz, S. Johnson and D. Smallbone (1998) *Warunki Prowadzenia Dzialalnosci Gospodarczej Przez MSP w Polsce i Krajach Europejskich* (*Conditions for Promoting SME Activity in Poland and European Countries*) (Warsaw: Polish Foundation for Small and Medium Enterprise Promotion and Development).

Popoff, F., and D. Buzzelli (1993) 'Full Cost Accounting', *Chemical Engineering News*, 11 January 1993: 8-10.

Porter, M.E., and C. van der Linde (1995) 'Green and Competitive: Ending the Stalemate', *Harvard Business Review*, September/October 1995: 120-34.

Preston, J. (1999) 'Lead dust in the wind withers Mexican children', *The New York Times*, 30 May 1999: 8.

Problemy Ocen Srodowiskowych (Problems of Environmental Assessment) (1998) 'Special Issue on Environmental Management in Business', *Problemy Ocen Srodowiskowych* 2–3.2 (Polish language).

Q SET (1999) 'A First ISO 9002 Certification for Sydney: Network Services pass the grade with flying colours', www.qset.com.

Rawls, J. (1972) *A Theory of Justice* (Oxford, UK: Clarendon Press).

Reforma (1999) 'No quieren ser candidatos', *Reforma*, 30 April 1999.

Regional Chairman's Task Force on Sustainable Development (1993) *VISION 2020: The Sustainable Region* (Hamilton, Canada: Region of Hamilton-Wentworth, February 1993).

Region of Hamilton-Wentworth (1999) *Summary of the Sustainable Community Planning Process, 1990 to 1999* (Hamilton, Canada: Region of Hamilton-Wentworth, March 1999).

Riglar, N. (1996) 'Environmental Management Systems: Current Status and Trends in Local Government', *Local Environment News* 2.8 (August 1996).

Rivière, A., J. Soth, R. Ketelhut and M. Braungart (1997) 'From Life-Cycle Assessment to Life-Cycle Development', in *Proceedings of the 90th Annual Meeting and Exhibition of the Air and Waste Management Association*, Toronto, Canada, 8–13 June 1997.

Robèrt, K.-H. (2000) 'Tools and Concepts for Sustainable Development: How do they relate to a framework for sustainable development and to each other?', *Journal of Cleaner Production* 8.3: 243-54.

Robèrt, K.-H, H. Daly, P. Hawken and J. Holmberg (1996) 'A Compass for Sustainable Development', *The Natural Step Newsletter* 1 (Winter 1996): 3-5.

Rorive, P. (1997) *A New Challenge for the Protection of Environment* (Brussels: Electrabel).

Rosenbaum, S.W. (1997) 'ISO 14001: Legal Advantages of Replacing Command and Control Regulation', *Practice Periodical of Hazardous, Toxic, and Radioactive Waste Management* 1.3 (July 1997): 124-26.

Rotherham, T. (1998) *Raising Stanards: IUCN and the Future of ISO 14001* (Poland: IUCN).

Rothery, B. (1995) *ISO 14000 and ISO 9000* (Aldershot, UK: Gower).

Saaty, T.L. (1980) *The Analytic Hierarchy Process* (New York: McGraw–Hill).

Saunders, D.A., G.W. Arnold, A.A. Burbridge and A.J.M. Hopkins (eds.) (1987) *Nature Conservation: The Role of Remnants of Native Vegetation* (Chipping Norton, NSW, Australia: Surrey Beatty & Sons).

Saunders, D.A., and R.J. Hobbs (eds.) (1991) *Conservation 2: The Role of Corridors* (Chipping Norton, NSW, Australia: Surrey Beatty & Sons).

Satz, R. (1991) *Chippewa Treaty Rights* (Eau Claire, WI: Wisconsin Academy of Sciences, Arts and Letters).

Schwarz, E.J., St. Vorbach and E. Grieshuber (1999) *Analyse des Nutzens unterschiedlicher Umweltmanagementsysteme* (Klagenfurt, Austria: Schriftenreihe des Bundesministerium für Umwelt, Jugend und Familie): 57-59.

Scott, A. (1999) 'Profiting from ISO 14000', *Chemical Week* 161.36 (29 September 1999): 83-84.

SETAC (Society of Environmental Toxicology and Chemistry) (1991) *A Technical Framework for Life-Cycle Assessment* (Pensacola, FL: SETAC): 7-30.

SETAC (Society of Environmental Toxicology and Chemistry) (1993a) *A Conceptual Framework for Life-Cycle Impact Assessment* (Pensacola, FL: SETAC): 9-24.

SETAC (Society of Environmental Toxicology and Chemistry) (1993b) *Guidelines for Life-Cycle Assessment: A Code of Practice* (Pensacola, FL: SETAC): 14-15.

SETAC (Society of Environmental Toxicology and Chemistry) (1994) *Life-Cycle Assessment Data Quality: A Conceptual Framework* (Pensacola, FL: SETAC): 1-15.

SFS (Swedish Code of Statutes) (1998) *Ordinance of Environmental Hazardous Activities and Public Health*: 899.

Sheldon, C., and M. Yoxon (1999) *Installing Environmental Management Systems* (London: Earthscan).

Spencer, C., and G. Francis (1998) 'Divisional Performance Measures: EVA as a Proxy for Shareholder Wealth', in A. Neely and D. Waggoner (eds.), *Performance Measurement Theory and Practice. Vol. 1* (Cambridge, UK: Cambridge University, Centre for Business Performance): 348-56.

Stares, J. (1997) 'Towards an Integrated Management System' (unpublished MSc thesis; Aberystwyth, UK: University of Wales).

Steer, A. (1996) 'Ten Principles of the New Environmentalism', *Finance and Development* 33.4: 4-7.

Suagee, D., and P. Parenteau (1997) 'Fashioning a Comprehensive Environmental Review Code for Tribal Governments: Institutions and Processes', *American Indian Law Review* 21: 297-328.

Switzer, J., and J. Ehrenfeld (1999) 'Independent Environmental Auditors: What does ISO 14001 registration really mean?', *Environmental Quality Management* 9.1: 17-33.

Thompson, M., R. Ellis and A. Wildavsky (1990) *Cultural Theory* (Boulder, CO: Westview Press).

Tibor, T., and I. Feldman (1996) *ISO 14000: A Guide to the New Environmental Management Standards* (London: Irwin).

Tomer, J.F. (1992) 'The Human Firm in Natural Environment: A Socio-economic Analysis of its Behaviour', *Ecological Economics* 6.

Trotman, J. (1996) 'Policy Letter No. 17: Protecting Health and the Environment', *Ford Motor Company's Environmental Management System Pocket Guide*: 5-6.

Tucker, R., and J. Kasper (1998) 'Pressures for Change in Environmental Auditing and in the Role of the Internal Auditor', *Journal of Managerial Issues* 10.3 (ABI/INFORM edition): 340-54.

UBS AG (1998a) *Environmental Policy* (Zurich: UBS AG, 18 July 1998).

UBS AG (1998b) *Kreditweisung Umweltrisiken* (Zurich: UBS AG, December 1998).

UKOOA (United Kingdom Offshore Operators' Association) (1993) *Guidelines on Safety Management System Interfacing* (Aberdeen, UK: UKOOA).

UNEP (United Nations Environment Programme) (1994) 'What is Cleaner Production and the Cleaner Production Programme?', *Industry and the Environment* 17.4: 4.

UNEP (United Nations Environment Programme) (1998) *Eco-labels in the Tourism Industry* (Paris: UNEP).

Van Berkel, R., W. Willems and M. Lafleur (1997) 'Development of an Industrial Ecology Toolbox for the Introduction of Industrial Ecology in Enterprises: I', *Journal of Cleaner Production* 5.1-2: 11-25.

Verein für Konsumenteninformation (1998) *Umweltzeichen Richtlinie UZ 26 Mehrweggebinde für Getränke und andere flüssige Lebensmittel* (Vienna: Verein für Konsumenteninformation).

WCED (World Commission on Environment and Development) (1987) *Our Common Future* (Oxford, UK: Oxford University Press).

Weaver, J. (ed.) (1996) *Defending Mother Earth: Native American Perspectives on Environmental Justice* (Maryknoll, NY: Orbis Books).

Western, D.J. (1994) 'Nuclear Electric's Approach to Environmental Management Systems', *Nuclear Energy* 33.2: 111-18.

Wilkins, D. (1997) *American Indian Sovereignty and the US Supreme Court: The Masking of Justice* (Austin, TX: University of Texas Press).

William McDonough Architects (1992) *The Hannover Principles* (New York: William McDonough Architects).

Williams, R. (1990) 'Encounters on the Frontiers of International Human Rights Law: Redefining the Terms of Indigenous People's Survival in the World', *Duke Law Journal*, 1990: 660-70.

Wilson, C.L., and W.L. Thomas (1998) 'ASARCO–EPA Settlement Agreement: Understanding the Value of a Corporate-Wide EMS for Regulators and Strategists Alike', *Corporate Environmental Strategies* 5.4 (Summer 1998): 4-17.

World Bank (1999) *Poland: Complying with EU Environmental Legislation* (Final Report WB, ECA Environmental Unit; Washington, DC: World Bank).

Yap, N.T. (1988) 'The Private Pursuit of Public Interest: A Framework for Low-Waste Pollution Control Policy' (thesis submitted to Dalhousie University, Halifax, Canada).

Young, M.D., N. Gunningham, J. Elix, J. Lambert, B. Howard, P. Grabosky and E. McCrone (1996) *Reimbursing the Future: Part 1* (Biodiversity Series, Paper No 9; Canberra: Biodiversity Unit, Department of Environment Sport and Territories).

Yoshiki-Gravelsins, K.S., J.M. Toguri and R.T.C. Choo (1993) 'Metals Production, Energy and the Environment. II. Environmental Impact', *Journal of Materials*, August 1993: 23-29.

Zuckerman, A. (1999) 'Using ISO 14000 as a Trade Barrier', *Iron Age New Steel* 15.3 (March 1999): 77.

ABBREVIATIONS

ALARA	as low as reasonably achievable
Al	aluminium
ALGA	Australian Local Government Association
BEA	Business Environment Association (UK)
BOCAIB	*Boletín Oficial de la Comunidad Autónoma de las Islas Baleares*
BOD	biochemical oxygen demand
BS	standard of the British Standards Institution
BSI	British Standards Institution
BVQI	Bureau Veritas Quality International
CEC	Commission of the European Communities
CEO	chief executive officer
CF_4	carbon tetrafluoride
CFT	cross-functional team
CFC	chlorofluorocarbon
CH_4	methane
CHMM	Certified Hazardous Materials Manager (USA)
CI	criticality index (Mazzucconi SpA)
CO_2	carbon dioxide
CoA	Commonwealth of Australia
COAG	Council of Australian Governments
CoC	Code of Conduct
COD	chemical oxygen demand
COPERBO	Companhia Pernambucana de Borracha Sintética (Brazil)
CP	cleaner production
CPC	Camaçari Petrochemical Complex (Brazil)
CPM	Capital Program Management department of New York City Transit Authority
CTPID	Center for Technology, Policy and Industrial Development, MIT
dBA	decibels on the 'A' scale
DEHOGA	Deutscher Hotel und Gaststättenverband eV
DfE	design for the environment
DOE	US Department of Energy
DOGC	*Diari Oficial de la Generalitat de Catalunya*
EA	European Co-operation for Accreditation
EA	environmental aspect
EAA	European Aluminium Association
EAF	external amplifier factor (Mazzucconi SpA)
EARA	Environmental Auditors Registration Association
ECA	environmental cost accounting

ECOTUR	Ecology and Tourism (*Ecología y Turismo*) (Spain)
EED	Environmental Engineering Division (of NYCTA)
EEK	Estonian kroon
EHS	environment, health and safety
EHSMS	environment, health and safety management system
EI	environmental impact (Mazzucconi SpA)
EI	Environment International Ltd
EIB	European Investment Bank
EMAS	Eco-management and Audit Scheme
EMP	Environmental Management Program (of NYCTA)
EMPOST-NET	The Emerging Paradigm of Sustainable Tourism: A Network Perspective
EMS	environmental management system
ENDS	Environmental Data Services
EnAcT	Environmental Action Team (of Microelectronics)
EPA	Environmental Protection Agency (USA)
EPA	Environmental Protection Administration (Taiwan)
EPE	environmental performance evaluation
EPEA	Environmental Protection Encouragement Agency (Germany)
EPI	environmental performance indicator
EPS	expandable polystyrene
ERM	Environmental Resources Management
ESH	environmental, safety and health
ETH	Swiss Federal Institute of Technology (*Eidgenössische Technische Hochschule Zürich*)
EU	European Union
EWEB	Eugene Water and Electric Board (USA)
FDA	US Food and Drug Administration
FTSE	Financial Times Stock Exchange
GANA	Brazilian Environmental Standardisation Support Group
GDP	gross domestic product
GmbH	Gesellschaft mit beschränkter Haftung
H_2SO_4	sulphuric acid
HACCP	Hazard Analysis Critical Control Point
HCFC	hydrochlorofluorocarbon
HEG	Hackefors Environmental Group (Sweden)
HMSO	Her Majesty's Stationery Office
HSE	health, safety and environment
HSEQ	health, safety, environment and quality
IAF	internal amplifier factor (Mazzucconi SpA)
ICHE	Institute for Hotel Quality (*Instituto para la Calidad Hotelera Española*) (Spain)
IDB	Industrial Development Bureau of the Thai Ministry of Economic Affairs
IEMA	Institute of Environmental Management and Assessment, USA
IER	initial environmental review (Mazzucconi SpA)
IFC	International Finance Corporation
IIP	Investors In People (UK)
IMNC	Mexican Institute for Normalisation and Certification
INEM	International Network for Environmental Management
IPA	isopropyl alcohol
IRMP	integrated resources management plan
ISO	International Organization for Standardization
IT	information technology
IWM	industrial waste minimisation
JJPS	Jebsen & Jessen Packaging Pte Ltd
JJSEA	Jebsen & Jessen Group of Companies (South East Asia)
LA 21	Local Agenda 21

LA-EMAS	Adaptation of the Eco-management and Audit Scheme regulations for UK local government
LCA	life-cycle assessment
LCD	life-cycle development
LEAG	local environmental advisory group (of Microelectronics)
LEED	Leadership in Energy and Environmental Design certification system of US Green Building Council
LIFE	European Community Financial Instrument for the Environment
LPG	liquid petroleum gas
LPG	liquid propane gas
LRQA	Lloyds Register Quality Assurance
MACT	maximum available control technology
MEH	Ministerio de Economía y Hacienda (Spain)
MESH	management environment, safety and health (Nike)
MIMA	Ministerio de Medio Ambiente (Spain)
MIT	Massachusetts Institute of Technology
MOEA	Ministry of Economic Affairs, Thailand
MPI	management performance indicator
MSDS	material safety data sheet
NAS	Naval Air Station (USA)
NASA	National Aeronautics and Space Administration (USA)
NAVSTA	Naval Station (USA)
NEMA	Network for Environmental Management and Auditing
NEFCO	Nordic Environment Finance Corporation
NF_3	nitrogen trifluoride
NGO	non-governmental organisation
NOPAT	net operating profit after tax
NPS	National Protocol System (Australia)
NRE	Department of Natural Resources and Environment (Australia)
NT$	New Taiwan dollar
NUTEK	Swedish National Board for Industrial and Technical Development (*Närings- och teknikutvecklingsverket*)
NYCTA	New York City Transit Authority
OHSAS	occupational health and safety standard
OPI	operational performance indicator
OSHA	Occupational Safety and Health Administration (USA)
OSM	Oki Semiconductor Manufacturing
OSS	Office of System Safety (NYCTA)
P2	pollution prevention
PCG	product composition guide (Microelectronics)
PET	polyethylene terephthalate
PFC	perfluorocompound
POLE	Pollution Offset Lease for Earth
PPE	personal protective equipment
PPG	Perusahaan Pelindung Getah (M) Sdn Bhd
ppm	parts per million
PSB	Productivity and Standards Board (Singapore)
PVC	polyvinyl chloride
QA	quality assurance
QMS	quality management system
R&D	research and development
RCM	resource conservation management
RMA	New Zealand Resource Management Act 1991
ROCE	return on capital employed

SA	Sociedad anónima
SEA	significant environmental aspect
SEBRAE	Brazilian Small Industry Association (*Serviço Brasileiro de Apoio às Micro e Pequenas Empresas*)
SETAC	Society of Environmental Toxicology and Chemistry
SF$_6$	sulphur hexafluoride
SFS	Swedish Code of Statutes
SGS	Société Générale de Surveillance
SIC	standard industrial classification
SIGA	Sociedade de Incentivo e Apoio ao Gerenciamento Ambiental (Brazil)
SME	small or medium-sized enterprise
SO$_2$	sulphur dioxide
STENUM	*Stoff, Energie, Umwelt*
TAP	technical assistance provider
TEMS	tribal environmental management system
TNS	The Natural Step
TUI	Touristik Union International
UBS	Union Bank of Switzerland
UKAS	United Kingdom Accreditation Service
UKOOA	United Kingdom Offshore Operators' Association
UNCED	United Nations Conference on Environment and Development
UNEP	United Nations Environment Programme
UNESCO	United Nations Educational, Scientific and Cultural Organisation
UNI	Italian National Standards Body
UNIDO	United Nations International Development Organisation
USAEP	United States–Asia Environmental Partnership
US AID	United States Agency for International Development
VOC	volatile organic compound
WACC	weighted average cost of capital
WBCSD	World Business Council for Sustainable Development
WCED	World Commission on Environment and Development
WDR	Warburg Dillon Read

BIOGRAPHIES

William (Jim) Altham is a Research Associate at the Centre of Excellence in Cleaner Production, Curtin University, Australia, with qualifications in economics and ecologically sustainable development. His research interests include the evaluation of environmental management systems, environmental performance indicators, benchmarking and environmental reporting.
althamj@resources.curtin.edu.au

Jonas Ammenberg has a degree in applied physics and electrical engineering with an orientation towards environmental techniques and management. He has extensive knowledge of implementing EMSs in companies. Currently, he is a PhD student conducting research on EMSs and teaches environmental management at Linköping University, Sweden.
jonam@ifm.liu.se

Natalia Anguera has a Master's degree in environmental sciences (Universitat Autònoma de Barcelona) and currently works as consultant in Randa Group, Barcelona, mainly on the topics of implementation of EMSs in tourist and industrial organisations. She is also experienced in designing software for environmental data management.
nanguera@randagroup.es

Silvia Ayuso is an environmental engineer (Technische Universität Berlin) and currently works as an consultant for Randa Group in Barcelona. She is currently undertaking a PhD thesis on sustainable tourism and has practical experience in implementing EMSs in hotels.
sayuso@randagroup.es

Mark Bekkering was, between March 1997 and September 1999, the environmental management system co-ordinator for the Regional Environment Department of the Regional Municipality of Hamilton-Wentworth, Canada. He is currently Senior Research and Policy Planner in the Policy and Research Division of the City of Toronto Urban Planning and Development Services.
mbekker@city.toronto.on.ca

Berit Börjesson is an environmental consultant and the central co-ordinator at Hackefors Environmental Group, Linköping, Sweden. She is a founder of joint EMSs and has played a key role in the environmental network at Hackefors.
berit@altea.se

Dr **Pamela J. Bridgen** is CEO of Environment International. She was one of the first in the USA to be certified as an ISO 14001 lead auditor and has assisted both public and private organisations in the development of ISO 14001 EMSs.
exec@envintl.com

Susan Burns is a Principal with Natural Strategies Inc., a US-based management consulting firm. She has over 15 years of experience working with businesses on sustainability strategy and implementation. She recently developed the screening criteria used to select sustainability leaders for a new mutual fund, Portfolio 21. She holds a Bachelor of Science degree in thermal and environmental engineering.
burns@naturalstrategies.com

Enrico Cagno PhD is a Research Officer with the Department of Mechanical Engineering, Politecnico di Milano in Italy. His primary research interests are sustainable product system design, environmental management systems, total quality environmental management and risk assessment.
Enrico.Cagno@PoliMI.it

Adrian Carter is Environmental Adviser at Amec Process & Energy, UK, and has ten years' experience of environmental work, covering environmental management systems, environmental impact assessment, environmental education, and coastal/marine ecology. Current areas of interest include oil platform decommissioning and the environmental impact of offshore wind farms.
adrian.carter@apel-a.amec.co.uk

Bruce Cockrean is an environmental management consultant based in the UK, working with local government and the service sector. Bruce worked at the London Borough of Sutton where he was responsible for the development of the first LA-EMAS-verified units in the UK. From 1996 to 1999 Bruce worked as an environmental consultant in New Zealand, where his work included the development of national guidance on ISO 14001 for local authorities.
bruce.cockrean@globaltolocal.com

Mark Curran is President of The Gauntlett Group and directly responsible for its environmental management systems (EMS) and environmental cost accounting (ECA) practice. Mark has over 15 years' experience in EMS design, development and implementation. He provides both strategic and 'hands-on' assistance to a number of both large and small corporations in the development and certification of their EMSs. Mark has worked extensively in Europe, Asia and the Americas assisting companies in the consumer products, electronics and automotive industries. He and The Gauntlett Group have undertaken significant research in developing EMS enhancement tools such as activity-based costing for environmental aspects and impacts and environmental costing software.
MECurran@aol.com

Anne Downey is a lawyer, and Senior Vice-President for Legal & Regulatory Affairs at Q SET International. As co-founder of Q SET, she was selected in 1997 as one of Europe's Top Five Women Entrepreneurs in IT.
anne_downey.qset@lnn.com

Dr **John Ehrenfeld** is the Director of the Technology, Business and Environment Program at Massachusetts Institute of Technology (MIT), USA, an ongoing project examining the way businesses manage environmental concerns. A Senior Research Associate at the MIT Center for Technology, Policy and Industrial Development (CTPID), he has additional appointments in the interdepartmental Technology and Policy Program and in the Departments of Chemical Engineering and Civil

and Environmental Engineering. He is author or co-author of over 70 publications and is an editor of *The Journal of Industrial Ecology*.
john.ehrenfeld@alum.mit.edu

Dr **Pam Evers,** an environmental law attorney and business professor, worked for the Bad River Band of the Lake Superior Chippewa Indian Tribe drafting environmental regulations and enforcement procedures. Her academic research and business consulting focuses on ISO 14001 implementation, toxic torts, and American Indian law. She is based at the Stephen F. Austin State University in Texas, USA.
pevers@sfasu.edu

Quentin Farmar-Bowers has qualifications in agriculture, agricultural economics and business studies and has worked in the environmental aspects of resource use for the past 24 years. He is currently undertaking research for a doctoral thesis in sustainable development at Melbourne University, Australia.
quentinf@mailhost.civag.unimelb.edu.au

Dr **Johannes Fresner** is managing director of STENUM. He is a chemical engineer who has been working in cleaner production since 1992, nationally and internationally for the United Nations International Development Organisation (UNIDO). His present activities include strategic consulting for the Austrian Ministry of Science.
j.fresner@stenum.at

Dr **Pere Fullana**, chemical engineer (Institut Químic de Sarrià), industrial engineer (Universitat Autònoma de Barcelona) and PhD in photochemical engineering (Universitat Ramon Llull), teaches environment at an International School of Commerce (Escola Superior de Comerç Internacional, Universitat Pompeu Fabra) and is Technical Manager of Randa Group in Barcelona. He is the Spanish Delegate to ISO TC 207/SC5 and member of the SETAC (Society of Environmental Toxicology and Chemistry)-Europe LCA Steering Committee.
pfullana@randagroup.es

Bettina Furrer heads UBS's Environmental Risk Management at UBS Corporate Centre in Zurich, Switzerland. She is responsible for UBS's environmental management system, environmental strategy and product innovation in the field of sustainability. She managed the project for global ISO 14001 certification at UBS.
environment@ubs.com

David Galbraith holds a Bachelor's degree in biology from Harvard University, USA. He co-ordinated the implementation of Proyecto Guadalajara for The Lexington Group Environmental Management Consultants, Inc. USA.
dgalbrai@erg.com

Naomi Gollogly has worked in various capacities at Nike as a copywriter for five years. She has helped develop the communications around Nike's efforts to reduce the company's environmental impact and issue a call to action for Nike employees and shareholders to take part in environmental initiatives around the world.
naomi.gollogly@nike.com

Richard Gould is an Environmental Specialist and an EMS Lead Assessor and EMAS Lead Verifier, formerly with the British Standards Institution and now based at the UK Environment Agency. He undertakes ISO 14001 certification assessments, EMAS verifications, product development and delivery of environmental training courses. Richard is an EARA-registered auditor.
richard.gould@environment-agency.gov.uk

David Harwood MSc has been involved with health, safety and environment for 12 years in the chemical and engineering industries. He has a particular interest in environmental chemistry and law. He is the ALSTOM Power Newcastle operations Corporate Manager responsible for quality, health, safety and environment.
david.harwood@power.alstom.com

Nancy E. Helm is a senior environmental protection specialist with the US Environmental Protection Agency, Region 10. She has worked in several programmes and has skills and interests in pollution prevention, incentives to compliance, environmental management systems and organisational structure.
helm.nancy@epamail.epa.gov

Wojciech Heydel became Associate President of BP Poland in 1997, having helped build up the retail and liquid gas business in Poland. He is currently working in the international division of BP Amoco in London, UK.
HeydelW@bp.com

Ruth Hillary PhD is the founder of the Network for Environmental Management and Auditing (NEMA) and UK expert to ISO TC207/SC 1 Working Group 2 feeding into the deliberation on ISO 14004 and ISO 14001. She is Editor-in-Chief for Elsevier's journal of environmental leadership, *Corporate Environmental Strategy*, and is the Series Editor of the Business and the Environment Practitioner Series. Her PhD is 'The Eco-management and Audit Scheme: Analysis of the Regulation, Implementation and Support', Imperial College, University of London. She is widely published and is editor of *Environmental Management Systems and Cleaner Production* (Wiley, 1997) and *Small and Medium Sized Enterprises and the Environment: Business Imperatives* (Greenleaf Publishing, 2000). She acts as a consultant to industry on ISO 14001 and has worked for the European Commission on EMAS and been project manager on many EU and UK projects. Her recent study for the UK Department of Trade and Industry was on the opportunities and barriers facing SMEs implementing environmental management systems such as ISO 14001.
rhillary@nema.demon.co.uk

Dr **Olof Hjelm** is an environmental chemist with an interest in environmental work at companies and organisations. He currently conducts research on EMSs at companies and local governments and teaches environmental courses at Linköping University, Sweden.
olohj@ifm.liu.se

Scott D. Houthuysen graduated from Rutgers University, USA, with a BSc in chemical engineering and has over 15 years' experience in the electronics industry. Scott has experience in environmental and process engineering and has completed his MSc in project management with Stevens Institute of Technology in New Jersey. Scott is a registered Professional Engineer in the State of New Jersey, a Certified Hazardous Materials Manager (CHMM) and a registered environmental auditor with the Institute of Environmental Management and Assessment (IEMA). Scott's current assignment includes

managing Microelectronics's business-wide ISO 14001-certified environmental management system as well as Group-level environmental projects and programmes.
houthuysen@lucent.com

Heinrich Hugenschmidt focused on the influence of environmental issues on industry competition in his PhD thesis. Since January 2000 he has been working with UBS e-services at UBS Warburg, Switzerland. Before that, he headed UBS's Environmental Risk Management Services for four years.
environment@ubs.com

Andy Hughes is an environmental strategy consultant at URS Dames & Moore, London, specialising in environmental performance evaluation, corporate governance and shareholder value-related issues. At the time of writing the chapter in this volume, Andy was an independent consultant, with an honorary attachment to Bradford University, UK, where he previously directed their Business Strategy and Environmental Management part-time MSc.
Andy_Hughes@URSCorp.com

Vicky Kemp is an independent consultant with over ten years' experience in corporate environmental management and consultancy. She specialises in advising major companies and government bodies on winning tangible business benefits from improved environmental performance, through environmental management systems aligned with their strategic direction. At the time of writing the chapter in this volume, Vicky was a Principal Consultant with Entec UK Ltd.
vicky@mantaray.org.uk

Dr **Riva Krut** is president of Benchmark Environmental Consulting, USA. She was consultant project manager on the implementation of ISO 14001 at New York City Transit Authority Capital Program Management (CPM) from March 1998 to present. She consults and has published widely on voluntary environmental management, EMS, ISO 14001, sustainable industrial development and corporate environmental reporting.
benchmark@mindspring.com

Kristian Eg Løkkegaard, partner in Ernst & Young, Denmark, and head of the environmental department, participates as Danish delegate in the standardisation of environmental management standards under ISO/TC207. The author has participated in the development of environmental auditing standards (ISO 14010/14011/14012) and environmental performance evaluation guidelines (ISO 14031). He was selected as convenor for the development of ISO TR 14032.
kristian.loekkegaard@dk.eyi.com

Dalia Maimon is Professor of Environmental Economics at the University of Rio de Janeiro, Brazil. He is a member of the Commission for the Follow-up of UNCED (United Nations Conference on Environment and Development) and of the UNESCO Biosphere Reserve Commission. He is also a member of the Board of Trustees of INEM (International Network for Environmental Management) and President of SIGA-INEM, Brazil. He is responsible for environmental management training for the MBA course at the University of Rio de Janeiro and Fundação Getúlio Vargas. He has also acted as co-ordinator of ISO 14000 series implementation for SEBRAE (the Brazilian Small Industry Association), where over 2,000 companies and implementers were trained. Dr Maimon is the author of *The Greening of Brazilian Business* (UNESCO, 1999), *ISO 14001 in Small and Medium-Sized Industry* (CNI/QualityMark, 1998) and *Green Passport: Environmental Management and Competitiveness* (1996), and also has a weekly television programme on energy conservation on Futura, the educational channel of Globo Television in Brazil.
siga@domain.com.br

Dr **Dora Marinova** is a Senior Lecturer at the Institute for Sustainability and Technology Policy, Murdoch University, Australia. She graduated in mechanical engineering, took a Master's in applied mathematics and a PhD in economics. Her research interests include innovation, technology transfer, R&D and economic growth.
marinova@central.murdoch.edu.au

David McCallum is the lead consultant assisting the Regional Environment Department, Hamilton-Wentworth, Canada, with development of its EMS. Since 1986, he has provided environmental planning and management services to a wide variety of clients and has assisted the Canadian Standards Association with the development of its EMS standards.
david@netaccess.on.ca

Matthew Mehalik is a graduate student and instructor in systems engineering at the University of Virginia, USA, where he is completing a PhD in systems engineering with concentrations in business ethics and social studies of technology. His research area involves investigating cases of environmentally sustainable design strategies for international businesses.
mmm2f@virginia.edu

Dr **Vicki Milledge** is Assistant Professor of Management at the University of Massachusetts, Boston, MA, USA. She holds a PhD from the University of California at Berkeley in organisational behaviour and industrial relations. She has over ten years' experience in human resources, with Coopers & Lybrand and with Apple Computer. Her research focuses on applying organisational behaviour theories to the management of environmental issues in organisations.
vicki.milledge@umb.edu

Dr **Paul F. Monaghan** co-founded Q SET in 1992, after a career devoted to environmental software development. As a consultant in Canada, he helped large corporations improve environmental performance. He became a professor at the National University of Ireland. As CEO, he has grown Q SET into a company with operations in the UK, USA and Ireland.
paul_monaghan.qset@lnn.com

Birgitte B. Nielsen has an MA in Tech. Soc. Econ. and is a Partner of Valør & Tinge A/S communication consultancy in Denmark. Her primary focus is operationalising environmental issues and sustainable development in organisations. She has specialised in environmental management systems, training, environmental dialogue and reporting.
birgitte@v-t.dk

Barry O'Brien has a BSc Honours degree from National University of Ireland, Cork. He joined Waterford Crystal in 1970 as a production engineer. He has held many positions within the company, including General Manager Manufacturing, and at present is General Manager Strategic Products and Quality Assurance.
bobrien@waterford.ie

Charlotte Pedersen has an MA in political science and works with Deloitte & Touche, Denmark. Her primary focus is implementation of environmental management systems and related management issues, along with knowledge (intellectual capital) management and reporting and other non-financial issues.
cpedersen@deloitte.dk

Dr **Anne Randmer**, of the Centre for Development Programmes in Estonia, specialises in environmental management issues, having specific experience in environmental impact assessment and auditing. She has directed 30 international projects. In 1996–98 Dr Randmer was the local assessor carrying out assessment of all Phare-funded programmes in Estonia.
emieco@estnet.ee

David Robinson is an Environmental Specialist and an EMS Lead Assessor with the British Standards Institution. As well as undertaking ISO 14001 certification assessments, David is involved in the development of new environmental products and the delivery of environmental training courses. David is an EARA-registered principal environmental auditor, EMAS Lead Verifier and a member of the Institute of Environmental Management (now IEMA).
david_robinson@bri.org.uk

Rafal Serafin became the Director of the Polish Environmental Partnership in 1996. He holds degrees in environmental sciences and geography from universities in Waterloo and Toronto in Canada, and East Anglia in the UK.
serafin@epce.org.pl

Jim Strycharz is the Director of the New York City Transit Authority (NYCTA) Capital Program Management (CPM) EMS and a Project Administrator in the Department of Internal Controls and Special Projects at the NYCTA CPM. He has over 20 years' experience in construction and engineering as a Project Manager and as Project and Financial/Accounting Auditor.

Jason Switzer is a Project Officer at the International Institute for Sustainable Development in Geneva, Switzerland, working on sustainability issues related to Trade Policy, International Security and Foreign Aid. The research for the chapter in this volume was undertaken while he was completing Masters' degrees in technology policy and in environmental engineering at Massachusetts Institute of Technology, USA, as a Research Associate for the Technology, Business and Environment Program.
swish@alum.mit.edu

Gill Tatum joined Groundwork Blackburn Trust, UK, in 1997 and has been responsible for developing the environmental management services trading company of the trust. She has worked in environmental consultancy for over ten years and specialises in environmental management systems.
gtatum@groundwork.org.uk

Jean-Pierre Tack is project manager at Tractebel Development Engineering and lecturer at the Catholic University of Louvain. He has worked as EMAS and ISO 14001 Consultant Team Leader in the Tihange nuclear power site and several other industrial plants.
jean-pierre.b.tack@tractebel.be

Mike Toffel is currently pursuing a doctoral degree in business strategy at the Haas School of Business at the University of California, Berkeley, USA. Until recently, he was Director of Environment, Health & Safety at Jebsen & Jessen (SEA) Pte Ltd, a highly diversified group of companies engaged in seven core businesses with operations across Southeast Asia. He holds Masters' degrees in Business Administration and Environmental Studies from Yale University, USA, and has worked at Arthur Andersen, Xerox, Arthur D. Little and J.P. Morgan.
toffel@haas.berkeley.edu

Paolo Trucco PhD is a Research Officer with the Department of Mechanical Engineering, Politecnico di Milano in Italy. His major areas of study are environmentally conscious design and manufacturing, green supply chains, life-cycle assessment and total quality environmental management. He is a member of the Technical Committee for the Environment of the Italian National Standards Body (UNI).
Paolo.Trucco@PoliMI.it

Paula Valero has worked at Nike for ten years and is responsible for leading the global strategic environmental management vision for effective integration into the business. This includes working with Nike-owned subsidiaries and contract manufacturing operations worldwide. Emphasis is on creating the infrastructure needed in order to build internal capacity and accountability, resulting in value added to the business through financial savings and reduced environmental impact. Following reorganisation at Nike, Paula is now part of the Corporate Responsibility Compliance department.
paula.valero@nike.com

Richard Wells, President of The Lexington Group Environmental Management Consultants, Inc., USA, holds a Master's of management science from the Sloan School at MIT. He has served as an expert on the US delegation to ISO TC 207 and has more than 20 years' environmental consulting experience in the US and Latin America.
rwells@lexgrp.com

Nonita T. Yap holds a doctorate in chemistry. She teaches and studies the relationship between technology, environmental sustainability and public policy. She has worked in Africa, Asia and Latin America. Her publications include two books: *Waste Management for Sustainable Development: Policy Planning and Administrative Dimensions. Case Studies from India* (Tata McGraw–Hill, 1995) and *Cleaner Production and Consumption in East, Central and Southern Africa: Challenges and Opportunities* (University of Guelph/Weaver Press, 2000).
nyap@rpd.uoguelph.ca

WEB RESOURCES

◢ ISO 14001/EMS standards

ISO 14001 Information Center	www.iso14000.com
ISO14000.org	www.iso14000.org
ISO Survey of ISO 9000 and ISO 14000 Certificates, 1998	www.iso.ch
ISO 14000 and Environmental Management Systems: A Foundation for Sustainability	www.trst.com
ISOft14000.com: ISO 14000 information source	www.isoft14000.com
ISO 14001 Speedometer	Downloadable from INEM (www.inem.org)
ISO 14000 NGO Initiative	www.ecologia.org/iso14000
American National Standards Institute (ANSI)	www.ansi.org
British Standards Institution	www.bsi-global.com/group.html
The EMAS Help-Desk (housed at European Commission DG XI)	http://europa.eu.int/comm/environment/emas/ *Holds the official list of EMAS-registered sites in Europe; list available by e-mail:* emas@dg11.cec.be
UK Competent Body for EMAS	www.emas.org.uk
UK Accreditation Services	www.ukas.com
Institute of Environmental Management and Assessment	www.iema.net/index2.htm
Voluntary Environmental Management Systems/ISO 14001	www.epa.gov/owm/wm046200.htm

www.ecology.or.jp/isoworld/english/analy14k.htm
Information on total number of registered sites

www.ncsi.com.au/
www.ncsi.com.au/enviro.htm
Sites of the National Association of Testing Authorities, Australia

www.qas.com.au/training.htm
Information on quality assurance in Australia

◢ General information, links and related sites

APEC Working party on sustainable development in the Asia–Pacific
www.apecsec.org.sg/workgroup/sd.html

Australian Cleaner Production Association   www.acpa.org.au
Information on the 2nd Asia Pacific Cleaner Production
Roundtable held in Brisbane in 1999, and membership information

Business and the Environment   www.cutter.com/bate/index.html

CO_2 Update
A weekly brief, produced by Deloitte Touche Tohmatsu, of news relating to emission
reductions. E-mail Andrew_Sharpe@deloitte.com.au and ask to be put on the list.

enviro-e-alert
A regular update, provided by Mallesons Stephen Jaques Solicitors, on legal issues and the
environment. It can be obtained by e-mailing the firm at enquiries@msj.com.au.

Environment International Ltd   www.envintl.com

The Environmental Law Institute   www.eli.org
An international research organisation, which maintains an ISO 14001 Pilot Projects web page
as a joint venture with the United States Environmental Protection Agency

Environmental Partnership for Central Europe   www.epce.org.pl

United States Environmental Protection Agency   www.epa.gov

Greenbuzz   www.greenbiz.com
A fortnightly e-mail update on what's new in the world of business and the environment.

Green Globe   www.greenglobe.org

Her Majesty's Stationery Office   www.hmso.gov.uk/stat.htm

International Institute for Sustainable Development (IISD)   http://iisd.ca

IISD: Business and Sustainable Development   www.iisd.org/business

New Ideas in Pollution Regulation

A monthly e-mail update, provided by The World Bank,
which can be received by e-mailing dshaman@worldbank.org.

PREPARE   www.prepare-net.org

Activities of the PREPARE network (preventative environmental protection
approaches in Europe), with a thematic group 'Cleaner Production and
Environmental Management Systems' focusing on the development of tools
for effective environmental management systems

STENUM GmbH   www.stenum.at

Information on industrial project, cases and research in the area of
fully integrated management systems covering quality (ISO 9000, ISO 9000/2000,
ISO 14001, VDA 6.1, VDA 6.2, health and safety, hygiene)

SustainableBusiness.com   www.sustainablebusiness.com

A source of interesting new information on the business opportunities emerging from the
transition towards sustainable development

United Nations Environment Programme (Production and Consumption Unit)

www.unepie.org/hp_pc.html
A range of information on cleaner production, etc. and industry

World Business Council for Sustainable Development   www.wbcsd.ch

Information on news, speeches, reports, etc. of member activities

The American Society for Quality   www.asq.org

Links to environmental management issues

www.webdirectory.com
Global web search engine on environmental matters

Green Channel   www.greenchannel.com/areas.htm

Links to other related sites

◢ National and local organisations related to chapters in this volume

Austrian eco-design   www.ecodesign.at

The platform for Austrian eco-design activities, providing up-to-date information and a
meeting point and discussion board on eco-design and related activities

Environment Department of Regional Catalan Government   www.gencat.es/mediamb

EMI-ECO, Estonia   www.emieco.ee

Official website of Poland   www.poland.pl

Spanish Ministry of Environment	www.mma.es
Taiwan Ministry of Economic Affairs Industrial Development and Investment Center	http://mail.idic.gov.tw
Institute of Environmental Analysis	www.epa.gov.tw/analysis
UK Environment Agency	www.environment-agency.gov.uk
UK Environment Agency pollution prevention guidelines	www.environment-agency.gov.uk/epns/ppgs.html
Western Australia Sustainable Industry Group Cleaner Production Unit	http://cleanerproduction.curtin.edu.au *Site visits, upcoming activities, seminar reports, links, etc.*

◢ Companies/organisations discussed in this volume

BP	www.bp.com
Electrolux	www.electrolux.se
Electrolux environmental training	www.electrolux.co.uk/node423.asp *An on-line corporate environmental training programme*
Engineering Ethics at the University of Virginia	http://repo-nt.tcc.virginia.edu/ethics/ethics_home.html
Eugene Water and Electric Board	www.eweb.org
Groundwork	www.groundwork.org.uk
Interface	www.interfaceinc.com
Micron Technology Inc.	www.micron.com
Natural Strategies, Inc.	www.naturalstrategies.com
The Natural Step	www.naturalstep.org
Naval Air Station Whidbey Island	www.naswi.navy.mil
Naval Station Everett	www.everett.navy.mil
Oki Semiconductor Manufacturing	www.okisemi.com
Rohner Textil, Climatex	www.climatex.com
Sånga-Säby Kurs & Konferens	www.sanga-saby.se

US EPA American Indian Environmental Office   www.epa.gov/indian/
*Discusses co-operative programmes between the United States
government and Indian nations*

NativeWeb   www.nativeweb.org
An on-line information site concerning indigenous issues

The National Congress of American Indians   www.ncai.org
*The largest and most representative Indian organisation
serving the American Indian and Alaska Native governments*

National Tribal Environmental Council   www.ntec.org/links
Maintains a link page to American Indian resources and information

World Tourism Organisation   www.world-tourism.org

World Travel and Tourism Council   www.wttc.org